April 1988

To keep

while

recuperate

to full health

Best wishes

Michael

A REFUGE FROM DARKNESS

A REFUGE FROM DARKNESS

WILFRID ISRAEL AND THE RESCUE OF THE JEWS

NAOMI SHEPHERD

PANTHEON BOOKS
NEW YORK

To Yosef Amir (Friedrich Altmann) and Hans Feld

Published in the United States by Pantheon Books, a division of Random House, Inc.,
New York, and simultaneously in Canada
by Random House of Canada Limited, Toronto.

Originally published in Great Britain as
Wilfrid Israel: German Jewry's Secret Ambassador
by George Weidenfeld & Nicolson Ltd., London.

Library of Congress Cataloging in Publication Data
Shepherd, Naomi.
A refuge from darkness.
Includes index.
1. Israel, Wilfrid. 2. Jews—Berlin (Germany)—
Biography. 3. Refugees, Jewish—Great Britain—Biography.
I. Title.
DS135.G5I847 1984 943.1'55004924024 [B] 83-22000
ISBN 0-394-52503-5

Manufactured in the United States of America
First American Edition
Designed by Naomi Osnos

Contents

Illustrations

(between pages 116 and 117)

Acknowledgements

This book could not have been written without the help and encouragement of Wilfrid Israel's friends, colleagues and relations, who so generously provided personal reminiscences, letters and suggestions for further contacts. My first thanks, then, to the following: Marion Alward, Yosef Amir, David Astor, Uri Baer, Sir Harold Beeley, Eliezer Be'eri, Salka Behr, Bertha Bracey, Rafael Buber, Milein Cosman, Hans Feld, Gunther Friedlander, Alfred Front, Lola Hahn Warburg, Arieh Handler, Bertha Heilbut, Ruth Herzberg, Elsa Hirschberg, Rita Luedecke Hodge, Diana and David Hopkinson, Gustav Horn, Arnold Horwell, Professor Albert Hourani, Hans Hoxter, Ursula Joachim, Ruth Kew, Efrem Kurtz, Fritz Landshoff, Mathias Landshoff, the late Joseph Linton, Peretz Leshem, Dr Ernst Lowenthal, Eric Lucas, the late Professor T.H. Marshall, Dr Wolf Mattesdorf, Dr Dietrich Mende, Eva Stern Michaelis, Henry Myer, Thea Nathan, George Newman, the late Lord Noel Baker, Vivian Prins, Margot Pottlitzer, Dr Eva Reichmann, Tuvia Rechtmann, Dr Werner Rosenstock, Vera Schaerli, Agnes Schneider, Dora Segall, Vera Sharp, the late Mordechai Shenhabi, Ursula Borchard Sklan, Shiela Sokolow Grant, Flora Solomon, the late Dr Moritz Spitzer, Joan Stiebel, Professor Siegfried Stein, Peter Vansittart, Margret Wellington, Professor Leni Yahil, and Professor Walter Zander.

For the account of the N. Israel firm in Berlin before and during the Nazi period, I am indebted to the memories of those who worked there, who included: Leo Adam, Frieda Bune, Kurt Collisi, Frank Eiseman, Frieda Grimm, Else Kleditz, Emilie Maertens, Henry Ollendorff, Hans Paech, Hildegard Schubert, Eva Maria Schluter, Irmgard Smurka, Herbert Stern, Hans Walther, Imhoff Walli, Friedel Witt, Bernhard Wolf, and Bruno Wolff.

In the final chapter I have drawn on the memories of Yoel Durkan, Rudolf Jones, Minna Koss, and Shlomo Steinhorn.

The following kindly helped me reconstruct Wilfrid Israel's Berlin life by contacting German archives and finding historical material: Ernst Cramer, Dr Cecile Lowenthal-Hensel, and Gunter Scholl; I am grateful to Dr Clarita von Trott zu Solz for Wilfrid Israel's letters to her husband.

For their patience in answering questions about different aspects of the period, I am indebted to Dr Steven Aschheim, Professor Yehuda Bauer, Judith Tydor Baumel, Professor Gabriel Cohen, Dr Gideon Cohen, Professor M.R.D. Foot, Recha Freier, Dr Anthony Glees, Dr Azriel Hildesheimer, Dr Gerhard Hirschfeld, Dr Jorge Haestrup, Daniel Johnson, Helga Keller, Dr Lothar Kettenacker, Professor Konrad Kwiet, the late Lieutenant-Colonel J.M. Langley, Barnett Litvinoff, Dr Avraham Margalioth, Stefan Mendelsohn, Yochanan Meroz, Professor Baruch Ophir, Dr Anthony Polonsky, Gideon Rafael, Sir Frank Roberts, Professor Norman Rose, Lord Sherfield, Dr Herbert Strauss, Professor Bernard Wasserstein, and Dr Ronald Zweig.

Jean Cowen, Erwin Lichtenstein, the late Thea Pollack, Miriam Spielmann, and the late Chanan Yatir provided valuable information, documents and photographs.

The Friedrich Ebert Stiftung, Bonn, provided the financial help which made a stay in Germany possible.

Documents concerning Wilfrid Israel were buried deep in archives in several countries; my particular thanks to the following for their patience and help: Dr Michael Heymann, Israel Philipp, Yoram Maiorek and Esther Meron of the Central Zionist Archives; Malcolm Thomas of the Friends Library, London; Dr Sven Welander of the UN Library Archives, Geneva; David Massar of the Board of Deputies of British Jews Archives, London; Rose Klepfisz of the Joint Distribution Committee Archives, New York; Hanna Nehab of Kibbutz Hazorea Archives; Eva Mitchell of the Central British Fund, London; Mr Kay of the ICA Archives, London; the staff of the Public Record Office, London; the Leo Baeck Institutes in London, New York and Jerusalem; the YIVO Institute, New York; the Wiener Library, London and Tel Aviv; the Friends of the Hebrew University, New York, for permission to reprint parts of Israel's letters to Einstein; the Swiss National Archives, Berne; the Lambeth Palace Library Archives, London; Chatham House, London; Kibbutz Artzi Archives, Kibbutz Merhavia; Geheimes Staatsarchiv Preussischer Kulturbesitz, Berlin, Dahlem; Auswartiges Amt Research Department, Bonn; Friedrich Ebert Stiftung, Bonn; and the Bundesarchiv, Koblenz.

Dr Gideon Cohen, Dr Martha Bickel and Heidi Bastian helped me with translation and interpretation from German; Richard Nowitz saved many old photographs. Heidi Bergemann typed the manuscript. Linda Osband saw the book through the press.

Martin Gilbert encouraged my initial interest, put his Jerusalem library at my disposal and read the manuscript in typescript. Professor David Wyman also read the MS and made valuable corrections.

Finally my deepest gratitude to my husband, Yehuda Layish, for his unfailing and stalwart support, and to my three children, who tolerated a sixth presence in their home for over three years.

Wilfrid Israel's Family Tree

(Simplified Version)

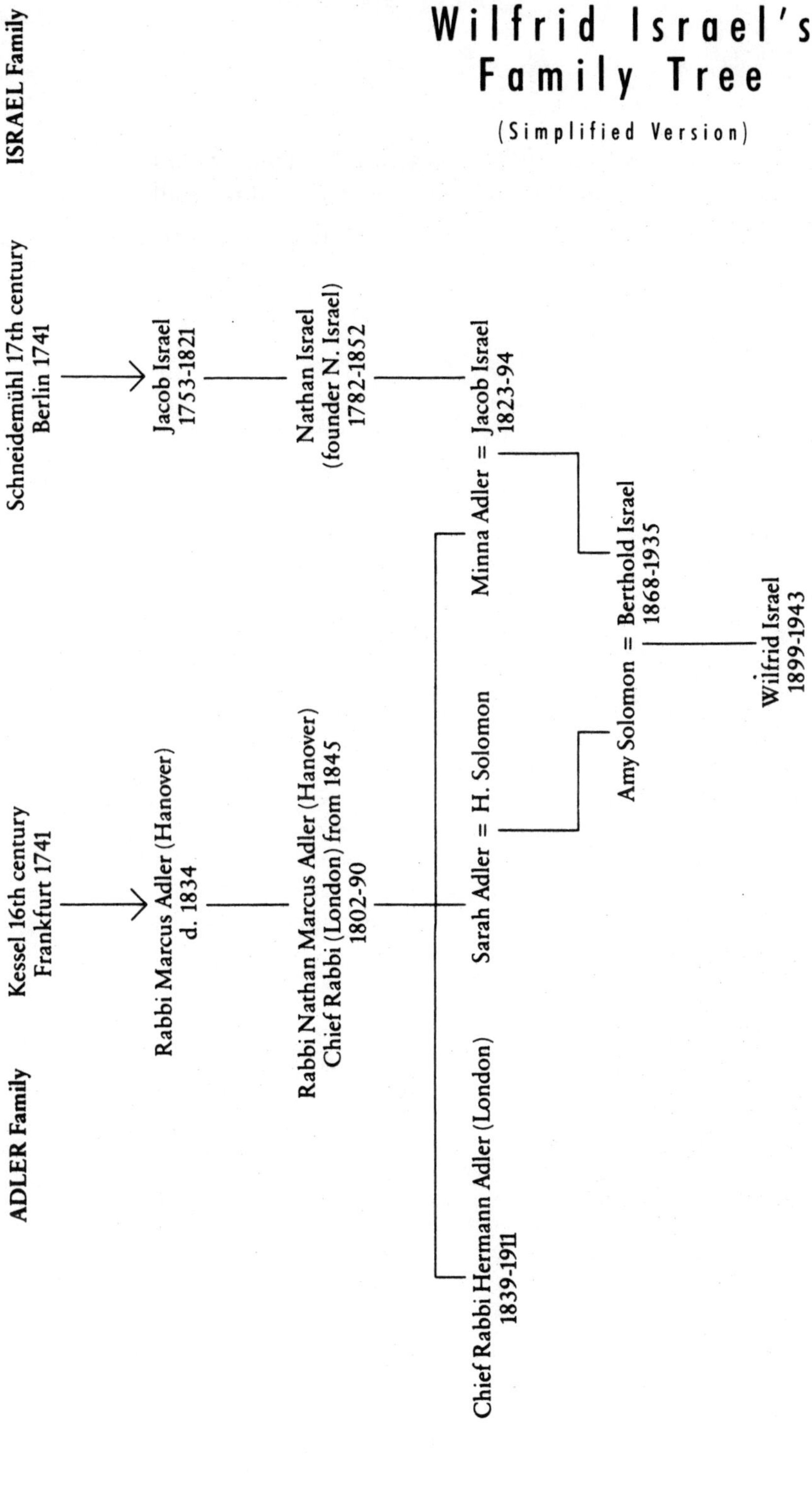

'Wir spricht von Siegen? Überstehn ist alles.'
'Who speaks of victories? To endure is all.'
Rilke, REQUIEM

1
Prologue: In Search of Wilfrid Israel

On 1 June 1943, an unarmed passenger plane flying from Lisbon to Bristol was intercepted by a Luftwaffe fighter patrol over the Bay of Biscay and shot down in flames. Everyone on board was killed. Four men among the thirteen passengers were rumoured, at different times, to have been the target of the attack.

One was Leslie Howard, a world-famous actor and hero of many war films, who had been singled out for propaganda attacks by Goebbels himself. Howard's accountant and escort, Alfred Chenhalls, a stout man who smoked cigars, resembled Winston Churchill, then due to return to England from North Africa. A third man, Tyrrell Shervington, was subsequently named by the Germans as a British intelligence agent. The fourth passenger, whose name was not mentioned at first, was returning from a relief mission to the refugee camps in Portugal and Spain. His obituary in *The Times*, a week later, described him as 'a British-born businessman with a prominent position among the Jews of Berlin, who had devoted himself, after leaving Germany just before the war, to the rescue of Jewish children from Nazi hands, and ... who had placed at the disposal of the British government his deep and extensive knowledge of German affairs.'[1] His name was Wilfrid Israel.

Lisbon was a wartime centre of espionage and counter-espionage. German agents planted microphones in Portuguese government offices, followed visitors in the streets, and sifted the waste-paper baskets of hotels. British travellers were warned never to talk about their schedules and itineraries – to some extent a pointless precaution, since, for the price of a cup of coffee, anyone could sit on the airport terrace and watch passengers boarding every flight. But British agents detected the German buggings, and they watched the watchers.[2] Thus it was curious that none of the rumours about the four men was ever confirmed, and the full story of the plane's mysterious end was never revealed.[3] As for the British-born German businessman, he was swiftly forgotten. His spectacular death appeared to have been the only public event of his life.

Nearly forty years later, in August 1980, Wilfrid Israel's name appeared in an American literary review. Stephen Spender, a British poet and writer who had spent several years in Weimar Berlin, recalled that Israel was the original of one of the characters in Christopher Isherwood's early novel *Goodbye to Berlin*. Bernhard Landauer, as Isherwood calls him, a world weary, faint-hearted young Jewish businessman, who reacts to Nazi threats with indifference, is a 'culture devotee' who sleeps with a sandstone buddha at the foot of his bed. According to Spender, Isherwood later regretted the portrait as an injustice to Israel, a courageous man, and attempted to set the record straight in a later book. Spender added that Wilfrid Israel's memory in Israel was still a legend.

The standard reference works allotted Israel no more than a paragraph or two, describing him as businessman and philanthropist – no legend there. A first search in the Central Zionist Archives produced only the thinnest of files, containing a lone document and its carbon copy. However, this document was a signed tribute by Chaim Weizmann, head of the Zionist movement from the First World War and first President of the Jewish State. Written a year after Israel's death, it suggested that the two men had known one another for many years. Israel had gone to Portugal, Weizmann wrote, to distribute emigration certificates to Palestine among Jewish refugees – a routine task assumed willingly by a man who had undertaken more important missions. Yet the obituary was ambivalently worded: 'Though Palestine appealed to the artist and idealist in him,' Weizmann remarked, 'I doubt whether he would have called himself a Zionist.'[4]

Who was Wilfrid Israel, friend to both Isherwood and Weizmann? Though, in 1930, these last two might have passed one another in a Berlin street, the living distance between them was great. Weizmann was a professional politician – albeit without a country – whose work took him between the congress halls and grand hotels; Isherwood, an obscure and penniless young expatriate writer recording the grotesque decline of pre-Nazi Berlin, was a critical occasional visitor in the homes of those wealthy Jews whose support Weizmann canvassed. And why did Spender think, quite wrongly, that Wilfrid Israel was a 'legend' in the Jewish state?

There is only one place in modern Israel where his memory still lives – Hazorea, a kibbutz lying in the crook of wooded hills on the edge of the great plain called the Jezreel Valley. Here, beyond the factories and the cowsheds, at the far side of a central lawn, is a small pavilion with a columned patio and tiled roof, whose style is a subtle hint at the collection of oriental art housed inside. The sculptures in the collection, from Cambodia, India, China and other parts of the Far East, include the twelfth-century Khmer buddha which Isherwood described as standing at the foot of Bernhard Landauer's bed in Berlin.

In a will written the night before he left for Lisbon, in March 1943, Wilfrid Israel bequeathed his art collection to the kibbutz. The settlers received the news with mixed feelings. At that time, Hazorea was still a Spartan place. The hills now so thickly wooded were bare; the farmers coaxed meagre crops from hastily planted and waterlogged fields, and many still lived in shacks and tents. An art collection coveted, so they heard, by the British Museum, was an unnecessary responsibility.

But the founders were committed to their friendship with Wilfrid Israel, which went back to the first days of Nazi rule in Berlin. They were all cultivated people, whose life as farmers had begun as much by intellectual choice as from necessity. When the kibbutz assembly met to vote on whether to accept the bequest, there was a struggle. Wilfrid's friends won by a third of the votes. Through wars and through hard times, the Khmer Buddha and his fellows remained in Hazorea, witnesses to the personal influence of Wilfrid Israel, and the loyalty he inspired for decades after his death.

My search for Wilfrid Israel began in Hazorea, and led me to the men and women in three continents who had known him personally and remembered something of his life and work. Business colleagues and employees, Quaker relief workers, German intellectuals, English clergymen, German aristocrats, Oxford dons, British Foreign Office officials and others described him in similar terms. He was gentle and courageous; a man who avoided public office and shunned publicity, but who had an almost hypnotic ability to influence his friends and his colleagues in private conversation. A few people saw him as Bernhard Landauer: effete, 'over-refined'. But all thought him a man of infinite and baffling contradictions.

Even the first posthumous tributes which appeared were puzzling. Israel earned equal praise, in 1944, from colleagues as politically opposed as Weizmann and Harold Beeley, an Oxford don turned Foreign Office official, already known as a pan-Arabist and enemy of Zionism. Israel elicited equal trust, on important missions, from men as different as Max Warburg, the German-Jewish banker who believed that his German and Jewish loyalties were compatible, and Weizmann, who attacked Warburg in his autobiography as 'the usual type of Kaiser Juden – more

German than the Germans, obsequious, super patriotic, eagerly anticipating the wishes and plans of the masters of Germany'.

The indolent, self-centred Landauer was also the original of another portrait, *Zug in Wilfrid's Bild* (*Traits in Wilfrid's Portrait*), a prose poem by the philosopher and theologian Martin Buber, who described Wilfrid Israel as a man of great moral stature, dedicated to the service of others. The man Albert Einstein called 'a living work of art', directed a business with 2,000 employees. The man a scholar colleague in wartime England, Albert Hourani, saw as 'totally lonely and unhappy', had friends in every continent and was known for his ironic humour and love of mild practical jokes. The man a German journalist thought possessed a 'puritanical English streak', was described by an English writer friend as an inscrutable oriental. The man who spent the pre-war years rescuing the persecuted from Germany was a close wartime colleague of George Bell, the controversial Bishop of Chichester, Eden's 'pestilential priest', known as much for his German sympathies as for his anti-Nazi speeches.

Israel left no diaries or memoirs to help realign these confusing signposts. Only tributes and the memories of friends remained, but these were equally difficult to reconcile. For Wilfrid Israel's friends not only belonged to different worlds; they usually knew little or nothing of one another. His closest personal friends were not told of his public work. Two men who, in succession, had shared his London flat at the beginning of the war had no idea where he went or what he did during the day. He did not invite questions. 'Wilfrid was noble, but intangible,' said one old friend. 'A set of Chinese boxes,' said another. Not only was he contradictory; he was also intensely secretive.

Yet his name was not unknown. By the fourth decade after his death, it had appeared in a score of books about the Nazi period: memoirs, biographies, scholarly monographs, histories of refugees and of rescue attempts during the Holocaust. But in almost all the books he enters without introduction and leaves without explanation, a Berlin businessman always intent on some plan of rescue; a man who works alone, in the background, about whom no writer knows enough to say what he achieved, or even who he was.

In 1954, Sir Michael Bruce, a gentleman adventurer with no capital but his Scottish pedigree, published a book of memoirs which included his experiences in Vienna and Berlin after Germany's annexation of Austria – the period of the most violent pre-war Nazi excesses. Bruce was sent to Berlin by Jewish leaders in London to report on the plight of German Jewry during the Kristallnacht, the anti-Jewish pogrom of November 1938. The man with whom Bruce claimed to have made clandestine contact, and whom he praised for his exemplary courage, was Wilfrid Israel.[5]

Three years later, a journalist called Ian Colvin, who had written on the Chamberlain Cabinet, Berlin in the 1930s and German Intelligence, investigated the plane crash of 1943. He discovered that Leslie Howard and Wilfrid Israel had met in Madrid, at a British luncheon at the Cork Club. In Colvin's book, *Flight 777*, Howard tells Israel: 'But you *are* the Scarlet Pimpernel; I've only played the part.'

Colvin claimed that Israel, 'the Jewish agent', was well known to both German and British Intelligence, and that he personally had seen a 'Confidential Wehrmacht List' on which Israel was described as a British spy. British Intelligence sources, Colvin wrote, refused to discuss him. German Intelligence, he suggested, might have planned his death.[6]

Colvin's account of Israel's life was clearly taken from a privately printed, and privately distributed, volume of personal recollections published in London the year after his death. Apart from tributes by Einstein, Buber, Bell and Weizmann, other, less famous friends, leading figures in Jewish relief work during the 1930s, claimed that Wilfrid Israel had played a leading role in the Hilfsverein der Deutschen Juden, the German-Jewish emigration office which organized the transfer of Jews to countries abroad, apart from Palestine. The Hilfsverein enabled some 52,000 Jews to leave Germany during the pre-war period – more than any one other organization.[7] But no confirmation appears in any study of German Jewry during the time.

In mid-1956, Wilfrid Israel surfaced again in the British Press, posthumously summoned as character witness in a controversy surrounding Adam von Trott zu Solz, one of the best known figures in the anti-Nazi opposition groups in Germany. Trott, who had attempted, both before and during the war, to find allies in England and America, was suspected of duplicity by his old Oxford friends, and only rehabilitated, in British eyes, when executed by the Nazis in 1944. In 1956, a newly published document revived old suspicions.

David Astor, among those who came to Trott's defence, argued that two political confidants and friends of Trott's in wartime England had never doubted Trott's integrity or questioned his anti-Nazi credentials: Stafford Cripps, Labour politician and by 1942 a member of the War Cabinet, and Wilfrid Israel. Israel, Astor argued later, a courageous Jew and victim of Nazism, could not have befriended a man whose German nationalist loyalties were thought to have compromised his anti-Nazi sentiments. Israel appeared thereafter, in his usual disjointed way, in subsequent biographies of Trott. Christopher Sykes, whose biography of Trott appeared before the British records for the period were opened, remarked confidently that Israel's work for his fellow Jews was 'strictly legal', thus ineffective; the book cast no further light on the two men's friendship.[8]

In 1958, a monograph on the Israel family appeared in one of the first of a series of scholarly volumes commemorating German Jewry. The author, Hans Reissner, was uniquely qualified to write about Wilfrid Israel, having worked at his side as secretary to the executive of the Israel firm in Berlin, and was now teaching history at Princeton. However, the narrative faltered as it reached Wilfrid Israel himself, either from reticence, or – as appears more likely – from lack of detailed knowledge.

Like Buber's prose poem, Reissner's monograph was studded with dark hints about a mystery in Israel's personal life. Moreover, Reissner added: 'In order to survive, he had to develop a particular *joie de vivre* bordering on the perverted. In these circumstances, conspiracy and counter-conspiracy, which an individual would normally despise, may have come to him quite "naturally".' Reissner then relegated the 'supposed links' between Wilfrid Israel and members of the German opposition to a footnote. He recalled only one meeting between Israel and Hans Schönfeld, a Lutheran well known as an anti-Nazi, 'in or about 1937'. Despite the intimacy he claimed, Reissner was obviously not in Israel's confidence, though he knew who went in and out of his employer's office.[9]

During the next decade, Wilfrid Israel's name was rarely mentioned. It was only when the official British records for the 1930s were opened to historians, after the thirty-year ban lapsed, that he reappeared in documents related to Germany in the last year before the outbreak of the Second World War, and to the period in late 1942 and early 1943 when the extent of the massacre of European Jewry was publicly recognized, and belated rescue attempts finally launched – two of them from London.

The first historian to provide a documentary account of the famous November pogroms of 1938, and the political events surrounding them, Lionel Kochan, now named the 'representative of principal Jewish organizations, who is British born', described in British diplomatic papers as having called on the British Embassy in Berlin on the day before the pogrom to warn of impending violence. A few years later, in a survey of British policy towards refugees in the pre-war period, another historian, Joshua Sherman, noted Israel's repeated representations to the British Foreign Office on behalf of German Jewry, including several detailed proposals for action. But both writers were concerned with the pattern of events, and not the role of individuals, particularly one of whom so little was known.[10]

Wilfrid Israel's mission to Portugal and Spain was more fully reported;

but because it aborted with his death, and because he took whatever plans he had into the waters of the Bay of Biscay with him, little attempt was made to explore its context.[11]

British friends continued to describe Wilfrid Israel as exotic, oriental, and, invariably, 'dark-eyed'; in fact, Israel was tall, fair and blue-eyed, but Isherwood's original description had irrevocably established both Israel's inscrutability and his pigmentation in the literary imagination. A young writer, Peter Vansittart, who became Israel's personal friend in wartime London, described him as belonging to the type of 'heroic dandy'. For Vansittart, who had a copy of Isherwood's novel in his pocket when he first met Israel, he was like 'Wilde, Disraeli, Brummel, Robespierre, Saint Just, and their popular counterparts – P'smith, Raffles, Sir Percy Blakeney'. When Isherwood, taking up a reference in Spender's autobiography which reported Israel planning passive resistance to Nazism as early as 1932, finally published his reappraisal in 1977, he did not deny his original perceptions of Wilfrid Israel. These were, he said, 'based on actual observation'. All he did was to re-examine what he describes as his own latent hostility to a man who had both interested and puzzled him.[12]

So despite the tributes of his distinguished friends, the sparse but striking references in the histories, and the embellishments of English writers, Wilfrid Israel – whoever he was – was consigned to history's button moulders.

Enter the specialists, the professional scholars who labour to reconstruct, from piecemeal evidence and scattered documentation, the last years of German Jewry. To these men and women, Wilfrid Israel's name is not obscure; but, for them, he is of least interest, a faceless man, whose name appears only on a handful of the surviving documents. Academic discipline precludes speculation about the role of a man who did not put his name to official reports or engage in official correspondence, and who was not, formally at least, a community leader or worker.

The German-Jewish community was completely destroyed, and so were many of the records for the Nazi period. The most complete set of documents recovered, those of the Reichsvereinigung, the Jewish organization reconstituted according to Nazi decrees in mid-1939, were found in the cellar of a ruined synagogue a few years ago. But these relate to the period after Israel had – officially – left Germany. If Wilfrid Israel had indeed played a leading role in the Hilfsverein emigration office, as several survivors maintain, this cannot be proved from such documentation, for the simple reason that most of the documents relating to that organization are lost. Moreover, the British records indicate that the most intensive period of Israel's work – that of the greatest mass emigration of German Jews – was the period between November 1938 and September 1939. Conditions were chaotic, Nazi pressures overwhelming, and no one could keep accurate track of all the activities of Jewish leaders.

Furthermore, three areas in the history of Jewish emigration from Germany have not yet been investigated systematically. These are: the contacts between German Jews and foreign diplomats; illegal activities; and contacts with the Gestapo.[13] Yet these are vital factors, for the success or failure of rescue efforts depended on the immigration laws of the countries of refuge and restrictive foreign currency regulations, which together prevented the emigration of nearly half of German Jewry; and the double role of the Gestapo, which both encouraged and hindered the expulsion of Jews from Germany.

Israel's surviving colleagues maintained that he was one of the chief links between the Jewish leadership in Germany and the outside world, and that foreign visitors seeking information on German Jewry always came to him. If this was so, then it was an advantage for him not to appear on official rosters. Jewish officials were answerable to the Gestapo, which attended most formal meetings. Moreover, as Israel's frequent sorties from Germany were ostensibly business trips, the less he was exposed to questioning the better. Nor would his meetings with foreign visitors have been recorded in Germany.

Thus the story of Wilfrid Israel's work for German Jews was not to be found in official records, but only in personal testimonies, or, perhaps, in isolated documents in any one of the score of archives in which the fragments of that dispersed community had come to rest.

Who was to testify? Most of Wilfrid Israel's closest colleagues – Otto Hirsch, Paul Eppstein, Cora Berliner and Hanna Karminski among them – died in the concentration camps. All had the chance to escape but chose to remain with those of the community who had no way of leaving Germany.

Yet a few of the leaders survived and, where they are concerned, there is probably another reason why the story of Wilfrid Israel, like many others, has not been told. Reissner's disapproving comment about 'conspiracy which an individual would normally despise' is revealing. It is typical of the tone of many surviving testimonies, particularly regarding the last period of German-Jewish emigration. Obedience to the law was bred in the bone of the German-Jewish middle class, and few were proud of breaking even the laws of their persecutors.

Furthermore, no one could work for the Jewish community during the Nazi period without daily contacts with men who were, at least nominally, Nazis. Rabbi Leo Baeck, the head of the central Jewish organization, the Reichsvertretung, and Max Warburg, head of the Hilfsverein until 1938, and arguably the most powerful man in German Jewry – both of whom survived the war (Baeck in Theresienstadt, Warburg in New York) – preserved an almost total silence on all such aspects of their work. Israel, too, swore his most trusted aide to secrecy – a vow the man could not bring himself to break completely even thirty years after Israel's death.

When Wilfrid Israel left Germany, days before the outbreak of war, and settled in London, he might have come out of the shadows into historical daylight. But everything conspired to consign him to obscurity, quite apart from the fact that he himself wanted no credit for anything he did.

During the great invasion scare in 1940, he had first worked, so colleagues maintained, as liaison officer between the German and Austrian refugees interned as 'enemy aliens', the refugee organizations at Bloomsbury House in London, the Home and War Offices, and – informally – the various public committees organized by those who tried to reverse government policy. Israel's secretary, Marion Schreiber, testified to the hundreds of letters she had typed to the Home Office and also for onward referral to the War Office; internees remembered his visits to the camps; Anglo-Jewish contemporaries remembered his presence at committee meetings.

But the majority of Home Office files remain closed, though the thirty-year limit is long past. The Home Office deny all knowledge of Mr Israel and his activities. Wartime internment was a stigma, and some years ago, under pressure from their old clients, the refugee organizations centred on Bloomsbury House destroyed all their files, except a small cache in an old people's home in North London. The committees dispersed. There is no mention of Israel's role in the release of internees in any of the several books written on internment policy and its results.

As for the 'knowledge that Wilfrid Israel placed at the disposal of the British government', all that was known about Israel's work, at his death, was that he had worked as 'consultant' to research on German and Jewish affairs for the Royal Institute of International Affairs, 'Chatham House', at the Foreign Research and Press Service at Oxford – then in the service of the Foreign Office. Though many of the papers prepared by the FRPS are now awash in the great swell of material in the Public Record Office, Chatham House has no documentation save advisory handbooks, with no details of personal contributions. Its records contain only the date of Israel's formal recruitment, and the notice of his death. A rare published study of Chatham House's contribution to

British policy on Germany mentions Israel anonymously, as '*eine geeignete mittelsmann*' (a convenient intermediary) between the Institution and the German political exiles in 1941.[14]

Israel's journey to Portugal and Spain in the spring of 1943, by contrast, was amply documented in office minutes, cables and published records. Yet, even here, there is a puzzle. While most documents referred, as Weizmann had done, to the task of distributing certificates to Palestine, two articles suggested that Israel had another mission – to explore the feasibility of collective transports for children from Nazi-occupied territories into Spain. Israel sent no report back on this aspect of his work. Moreover, in the published histories, there is no indication of the context of such rescue plans. Most Jewish efforts were concentrated in the Balkans, within easier reach of Palestine.

Finally, the question remained: was there any truth to what Colvin had written? Might Israel have been the object of the attack on the civilian plane? And why, indeed, was that plane singled out for destruction, as popular myth had it?

To call a man an enigma is subtly to devalue his personality. The first task of research was obviously to recreate Wilfrid Israel's early years and personal experiences, in the light of which at least some of the apparent contradictions might be resolved. Forty years ago, friends seeking to perpetuate his memory were unable even to assemble a collection of his letters. Israel's executor answered requests for help sternly: 'Don't forget that when Wilfrid left [Berlin] in 1939 he did not take a single piece of paper with him, so that there are only a few notes since that time.... I think you know very well how little Wilfrid liked publicity of any kind, so no copies are kept of most of his personal letters.'[15]

But many letters were kept by his personal friends. Four hundred, at least, have survived, for Israel was an assiduous letter writer, even referring, near the end of his life, to his *renommé* in dashing off notes. The letters which remain display the familiar contradictions. The handwriting, bold and beautiful, is almost aggressively legible, the hand of a man who wants no misunderstanding. The style, however, is veiled, hesitant, often disjointed. One reason, undoubtedly, is that he knew most of the letters written in the last ten years of his life would be read by enemies or strangers – by the Gestapo or by British wartime censors. Nevertheless, they authenticate, in many cases, what would otherwise remain speculations about his experiences and intentions, and test the accuracy of his friends' memories.

His London papers, too, are far more than 'a few notes'. After his death, they were vetted by the Foreign Office, and much is the clutter of a busy man's desk. All personal letters were removed. Nevertheless, they reward close scrutiny. Israel wrote out, carefully dated and signed with his initials, draft papers on all the major issues he discussed with his British colleagues: his views on the failure of German democracy; the anti-Nazi groups in Germany; British post-war policy for Europe; Zionism; Palestine; and the post-war future of Jewry. The papers also contain over forty Chatham House reports, on many of which he worked, with his annotations, and minutes of discussions with his own contribution carefully marked. Even stray papers are significant: scribbled lists of names led to survivors of committees long disbanded; once destitute refugees now living under different names; and old employees in the family business.[16] Finally, every archive where there was a chance of finding further evidence of Israel's work had to be scanned.

Very slowly, the life of Wilfrid Israel began to take shape, its contours shifting and settling like a wreck beneath water. Some details were erased – for instance, the circumstances in which Israel met Gorki's wife; the names of those who were his informants in the German political police; and the reason why he might have visited the Soviet Union in the winter of 1943. Yet despite all this, the pattern of his life and, whatever the contradictions of his personality, the essential simplicity of his intentions stand out clearly.

Nothing in the following narrative is invented, or artificially restored. There are no concessions to fiction, no invented dialogues; necessary speculations are not disguised as fact. Based on archival sources, personal testimonies and Israel's own surviving letters and notes, it is a brief portrait of a man and his times; a man who, in the words of a letter to Adam von Trott in November 1939, said that he, like Trott, had 'felt the burden of his time too ardently', and whose adult life was mostly concerned with the casualties of that time.

2
The Last Heir

When Wilfrid Israel was born in London on 11 July 1899, his father was the owner and director of one of the most famous business houses in Imperial Germany, and his mother's grandfather, Hermann Adler, was Chief Rabbi of the United Hebrew Congregations of Great Britain. Both families, which had twice intermarried, were able to trace their ancestry back for centuries: Wilfrid's maternal great-grandfather's family, the Adlers, to rabbinical scholars in the sixteenth-century ghetto of Frankfurt-on-Main, and his father's to a small group of Jewish traders who had lived on royal sufferance in Berlin from the mid-eighteenth century. Together, the families exemplified the intellectual and material progress of European Jewry over 300 years.

At the turn of the century, the Israels in Germany and the Adlers in England were firmly established as patriots and monarchists. When there was a break in the Israel family tradition, it was towards a more intense conservatism still: Moritz Israel, Wilfrid's great-uncle, declined his share in the family firm, bought a *Rittergut*, a manorial estate, at Schulzendorf in East Prussia, studied agriculture and became a gentleman farmer; his son and heir, Richard, served as an Oberleutnant on Hindenburg's personal staff during the First World War.[1]

The Adlers, meanwhile, had become equally loyal Englishmen. Nathan Marcus Adler, the first British Chief Rabbi, had emigrated from Hanover (formally under the British Crown) in 1844 and delivered his first sermons in German. But his son, Hermann Marcus, wore the robes of an Anglican prelate, officiated at the marriages of the Anglo-Jewish merchant elite, and kept his distance from the new immigrants from Eastern Europe who congregated in the East End of London. In 1896, he deplored the revolutionary ideas of Zionism, outlined in Herzl's *Judenstaat*, as 'impracticable and at the same time dangerous'.[2]

In the year in which Wilfrid Israel was born, his great-grandfather Adler was preaching in support of the British campaign against the Boers in South Africa, with illustrations from the Old Testament, adding that 'of all the policies none is more dangerous, none more calculated to sap a nation's greatness, than the advocacy of peace at any price ... the government of our queen had no alternative but to resort to the fierce arbitrament of war'.[3] Germany, meanwhile, viewed the Boers as the outriders of German culture.

In the same year, the Israel firm in Berlin began issuing an annual series of sumptuously produced albums for its customers, glorifying German arts and sciences, the enlightened rule of the Hohenzollerns, and the position of the N. Israel business house as one of the jewels in the crown. The 1901 issue was dedicated to the German colonies, written by the director of the German Colonial Museum, and later volumes appeared on subjects such as the German theatre, education and 'the age of woman's energy' (the athletic and intellectual achievements of women over the previous century).[4]

Behind the Israels' and the Adlers' earnest affirmation of support for their sovereigns was the consciousness that even the most privileged Jews were not immune to criticism for their birth, their separate creed and, above all, their success. The majority of the Jews in Britain were still conspicuously foreign, and frequently suspected of foreign loyalties. In Germany, the economic crisis twenty years earlier had precipitated the first appearance of racial, as opposed to religious, anti-semitism, and the 'Anti-Semitic' political party was to win sixteen seats in the Reichstag in the 1907 elections.

In England, Rabbi Adler joined battle with an Oxford professor of history, Goldwin Smith, who had argued that Jews, with their 'international background', could not be patriots.[5] Adler's remarks about 'undesirable elements' among Russian-Jewish emigrants were pounced on by anti-semitic writers. He defended adherence to Jewish tradition while rejecting Gentile accusations of 'exclusiveness'; he also warned Jewish traders against 'double standards' for Jewish and Gentile customers – indicating how far both he and his congregation were on the defensive.[6]

Berlin Jews were even more vulnerable. By the 1880s there were more Jews in Berlin than in all England, conspicuous above all for their role in commerce. The message of the Israel albums was that the firm was not only a business, but a purveyor of German good taste, vital to the economic health of the *Weltstadt* (big city). Above all, it stressed the Israels' German pedigree. The chief editor of the albums, the writer Conrad Alberti, pointed out that 'unlike its rivals, N. Israel had a history dating back to 1815'. In the album for 1902 dedicated to the Kaiser Wilhelm, in an essay entitled 'The Development of Berlin and the N. Israel Emporium', Alberti plays Virgil to an imaginary visitor. From the white mass of the Reichstag, fronted by a bronze statue of Bismarck, they stroll past the double row of statuary in the Siegesallee and, having inspected the Linden avenue, the cathedral and the royal palace, arrive at the Schlossplatz with its statue of the old Elector, and finally see the old town before them, a 'teeming wellspring of modern life', with its shops and industries, and, at its heart, opposite the red brick town hall, the five-storey 'citadel of commerce' – N. Israel.

Conrad Alberti was no ordinary hack. He was a well-known writer, best known for his novel *Die Alten und die Jungen* (1902), and, as co-editor of the liberal journal *Die Gesellschaft*, dedicated to spreading the ideas of Zola and attacking the evils of industrialism. Not only did the central character in Alberti's novel excoriate, on behalf of younger Jews, the 'superfluousness, harmfulness and rottenness of Jewry'; but in 1882 Alberti had published a violent attack on German Jewry, arguing that as religion was declining and Jewish separatism was obsolete, Jews must assimilate totally. If Germany encouraged this, he wrote, at some time in the future 'the last Jew would be exhibited as a rarity'.[7]

The Israels could not have been more strongly identified with the Jewish community. In 1902, the Israel firm was still closed on Saturdays and the Jewish High Holy days; Berthold Israel, Wilfrid's father, was a warden of the fashionable Lutzowerstrasse synagogue, and Mrs Israel's ancestry was well known. Had anyone charged Alberti with inconsistency – or venality – he might have pointed to the closing paragraphs of the article, which described the exceptional welfare benefits the Israels provided for their employees: the extra pension scheme, the recreational facilities, and the long weekend holidays. Jewish paternalism, in the form of their own bonus schemes, combined with the Bismarckian social services to provide benefits to employees unique in the Europe of the time. The Israels prided themselves on being progressive employers; their motto was '*Reélitat*' (honesty) and this referred not only to services to the customers, but the treatment of their employees. Alberti's essays, however, revealed the worm of uncertainty at the heart of Jewish success, as well as the typically German-Jewish belief that probity and industry – and self-criticism – could ward off attacks from outside.

This, then, was the family into which Wilfrid Israel was born, in which the consciousness of power and its responsibilities was uneasily balanced with the knowledge of vulnerability. Cosmopolitan, yet intensely loyal to their different countries, the Israels and the Adlers were typical of the great European Jewish families scattered across the Continent at the turn of the century.

Throughout his life Wilfrid Israel was ambivalent about his role as a businessman. In his view, the too rapid industrialization of Germany – which had naturally contributed to the rise of the Israel firm – was one of the main causes of the breakdown of German civilization in the 1930s, and he believed that only socialism, and an end to the old monopolies on the land and in industry, could help create a stable German democracy. He also had the German conservative and romantic view of the need for an escape from the city and a return to the virtues of an agrarian society. Such ideas were conventional enough at the time, if contradictory and odd when held by a Jewish businessman.[8] But Wilfrid was unlike other German-Jewish businessmen. The two traditions of Jewish paternalism and German *Sohnespflicht* (filial duty) had thrust him into a role to which, though he fulfilled it faithfully, none of the friends of his youth thought him suited. When he finally liquidated the firm in 1939 and left for England, he did so with both regret and relief; henceforth, he was to dedicate himself to study and research.

Whatever the attractions of the Adler heritage, however, Wilfrid's role in German-Jewish life during the Nazi period was dictated by his sense of the tradition the firm represented and its importance to the self-respect of the Jewish community. N. Israel was not one of the larger Jewish firms; it had no branches, unlike the huge chain-stores Tietz, Wertheim, Schocken or the Kaufhaus das Westens. Its architecture was solid rather than striking like Wertheim's new façade in the Leipzigerstrasse, which had been designed by Alfred Messel and dubbed 'the consumers' cathedral'. But N. Israel was a Baedeker landmark. The first of the great Jewish business houses in Berlin, it was the last to close its doors.

It was also a base for Wilfrid during his work for German Jewry. Like his father, Wilfrid Israel was well known in international business circles and this – rather than his British passport, which afforded him no real protection in Germany – ensured that whatever happened to him or his family was immediately known abroad. Moreover, N. Israel maintained close links with its provincial customers throughout Germany; the peculiarity of the firm was that it had always combined retail and wholesale trade, and its Gentile customers were dispersed all over Germany and in Eastern Europe. Many had sent their sons for training in the Israels' trade school in Berlin. Thus Wilfrid's potential sources of help and information covered the entire country.

In 1935, Kurt Tucholsky, the Jewish writer and satirist, wrote of German-Jewish businessmen, in a much quoted passage: 'Now they slink out, gloomy, soundly thrashed, in shit up to their ears, bankrupt, their money robbed – and without honour.'[9] Tucholsky, like many other writers and historians – Hannah Arendt is the most celebrated among them – could see no dignity in those who remained in Germany under Nazi rule. The case of the Israels indicates that the issue was not so simple. In the first years of Nazism, it would have been easy to liquidate the Israel firm with profit to all involved, since one of its chief executives was British. But Wilfrid Israel fought a rearguard action against the Nazis both outside and inside the firm, helping Jews from the firm's funds, and running the business into the ground in the process; its continued existence was a mark of defiance. The rise of the firm had mirrored, step by step, the emancipation of German Jewry, as both Jews and Nazis recognized, and it was this, rather than the loss of the family fortune, which made the fate of N. Israel more than one more financial casualty of a business community whose fall was far more rapid than its rise.

Writing from Berlin to a friend in Palestine in the spring of 1937, Wilfrid commented: 'To liquidate the existence of five generations on one's own, without going to the dogs oneself, isn't so easy.'

Alberti, in his public relations efforts, had claimed only four Israel generations. N. Israel was officially founded in 1815, and, counting forward from that point, Wilfrid and his brother Herbert were the fourth generation of Berlin merchants. By taking the family history one generation further back, Wilfrid recalled a time when the family were, in fact, no more than old clothes' dealers. This, together with pawnbroking, was the only occupation open to Jews in Berlin at the time, and the Jewish rag merchant was a famous figure not only throughout Europe but in the Far East as well. Among Wilfrid Israel's collection of Cambodian buddhas, Ghandara and Gupta sculptures from India, and Ethiopian textiles, is a Chinese T'ang statuette dating from the seventh century, entitled 'Western merchant', which is a fine example of a traditional figure known to collectors. It is a bent, sad figure with a recognizably Jewish face and distinctively Jewish clothing, hauling a sack on his back. It stands out in a collection chosen for its beauty, perhaps a talisman against arrogance, like the skulls which used to lie on the desks of Renaissance rulers as a reminder of mortality.

Before 1812, the Israels had neither a fixed name, nor the permanent right of residence in Prussia.[10] The first Prussian Israel, Jacob, was sworn in as a municipal citizen of Berlin in April 1806, three years after the victory of Napoleon over Prussia brought freedom to all Prussians, regardless of their faith. On 11 March 1812, equal rights and privileges were extended to the Jews of Prussia and the special taxes imposed on them until then were abolished. Jacob was now declared a native Prussian citizen. Had he so wished, he might have changed his trade. He was no longer bound by Mosaic law in family and inheritance matters and his sons became liable to military service. He was also obliged to choose a fixed surname, like all Jews of the period.

But he was nearly sixty, disposed neither by age nor temperament to drastic change. He continued to deal in second-hand clothes and did not join the Jewish trade associations, which, in 1805, had merged with the Christian merchant guilds. Despite the growing secularism in the Jewish community, and the fact that many Jews at this time adopted German surnames (and first names), Jacob Israel insisted that the family name should remain that of his father, the first of the family to settle in Berlin. Jacob's son also stipulated in his will that the inheritance depended on the retention of the name Israel; after that period, the firm was so well known that to change the name would have meant a loss of goodwill. This was the reason why, over 120 years later, when the Nazis ruled Germany, the name N. Israel flashed out every night over one of the main squares of Berlin, until in 1939, at a time when the Nazis forced male Jews to adopt Israel as their middle name as a stigma and badge of their race, Goering insisted that the owners of 'Aryanized' firms remove the names of their Jewish founders from their shop fronts.

The official founder of the firm was Jacob's son Nathan. His shop was in the Molkenmarkt, where, after three years among the old clothes dealers in the Judenstrasse, Nathan set up a business in Silesian linen fabrics.

During the lifetime of Nathan's son and Wilfrid's grandfather, Jacob Israel, the population of Berlin increased nearly ten times. It was now not only a garrison town, but the industrial capital of Imperial Germany, demanding recognition, after the country's unification, as a *Weltstadt* like Paris and London. Deplored by Bismarck and conservative German writers as an upstart among cities, Berlin became the home of the majority of Germany's Jews, who, by 1905, numbered over 130,000, or more than 4 per cent of the capital's population – as high a percentage as they were ever to reach. N. Israel now supplied linen and furnishings to hotels, clubs and theatres, to barracks and officers' messes, to hospitals and churches. At the death of Wilhelm I, in 1888, the firm provided the black crêpe decorations strung all along the royal funeral route.

By this time, N. Israel occupied four floors in a block facing the Berlin Municipality, had 250 employees, including a team of travelling salesmen, and produced one of the first mail-order catalogues on the American pattern. Many of its provincial customers even deposited their surplus funds with the firm for safekeeping: N. Israel was an active member of the Berlin stock exchange until the First World War.

Jacob Israel, Wilfrid's grandfather, having earned the title of 'Royal

Merchant' of Berlin (*Köeniglicher Kommerzienrat*) in 1886, married Minna Adler, the daughter of the Chief Rabbi of England. He remained an unpretentious observant Jew, giving generously to charity but living modestly – travelling to work by bus, bringing sandwiches for lunch in the office, switching off gas lights when they were not needed, and often showing customers to the door himself with the query 'Did you find what you were looking for?' He caught pneumonia while attending the funeral of a Gentile employee. As the funeral took place on the Jewish Sabbath, he walked to the ceremony on a cold March day, and died two weeks later. But in his will, he specified that if his sons thought it necessary, to meet competition, the business could be opened henceforth on Sabbaths (though not on High Holy days) if, in atonement (the Hebrew *kofer*), his heirs were to donate a substantial sum to charity. This happened only in 1907; the exact sum donated is not on record, but it was a Berlin-Jewish legend that Berthold Israel had deposited the equivalent of a million reichsmarks in gold in the community chest.

While the Israels, who by the turn of the century were no longer observant orthodox Jews, had kept their Jewish name, the rabbinical family of the Adlers, like many other German Jews, had adopted the name of the German eagle.[11] Originally named Kayn (or Cohen, of the Jewish priestly sect), the family had settled in Frankfurt-on-Main at the beginning of the sixteenth century; at the time of the notorious Fettmilch pogroms in 1614, the family escaped together with another thousand Jews and – according to family legend favoured by their British descendants – when the Emperor Mathias restored the Jewish community two years later, one of the Kayns marched at the head of the returning Jews carrying the royal standard. Whether the story was true or not, the imperial eagle continued to decorate the Adler family's cutlery well into the twentieth century, as well as the bookplates of Wilfrid's bibliophile great-uncle, Elkan Adler, a solicitor and scholar, who was among the first travellers to identify and purchase some of the Cairo Genizah fragments of ancient Jewish scrolls. He was so often abroad that, on one occasion, his business partner embezzled all the firm's cash and Adler had to sell most of his collection of manuscripts to pay his debts; during a trip in 1924 with Wilfrid and another nephew, he borrowed from them to pay for further purchases.

The first distinguished Adler rabbi was born in Frankfurt in 1741 – the same year the Israels settled in Berlin. His son, Mordechai Adler, became Chief Rabbi of Hanover, then under the British Crown, and his grandson, Nathan Marcus, after inheriting his father's position, became the first Chief Rabbi of the United Congregations of Great Britain in

1845. At that time, there were only 20,000 Jews in Britain, deeply divided by communal schisms, and while German Jewry was already heir to a long tradition of scholarship by rabbis, philosophers and historians, British Jewry had produced mainly bankers, merchants and philanthropists. Half of the population of Britain at that time was illiterate, and the education of British Jews could not compare with that of their German co-religionists. Though Oxford and Cambridge admitted Jews officially from the 1850s, very few took advantage of the concession. The colleges were Christian foundations; the social atmosphere was hostile to Jews, and continued to be so well into the first decades of the twentieth century.

Nathan Adler, who had a classical humanist education from Gottingen and Würzburg universities as well as rabbinical training, immediately attempted to organize Jewish schools in Britain which would provide both boys and girls with general and Jewish education. Even before he had mastered English, he ordered questionnaires sent out to all the Jewish communities; there were already free schools for poor Jews, but these were of a Dickensian grimness, with one teacher for 600 pupils and lessons relayed from group to group through huge halls by 'monitors'. Adler travelled widely throughout Britain, enlisted the support of wealthy Jews in the City, such as the Montagus and the Rothschilds. After ten years, he had set up twenty schools for 3,000 children - half of all the Jewish children in Britain - and established Jews College, for the training of rabbis, teachers and lay leaders, which he wanted to integrate with London University. Adler was asked to contribute his views on education to the parliamentary commission of 1861 on popular education: among his proposals was the free compulsory education of boys and girls to the age of fourteen.

But Adler's idea of a separate but equal status for Jewish children, within a state system, was not in the spirit of the times in Britain, and was favoured neither by the wealthier Jews - who wanted their children to be educated together with Gentiles - nor by the provisions of the Education Act of the 1870 Liberal Government, which set up non-sectarian schools financed by municipal taxation. Before leaving Germany in 1844, Adler had spoken bitterly, in his last sermon, of German political illiberalism: 'We know not whether we are citizens of this land or foreigners, for we must beg even for the smallest parcel of land we wish to acquire.' Like most European Jews, he regarded Britain as the most tolerant country in Europe. But he could not see that British liberalism - which would ultimately encourage that trend to assimilation he deplored and feared - and the relative stability of England, which was the main cause of tolerance, worked against his ideas.

Thus, paradoxically, in the country which offered so many Jews asylum, there was to be no specific tradition of Jewish intellectual brilliance to compare with that which flourished in the far less tolerant political climate of nineteenth-century Germany – as Wilfrid Israel was to note, with disappointment, when he finally came to live in England in 1939.

Hermann Adler, the Edwardian Chief Rabbi, inherited all his father's conservatism without his reforming energy. The Adlers became part of the British Establishment, anxious to stress their relationship to the Anglo-Jewish nobility: the Rothschilds and Montagus were distant relations. While the Jewish tradition that commerce should support scholarship continued, marriage between rabbinical and merchant families was no longer so strong an institution in Western Europe.

The marriage of Wilfrid's parents, Berthold Israel and Amy Solomon, celebrated under the traditional canopy on the lawn of the Solomon mansion at Kensington Palace Gardens in 1893, was certainly not such a marriage. The Solomons had initially opposed it because the two were first cousins, fearing for the health of the couple's children. Berthold, together with his brother Hermann, had inherited the family business only a few months earlier; he had spent the previous year, since his engagement, on a grand tour around the world. He dressed like a City stockbroker, and – unlike his father and grandfather, who had only received elementary education, though they studied the Torah privately – had attended one of Berlin's most famous secondary schools, the Französische Gymnasium.

Amy Solomon, the Chief Rabbi's granddaughter, was the youngest of nine children of a wealthy businessman from Exeter, who had made his fortune by manufacturing the steel pens which were replacing quills in city offices, and was now in the import and export trade; Amy's second name, Josepha, was that of the ship in which his cargo was travelling at her birth. Amy was a self-willed young woman, with intelligent eyes and a rapacious mouth. She was widely read, liked the company of actors, musicians and intellectuals, and, in Berlin, terrified the more sedate wives of businessmen by quoting from contemporary French poets; she signed herself 'Aimée'. No quiet bluestocking, Amy had no compunction about displaying the Israels' great wealth. The couple lived first in the Hohenzollernstrasse, and then in the Hildebrandstrasse, two short parallel avenues leading into the Tiergartenstrasse, which bordered on Berlin's central park – according to the observer's view, the most fashionable, or the most pretentious, quarter of Berlin. The Israels entertained in the formal style which Berlin Jewry believed was English, with a butler and a team of other servants. Artists, opera singers and diplomats, as well as business friends, were always Amy's guests on her birthday, 1 January, when she wore a favourite emerald necklace. She was an eccentric rather than an elegant woman, one of the first to wear trousers; and, like her husband, she sat for her portrait by the Berlin society painter, Josef Oppenheimer.

The family travelled in a carriage and pair, with a horse-drawn sleigh for the Prussian winter, before the age of the Mercedes or the Rolls, which they used for formal occasions. Even their chauffeur had distinction: he wrote a motoring column for a Berlin newspaper.

Berthold had inherited the caution and, on occasion, even the parsimony of his Israel father and grandfather. He was driven to work each day in an old and rather shabby car, fitter for an employee than the director of the firm. His clothes were made by one of the firm's resident tailors, whom he instructed not to exaggerate fashionable lapels or padding, as the suits would have to last for years. He had a good winter coat, but the fur was on the inside. His style, one acquaintance commented, was 'calculated simplicity', and when he travelled alone, he was as likely to eat in a railway station buffet as in the nearest good restaurant.

In business, Berthold was cautious and resistant to change. Although he spent less time than his father had done talking to customers, he frequently visited his competitors' firms, incognito, to compare prices and conditions of sale. Under his directorship, the Israel firm expanded and became a modern department store. Chaim Weizmann, in a letter to Lord Perth in 1939, described it as having been 'something corresponding to Harrods here, but older established';[12] by the early 1930s it employed over 2,000 people.

Wilfrid Berthold Jacob Israel, the second of three children and the first son, was born, as his name indicates, with the whole weight of family tradition on his shoulders. He was given a first name equally familiar in Germany and England, with the result that it was misspelt by everyone but his closest friends. He was born in London, because his mother was determined that he should be British. His German friends all insisted that he profited from a triple culture: German, English and Jewish. The reality was somewhat different.

Amy Israel disliked Germany. She had made it a condition of her marriage that she should visit England frequently, and, although she spoke fluent German, she refused to have it spoken at her dinner table unless her guests knew no English, announcing 'German is for the servants'. This did not endear her to German Jews proud of their national culture. Both her elder children were taught at home by an English governess and the almost exclusive influence of his mother until puberty, as well as his physical frailty, meant that Wilfrid had little in common with other boys of his age by the time he reached the Gymnasium.

Few German Jews can have received the complete works of Sir Walter Scott as a barmitzvah present, and few boys of any nationality would have been offered a tour of Italy's art galleries at the age of thirteen. From the age of eight, Wilfrid received tuition in Hebrew and Bible studies from Arthur Levi, a young rabbinical student, but most of this knowledge evaporated once his barmitzvah was passed; his uncle Elkan Adler regarded him as ignorant of Jewish culture.

Amy was a strict disciplinarian, and she dominated the household. The Israel children were expected to dress up and perform sketches they had composed on the occasion of their mother's birthday, before the grand company arrived. Agnes Schneider, a young American who came to Berlin to study singing in 1911 and lived with the family from 1914 for nine years, remembered that Herbert, the younger brother, hated all this and would burst into tears; Wilfrid, however, was always perfectly controlled. Later in life, he was punctilious in remembering friends' birthdays, but refused to give presents on anniversaries or to celebrate his own birthday. He brought gifts spontaneously, but hated formal occasions, and it is hard not to connect this with the style of the Israel household, where nothing controversial could be discussed at mealtimes, mother's word was law, servants were always on hand, and no one could be invited home without Amy's prior consent.

Family portraits show Wilfrid as a solemn little boy, in the stiff poses of the time – one in a sailor suit in which he attended dancing classes, in what he called 'my most militant and successful days' – and in later pictures as an overgrown and melancholy adolescent. His cousin Hilda – the daughter of Richard Israel, the army officer – who grew up with horses and cows on the family estate, dreaded the visits to the town Israels, for which she had to dress in uncomfortable clothes, and where the fashionable *canapés* Amy's white-gloved servants handed round were far too small for a hungry child. She never saw Wilfrid smile, and thought he looked right through the servants.

Amy played hostess frequently to visiting musicians and actors. Berthold preferred business trips to hotels whose furniture he had supplied. One of Wilfrid's English cousins, Henry Myer, who visited Berlin in 1908 and 1911, remembered being taken to the May Parade in Potsdam where the Kaiser's daughter went about in a carriage and pair selling marguerites; the Israels' journey then continued to Dresden, to inspect a new hotel the firm had equipped.[13] It was clear that Wilfrid was being prepared, even then, to inherit his father's place in the business. 1911 was the year of Agadir, when a German gunboat was sent to Morocco in a futile effort to challenge the other colonial powers, and Berthold, when questioned about German rearmament, said that 'if the Germans were taxed so heavily to pay for armaments, they couldn't do otherwise than to make war'. Berthold himself was rumoured to pay higher taxes than any other Jew in Berlin.

Taken to Tuscany, Rome and Venice, Wilfrid dutifully recorded his impressions of every museum and cathedral.[14] The itinerary suggests that the family drove rather than walked through the galleries: more than a decade later, when Wilfrid was writing to a favourite aunt, explaining the political background to Botticelli's *Calumnia* in the Uffizi, he added, 'I know by experience how enthusiastic one is after having visited the Umbrian towns. ... I am so glad that you did not have to rush.'

He was to return regularly to Italy – to Venice and the Villa Ruffolo in Ravello – like many cultivated Germans, to escape the Prussian climate and to revisit favourite paintings such as Bellini's *Madonna degli Alberetti* – 'Meine Lieblingsmadonna' – in the Venice Accademia, always finding time for the galleries, which he visited in peace and in war, on whatever mission, until a few days before his death. In adolescence he began to sketch and model in clay, and daydreamed of becoming a sculptor. By now he was attending the Mommsen Gymnasium with his brother Herbert; most of his spare time was spent sketching at the easel in the basement of the Hohenzollernstrasse house, and writing poetry. Fritz Landshoff, a schoolfriend who walked home with him every day, doubted that he ever seriously believed he could become a sculptor. Other friends said it was a frustrated hope. What is certain is that he bitterly regretted that his studies were cut short before he could attend either art school or university.

In 1941 he wrote to a young refugee friend in England whose university career had been interrupted by the Nazis and who was working on a farm: 'I know from my own experience how depressing it is not to have a real finish to one's education. I was never able to do my matric and always felt it.' That same autumn, when he was working regularly with a team of scholars under Arnold Toynbee at Balliol, he wrote: 'This contact with Oxford is something that has played a big part in my imagination since boyhood; now, in these advanced years, it has become reality, under such strange circumstances.'[15] In many other letters, he confesses that he has a 'disorganized', 'dishevelled' mind, that he lacks training in and basic knowledge of all the subjects he wanted to master, from the history of Jewish emancipation to the Hellenistic origins of the art of Ghandara. The disability of Jewish youth in Nazi Germany, evicted from schools and universities, was one which Wilfrid Israel felt especially keenly: privileged in all else, he had been deprived of an education.

In Germany, at that period, a young man with artistic ambitions did not necessarily attend university; but Wilfrid was not allowed to become an artist. Moreover, though he was heir to the business, it was his brother Herbert who studied economics in Berlin and was later sent to the United States to study business administration. The First World War broke out when Wilfrid was fifteen, and all that followed put an end both to his chances of further education and to any compromise over his own ambitions.

Henry Myer had noticed that Wilfrid was 'not soldiering material. He was incapable of any sort of anger or of losing his temper.' Wilfrid became a convinced pacifist and, by the time he reached military age, he wanted to declare himself a conscientious objector.

Pacifism had existed in Germany as an organized movement since the Franco-Prussian War, but it was the creed of a small group led by privileged idealists, such as Bertha von Suttner. There was no tradition of political non-conformism, no belief in bearing personal witness, or of individual protest, like that of the Puritans and Quakers in Britain and the United States, whose members included thousands of conscientious objectors during the war. Though Wilfrid Israel was to meet many leading British pacifists in the years following the war, he was too young to have met them at that time, although he may have heard of their ideas. The men to whom he looked for guidance in 1917 and 1918 were Albert Einstein and Maximilian Harden, the brilliant and iconoclastic Jewish publicist who edited the weekly *Die Zukunft*, and who, after initially supporting the aims of the war, turned against it in mid-stream.

Einstein had left Switzerland in 1914 and settled in Berlin; he was then thirty-five, already a famous mathematician and physicist, and when German intellectuals (including many Jews) issued the notorious *Manifesto to the Civilized World* in October 1914, defending German militarism and nationalism, Einstein was one of the three men who issued a challenge and proposed a European anti-war union. In November 1914 he helped found the Bund Neues Vaterland, whose policy was peace without annexations; though the organization frequently petitioned the Reichstag and carried on a correspondence with British pacifists, it was only officially closed down in February 1916. Einstein refused to take part as a scientist in the war effort, unlike his fellow Jews Walther

Rathenau and Fritz Haber, who respectively reorganized the German armaments industry and contributed to the development of explosives.

As an adolescent, Wilfrid was a frequent visitor to Einstein's house. He had a great admiration for the man and his determination to stand up for his principles, whatever the odds against him. In later years, Wilfrid was to send his friends to hear Einstein's lectures, even when they protested they could not understand a word he said. 'Go just to experience his personality,' Wilfrid told them.

But the Israels had no intention of allowing Wilfrid to appear before a tribunal. When he received his mobilization papers in the autumn of 1917, his parents summoned three doctors, strangers to the family, to testify that he was medically unfit to serve. Wilfrid did not get the chance to make a heroic stand, and his distress is apparent in a letter he wrote a few months later to Maximilian Harden, who had already forecast the collapse of the monarchy (which he had previously supported), condemned the German war aims (which he had previously approved) and outlined a peace plan of his own, including anti-capitalism and militarism, self-determination for small nations and the integration of Germany into the new Europe.

On 15 April 1918, Wilfrid wrote to Harden:

> Your world of ideas seems to offer the only true oasis in our pitiful desert, the sole remedy for the madness which dominates our world.
>
> From day to day thoughts and ideals gain force within me, and the more I encounter shocked opposition the more determined I am to carry on my fight.
>
> The terrible truth is that inhuman forces are ruling us. However, there are still *a few human beings* among us, and it is these for whom the world must be saved with the cry 'Retour à la Nature!' Are you aware what weight your voice, your words have here and even more in the neutral countries, in England, in America, and what wonderful and restoring influence you could exert? I am not twenty years old, yet I already feel and am convinced that the echo of your voice will not disappear unnoticed. Now we still hear 'The battle continues!' When will we hear 'Humanity has awakened!'[16]

The letter was written, not from the Israels' house, but from the Pension Rankeplatz, a sign that Wilfrid probably knew that *Die Zukunft* was not a paper that the Israels would have allowed inside their house. Wilfrid was not the only young man to admire Harden; many of his generation followed Harden's somewhat inconsistent lead – the writer Theodor Lessing had run away from home to join his hero. Though there is some adolescent bravado in Wilfrid's claim to rebellion, the reference to 'shocked opposition' was true in the wider sense, for to Wilfrid's class Harden was a dangerous revolutionary. But there was more to the Israels' family hatred of Harden, and what he stood for, than this.

Thirteen years earlier, a scandal of regal proportions had threatened to destroy the Israel family. Hermann Israel, Berthold's elder brother and the heir to the dynasty, was accused by an ex-lieutenant in the Prussian army of having forced him to have homosexual relations, a criminal offence under Prussian law. Hermann denied the charge on oath, but the lieutenant was not to be shaken off; he pressed a further charge of perjury. Rather than stand trial in a public court, though he continued to deny all the charges against him, Hermann boarded his yacht, and – positioning himself so that he would fall into the water – shot himself through the head. The Berlin papers carried nothing of this story but the notice of his death; but Harden, in two articles which attacked both the press, for its silence, and the brutal laws which forced a man to take his own life rather than face condemnation by society, revealed the whole story to the world at large.[17]

It is likely that Wilfrid knew of the episode, though it is possible that he did not know of Harden's part in it; Harden was far more famous for having exposed the homosexual *kamarilla* of his political enemies in a circle near the Kaiser, three years later. But adolescence is the time for ferreting out family secrets, and Wilfrid hated what he already saw as the hypocrisy and corruption of bourgeois society; this was just as strong an emotion as his family loyalties. He saw conformism, too, as the main cause of the German Jews' support of the war, though there were many Jews among the pacifists, as in all *avant-garde* groups.

Leading Jewish organizations urged the Jews to join the ranks at the outbreak of war. One hundred thousand Jews, about one-fifth of the Jewish population, had served in the Kaiser's army, and 12,000 were among the the casualties.[18] Their loyalty did not help them; in October 1916, the anti-semitic Prussian First Quarter-Master General Ludendorff ordered a census of Jews, the notorious *Judenzählung*, to find out how many were actually at the front.

But for Wilfrid, with his uncle Richard and his cousin Ernst on one side of the battlefield, and his cousin Henry on the other, the horror was unbearable. Shortly before his death, he was to write: 'The second world war has emphasized the tragic situation of the Jews among the peoples. But in the midst of this tragedy there is perhaps one redeeming point: the fact that at least, in this second world war, Jew is not fighting Jew.'[19]

All divisions between Jews appeared tragic to Wilfrid. The war which had set English against German Jews had, however, brought the Jews in the German army closer to the Jews of Eastern Europe. 'Before 1914,' Wilfrid wrote later, 'the abyss between Jews in the East and Jews in the

West seemed unsurmountable. ... Western Jews, including the German Jew, considered the Eastern Jew to be something alien, in every respect something distant.... Berlin was certainly a centre, a bastion of this superficial and disruptive arrogance.'[20]

Before the First World War, when hundreds of thousands of Eastern European Jews fled to Germany, as they had to England to Wilfrid's great-grandfather's concern, as a result of the pogroms in Tsarist Russia, the role of German Jewry was to provide them with charitable support and, where possible, escort them across Germany to Hamburg, where they were helped to embark for the New World. The Hilfsverein der Deutschen Juden, which, ironically, was to help the German Jews themselves emigrate in the late 1930s, was founded in 1903 to help these refugees from the East: Berthold Israel became its honorary treasurer after the First World War.

Those Eastern Jews who remained in Berlin during Wilfrid's childhood settled in the Scheunenviertel, an old barn area which was practically in the Israel firm's backyard. Their clothing was distinctive, whether labourers or orthodox Jews who, with their untrimmed earlocks and beards, Yiddish speech and traditional style of worship and study, were entirely different to the observant German Jews, for most of whom the Reform movement had subdued and westernized the old rituals. Religion, for most German Jews, was confined to the occasional visit to the synagogue on High Holy days and a few family rituals: in the larger cities, the rate of intermarriage had now reached 40 per cent of all Jewish marriages. The *Ostjuden*, with their little shops and stalls, the pedlars with their sacks of old clothes on their backs hawking their wares at street corners, were an embarrassment to the old Jewish community which believed itself barely distinguishable from Gentile Germans.

But as Wilfrid commented in 1943, the war changed the attitude of some liberal middle-class Jews. Young Jews serving in the army had visited the heartland of Jewish settlement in Russian Poland, Lithuania and Latvia, and found not only that an alternative Jewish culture, one far more vigorous than any in Germany, existed, but that the younger generation embraced new socialist ideas and wanted to break away from the dogmatic orthodoxy of their elders.

A young doctor who had served as a non-combatant in the army, Siegfried Lehmann, who was to become one of the closest of Wilfrid's colleagues, founded the Jüdische Volksheim, or people's settlement, in the Scheunenviertel in May 1916; its existence suggested to Wilfrid, as to other young liberal Jews, that the 'superficial arrogance' of German Jews could be overcome. The intellectual patron of the Volksheim was the socialist philosopher Gustav Landauer, and its rationale was influenced by non-Jewish movements as far apart geographically as Tolstoy's followers in Russia and the East End settlement work at Toynbee Hall in London. The Volksheim was primarily a social welfare institution for children and young people, but in the evenings, visitors such as Wilfrid attended lectures on Eastern Europe or Zionism. The Volksheim idea was to reach the *Ostjuden* of Germany through their children - but it proved too intellectual and patronizing to succeed. Gershom Scholem noted unkindly that visitors sat round on chairs, while the immigrants were grouped picturesquely on the floor; he advised Lehmann to learn Hebrew instead. Kafka, whose fiancée Félice Bauer was among the Volksheim's protégés, doubted that the 'symbiosis' could succeed. Scholem and Kafka were right. The young Jews in Berlin slums became Jewish nationalists and Zionist pioneers; liberal Jewry became increasingly entrenched in its own defence of its rights and privileges. The result was that men such as Lehmann and - later - Wilfrid, became increasingly drawn to Zionism as a social ideal.[21]

Thus, by the time Wilfrid was nineteen, it did not look as if he was going to follow in the footsteps either of the Israels or of the Adlers. He shared none of their basic commitments to the old order. His enthusiasm for pacifism and internationalism, socialism and Zionism made him an unlikely candidate for membership of the conservative Jewish middle-class community. He was not to join the family firm until April 1921, and the harness was to hold him very loosely until 1926.

But, because of the essential gentleness of his personality, there was no dramatic breakaway, no open confrontation with his family. During the next four years he was gradually to acquiesce in his family's plans for his future. The price of this acquiescence was a permanent ambivalence and uncertainty about his place in the German-Jewish community which was to persist until the Nazis came to power.

3
The Apprentice

The Israels had kept Wilfrid away from the army tribunals. But there was no chance of his studying or joining the business while all he saw around him in Berlin, in the last phase of the war, was hunger, human misery and the beginnings of revolt against the old order. During the notorious 'turnip winter' of 1917 there had been increasingly severe food shortages; now all fresh food was unobtainable save for those who could 'hamster' in the country, buying from peasants. Some bought from profiteers, or stole. Coal and cloth were scarce; fats were skimmed from the dishwater in hotels; paper was used as bandages; and relief workers spread the story of an officer who, returning home, tore the cotton backing from his precious war maps to change his baby's nappy. The German children suffered most: born to undernourished mothers or reduced to rachitic apathy by semi-starvation, hundreds of thousands died or were permanently stunted.[1]

Compared with such misery, the privations of the rich were negligible. Berthold Israel was able to purchase a plot of land on the Wannsee lakeside for a country villa in 1916 and, in 1918, to commission an architect to draw up plans for its construction. The Israel country cousins were more directly affected: Richard's wife, Bianca, and her daughter worked in the fields, and her modern nickel bath was commandeered for scrap metal – but fortunately proved too large to fit the local smelting furnace. Jewish families such as the Israels, conscious of the example they had to set, eked out their rations in strictly legal ways; soon after the war, visitors to the Robert Mendelssohns, the Jewish bankers, noted the cabbages and peas growing opposite the front door of their Grunewald mansion as well as the Van Gogh hanging in the drawing-room.[2]

The armistice of 11 November 1918 marked the official end to the fighting, but the Allied blockade of Germany continued for another seven months, until the Treaty of Versailles was signed. Fishing in the North Sea was banned; without imported fertilizers harvests were poor and children stood on the Rhine bridges begging for milk.[3]

Having lost an entire generation of young men in the trench war, however, the Allies were in no mood to be merciful, and the British press attacked the 'Hun Food Snivel' hysterically.[4] But by March 1919, a first breach in the blockade had been made by two small groups of determined people (most of whom were women) in England and Germany, who had remained in touch with one another throughout the war; Wilfrid Israel was among them.

Two committees – the Quakers in England and an independent body in Berlin working together with the International Red Cross – had supervised the welfare of interned enemy civilians in both countries and maintained contact between families separated by war.[5] One of the leading figures on the Berlin committee was Dr Elisabeth Rotten, a well-known pacifist who had been threatened three times with exile because of her links with Britain, but who, with the help of influential friends in office, had remained active. She was the daughter of Swiss-Jewish parents, educated in Germany and at Cambridge; at the outbreak of war she had been teaching education and psychology in Berlin. In mid-1915, she had set up an emergency welfare organization, the Auskunft und Hilfstelle, to distribute food and clothing to mothers and children in distress; in 1918 the 'inner circle' of her helpers was four women and a young man of nineteen – Wilfrid Israel.

Throughout January and February 1919, the British Quakers negotiated with the Inter Allied Food Council in Paris for permission to send supplies of powdered milk and baby clothing to maternity and children's hospitals thoughout Germany, through Dr Rotten (who was *persona grata* in England because of her wartime services for British prisoners of war and internees). Though their appeal received the almost immediate sanction of the Allied Supreme Council in Paris, the Quaker Emergency Committee's efforts met with bureaucratic obstruction and public opposition at home. They were forced, at first, to keep their work secret – forbidden to make public appeals or publish any report of their work in the press – and no members of the Emergency Committee were allowed to visit Germany. When they finally printed circulars, they were dubbed 'Hun Coddlers', and the Home Secretary was asked in Parliament whether the 'appeal for clothing, food and luxuries' had his sanction. The London office of the Inter Allied Food Council held up supplies already sanctioned by Paris; first the British, and then the American Red Cross refused help with transportation; the War Trades Department would not issue an export licence until the formal approval of the Foreign Office was received. It was only after the intervention of Lord Robert Cecil, the Archbishop of Canterbury and finally of the Prime

Minister himself, Lloyd George, that the consignment of food and clothing left Britain for Germany.[6]

This was Wilfrid Israel's first strategic lesson in saving lives, despite political opposition and official obtuseness – something he was to struggle against all his life. It did not embitter him against England. Dr Rotten wrote later to the Quakers:

> I have in Wilfrid Israel a model of what high-spirited youth may be. I cannot tell you what this boy of 19 who is my very next friend and helper amongst all my dear and unfailingly faithful fellow workers means to me. I wish he could come over to England and talk to you about our hopes for future co-operation with your society which are in our daily conversations. I am sure you would find him worthy of your finest spirit. If ever my courage or faith might fail, he would no doubt cheer me up and make me strong and plucky again.[7]

Dr Rotten's contact with the Quakers was not the only unofficial effort to break through the blockade and reach public opinion in England. A related episode was to influence Wilfrid's life. During the abortive German revolution between the autumn of 1918 and the spring of 1919, which began with the revolt of sections of the German navy, *ad hoc* workers' and soldiers' councils surfaced all over Germany in an attempt to force through social and political change. Berlin remained quiet until 9 November, when factories closed down, soldiers left their barracks, epaulettes and cockades were torn from officers' uniforms, and the German Republic was proclaimed from the balcony of the Reichstag. For a short period it looked like a real revolution; the Kaiser, then on the royal train on the Belgian–Dutch frontier, abdicated, the armistice was signed, and one of the soldiers' councils stationed men at the opened gates of Ruhleben, the British internment camp. The soldiers handed all those who left a stencilled document. 'Gentlemen,' it began:

> In this historical moment when you are regaining your freedom by the opening of the gates at Ruhleben, we are asking you to take these lines with you to England to let them be known to your countrymen. You are the crown witnesses [*sic*] of the revolution, you are the first ones who leave our country after it. . . . It took four years of endless privations and sufferings to make our people realize that they had been ill guided and misled.

The prisoners had suffered, the revolutionaries recognized, but, they added: 'Do not hold the German people responsible; it has suffered more than you.' They asked the released prisoners to tell England what they had seen in Berlin and during their journey through Germany: 'Tell England order reigns, social democracy has achieved revolution', and asssured them that the soldiers 'did not intend to establish a new autocracy in the place of the one . . . swept away'. Finally, they asked them to act against the blockade which could 'drive many into the ranks of the terrorists. . . . Long live our newly acquired freedom, long live the Republic, long live the Society of Nations, long live Peace!'[8]

Among those leaving Ruhleben on that day in November was a young Englishman, Tom Marshall, who had been trapped by the war in Weimar and had spent four years in the camp. He was impressed by the document, and kept it; but his reactions were not quite those the soldiers had intended to arouse. To Marshall, it indicated the frightening rapidity with which the political wind in Germany could change, and the sincerity with which Germans could renounce policies which, until so recently, they had supported.

Over twenty years later, Tom Marshall became head of research on Germany at the British Foreign Office, and Wilfrid Israel, who had witnessed the revolution in Berlin from a very different vantage point, became Marshall's adviser.

Once the first supplies of milk and clothing began to reach Germany, Dr Rotten and her helpers handed over distribution to a larger German welfare body, the Wohlfahrtstelle, and she and her helpers divided their time between welfare work and what Rotten thought more important even than the despatch of food – contact between post-war Germany and England. The first meeting between Dr Rotten and the English Quakers took place in Holland in April. There she told them facts that she could not put into her letters: that the food shortages were not only the result of labour and transport problems caused by the war, and by the poor harvest, but by the inequitable division of the available food; that the peasants were selling their goods at a profit, particularly to the large hotels, with official sanction, to give the impression of prosperity to the outside world, and that the people were suffering from official attempts to hide the real situation. She made no secret of her sympathy for the revolutionaries; but by this time, fear of radicalism had led the new German Government to support the right-wing militias which were putting down the rebels.[9]

During the following months, Wilfrid Israel worked steadily to widen the contacts between German pacifists and liberals and their British sympathizers. He travelled between Germany, Holland and Switzerland, and when the Quakers finally arrived in Germany immediately after the signing of the Versailles Treaty in June 1919, he helped introduce them to officials and bankers in post-war Berlin, as well as to young Germans, 'who were eager to hear about Quakerism and pacifism and to tell about their own movement [the Frei Deutscher Jugend] which began among older school children'. This group, formed in 1913, had aimed at 'a kind of self-determination, a revolt against hypocrisy and untruthfulness in school and society'.[10]

Not all Germans welcomed the Quakers unreservedly; in hospitals they were shown starving children whose bones bent at the slightest pressure and told that this was 'England's work'; in the Plotzensee prison, where they admired educational and welfare work among young delinquents, they were accused of not having done enough to prevent the blockade. But the development of the feeding scheme, which the Quakers took over from the totally inadequate Wohlfahrtstelle in the autumn of 1919, was nourishing more than 500,000 German children by the middle of 1920 and ensured their acceptance in Germany.[11]

The popularity of the Quakers enabled them to remain in Germany – though often at some risk to their representatives – throughout the pre-war Nazi years. They established links at this early stage with Jewish organizations, and these were to be among Wilfrid Israel's greatest assets after 1933. Wilfrid chaperoned the Quaker women around in Berlin in a carriage and pair (there was no petrol for the Israel limousines), accompanied them to philosophical congresses, and introduced them to leading Jewish philanthropists.

Dr Rotten and the Quakers collaborated not only with the welfare committees caring for the German destitute, but also with those set up to deal with foreign refugees, in particular the Russian prisoners of war who were unable to return home after the 1917 Revolution, and the Polish refugees, among whom there were many Jews who had fled the pogroms of 1919 in Poland and Lithuania. American-Jewish charities were also involved; the money they contributed was spent on 'non-sectarian relief' without distinction between Jews and non-Jews, so that, as one of the leading German officials involved commented, 'amounts collected by Jewish organizations for international purposes could seldom be traced as such'.[12] Through his father's connections with the Hilfsverein, Wilfrid put the Quakers in touch with those philanthropists he knew were able and willing to give immediate help.

At a congress on adult education which he attended, with his Quaker friends, at Wetzlar in August 1919, Wilfrid first saw and heard Martin Buber, the Jewish philosopher and theologian whose teachings were to influence him throughout his life. Sitting in the audience at Wetzlar, sketching Buber's philosopher colleagues Paul Natorp and Ferdinand Tonnies, Wilfrid felt close to Buber, as he later wrote, for several reasons.[13] Buber had already popularized the Chassidic folklore of Eastern Europe, and this nourished Wilfrid's literary and romantic view of the Jews of the East. But perhaps more important was the fact that

Buber's interpretation of the Jewish heritage was intellectually exciting to Wilfrid, who was not an orthodox Jew. Moreover, Buber's ideas were linked with an interpretation of socialism and Zionist idealism which Wilfrid eagerly accepted. As Buber mentioned in an exchange of letters with Wilfrid years later, 1919 was critical to his own intellectual development.[14] It marked his final rejection of state socialism and his adoption of the idea of socialist individualist communities in Palestine – what Buber was to call 'Hebrew humanism'.

At this period, both Buber and Elisabeth Rotten were leading European educationists. The 'New Education Fellowship', of which Rotten was a founding member, organized conferences all over Europe to discuss new ideas on the upbringing of children: greater freedom for the child at home and school, coeducation, participation of children in school government, and an end to the spirit of competition. Brought up under strict discipline at home, and then schooled in a Prussian gymnasium, Wilfrid responded eagerly to these new ideas and put some of them into practice when he came to set up his own business school in 1926.

Five weeks after the armistice, Mathias Erzberger, the politician who had signed for Germany, inaugurated a German internationalist society, the German League of Nations Union (Deutsche Liga für Volkerbund), announcing that the war 'had made the feeble literary idea of the unity of peoples into the political demand of the whole world'.[15] Long-term pacifists, including Rotten, refused to join the Union until Erzberger's resignation in the spring of 1919.[16] Germany was not to be admitted to the League of Nations itself until 1926, but the German Liga was the first link between Berlin and Geneva. Subsequently, through his work for the Liga, Wilfrid met the English internationalists Philip Noel Baker, Robert Cecil and Clifford Allen.[17] Allen was a former conscientious objector who had been imprisoned for refusal to do non-combatant duties. In 1939, during the British 'peace aims' debate, Wilfrid remarked: 'After the last war, I was one of those "mad idealists" who believed in the birth and reality of the League of Nations ... and I fear I have remained one of those blissful fools to this day.'[18] The Liga, however, included not only 'blissful fools' but, by 1922, many hard-headed conservatives, such as Max Warburg and Hjalmar Schacht.[19] It was soon at loggerheads with its European counterparts. In April 1920, its bulletin pointed out that the entry of French troops into the Ruhr was an infringement of the League Covenant, and German and French pacifists clashed at international meetings not only on this issue, but on the post-war settlement as a whole.[20]

The socialist utopian ideas of the Buber circle, the version of Zionism which was neither nationalist nor militant, were eventually to be swept away by Nazism. But there were other warning signs even in the immediate post-war period that they were no answer to the problems of the mass of European Jewry. Later in life, Wilfrid tended to blame their failure on a lack of leadership by people like himself: 'I still believe in the truth of the old values which Buber expounded – but we did not personify them and realize them, and therefore were no example . . . for others – in most cases we failed utterly.' Yet even in 1917, when leading European socialists were canvassed on 'the coming peace and the Jewish question', they were receptive to the idea of political Zionism, not as an elite movement, but because they believed that the Jewish masses in Russia, Poland and Romania constituted a national minority which was not to be accommodated easily in the new Europe.[21]

In education, little changed within Germany. Teachers from 'progressive' schools in England who visited Germany in the early 1920s noticed that even those schools which adopted the new ideas in theory, remained authoritarian in practice. The Weimar curriculum continued to stress aggressive nationalism and praised the defunct monarchy; history books attacked the Republican Government and asserted that it had undermined Germany's undefeated armies. The youth movements which Wilfrid greatly admired – though he never joined one himself – were the signs of a genuine rebellion; but the cult of youth was exploited by the radical right. The youth movements became Hitler's most ardent supporters and were among the first to expel young Jews from their ranks.

Thus, all the brave new ideas which so fired the young Wilfrid Israel's imagination, promising freedom and tolerance to a boy brought up under such strict restraints, were to be fatally compromised within less than a decade.

Not only were the German and French internationalists and pacifists rapidly at odds on national grounds. The weaknesses of the League of Nations itself, and the anomalous situation of the Jews in the struggle for self-determination of smaller nations, became clear towards the end of 1920, when the League faced one of its worst post-war crises. Wilfrid Israel – whether as delegate of the German Liga or on a private visit to Lithuania, is not clear – was a concerned observer.

Since the end of the war the Poles and Lithuanians had been fighting for control of the Lithuanian capital, Vilna – like Kovno, a centre of Jewish culture, and a refuge for Polish and Russian Jews during the war. On 7 October, the Treaty of Suwalki, on the demarcation line between the two countries, and about 100 miles east of Vilna, was signed in the presence of inexperienced League delegates, only one of whom knew the language of the combatants. Within hours of the signature of the treaty, Polish troops under General Zeligowski once more advanced on Vilna, and the Lithuanian Government hastily withdrew to Kovno; the Jewish refugees had to take to the road again.[22]

According to one of his brief autobiographical notes, Wilfrid was in Kovno at the time. He wrote two accounts of what happened.[23] One was a dramatic version: Jews in a train travelling from Kovno to Vilna argue about the chances of peace; the organ in a former Russian Orthodox church in Vilna plays against the background of distant artillery fire; the flags of the Allied military commission flutter 'jeeringly' opposite the Red Flag of the Russians; the Government pulls out; shops are looted, and the houses of Jews barricaded against pogroms. Jewish refugees flee, dreaming of Palestine – 'Perhaps, in that far away land, the home of their longing?'

The other account was a sober message sent to the League of Nations. It ended:

> In Kovno refugees block the city ... the situation looks threatening to the whole state. It is feared that the recent events may lead to the breakup of Lithuania unless there is intervention at the last moment. The ruin that threatens would not only put an end to the reconstruction of Lithuania, but lead to unpredictable political complications and chaos in the economy of Eastern and Central Europe.

The report was acknowledged in Geneva, Wilfrid noted, with the remark that 'it had served a useful purpose'.

The League had played a weak and indecisive part which augured ill for the future. Vilna was eventually granted to Poland seven years later by an international body whose decision was of dubious legality. In 1927, Wilfrid added a footnote: 'We have lost all illusions that passions aroused and inflamed for more than seven years can be controlled and channelled by "reports".' The experience affected him deeply. In his research papers for the Foreign Office in 1941, he argued that the surrender to force in the case of Vilna, as in other parts of Eastern Europe at the time, had encouraged the growth of the fascist movement in Germany.

In the period immediately following his visit to Lithuania, however, Wilfrid still believed that privileged observers like himself could elicit official action, and, when he returned to Eastern Europe in the following summer, he sent one of the first authoritative reports of events surrounding a much greater disaster: the Russian famine of 1921.

By this time, Wilfrid had finally been shoehorned into the Israel business. The emotional pressures from the family in early 1921 were overwhelming. Wilfrid's elder sister Viva, who had married and gone to live in London, had died in childbirth leaving a son. Herbert, Wilfrid's younger brother, was finishing his schooling, and was to enter the Friedrich Wilhelm University to study economics. Post-war inflation sent the crowds scurrying into the shops to exchange their marks for goods; but only firmly established businesses, with solid credit facilities, survived. It was important to demonstrate the firm's continuity, and the Israels, who closed ranks in time of trouble, were reluctant to bring an outsider into the management. Wilfrid could hardly have been of much practical assistance to his father, as he had neither enthusiasm, nor business training. But he was, after all, the heir apparent.

So in April 1921, Wilfrid Israel was officially recruited to stand at his father's side. On 8 March 1922, he finished his period of apprenticeship and was formally pronounced Einzelprokurist, confidential clerk (general manager), a title which enabled him to sign documents and attend meetings of the board of management.

Meanwhile, barely three months after joining the firm, he was back in Eastern Europe, this time in Latvia, sending more reports to the League. This could have been justified as a business journey; the Israels supplied linen to the German Red Cross, and the International Red Cross operated a camp for refugees in Riga which Wilfrid visited. N. Israel was also exploring export outlets in Riga and in Kovno. But this was scarcely Wilfrid's main concern.

During his stay in Riga, reports began to filter through from Soviet Russia of a famine in the Volga region. Tsarist Russia had known similar disasters in the past, the result of primitive farming methods and the lack of irrigation systems. But other factors led to the famine of 1921: world war and revolution had destroyed much agricultural machinery, 50 per cent of which was imported; replacements were currently blocked; labour was inadequate, and an exceptionally severe drought had set in during the spring.

Communist Russia was still a pariah state; the West was demanding that the Soviets meet debts incurred by the Tsarist Government; the Soviets did not recognize the League. Meanwhile, millions were dying. The first relief missions, which included Quakers sent east from Germany, sent back horrifying accounts, including photographs, of the plight of the Russian peasants. They ate grass seeds, straw, leaves, clay, horse dung and crushed bones. The bodies of peasants and animals lay unburied on the roads; then there was a typhoid epidemic, which was to kill many of the relief workers, spreading slowly only because mass immunity had followed the death of millions in 1919 from the same disease.[24]

At this period, there existed no international administration for relief, famine or health control, such as that set up after the Second World War by the United Nations. Only one mass venture of this kind had been undertaken – the repatriation of nearly 500,000 Western prisoners from the Soviet Union by the patient diplomacy of Fridtjof Nansen, the Norwegian Polar explorer and statesman, from the spring of 1920.

Nansen was acceptable to the Bolshevik Government because, from the time of the Versailles Treaty onwards, he had attacked the policy of ostracizing the Soviet Government, maintaining that the Allied blockade and political boycott of the Soviet Union threatened not only the population of Russia, but the newly established peace of Europe. In April 1919, he had suggested that the Allied leaders supply food to the Russians; this was accepted on condition that hostilities in the USSR cease. But the Soviets, still under attack from White Russian forces supported by the Allies, refused to down arms, and Nansen's project was abandoned. Now his worst forecasts proved accurate.[25]

The failure of the harvest in the Volga and Southern Ukraine threatened 20,000,000 Russians with starvation, but the Soviets did not immediately appeal for help. It was not until the end of July 1921 that various reports began to be received in the League offices suggesting that the Soviets would co-operate with relief projects originating in the West.[26] But the most important signal was a telegram from Maxim Gorki, the Russian writer, to Nansen. Reporting this to the League Nansen commented:

> As the Soviet Government has not hitherto been very willing to admit that the conditions in Russia were very bad ... I am inclined to believe that the situation is really very serious and that Gorki's description cannot be much exaggerated, for otherwise he would hardly be allowed to send the telegram, which is certainly not good propaganda for the Bolshevik system.

If the co-operation of the United States could be secured, Nansen concluded, he was prepared to return to the field.[27]

Only a few days later, Nansen received an independent confirmation of the situation from Berlin. On 2 August, Wilfrid wrote directly to Nansen:

> As I am myself endeavouring to be of service to all efforts preparing for relief work in Russia ... and having just returned from Riga, I am sending you the following short survey which I earnestly hope may help to bring about immediate help and united action of Europe for relief in Russia ... the reports published in the press are in no way exaggerated as the horror of the present

situation in the hunger-stricken districts is illuminated ... by the refugees from Russia and those passing through the International Red Cross camp in Riga which I had the opportunity to visit.

Wilfrid reported that the famine had already started in some districts in May, and that the measures contemplated by Hoover's American relief organization 'were definitely accepted by the Russian government and offered a sound basis for action'. A local committee had been formed in Riga and, together with the Latvian Red Cross and Quaker organizations' representatives in Moscow, formed the necessary link for relief work. Stressing that the German Red Cross was anxious to co-operate, Wilfrid added delicately that many non-communists – or, as he put it, 'individuals who are above all suspicion of harbouring a one-sided and narrow conception' – were prepared to help, and that 'Maxim Gorki's wife, at present staying in Berlin, would also warmly welcome an international humanitarian relief organization'. Israel himself was 'in continual touch with Riga and the wife of Gorki'. He suggested calling a conference and setting up an international body for relief work: 'Delay at this decisive moment would make Europe guilty of a crime never to be obliterated.'[28]

Wilfrid wrote at the same time to Philip Noel Baker at the League – who did not think that anything could be done – and to Hugh Massingham, the editor of the London *Nation*, who had published some of the first reports of the famine and was to support the appeal for private funds consistently.[29] Nansen left for Riga two weeks later, shortly after relief and Red Cross organizations had nominated him High Commissioner for Russian relief, and on 27 August concluded an agreement with the Soviets for the distribution of supplies; the Americans had signed an agreement the previous week.

But the League of Nations did not back Nansen. In September, in a famous address, he appealed to the nations of the League to set aside politics in the interests of humanity and support the system of international credits to Russia which he was convinced was the only way to check the famine. 'Is there any member of the Assembly who is prepared to say that, rather than help the Soviet Government, he will allow 20,000,000 people to starve to death?' he asked. There was: the Serbian delegate said it was better Russia should die than bolshevism survive, and was roundly applauded. Only Robert Cecil supported the idea of credits, and the motion that the League support Russia – to the cost of half a battleship, as Nansen observed – was defeated. League committees were established but never took action.

Nansen toured Europe raising private funds, a signal that he was not defeated, though he could not hope to raise money on a scale that the

League could provide. The toll taken by the famine, and the disease which accompanied it, was in his estimate 7,000,000 dead. He continued his work of repatriation despite accusations that many of the returning anti-bolsheviks went to their deaths. In 1922 he arranged a population exchange between Greece and Turkey, and later distributed the 'Nansen passports', documents for stateless refugees, which helped thousands of refugees find homes.

Nansen's giant figure dwarfed all those who subsequently worked for refugee relief; throughout the Nazi period, his name and example were constantly invoked. But he had no real successor.

Nansen was no bureaucrat, and the details of Wilfrid Israel's work with him have long since disappeared.[30] Throughout the 1930s his signed photograph remained on Wilfrid's desk, a reminder of the latter's second attempt, before he was twenty-three, to help breach the solid wall of indifference and political hostility which prevented help reaching the dying. In the Nazi period, some of Wilfrid's colleagues thought him naïve, or saintly, in his refusal to recognize obstacles to rescue. But, in his youth, he had learned the immorality of pessimism, and – unlike many of his fellow Jews – he never regarded indifference to Jewish suffering as unique. At the most impressionable period of his life, he had twice seen the deaths of millions silently tolerated.

The only documented sequel to Wilfrid's work with Nansen was his appearance, as representative of the German Liga, at a conference sponsored by the pro-bolshevik All Russian Central Executive in Berlin on the 9th and 10th of July 1922 – an event not recorded in the main newspapers in Germany. The conference acknowledged that the combined efforts of the Soviet Government and foreign relief organizations had limited the extent of the famine, and called on them to support the economic reconstruction of the devastated regions. Germany was represented by several charitable, pacifist and Jewish organizations; America by philo-Soviet groups, and Britain by a member of the Russian Red Cross. A member of the League of Nations office in Geneva attended but left after the second meeting, commenting that 'the conference in question appeared to me to be nothing but rather clumsy Russian political propaganda – it could do the League no good to underline the fact that it was represented at such a demonstration.' Perhaps this explains why the German Liga was represented by so very junior a member as Wilfrid Israel.[31]

As a young man in the Berlin commercial world, Wilfrid's revolutionary sympathies at this time were incongruous. But his wealth enabled him to support any and every cause or individual he thought worthy, from the

All Russian Central Executive to the White Russian refugees, from the Volksheim to the communist welfare body in Berlin, the Rote Hilfe. Wherever he could, he contributed anonymously, and before long Israel's sales managers became used to beneficiaries presenting themselves in the basements where surplus stocks were kept, with instructions from Herr Wilfrid to let them help themselves.

One of his chief 'customers' in these early years was Ernst Friedrich, actor, pacifist, writer and anarchist, who in 1923 opened a gallery for the work of revolutionary artists, and an 'Anti-War Museum' in the Parochialstrasse, a few minutes' walk from the Israel store. The friendship between Wilfrid and the flamboyant Friedrich went back to meetings of the Frei Jugend and the All Russian conference, at which Friedrich represented 'German anti-militarist youth'. Wilfrid backed both Friedrich's pacifist schoolbooks and the Anti-War Museum, which was formally opened in Easter 1925. It was a grand name for a tiny house sandwiched between two larger buildings. In four small rooms, Friedrich set out to demolish that glorification of war, which made generations of little German boys dress up in their fathers' steel helmets and decorations: the war worship which Heinrich Zille, one of Friedrich's artist friends, savaged in his famous drawing of a starving war widow glumly surveying her husband's Iron Cross. Outside the Museum were two steel helmets upended and used as flower pots; inside, war mementoes were displayed like the relics of a primitive tribe, beside horrifying photographs of shattered bodies and the hideously mutilated faces of survivors of the recent war. These were also reproduced in Friedrich's best-selling *War against War*, a tirade, written in three languages, against militarism and the role of 'international capitalism', which he saw behind it.[32]

Wilfrid was a frequent visitor to Friedrich's home in the Parochialstrasse, and even wrote him letters – scarcely necessary considering that they were next-door neighbours – which were later to endanger him. He admired the work of Friedrich's 'revolutionary artists', including Kathe Kollwitz, Otto Dix and Georg Grosz; but if he bought their work, he did not keep it. His own collection, begun in these years with the help of the famous dealers Paul Cassirer in Berlin and Dr Hauswedell in Hamburg, ranged from ancient Chinese sculpture to Italian Renaissance works. He recommended his friends to buy not only Kollwitz and Dix, but the work of an artist detested by Grosz and his friends – Oskar Kokoschka – dubbed the 'art whore', whom they had promised to hang from the nearest lamppost when their party came to power.[33]

His friendships in the early 1920s were just as eclectic. He had as many friends who had escaped from the Soviet regime as he had among anarchists or bolsheviks. One close friend was Efrem Kurtz, a young musician from an Odessa family, later to become famous as conductor of the Ballets Russes in Monte Carlo. Kurtz's family reached Berlin in 1921, where they lived in a bug-infested tenement in the Wittenburgstrasse, one of the poorer parts of East Berlin.

Though the Kurtzs had no friends in Berlin, Efrem's elder brother Edmond soon found work with another Russian family of musicians, the Spivakowskis, who had already made their name. One evening, young Efrem went to visit them in western Berlin. This was unknown territory to him, where the rich lived behind thick walls, off courtyards closed off from the streets by heavy entrance doors. Efrem had no idea how to enter the building and was about to give up and go home when a tall, handsome young man, wearing a superbly cut grey overcoat, appeared and, smiling, pressed a hidden bell. Wilfrid was to open many other doors for Kurtz, who was invited to Amy's 'Sundays' and introduced to leading Berlin musicians. His brother Edmond was taken to Leipzig by Wilfrid for lessons with a famous cellist; when Efrem collapsed one day in the street, Wilfrid located him and paid for private hospital care; and his sister Mary, who supported the family with her earnings as a violinist, was presented with a black velvet dress from the Israel store, in which to audition for a job with a women's orchestra in a night-club. Barely three years after his first meeting with Wilfrid, Kurtz was resident conductor with the Stuttgart Opera, and he had an almost superstitious awe of Wilfrid's powers of guidance.

By this time, economic conditions had stabilized. N. Israel was expanding. Berthold Israel, aware of his elder son's restlessness, offered him a journey round the world, and sent him off, at the end of 1924, with introductions to store and mill owners in America and India.

Wilfrid spent seven months abroad – the only time in his life that he enjoyed real freedom. He visited Palestine, Egypt, the United States, India, China and the Soviet Union, returning through Lithuania in the summer of 1925. America left little impression on him; it was his brother Herbert who was to admire the Americans and their business methods. When Wilfrid returned, he wore a Chinese kimono at home, set Indo-Chinese buddhas at his bedside, burned Indian incense tapers, and a procession of oriental friends returned his visit throughout the 1920s. But the journey was very far from being the cultural pilgrimage of a rich dilettante.

What has remained of a diary Wilfrid kept shows that it was in the East that he felt himself to be, most inescapably, a German and a Jew. His interest in the Far East and its culture, like his admiration for the Jewish pioneers in Palestine, and his enthusiasm for the Jewish farming settlements he visited in the Ukraine and the Crimea, was part of an attempt to break away from everything he found stultifying in German-Jewish life, and particularly in the world of commerce. He was excited not only by the art of the East, but by the beginnings of social change there, without the destruction of previous tradition. In his diary he mentions this qualification so often that it seems to be a reflection of his own family problem.

In the Indian diary, there is little mention of poverty and caste divisions; the sights and smells of the cities he explored thoroughly, usually on foot, stimulated rather than repelled him, and for a young man in allegedly delicate health, he survived the long train journeys, the heat and the spiced food remarkably well. He was in a constant state of elation which – according to his letters – he was never to recapture.[34]

In Ahmedabad, Wilfrid slept on the floor with Gandhi's disciples (Gandhi himself was away on a journey), who dressed in the homespun cloth which Gandhi had made a symbol of Indian revolt; he attended a Hindu wedding in Bombay, appropriately wreathed and anointed; and he witnessed elephant fights as a guest of the Maharajah of Baroda, in whose car he travelled and for whom he was temporarily mistaken by cheering crowds. He celebrated Holi, the Indian spring carnival, sleeping out in the garden of an overcrowded Delhi hotel, and suffered a brief dose of malaria – which he shrugged off as unimportant. A formal conversation with the poet Rabindranath Tagore was reported by a local newspaper and Wilfrid entered an ashram in Tagore's town, Shantiniketan. He only once recorded shock at the conditions of the working people – at the spinning and weaving factory in Bombay owned by the Sassoons – though he took care to add that these were, nevertheless, better than conditions in the small native workshops.

With Devadas, Gandhi's son, and the *Young India* journalists in Ahmedabad, he discussed the principle of non-violence, *ahimsa*. When he asked Devadas why his father had encouraged Indians to volunteer for military service during the war, he was told that Gandhi had not wished to force the British into concessions by open hostility.

> We discussed the way of life and traditions of the orient and the west ... about individualism there and the family as a social unit. Their wisdom ... teaches them not to create a conflict between the pleasures offered by life and the conditions of life as imposed by the family group. To sacrifice your own wishes and narrow interests in the interest of the family is regarded as a necessary and natural condition.

Wilfrid was clearly amazed to discover such similarity between his own problems and those of the Indians, who were fighting imperialism. 'It was difficult for me to grasp that these were the closest disciples of Gandhi himself. I had completely different ideas about the representatives of the so-called "revolutionary India".' Nor did he find any enthusiasm for communist ideas, which were 'met with a soft smile – the disciples of Gandhi reject any form of compulsion, wherever it may originate'.

For Berlin Jews, Wilfrid was always the symbol of 'British culture'. But in India, he did not use his British passport, and never mentioned his British nationality to the Indians he met – despite the fact that in Egypt he had been warned that should he present himself in India as a German, he would be followed by detectives constantly. He did not want to be identified in any way with the British raj, for whose representatives he had even less time than the Jewish mill owners he visited. 'Many Europeans who complain of the monotony of life here, and booze their way through the day, could with less arrogance and egotism interest themselves in Indian culture instead of in their chits in hotel bars,' he commented. From this time on, he hated to drink gin. When he was obliged to attend British dinner tables, he enjoyed setting traps for unwary memsahibs. The widow of a British official confessed her dislike of Germany. 'After a few minutes I managed to mention the fact that I happened to be a German citizen. Only the cool of the evening prevented a nervous collapse.' Later on, the same woman referred to the Viceroy's wife, Lady Reading, as 'a shabby Jewish intriguer'. This time the collapse and the subsequent apologies were inevitable.

The only Englishman with whom Wilfrid made friends was C.F. Andrews, Gandhi's closest British friend, whom he met on a train journey between Calcutta and Bolpur. Andrews told him of his life in South Africa, his realization that British rule in India was 'sterile', and his attempts 'to combine Christian ethics with the foundations of old Indian and especially Buddhist philosophy'. Wilfrid, for his part, gave Andrews his views on Judaism, Palestine, and the links between Western and Eastern culture. When they left the train to take a carriage together to Shantiniketan, Andrews invited Wilfrid to lecture about the Jews and Palestine to the Indian students of the local school of art. With the students clustered round him that night on the moonlit veranda, Wilfrid – who hated talking in public – was suddenly in his element:

> I started with the history of the Jews in the Diaspora, their persecutions in Eastern Europe, where they are the outcasts of the Western world, in danger of death when they try to practise their religion. . . . I told them how in the ghetto a rebellion arose against the fate of the Diaspora and their longing to return to Palestine.

On the following day, he told the Indians about the German youth movements, the Wandervogel and the Hohe Ueissner, and their cult of nature and of comradeship. He took care not to stress the generation gap, 'which would be painful to the Indians in view of their close family ties'. When he had finished, a young monk from a Buddhist seminary in Ceylon approached him, and announced that he would try to set up a youth movement of this kind when he returned home: 'such a revitalization was necessary to each true Buddhist religious community.'

Following Buber, who, some years previously, had published an essay on Judaism and the oriental spirit, Wilfrid saw likenesses between Eastern rituals and forms of prayer, and the Jewish rituals he had seen in Eastern Europe and in Palestine. The celebration of Holi in Bombay coincided with the Jewish Purim: 'In both cases, the ritual consisted in dressing up and re-enacting the killing of a tyrant who had threatened the community'; and in Jaipur, where, he said, he finally found the India he had been seeking, 'the children were seated like Buddhas . . . I thought I was in a Talmud Torah in Jerusalem.'

What he admired most in Indian art was Ghandaran sculpture: it was a significant choice, for the Ghandaran style is deeply influenced by the culture of the Eastern Mediterranean, in which Buddhist figures wear togas, and Graeco-Roman deities, putti and even scenes from Greek poetry appear on Buddhist buildings – a reflection of the mingling of cultures after the trade routes between China and the Roman Mediterranean were first opened.

From India, Wilfrid went on to China and the universities of Nanking and Peking, where, according to a speech he gave in Berlin in 1928, he again preached the Zionist gospel to the Chinese. Zionism, as Wilfrid saw it in those years, was not a nationalist doctrine, but a social experiment which would re-establish old Jewish links with the Orient; an intensely romantic concept only possible for a man who knew little of Jewish orthodoxy as it had evolved in Europe, and who believed that an intellectual synthesis of Jewish mysticism and German idealism could somehow be wedded to socialist reform.

These beliefs were strengthened by his journey to the Soviet Union, where he saw middle-class Jews tilling the Russian soil, in an extraordinary social experiment which convinced Wilfrid Israel that all the Jewish communities in Eastern Europe could share in and profit from revolutionary socialism. It was a belief that was to influence his entire attitude to Zionism for the rest of his life.

Other privileged visitors, at this period (very few were admitted to Soviet Russia in these years), admired the pioneering spirit of the new Jewish farmers who appeared to share the revolutionary ideals of the new Russia. Yet the origins of settlements in the Ukraine and the Crimea were fortuitous. Post-revolutionary Jewry in Russia was, it was true, freed from the restriction to the Pale of Settlement and the threat of officially supported pogroms. But the old Jewish middle class posed a problem to the Soviets. Jews could not compete for jobs in the professions and government offices with Ukrainians or other autonomous Russian groups. They belonged neither to the workers nor the peasantry now in power. The only work officially encouraged was work on the land.

Moreover, they depended essentially on capitalist financing – provided by American Jewry. During the immediate post-war period, the Joint Distribution Committee, the leading American-Jewish charity, spent millions of dollars on refugee relief – first independently, and then in collaboration with the Hoover project, which had assisted Nansen's attempts to alleviate the Russian famine. Finally, in order to help Russian Jewry to re-establish itself, the Joint representative, Joseph Rosen, concluded an agreement with the Soviet Government in 1922; loan cooperatives and vocational training schools were started, and a few thousand Russian Jews became revolutionary peasants. The settlements Wilfrid visited in the spring of 1925 were only a few months old and still in the experimental stage.

Living conditions were hard: many of the roads he travelled in the Crimea were impassable when it rained, save in Tartar peasant wagons. Some of the settlers had tuberculosis, and in the newer settlements the livestock was better housed than the settlers themselves. Among them were many young people, ex-students who shared in the revolutionary spirit and had chosen the collective as a way of life. The Zionist settlements, which eventually transferred to Palestine, were embryo kibbutzim. Bernhard Kahn, the Joint executive, who visited the settlements within a few weeks of Wilfrid's visit, praised the determination of the settlers, who in the Crimea were living in old shacks and barracks and in the Ukraine under canvas on the open steppes; he also noted that they had little choice. Under Soviet law they could neither sell nor mortgage their land; moreover, the AgroJoint, as the American organization was called, demanded some small investment – probably all the funds the settlers possessed in the project – 'otherwise the likelihood is that with the least discouragement they will drop the work and leave the land and ... we will soon find refugee camps instead of agriculturalists on the steppes of Russia'.[35]

On his way back to Berlin, Wilfrid revisited Kovno, and, as he put it, 'knocked up against' Siegfried Lehmann, late of the Berlin Volksheim. For the past four years, Lehmann had been running an orphans' home in

Kovno, as Wilfrid wrote, 'for children facing moral and physical destruction. Lehmann and his friends took them away from the streets, from the heaps of debris in which they made their so-called homes'. But while Lehmann succeeded with isolated cases, Wilfrid wrote: 'he realized that they could not stay in their environment in Lithuanian Kovno. Poverty, famine, illness would have pushed them back into their former state of human degradation.'[36] Lehmann decided to take the children with him to Palestine. His meeting with Wilfrid was providential; as soon as he reached Berlin, Wilfrid persuaded his father to contribute a substantial sum to the Jewish National Fund for part of the construction of a youth village in Palestine, Ben Shemen. The transfer and settlement of the Kovno home was financed by a Berlin Orphan Fund (Waisenhilfe) which supported both the Kovno home and Ben Shemen; Wilfrid became its chairman, and hence the godfather of the village. This was the first step in the transfer of Jewish children from Central and Eastern Europe to farming settlements, not to orphanages in the Holy Land - an old tradition.

But Lehmann, showing Wilfrid round Kovno and its Jewish suburb Slovodka in 1925, did not believe that the 'Jewish question' played an important part in his life; nor did he know that Wilfrid had discussed Jewish problems with the 'influential pacifist circles' he had met in Europe or India. 'What relation existed at that time for this young man between the world of beauty at which he aimed and the dirty, poor and unlovely Jewish quarters which I was able to show him during our walks in Slovodka?' [37] Lehmann discovered this only in the years that followed.

Wilfrid was equally misjudged by his friends and relations on his return to Berlin. He was anxious to share with anyone who was prepared to listen the problems of India, China and Soviet Russia, as well as his concern about German Jewry and its future. But he found no response at all. 'It was sad,' he told a friend in 1926. 'I was full of what I had seen and lived through, and brought pictures back of all the new and future world - but at home I found everything unchanged. People smiled ironically, and most of them did not even want to listen to what I had seen in those distant countries.'[38]

4

Wilfrid in Weimar

On his return from the East, Wilfrid entered what he liked to call 'the vicious circle of stability'. Its centre was the directors' suite on the second floor of the N. Israel block, where oil paintings of Jacob and Nathan Israel decorated the main conference room, and Wilfrid's windows looked across the street to the offices of the Mayor of Berlin. The print on another wall, Feigl's famous *Terra Sancta*, was Wilfrid's *mizrach*; the sign that in that direction, beyond the Scheunenviertel, lay the East.

Wilfrid now assumed responsibility for a small but varied Berlin community, the 2,000 employees of N. Israel: frock-coated department managers and clerks who had served the family for decades, some for fifty years and more; ambitious young salesmen who aimed at the few executive positions not reserved for the family; the daughters of the impoverished middle class, who worked as seamstresses or cashiers; provincial apprentices, the sons of the Israels' wholesale clients; and a brigade of uniformed commissionaires. Gentiles and Jews (who made up about a quarter of the staff), Social Democrats and fledgling Nazis, worked side by side among the rows of show cases ranged in tiered galleries around the main glass-roofed stairwell, in the spacious show-rooms leading off it, and in the workrooms, storerooms, delivery and mail-order departments dispersed in neighbouring buildings.

Berthold's concession to Wilfrid's obvious lack of interest in balance sheets, in the early years of his employment, was to put him in charge of the employees as personnel manager. He interviewed candidates for jobs and supervised their work, not through the heads of departments, but by spending most of his working hours not in his office but walking the floors, watching and learning, studying the behaviour of his employees with as obvious an interest as he had shown in the customs of the Indians or the Chinese – for until now they had been almost as strange to him.

The boy who had run international errands for the Quakers; the young man who believed that inaction over crying wrongs could be remedied by 'reports'; the world traveller who had tried to explain both

Jewish and German youth to the social revolutionaries of the East, now realized that, in the little community under his control, he could try to put some of his own ideas into practice. He learned all he could about each of his employees – their family circumstances, personal ambitions, problems at work. He told his friends that he was trying to put Buber's principles of 'dialogue' and mutual human respect to the test of reality. At first this caused some dismay. There was a strict hierarchy in N. Israel, as in all German institutions, and Wilfrid paid the same attention to a cashier or a commissionaire as to a department head or buyer on his walks; in fact, he paid them more attention, because he was unlikely to see them in his office. He did not announce himself; a cleaner in a corridor one day, who did not recognize him, called him over: 'Here, young man, you're so tall – straighten that picture, will you?' He obeyed. He assured a buyer in the leather goods department, during the Depression, that if he was laid off – in addition to the pension scheme – he would help pay for his son's education. To the irritation of the Social Democrats on the staff, when a young Nazi came to him in distress after his mother died, he lent him money.

But Wilfrid was not a crank, and he would not be manipulated. He had his own system of checking on his employees: one young man, for instance, was told to report privately on the work of his department head. Wilfrid knew whom he could trust – and this proved important during the Nazi period. His continuous *tours d'horizon*, from the early morning until the last survey of the huge display windows from the pavement outside, at seven in the evening, unnerving at first for the older employees, served as an incentive for the younger. Werner Behr, who eventually became the firm's financial director and Wilfrid's closest aide, began his career as a cashier in the late 1920s. He suggested a new method of getting information from the cash desks to the management, and was immediately promoted.

Wilfrid's most important experiment, however, was the private business school he founded, with his own curriculum and teaching methods. When it was formally opened, in Easter 1925, he was still in India; he hated ceremonies and speeches.

The N. Israel Hochschule was the only private school of its kind in Germany, though all trainees for management were obliged to attend municipal courses financed by taxes on employers. It was an expensive adventure, for the firm also paid its regular Berlin dues. Wilfrid's idea was that every trainee should be familiar with every stage of the manufacture of the goods N. Israel sold, from the raw material stage to the finished product. The first trainees in the linen and cotton departments were sent to factories in Bavaria from which the company bought its supplies. They rose at dawn to go to work with the factory hands, stood beside them at the looms of the Mecanische Waeverei in Augsburg, studied bleaching and dyeing at the Martini firm nearby, and the techniques of printing cotton at Gladbach, near Munich. Others attended a weaving school in Berlin.

The Hochschule taught science, economics, civics and gymnastics, apart from the routine business courses. The trainees were rotated as apprentices, in one department after another. At the end of three years, after talks with Wilfrid, they were finally placed; women were usually chosen for bookkeeping and accountants' posts rather than as buyers, but otherwise had similar training. Teaching methods were unusual for the time: the teachers sat among the students, and practical work was as important as theory; there was a model training shop for trainee salesmen apart from work in the store itself. In the evenings, they could attend lectures or meet in the school's social club; they ran their own theatrical circle, and took part in the firm's sports. The N. Israel rowing club exercised every Saturday on the Spree. Wilfrid accompanied its team to all its competitions with other big Berlin firms.

The Hochschule was a natural development from the firm's existing welfare and recreation schemes. But there were other models, which the Berliners believed were English: friends associated his work with Robert Owen's model working community and Ruskin's ideas on the reform of labour, for instance; yet management trainees were not working men, and the Hochschule was good business as well as educational innovation. The school rapidly became famous and N. Israel attracted somewhat envious praise: 'The commercial school established by N. Israel', a Berlin trade journal reported in 1928, 'has proved that there is no danger in this type of institution; on the contrary, it has done pioneering work in business circles by introducing a new economic and scientific form of training and educating young future businessmen.' The N. Israel method ensured that 'young people are not drilled, but encouraged to become versatile, well-educated businessmen, an aim not only in their own interests but in that of the firm that employs them'.[1] Other firms might offer higher salaries to trainees (the Israels paid a fair but not a high wage), but none could offer similar training or conditions.

With its private pensions and sick funds, training school, theatre group, rowing team, and even its own burial fund, N. Israel was a model society. Despite Wilfrid's innovations, however, it remained intensely conservative in its business methods until 1928.

Berthold Israel had not followed the example of Wertheim, Tietz and other department store owners who had branched out in other cities; he refused even to open a subsidiary in the fashionable new Kurfurstendamm, in Berlin's West End. N. Israel clung to the name of 'Das Kaufhaus im Zentrum' even though eastern Berlin was no longer the shopping centre of the city. The decision to remain in the Rathausplatz was part of the firm's loyalty to a traditional clientele: the landowners of the Brandenburg district; army families; the Berlin upper classes on whose linen the Israel seamstresses embroidered personal monograms. The poor nobility bought there, too, because the goods were elegant, but reasonably priced. Generations of Berliners had bought their trousseaux and furniture in the store, and, for regular customers, Berthold would order a special consignment of wood or silk, or send his own interior decorators to copy a model of a chair or table elsewhere in Berlin. In 1926, an American company offered a record figure of 26,000,000 reichsmarks to purchase the firm. Berthold turned it down; the Israels did not sell.

1926 was the year that one of the oldest executives, Julius Salinger of the clothing department, reached his sixtieth jubilee with N. Israel. This was the second time Israels had held a jubilee for old Salinger, who gave no sign of retiring. It was celebrated with an all-male dinner in a big hotel under chandeliers the firm had installed, at tables loaded with N. Israel linen and cutlery. One of the executives read out a specially commissioned ode beginning:

> In measured tread, from patriarchal times of old
> The records of this simple merchant house unfold
> Within the city where the thunder of the world resounds
> Salute the house where commerce new and proud abounds!

Then, to the folk tunes of 'Ich bin eine Preusse, kennt ihr meine Farben' and 'Der Jager aus Kurpfalz', they sang parodies about 'Herr Julius the buyer/Of sportswear attire'. In a formal photograph of the management, Wilfrid sits, not beside his father in the front row, but among minor employees.

But such idyllic scenes were shattered by the return of young Herbert Israel from a period of study and training at Columbia University and Macy's in New York. He told his father that if the firm was to survive the fierce competition of the late 1920s, they would have to revolutionize their accounting and sales techniques. It was absurd, he said, that the only available list of stocks should be kept in the heads of trusty old employees such as Salinger, or in handwritten inventories. For the first time, the N. Israel executive heard of cost analysis, profit and loss accounting, and statistics. To be certain that his ideas were put into practice, Herbert had brought back a small team to run the new statistical office – headed by a woman, Irene Witte. Equipment was modernized; Herbert, who had played with electric trains while Wilfrid preferred Meccano, even replaced the old typewriters with new electric models. Advertising was expanded and press conferences held. Alberti's literary essays, or their equivalent, were out; 'slogans' were in (one, admittedly, adapted from a Goethe quotation). The photograph of Hans Albers, a new Berlin film star, was plastered on the side of buses on lines passing the Spandauerstrasse, telling Berliners to 'Buy at N. Israel!', and the builders and renovators moved in.

All this caused fear and resentment among the older staff members, who thought it reflected on their personal honesty and efficiency. With one brother engaged in 'dialogues' with lift attendants and the other literally tearing the old store apart, the veteran staff's world was disintegrating, and it was not surprising that Wilfrid now had to take on a trained social worker to deal with staff problems. He also opened a bargain basement.

For, almost at the same time as Herbert's overhaul took place, the economic depression which had struck America began to affect Germany. Employees' wages were cut by up to 10 per cent, and the firm's turnover fell dramatically.

Israel's ploughed steadily through the Depression, perhaps due to Berthold's caution. The only gamble he had allowed himself was to let Amy open her own little boutique in a corner of the ground floor. Sadly for a patron of the arts, Amy had little taste. Her boutique was full of theatrical kitsch - hats, bags and jewellery - that the Israel clientele would not buy, and which sat oddly in the store's elegant shopping halls. Every Christmas, at the end of the decade, Berthold would beg his wife to turn over that floor space to the adjoining departments. Herbert's modern methods of feedback meant that Berthold knew exactly how much the loss of those few square feet was costing him. But Amy was adamant; she would have her boutique.

During these years, Wilfrid's position in his family and in Berlin-Jewish society was ambivalent. On the one hand, he was the dutiful son, the respected member of the community, like his father. But he remained a gentle rebel at heart.

Politically, father and son were far apart; Wilfrid with his socialist friends, Berthold supporting the ultra-right Deutsche Nationale Volkspartei which, though it had forced out its anti-semitic wing after Walter Rathenau's murder in 1922, was still far too reactionary for most Jews who, like Richard and Bianca, supported the Catholic Centre Party, the German Democrats (liberals) or the Social Democratic Party.

In communal Jewish affairs, though he had given way to Wilfrid on

Ben Shemen, Berthold would not support anything which looked like active Zionism rather than philanthropy. Wilfrid, meanwhile, drew closer to Zionist circles, partly because of his admiration for pioneering agrarian socialism, partly because of his growing alienation from those Jews who could not see the precariousness of their own position in Germany.

Berlin Jews had 'smiled ironically' at Wilfrid's youthful enthusiasm for world revolution. His answer was to smile, ironically, back at them. From a serious, naïve youth he became the elegant, urbane young man of the world whom Isherwood describes, confronting Berlin society – as his photographs from the period demonstrate – with a constant, defensive smile. There were to be no more spontaneous confessions of his beliefs; on the rare occasions when he spoke in public, he was nervous and banal. Accessible to his employees, and to anyone who needed his help, he refused to be drawn out by those who sought intimate confessions. His philanthropy, unlike that of most rich Jews, was as private as he could make it. He set part of his salary aside every month for whatever group or cause was most in need, often through a third party, and conveniently forgot to reclaim loans to friends.

Wilfrid was a well-known figure in Berlin-Jewish society during the 1920s, but he eluded all efforts to enlist him in community affairs save those of his own choice, such as the Waisenhilfe. Present at formal gatherings, at art auctions, visible at concerts and the Berlin theatre, his private life was a total mystery to his colleagues and his parents' circle.

When his parents moved to the Hildebrandstrasse in 1923, Wilfrid moved to a small flat of his own; scarcely a dramatic separation, for the the flat was in the street immediately parallel, the Bendlerstrasse, next door but one to the War Ministry. Yet the move was significant, allowing him to appear at his mother's elaborate entertainments and then retire to the comparative austerity of the Bendlerstrasse apartment.

It was on the top floor of the building, with no elevator, and visitors commented on the eerie silence Wilfrid had produced by installing double windows. He never entertained more than a handful of close friends there; a housekeeper, Marie, cooked simple meals and took messages. At weekends Wilfrid would sometimes take the night train, alone, on Friday afternoon, to a small town or village in the mountains, walk all weekend, and take the night train back to Berlin on the Sunday night.

More often, however, he spent weekends at 'my parents' little country place', as he called it, a big villa on the Wannsee at Schwanenwerder, half an hour's drive from Berlin. When his parents were not in residence, he would invite friends to the villa, 'mon Bijou', on one of a dozen or so wooded properties which sloped steeply down to the lakeside. A narrow road, dipping through perpetually damp woods, led into Schwanenwerder, a small peninsula owned almost entirely by wealthy Berlin Jews, past a strange imported ruin: a fragment of the Tuileries masonry, brought back from the Franco-Prussian War; it bore the inscription: 'This stone from the banks of the Seine, planted here in German soil, warns you, passer-by, how quickly luck can change.'

Wilfrid wrote frequently in praise of the English 'weekend idea', which he tried to practise at Schwanenwerder. But, as his English friends noticed, he dressed there with a most un-English country elegance, in fine flannels and a pullover, the Chinese kimono being kept for the Bendlerstrasse. In photographs, Wilfrid always stood with his right hand thrust into his trouser pocket – the same position he had adopted for the camera as a self-conscious small child.

Schwanenwerder was Wilfrid's retreat, but it was not really a 'country home' in the English sense, for the Israels had no roots in the Prussian countryside. Nor was Wilfrid's 'English' *alter ego* real, save in his own mind: 'My Anglo-Saxon education and behaviour put barricades around my heart, as you know,' he wrote to a close friend. The English façade was none the less more of a defence than the root cause of Wilfrid's reserve.

For where his daily life was concerned, Wilfrid often quoted the sixth of Rilke's *Letters to a Young Poet*, in which the writer advises the young Lieutenant Kappus to cultivate solitude, 'to be alone as a child is alone', and to look out at the world 'as something alien'.[2]

Though Wilfrid had been concerned with educational reform from his youth, and was to work for children all his life, he had no common language with the very young. The daughter of a woman friend remembered him, at Schwanenwerder, painfully ill at ease in a little girl's company, reluctant even to 'race her down the garden path', though he won her heart by telling her – with illustrations in the gravel path – how he had been chased by a snake. When he once begged a woman friend to be lenient with a disobedient child, and was told that he too would be strict when he became a father, he blushed painfully; she realized, too late, that she had wounded him, that he would never be a father.

Those with whom he continued to feel sympathy, and to befriend, were adolescents. Wilfrid understood best the time of life when everything is possible and nothing attainable. The odd boyishness many people noticed in him, well into middle age, was characteristic of an uncertainty and eagerness he could disguise, but never put aside altogether. Most of his friends, as distinct from his colleagues at work, were much younger than himself, and often outside his parents' social circle: writers, artists, Zionists.

As to his daily work in the firm, Wilfrid told a friend that he felt one passage in the same letter of Rilke's had been addressed personally to him:

> I know your profession is hard and filled with contradiction of yourself.... I can only advise you to consider whether all professions are not like that, full of demands, full of hostility against the individual, saturated ... with the hatred of those who have reconciled themselves mutely and morosely to their own insipid duty.

Thus Wilfrid Israel, despite his privileges and apparent sophistication, was a painfully vulnerable and lonely man. After his death, his German-Jewish colleagues eulogized him in terms that were all too revealing. Buber, who himself had had a deeply unhappy childhood, described him as 'exposed to life like a victim, but looking like one who masters life with ease ... there always was a pointed sword 'twixt him and what he loved'. In Buber's poem, what Wilfrid loved is Palestine; but the metaphor is clearly sexual. In one obituary, Reissner wrote: 'Underneath the ... outer layer of political opinion and charity is ... an elementary desire to love and be loved', and he noted to one of Wilfrid's friends, after his death, that the tragic truth of his life could never be revealed. What Reissner and others would only hint at, but not say, was that Wilfrid loved young men.

For the Berlin-Jewish community, this was unmentionable. The famous permissiveness of Weimar Berlin did not touch the Berlin merchant society in which Wilfrid spent most of his time. While Wilfrid was still a very young man, a close friendship with a beautiful young girl, the daughter of friends of his parents, created the rumour that he was engaged to be married. This relationship, in fact, probably indicated to him that he could never love a woman. As the years passed, and Wilfrid did not marry, his diffidence did not however discourage the young women who pursued him vigorously. He was strikingly handsome and attractive to women, and with those who were sensitive enough to respect his privacy he enjoyed long and affectionate friendships. But any unsolicited invasion of the Bendlerstrasse sent him to the telephone with requests to men friends to 'rescue' him.

The students in the Hochschule, the young men and women in the Zionist youth groups whom he began to meet in the late 1920s, and Berlin Jews at large gossiped furiously – and sometimes maliciously – about his close friendships with young men. No scandal ever touched Wilfrid, but he was aware that people talked. The story of Hermann

Israel's disgrace and suicide was never forgotten, and must have made Wilfrid even more sensitive to gossip. The more he protected his privacy, the more speculation he aroused. Hence the passion for secrecy noted by all his colleagues. By the time the Nazis came to power, this had become second nature.

The ambivalence of his emotional life and his sensitivity to gossip meant that Wilfrid came to distrust the world around him profoundly. His few really close friends, who knew of his dilemma but did not criticize him, were doubly precious: 'The purity and single-mindedness of your friendship puts me, the unbeliever, to shame,' he wrote to one such friend near the end of his life. Ambivalence also came near to making him inarticulate. Perhaps unconsciously echoing Buber's phrase about 'honest stammering' in Buber's 1929 essay 'Dialogue', he told a close friend that 'stammering is more eloquent than speech', and from this sprang another contradiction in his character. While he could outline a factual argument concisely and with great force, he became almost incoherent if asked to explain his deepest belief, or when trying to express his deepest feelings.

Yet in the letters which have survived to the young men for whom he cared so deeply, two characteristics stand out. For Wilfrid, the impulse to love meant the desire to shelter and to protect. Just as those who intermittently shared his life remembered only the most delicate physical touch – a hand on a shoulder, a handshake, an arm rarely taken in a gesture of reassurance – the letters indicate a much fiercer desire for possession – the building of protective walls, excluding the outside world. This was perhaps linked, in Wilfrid's character, with his passion and compassion for the persecuted and the hunted.

But together with this, in many letters to young men, was the advice to protect themselves from the assaults of the world – as he himself had tried to do – and to keep away from other people at times of stress. And a theme that constantly recurs in Wilfrid's letters to all his friends is his temptation to withdraw into himself – 'the ostrich policy' – and the comfort of hiding behind curtains of falling rain at Schwanenwerder, mists and fog approaching 'lovingly' to conceal him from the outside world. It was no wonder, then, that his friends thought Wilfrid ill-equipped to face the stresses of life under the Nazis a few years later.

He had been a fragile child; he was an ailing man. Friends thought most of his illnesses psychosomatic, but he had at least one real physical problem, connected with his sense of balance. He was continually in and out of sanatoria, always under doctors' orders. His letters refer to 'unpleasant heart trouble', 'weakness', 'lack of *élan vital*' (a favourite phrase) and long periods spent on his back. He suffered badly from insomnia, slept with a black velvet band over his eyes, wrote most of his letters in the small hours, and would ring friends after midnight to talk. But whatever the source of his physical problems, he always managed to overcome them at times of crisis. A familiar phrase in his letters of the 1930s was to be: 'We must not break down at the wrong moment.'

Discretion and secrecy - even when it was not necessary - had now become Wilfrid's second nature. This, with his absence of personal ambition, his gentle receptiveness, and his willingness to play the intermediary in any Jewish dialogue, now made him the perfect confidant to such giants of the Jewish world as Weizmann and Einstein, during the turbulent years at the end of the 1920s.

Robert Weltsch, the famous German-Jewish journalist from Prague, claimed in 1928 that 'the whole of Jewish life orients itself around Zionism'.[3] In fact the Zionist movement in Germany numbered only 25,000 supporters among Germany's 500,000 Jews, and of those, only a tiny minority were prepared to leave Germany for Palestine. Yet in the intellectual sense there was some truth in Weltsch's phrase. Many of the Zionist classics were written in German and the great Zionist charities, the Palestine Land Development Corporation and the Jewish National Fund among them, were developed and administered by German-speaking Zionists in Berlin and Vienna. As Richard Lichtheim was to write to Nahum Goldmann in 1942: 'We were only a small minority within our own more or less assimilated communities, but at that time ... we were proud to be the organizers and officers of the people, the real people, the eight million Jews in Eastern Europe in whose name we were speaking and acting.'[4]

By 1928, both Weizmann in London and Ben Gurion in Palestine - Zionism's diplomatic and grass roots leaders - were aware of the need to widen both the financial and the ideological foundations of Zionism. Throughout the 1920s, Weizmann sought the support of the 'non-Zionists' all over the world to boost what was still a small and often poverty-stricken settlement effort in Palestine. Ben Gurion and other Zionist Labour leaders sought the sympathy and interest of Western socialist parties. The first conference for the international League for Working Palestine was to take place in late 1930, at Ben Gurion's insistence; its committee, which had been established in Brussels two years earlier, included the Belgian socialist leader Emile Vandervelde, Eduard Bernstein, the German-Jewish socialist and pacifist who had been one of the leading members of the German Liga, and Arthur Henderson, the British socialist who was to become Foreign Secretary in the 1929 British

Cabinet.[5] These were the men whom Wilfrid, too, sought to interest in the Zionist idea.

In December 1928, a preparatory conference was held in Berlin at which Wilfrid Israel made what appears to have been his only speech in a public forum. He chose as his theme Edith Cavell's famous dictum 'patriotism is not enough' – the words of a brave English nurse who was executed by the Germans for her role in helping British soldiers escape in the First World War. Wilfrid argued that 'Zionism is not enough'. Jews could not be passive supporters of the Zionist ideal, but ought to support actively the new socialist movement in Palestine, for two reasons. Firstly, for their own self-respect: all Jewish communities were in fact one ('being a Jew requires the individual always to subject himself and adapt himself to the community') and were regarded as one by the outside world ('the world at large does not distinguish between Zionists and non-Zionists; the world at large knows only Jews'). Secondly, because, he thought, the social experiments in Palestine might prove a model for those countries in the East emerging from Western domination – including those he himself had visited, India and China, whose intellectual leaders were watching the fate of the new socialism in Palestine with 'acute awareness'.[6]

The hope of international socialist support for Zionism was dashed almost immediately. The British Prime Minister Ramsay MacDonald told Ben Gurion just a year later that Bengali Moslems were already pressing the Colonial Office to grant concessions to the Arabs against the Jews;[7] Ben Gurion's expectations of support from British socialists were rapidly disappointed.

Yet the aim of widening Jewish support for Palestine succeeded. Weizmann's six-year lobbying of American Jewry in order to enlarge the Jewish Agency, the administrative body which functioned under the Mandate Government, produced results a few months later. Meeting in Zurich in the summer of 1929, the sixteenth Zionist congress approved a new Agency constitution to include 'non-Zionist' members. The great Jewish financiers of American and British Jewry now became official patrons of the Zionist movement.

A few days later, however, events in Palestine proved how fragile hopes of increased prosperity and political stability had been. Arab nationalist leaders saw the Zurich congress as a threat; a relatively small incident at the Wailing Wall in Jerusalem, exploited by Arab extremists and accompanied by right-wing Jewish demonstrations, led to Arab massacres of the veteran Jewish population in Hebron and Safed, towns where Jews had lived continuously as communities since the fifteenth century. Many Arabs were killed in subsequent British police actions.

After this, the most serious outbreak of violence in Mandate Palestine, the new Labour Government in Britain revealed itself as basically unsympathetic to Zionism in the investigations and commissions which followed. The newly appointed non-Zionists were shaken by the revelation that the Jewish settlements were so vulnerable, and reconsidered their investments. Many European Zionists, particularly among the influential German group – men such as Weltsch and the Zionist leader Kurt Blumenfeld – felt that Weizmann had not done enough to tackle the problem of Arab hostility. Felix Warburg in New York, the famous banker and newly appointed president of the Administrative Committee of the Agency, and Einstein, whose international prestige made him an important supporter, voiced criticism in letters to Weizmann.

Weizmann's diplomatic efforts in London to ensure an impartial enquiry, and his newly found support in Jewish America, were endangered by the amateur diplomacy, in Jerusalem, of the chancellor of the recently founded Hebrew University, Yehuda Magnes, who was a member of the Brith Shalom group which favoured a bi-national state. Magnes played politics between the British adventurer St John Philby and Sir John Chancellor, the British High Commissioner in Palestine, and misrepresented his talks with the latter to Felix Warburg, whom he asked to use his influence with Weizmann to force through a proposal for a legislative assembly including Jews and Arabs – something desired by neither group.[8]

To cap Weizmann's problems, the funds already endorsed by the new Zionist administration abroad were blocked while the crisis lasted. Weizmann wrote to a close friend, 'Hundreds of thousands are lying idle now and our work is starving to death. My personal position (in the financial sense) is impossible. . . . This is shameful and indecent. . . . I shall have to spit upon it all and leave . . . if things do not improve.'[9]

At this moment, Wilfrid was also in London. He proved the perfect intermediary between Weizmann and the powerful bankers in Berlin, Max Warburg – Felix Warburg's brother – and the chairman of the Keren Hayesod, the Jewish National Fund subsidiary, Oskar Wassermann. After extensive talks with Weizmann he returned to Berlin on 27 November and three days later wrote to Weizmann:

> As soon as I returned to Berlin I arranged talks with Mr Wassermann and Mr Warburg. In the interim period [before Weizmann's projected visit] I believe I have succeeded in clearing up several things, and the subjects you suggested have been discussed fairly thoroughly . . . the day after my return, I had quite a long talk with Oskar Wassermann . . . apart from political questions we dealt mainly with the financial questions. My point that very soon we would not be able to pay salaries regularly made an impression. Though Mr

> Wassermann pointed out that this kind of situation had happened before, I could easily show that lack of funds at this moment, with all its consequences, would not only be disastrous for the people involved; it would also create a situation which politically, from the English as well as the Arab side, would be turned against us. I also made it clear that lack of funds seriously handicaps your political work.

Wilfrid also explained to Max Warburg the background to the Magnes affair. Warburg, who had not initially wanted to be drawn into internal Zionist affairs, was brought round by Wassermann. 'All were agreed that the one-man action of Dr Magnes, his kind of "unpolitical politics" could only cause damage, and that all initiative should be left solely in your hands.' Wilfrid had then proposed, and the bankers had agreed, that the money in the Emergency Fund (raised in the wake of the massacres) could be used freely not only for the victims of the riots but as loan funds for industrialists and merchants, and for the purchase of additional land to safeguard the security of the existing Jewish settlements.

Wilfrid assured Weizmann that Max Warburg's involvement had increased; very delicately, he suggested that Weizmann's own meeting with Warburg should take place not in Frankfurt, as Weizmann had wished, but in Warburg's own fief, Hamburg. He promised that Wassermann would do all he could to increase Weizmann's own political funds, and that both men would show flexibility on the commission which would decide the division of the money. Finally, he recommended co-opting his friend, Werner Senator, who had been nominated for membership of the Jewish Agency in Jerusalem, as treasurer. 'He is a person who is ready to dedicate himself unconditionally to any task he has accepted ... in the spirit of absolute dedication to your work and ideas.'[10] Senator, who was to remain in close touch with Wilfrid for the rest of his life, was to prove one of the most independent-minded spokesmen for German Jewry throughout the pre-war Nazi period.

When Weizmann visited Germany the following month, the Zionist leader and his young admirer had further meetings, and Wilfrid subsequently wrote thanking Weizmann 'for the extent and intimacy of your trust in me'.[11]

It was more difficult, however, for Wilfrid to keep the peace between Weizmann and Einstein, who was a whole-hearted supporter of Magnes and the pacifist bi-nationalists. After the August riots, Einstein had supported the mainstream Zionists fervently in the British *Manchester Guardian*. But when the Mandatory authorities pronounced a death sentence on the murderers of Hebron and Safed, Einstein signed Brith Shalom's petition for an amnesty. This infuriated Weizmann, who attacked them as 'extremists who would like to scuttle and give up everything', and was sorry to see 'that Einstein is lending them his moral support'.[12] To make matters even worse, Einstein wrote to Weizmann complaining of the behaviour of leading Zionists, who had sown the whirlwind by dealing 'superficially' with the Arab problem. 'If we don't find a way to co-operate with the Arabs, then we have learned nothing from the Via Dolorosa of two thousand years, and deserve our fate,' Einstein wrote.[13] He warned against too much dependence on the support of the British Government, and foretold that, if no accommodation was reached, the British 'would let the Jews down' in the end.

Weizmann responded bitterly, reproaching Einstein for his friendship with the Brith Shalom, who, he said, 'broke the united front of Zionism', and arguing that it was impossible to negotiate with murderers.[14] Einstein replied that the crimes had been provoked; without honest co-operation with the Arabs there would be no peace or security. 'Even if we were not so defenceless, it wouldn't be consonant with our dignity to prove nationalists à la Prussienne.'[15] Nevertheless, this letter was conciliatory; and, like Weltsch in an earlier letter, Einstein promised not to interfere further.

However, it soon came to Einstein's notice that the Palestinian weekly, *Falastin*, in its English edition, had heavily criticized his letter to the *Guardian*. In a front-page article entitled 'Relativity and Propaganda' it attacked Einstein as just another Zionist propagandist, a scientist 'who does not know anything about the world he lives in but its external curve'. Jewish attempts at friendly relations were hypocrisy, *Falastin* wrote. 'The Jews were determined to rob the Arabs by the latest civilized dodges'; Zionist propaganda was all 'lies and distortion', because Jews throughout the ages had 'resorted to falsehood to preserve their lives'.[16]

His vanity needled, Einstein decided to respond, but first he sent a copy of his letter to Wilfrid, asking him to translate and comment on it. Wilfrid was tactful. He knew Einstein well enough to suspect that outright discouragement would be counter-productive. His own opinion apart, he said, it might be a good idea to respond. But he felt he should warn Einstein of subsequent criticisms. 'There will be voices within the Executive Committee [of the Agency] who will be surprised that you express yourself again on this subject', after being publicly reviled. 'Perhaps it is too great an honour for *Falastin* that your answer should appear there – it is a cheap rag; perhaps it will be given too much importance by your comments.' Moreover, Einstein's remarks could be regarded by the Zionists as a political action – the prerogative of the executive itself.[17]

Einstein rejected Wilfrid's advice. *Falastin* printed his letter, jeering at him again and pointing out that while Einstein claimed to represent the Zionist movement, 'Weismann' was taking precisely the opposite view at the congress in Germany. The paper rejected Einstein's appeal for understanding and refused to take back its abusive remarks about Jews.[18]

The letters between Wilfrid and Weizmann during the following weeks indicate that Wilfrid attempted to soothe tempers.[19] But relations between the two great men never radically improved.

The Palestine riots, and the Zionist crisis of 1929, had not only shaken the professional Jewish politicians. The shock waves reached Berlin Jewry's intellectual circles and endangered their support of the Hebrew National Theatre, Habima, then in its nomadic infancy, and one of whose nurses was Wilfrid Israel.

Habima was the stepchild of the Hebrew revival in Eastern Europe. The highly romantic project to revive the Hebrew language on the stage and popularize Eastern European-Jewish culture had begun before the Russian Revolution, in Warsaw, where there was a potential audience of Hebrew speakers. From 1917 the company trained in Soviet Moscow, under the direction of one of Stanislavski's pupils, Vaghtangov, before setting off on a world tour of Europe and America. From the outset it had difficulty in finding patrons: the Joint Distribution Committee, so generous in other respects, did not see theatrical shenanigans as a deserving cause. In 1923, Cyrus Adler, the Joint leader, declared that, while they were prepared to support Jewish learning, education and religious life, the theatre was 'a construction of cultural work broader than the committee was willing to allow'.[20] When Habima arrived in Berlin at the end of 1927 on its second tour, it was already famous but desperate for money. Some of the actors had dropped out in the United States; many were homesick for the Soviet Union; others coveted a permanent place in Berlin's brilliant theatre life. The sands of Tel Aviv looked less attractive. The actors lacked even money to decorate the stage, let alone pay their rent in Berlin boarding-houses or the cost of further studies.[21]

Three wealthy young Berliners, dubbed 'the millionaires' children', adopted the vagabond players: Margot Klausner, daughter of the owner of the Leiser chain of shoe shops, and a left-wing Zionist; Lola Hahn Warburg, Max's beautiful daughter, and Wilfrid Israel. The three took over the feckless Russians, solicited funds furiously in the marble lobbies of Berlin's Jewish millionaires and with any other foreign Jews who came their way. Wilfrid organized benefit dinners at the Kaiserhof (where Hitler also liked to stay on his visits to Berlin), and gave the Russians the run of N. Israel for any materials they needed for their decor. He also spent hours discussing their repertoire – urging them to enlarge it to include foreign classics – and tried, with Klausner, to encourage them to emigrate to Palestine.

Klausner accompanied them on their first tour of Palestine in 1928. But by the end of the year they were back in Berlin, penniless as ever, and the three friends had to begin again. Towards the end of 1929 Habima appeared with a new repertoire ranging from Shalom Aleichem to Shakespeare. But both the real drama in Palestine and the worsening situation for Jews in Germany overshadowed the success of this new season.

Wilfrid and Klausner organized two benefit evenings for Habima at their parents' mansions, and invited all the most famous intellectuals of Jewish Berlin, including Buber, Alfred Doeblin, Arnold Zweig, Rudolf Kayser and Arthur Holitscher, as well as the Hebrew poet Chaim Bialik. One after another they rose to deliver their intellectual blessings on the infant theatre, like so many fairy godfathers in frock coats. Bialik, speaking in Yiddish, recalled the histrionic talents of the prophet Ezekiel, and exhorted Habima to raise the cultural tone of the Palestine community; Buber called on the actors to play Shakespeare and Schiller and reach 'all humanity'. Rudolf Kayser, a famous Berlin editor, thought Habima should act out 'Jewish suffering'; Arnold Zweig, who had written his own 'Jewish drama', made it clear he was annoyed at having been passed over. Then Holitscher, a socialist novelist and essayist who, like Wilfrid, admired the AgroJoint settlements in Russia, rose to his feet. 'Habima has only one task left. Pioneering Israel of our idealistic dreams is in ruins. All that is left to "Habima" is to lament Israel's passing on the stages of the world!'

As Klausner recorded in her diary, 200 intellectuals went into shock; she and Wilfrid sat 'paralysed' on the central staircase. However, Buber kept his head and announced that refreshments would now be served. A soprano sang 'Joshua fit the battle of Jericho', Buber reproved Holitscher for being a Jewish Cassandra, and the evening was saved.

But the middle-class Berlin community as a whole was far from happy with Habima's repertory. One of the plays they put on in December 1929 was Shalom Aleichem's *HaOtsar* (*The Treasure*), the story of a little Jewish community in the Russian Pale of Settlement, which goes on a false treasure hunt, hoping for easy money. The director, Alexander Diki, had reproduced the Jewish *shtetl* in all its squalor, superstition and backwardness. Berlin Jewry, which wanted plays about heroic pioneers in Palestine or at least dignified Biblical drama, was appalled. Even Klausner, whose father came from Galicia, admitted her discomfort. Alfred Tietz, one of the Berlin chainstore owners, who had refused to donate money to Habima, left his theatre box in demonstrative disgust:

'How dare they put this - this ghetto, these rags, this filth - on the stage here in Berlin, of all places!' he proclaimed, and left the theatre.

Wilfrid and his friends managed to launch Habima on one last European tour, including London (where an English friend of Wilfrid's, Jack Isaacs, a professor of English at London University, helped them hire a theatre), before the company settled in Palestine, to everyone's relief, in 1931. During this last, far less successful year in Berlin, it was Wilfrid who provided the funds for Habima's survival - something that the actors and even his fellow patrons only discovered years later.

In 1930, through Margot Klausner, Wilfrid met a young Romanian-born Palestinian socialist, Mordechai Shenhabi, who offered to take him on a tour of the Jewish townships of Poland. Wilfrid had seen the slums of post-war Kovno, the newly emancipated Russian Jews of the Crimea and the Ukraine, and the ostracized Jewish working class of Scheunenviertel. But, except on the stage, he had never seen the *shtetl*, where, as a leading British Jew, Neville Laski, remarked a little later, 'history is calculated from the date when the synagogue was last burned down.'[22]

Shenhabi was a member of one of the first kibbutzim in the Jezreel Valley - Mishmar HaEmek - and for several years the peripatetic envoy of the Marxist Hashomer Hatsair movement, who travelled about recruiting young pioneers in Eastern Europe. He thought that for Wilfrid to understand Zionism truly, he should see for himself the lives of the huge Jewish minority in Poland, who lived not only in the cities, where many had entered trades and professions and where they even played a role in national politics, but in the *shtetl*, where bitter fights were dividing religious and secular Jews, parents and children, over Zionism.

With Gustav Kroyanker, a well-known Berlin Zionist, Wilfrid and Shenhabi set out on 15 May for a ten-day journey; from Polish stations, they took the old stage coaches which travelled rough roads. They stayed at drab wayside inns, wrapped in thin blankets at night, and ate poor, doughy Polish fare. Once again hard travelling made Wilfrid communicative; he told Shenhabi that, while bound and indebted to his family, he was not part of their lives. Shenhabi, who became a good friend, took this with a pinch of salt; even Wilfrid's simplest clothes were so conspicuous that people in the villages they visited asked why, if Shenhabi was recruiting for farming pioneers, he should have brought with him so elegant a gentleman.

The three men visited tens of small villages, in an area where many Jews were employed making brushes from pigs' bristles. As many as eighty young men between seventeen and eighteen, from the local Zionist 'cell', would crowd into the largest room in the village to meet Shenhabi.

Knowing that the Zionists were godless, the elders did not ask for donations to the local synagogues, despite Wilfrid's obvious wealth. But he managed to make contact with the young people, who spoke in Yiddish and Polish with a little German thrown in.

The older people kept their distance; the women crowded into back rooms, peering round the door. The young people told the visitors that they felt they had no future in Poland; their only chance was to study Hebrew and then to leave the village, and the country. Shenhabi enrolled many new candidates.

But he could see that for both Kroyanker and Wilfrid, the visit was a blow to their earlier romanticism about the culture of Eastern Jewry. The behaviour of the older people, their evident hostility to Zionism, convinced both men that only the young and rebellious could contribute to a progressive Jewish state. Wilfrid saw the extreme orthodoxy and dogmatism of the elders as medieval anachronisms. To move such people to Palestine, he thought, could only compromise what had already been achieved; they would be a dead weight on the development of the national home. Thus his visit to Poland produced a belief in selective immigration which was to remain constant until his death.[23]

Wilfrid had already confessed to Einstein that he knew little of what was happening in the Arab world; he learned a little more by acting as intermediary between Weizmann and Rudolf Said-Ruete during the same year as his visit to Poland. Said-Ruete was the grandson of the Sultan of Zanzibar, half Arab, half German, who had approached Weizmann at the end of 1929, after hearing him lecture to the Royal Asian Society in London. Well connected, with expensive tastes, Said-Ruete proposed to Weizmann that he should use his connections to take soundings of Arab opinion in Cairo and Palestine, and – as honest broker – arrange meetings between Weizmann and Arab leaders.[24]

Weizmann was deeply reluctant, at this stage, to spell out Zionist policy towards the Arabs. However, under attack both by Zionists and non-Zionists for his lack of interest in the Arab case, it would have been unwise for him to reject the offer out of hand.

One of Said-Ruete's written conditions before undertaking the mission was that he receive instructions from, and communicate with, no one but Weizmann. From the outset, however, Wilfrid was discreetly in the picture, as financial intermediary, who had several opportunities to meet the envoy and discuss his impressions and views.[25]

Nothing in Said-Ruete's reports, despatched between December 1929 and March 1930, could have encouraged Weizmann to undertake further meetings. Said-Ruete warned Weizmann that the Zurich congress had set Jewish-Arab relations back, and that the Palestinian Arabs were now frankly alarmed that their rights were threatened. From Cairo he reported that the Egyptians backed the Palestinian Arabs all the way, although they were more preoccupied by the effects of the Depression. He thought only the Jews and Arabs in Egypt, acting together, could perhaps form a bridge between the Arab people and the Jews of Europe. Reaching Palestine in the New Year, he found no sympathy at all for Zionism; the only hope was for local Arabs and Jewish settlers to arrive at a compromise, without pressure. The Zionist executive, he wrote, was in danger of sacrificing the well-being of the 160,000 Jews already in Palestine to the prospect of 1,000,000 Jewish emigrants over the next thirty years.[26] In September 1930, Said-Ruete wrote to Wilfrid asking his help to find understanding for a 'bridge between the two sides', and offering himself (at a price) as an expert guide.[27]

Wilfrid had his own contacts among Jews in Egypt and Palestine, and clearly had a poor opinion of Said-Ruete.[28] But he feared the neglect of relations with the Arabs and was pessimistic about the future of the Jews in Europe. The surviving correspondence to Werner Senator, since 1929 on the Agency executive in Jerusalem as a non-Zionist, clearly conveys the dilemma of two men who saw, as they did, the coming storm, but who also realized that the solution of a mass transfer of Jews to Palestine would cause open conflict. Both men sympathized with bi-nationalism but saw that the Brith Shalom movement was powerless and doomed; both admired Weizmann but criticized what they saw as his lack of courage. Senator recommended concessions to the Arabs and the recognition of the Arab tenant farmers' rights, but recognized that no leader had the courage to adopt this policy. In July he argued that Wilfrid, with moderate Zionists such as Buber, Weltsch and others, should try to influence Jewish circles in Europe and plead for greater moderation. But as the Nazi menace grew, both men recognized that moderation, a cautious settlement policy and a dialogue with the Arabs were aims that would be swept aside by events.[29]

Weizmann was unseated as leader of the Zionist movement at the Zionist congress of 1931, defeated by the right-wing Revisionist Party, but succeeded by a close colleague, Nahum Sokolow. Wilfrid continued to meet Weizmann on business visits to London, but the friendship ossified now that Weizmann was out of office. Shenhabi, on a mission to London in November 1932, wrote that Weizmann's 'tragedy' was that he had realized too late that only a strong socialist movement in Palestine could save Zionism from right-wing extremists. Shenhabi, Weizmann's blunt settler friend, thought that 'he spent too much time with his enemies', the Revisionists. He urged Wilfrid, as Senator had done, to try to renew the international links between moderate Zionists and the socialist leaders in Europe who had founded the League for Working Palestine. But by now, Wilfrid was entirely preoccupied with events in Germany.[30]

Nothing could be more misleading than Isherwood's characterization of Wilfrid, during this very period, as a man who shrugged off the dangers to the Jews in the early 1930s with a combination of boredom and arrogance. In all other respects, the portrait of Bernhard Landauer is superficially precise. Landauer, with his weary ambivalence towards the business, his elaborate defences against the outside world, his mannerisms and disguises, is as instantly recognizable as the description of the statues and books in the Bendlerstrasse, or Bernhard's account of Wilfrid's travels. Isherwood was later to argue, in his semi-autobiographical *Christopher and his Kind*, that their friendship was tinged with hostility.

> I believe Christopher suspected that Wilfrid was a severely repressed homosexual, and that, as such, he condemned Christopher for his aggressive frankness about his own sex life. If Christopher did indeed suspect this, it would have been characteristic of him to be extra frank with Wilfrid, in order to jolt him into frankness about himself.[31]

But there were other reasons why Isherwood and Spender, two young writers 'leading our life in which we used Germany as a kind of cure for our personal problems', as Spender puts it, spoke Wilfrid's language only in the most rudimentary sense.[32] He was shackled to family life and commerce where they were free; but he also knew not only the ambivalence of that apparently primeval freedom Spender describes in his autobiography - naked bathers stretched out on the beach while the Storm Troopers trained in the woods behind them - but also the slow betrayal of the rebellion he had witnessed over a decade earlier. Isherwood sensed Wilfrid's sexual vulnerability, but it was to Spender that Wilfrid spoke of the coming ordeal of the Jews.

> In the summer of 1932 ... Wilfrid Israel came to stay with us in Sellin. One day, he and I went for a walk together through the forest.... Wilfrid Israel surprised me, during our walk, by outlining a plan of action for the Jews when Hitler seized Germany - an event which he seemed to anticipate as certain. The Jews, he said, should close their businesses and go out into the streets, remaining there, as a protest, and refusing to go home even if the Storm Troopers fired on them. It was only such a united action, within a hopeless situation, which would arouse the conscience of the world.[33]

In the state elections of April 1932, the National Socialists emerged as the strongest party in all the federal governments in the Republic. The day after the elections, Wilfrid wrote to Senator in Jerusalem:

> Prussia will have no other alternative but to form a neutral front or to create a coalition between the centre and the Nazis, but this idea is not yet voiced out loud. I suppose that this sort of arrangement will be a precedent for the whole country, if only because of the problem of reparations which isn't going to be worked out without Nazi action, and the enormous strengthening of the National Socialist movement. In other words, everything is still plunged in darkness. The only thing that is clear is just this darkness.
>
> Watch the forming and development of forces of the so-called fifth class, the huge army of unemployed. I'm not going, of course, to identify this army with the Nazi party; that would be an error. Nevertheless, there are, in right-wing circles, people with more understanding for the mental constitution of these desperate human beings than the left-wing parties and the trade unions.[34]

In July, at Lausanne, Germany's creditors waived the right to claim 90 per cent of Germany's remaining reparations payments; and in November the Nazis lost votes for the first time. But the visible darkness was closing in. Wilfrid still wanted to believe there was hope: a radical reorganization of the economy, a move towards European integration might stave off disaster: 'Meanwhile we are inevitably in a state of chaos, and there is no quick way out.'

Unlike the majority of German Jews, however, Wilfrid had no doubts as to the threat the Nazis posed to him and all his fellow Jews. In mid-1932, he became one of a group of younger Jews who, even before Hitler came to power, despaired of the conformism of their elders and realized the need for a leadership and new policies for German Jewry.

The last years of Weimar had seen a mending of fences between the Jewish liberals and the Zionists. A minority in the Central Verein, the main liberal organization, had for years worked to counter opposition to charitable work for Palestine. The growth of Nazism hastened the *rapprochement*, not because more than a minority contemplated emigration, but because the Zionists advocated a more positive Jewish commitment, and suggested at least one form of action to protect those immediately threatened by the Nazis.

Among the groups most vulnerable to the increasing effect of Nazi anti-semitism were young men and women who found themselves excluded from Gentile youth groups, and others whose families had been impoverished by the effects of post-war inflation even before the Depression and could find no work. One-third of the Jewish population of Germany was too poor to pay taxes at this period, and many young Jews were unemployed even before Hitler came to power in 1933. The man who did most to raise these young people's hopes was Ludwig Tietz, a member of the Central Verein board who had founded the first Jewish union for youth, the Reichsauschuss der jüdischen Jugendverbände, in 1927; he supported the non-Zionists' participation in the Jewish Agency in 1929, and in 1930 he headed a new 'positive' liberal party at the Jewish communal elections in Berlin – which promptly failed to win more than a handful of votes.[35]

Despite obvious differences in their personalities – Tietz had fought in the First World War, regarded left-wing Zionism as para-communist and was a born public leader – Tietz and Wilfrid became close friends. They shared a similar background – Tietz, a doctor, was a relative of the Israels' commercial rivals – and both felt responsibility towards the *Ostjuden* and the Jewish poor; the Reichsauschuss sponsored social work in East Berlin. Both believed that the Jews should affirm their unity rather than debate and protest against their persecution, the standard Central Verein response. Both were in favour of retraining Jewish youth for vocations and trades hitherto shunned by Jewish families who favoured the professions. But in Germany they were in a small minority, and they sought support abroad.

One of the first people Wilfrid tried to interest in the Tietz group was Werner Senator. After one of his first meetings with Tietz, Wilfrid wrote to Senator offering him work with the group which, he said, would try to get funds from abroad for welfare and retraining in Germany. Senator, while recognizing that this was indeed 'the bleeding heart of Jewish work', refused reluctantly, for personal reasons. He wrote:

> The Jewish people are now terribly divided. There is no Jewish leadership. The German Jews, who once played a leading role, are crushed . . . what they did is neglected, and American Jewry, who will unfortunately have to take up the leadership, are not yet ready to do so, because of the financial crisis . . . more than all else the shadow of war hangs over the future.[36]

The Tietz group was to spearhead the first practical efforts to rally German Jewry behind a policy of self-help in April 1933. Wilfrid, meanwhile, lent his help to another plan for Jewish youth, which grew naturally out of his earlier work for Ben Shemen and Lehmann's rescue of Eastern European orphans.

In the summer of 1932, Recha Freier, a Berlin rabbi's wife and student of anthropology, had a visit from a group of unemployed Jewish adolescents who wanted advice about their future. Training camps for Zionist youth already existed, but for adolescents there was no programme. Knowing of Wilfrid's work for Ben Shemen, she sought his help. Wilfrid and Lehmann had already, some months earlier, discussed a project for a training camp for young people in Ben Shemen. Wilfrid had written to Shenhabi that, if the plan was realized, it would be of value for young people in Germany 'as a living contact with Palestine, where otherwise there would be no possibilities for emigration'.[37]

Recha Freier and Wilfrid organized the emigration of a group of twelve Berlin boys, the pilot project for thousands of German-Jewish children who were soon to leave their sheltered lives in middle-class homes in Germany for the unknown rigours of life in Palestine. There were several hitches; a friend of Mrs Freier's pawned some jewellery to raise funds, and, at the last moment, the parents raised an unexpected objection; the boys had no overcoats. In the semi-tropical conditions of Ben Shemen in the Palestinian coastal plain there was no need for heavy overcoats in any season; but parents in chilly autumn Berlin were worried. Twelve tweed overcoats, with velvet collars, were taken off their hangers in N. Israel's junior clothing department, and presented to the apprehensive pioneers, and Recha Freier and Wilfrid Israel, the children's parents, and a small choir, sent them on their way from the Anhalter station in Berlin on 12 October 1932.[38]

The emigration of children to Palestine developed into what was known as the Youth Aliya movement. This was the first sign that rather than see their children forced into idleness and penury, thousands of German-Jewish parents were prepared to part with them – perhaps for good. It was the beginning of Wilfrid Israel's work for the rescue of thousands of his fellow Jews.

5
The Visible Darkness

'When the Nazis began to rule with thunder and lightning, when the Storm Troopers were once again marching untiringly through the streets of Berlin, a few people were sitting in the office of the Ben Shemen organization, discussing the necessity of saving the children. It was the evening of January 30th, 1933.'[1] Adolf Hitler had just been appointed Reichschancellor.

The meeting Wilfrid Israel thus recorded, ten years later, was the first tiny sign of a Jewish strategy of survival. 'Thunder and lightning' was the intimidation and murder of all those seen as potential opponents of the National Socialists, which was to continue from that night until the summer, when all political opposition had finally been crushed and the rule of terror could be institutionalized. It was during this period that the first campaigns to outlaw the Jews from German society began, and these ever-loyal citizens found that all the rules by which they had lived were suddenly changed.

During these months, Wilfrid was in danger of his life from the Storm Troopers' squads which roamed Berlin at will. He was triply vulnerable: firstly, as an ex-'leftist' and pacifist; secondly, as head of a prominent Jewish firm; and, thirdly, as member of the little group of Jewish activists around Ludwig Tietz.

Typical of the *wilden Aktionen*, the uncontrolled assaults of the Storm Troopers, was the attack on Ernst Friedrich's little museum, which led to Wilfrid's first arrest. On the night the Reichstag was burned down, 27 February, five regular policemen arrived at the Anti-War Museum, where the Friedrichs also lived, under the ludicrous pretext of searching for arms. Friedrich was dragged out of bed, arrested, and charged with high treason, while his wife and daughters took refuge with her parents. On 10 March, the Storm Troopers closed the streets leading to the Parochialstrasse and threatened to shoot any neighbour who opened their windows; they broke into the museum, which they vandalized, and took away all papers on the premises, including Wilfrid's letters. When Mrs

Friedrich and her daughters visited their home the next day, a Sunday, to salvage what they could, they found Wilfrid under interrogation by the Storm Troopers, who had converted the premises into one of their detention centres, erasing the 'Anti' from the sign outside.[2]

Wilfrid was arrested for the second time on 30 March, two days before the anti-Jewish boycott was to take place. Of this period, Werner Behr was to write:

> In 1933, Wilfrid realized at once that no further possibilities were open to Jews in Germany. It would have been an easy matter to secure personal advantages to his family by a speedy liquidation of the firm. This, however, would not have been in the interests of the Jews, and in particular of the Jews of the business world. Therefore, any such idea was renounced.[3]

This was part of a more complex story.

Berthold Israel's reaction to the threat of Nazism was typical of that of the Jewish middle class as a whole. Businessmen had, throughout the Weimar period, contributed to party political funds in the hope of influencing their policies, and the Jewish organizations had done all they could to shore up German democracy financially; in 1930 alone, it is estimated that the Central Verein spent 3,000,000 reichsmarks on contributions to the Centre party (for which most Jews traditionally voted) and the Social Democrats.[4] Berthold Israel went further. In February 1933, he was approached by Baron von Lersner of the German National People's Party (Deutsche Nationale Volkspartei), the Nazis' coalition partners, for a contribution to their election campaign. The DNVP, at this stage, were clearly Hitler's accomplices – though shortly destined to be wiped off Germany's political map – but Berthold consented, though protesting that he hoped the party would do what it could to modify Nazi anti-semitism. He was rewarded by an insult: a receipt from ex-Chancellor von Papen which did not even specify the donor's name.[5]

Berthold's precautions did not help protect his elder son. On the morning of 30 March, one of the most feared Nazi squads, the Wecke group, already known abroad to have carried out death sentences on those most hated by the Nazis,[6] arrived at the Israel firm and demanded that Wilfrid, who was in charge that day, dismiss all his Jewish employees. He refused. Hauptmann Walther Wecke, the squad head, told Wilfrid that he, Herbert and Werner Behr were under arrest. When Wilfrid asked on whose authority the arrests were made, one of the squad raised his revolver. Only Wecke's shouted order prevented Wilfrid's death on the spot. Years later, describing this to a young friend, Wilfrid said his courage was due only to surprise. 'I hadn't realized', he said, 'that they were using guns.'[7]

The three men were driven off to one of the Storm Troopers' detention centres, where they were threatened for hours; Wilfrid stood his ground. Paul Krentz, the Gentile head of the Hochschule, knew that the men could only be released with Nazi help, and sought the intervention of a Nazi in the *Betriebszelle*, the firm's works' committee, realizing that the arrests had clearly been made in co-ordination with Nazis inside the firm. In the late afternoon all three were freed.[8]

The political tensions in N. Israel, at the shop-floor level, had been evident for some time. The older generation of employees was conservative, but among the younger men and women there were many Nazis - who represented about 20 to 30 per cent of the employees - and a number of Social Democrat (SPD) supporters, who had, on at least one occasion, infuriated the Nazis by distributing anti-Nazi leaflets on the pavement outside N. Israel before the 1933 elections. Immediately after Hitler's accession to power, Nazis had taken over the key positions in the works' committee, though the trade unions and the SPD were not formally outlawed until early summer. The most powerful Nazi in the firm, the new *Betriebsrat*, or works' committee foreman, was a buyer in the carpet department, Kurt Liepert, who throughout the 1930s was to play a double role in N. Israel house politics - continually testing his strength against the executive, on the one hand, and, on the other, stepping in to warn or bail out Wilfrid. For the Israels were, in the last analysis, the sole owners of the firm, and paid the Nazis' salaries; although Liepert had no way of knowing how much English money was invested in the firm, and what form of intervention there might be, he played his cards carefully. Wilfrid's policy, from the outset, was to reject all demands made for the dismissal of employees, whether Jews or Social Democrats, though he could not stop bullying and intimidation behind his back.[9]

This began almost immediately. Nazi employees had surfaced in every department. Juniors turned against some of the buyers and department heads, warning them that unless they co-operated with the Nazis, their lives would be at risk. Leo Adam, the nephew of the liberal Rabbi Leo Baeck, one of the first trainees of the Hochschule and now a buyer in the cotton department, was ordered to train a Nazi as his successor. As a consequence, many Jews prepared to leave.

Berthold was badly shaken. He had been away when his sons were arrested, and, after their release, he made another attempt to buy off the Nazis. That evening, he called on the legal adviser of the Storm Troopers, Justizrat Lutgebrune, at his home, introducing himself by giving his Prussian ancestry, both rabbinical and commercial. Lütgebrune responded by explaining his own Protestant credentials, in what must have been a grotesque exchange. The next day, he sent Berthold 'protective papers' for himself and his sons, which attested that the bearers 'were not suspected of any subversive activity', and that anyone intending to take action should check with Lütgebrune's office first.[10] The record of Wilfrid's subsequent problems suggests that he never used them.

On 1 April, the day of the anti-Jewish boycott throughout Germany, Storm Troopers picketed the N. Israel building. As Isherwood, who was still in Berlin, but no longer in touch with Wilfrid, recalled, it was not an impressive performance: 'Two or three uniformed Storm Troopers were posted at each of the entrances. Their manner wasn't at all aggressive; they merely reminded each would-be shopper that this was a Jewish store.'[11] Rosa Dukas, an employee, heard a Gentile woman telling the indifferent Nazis that her grandparents had bought all their purchases there and that she intended to do the same.[12]

On the second floor, meanwhile, a stormy meeting between the management and the works' committee was in progress. The Nazis, headed by Liepert, demanded the resignation of five leading executives, three of whom were Gentiles, and one a Jewish convert to Christianity.[13] But, of the 500 Jews in the firm, only two are known to have lost their jobs in the entire Nazi period: Martin Buber's son Rafael, who was general sales manager, and a young Jewish trainee named Alfred Front.

Buber had worked at the Schocken department store before joining the Israels in 1930. It had not escaped the notice of the Nazi employees that Wilfrid had delegated Buber to distribute clothes, materials and blankets from the firm's stocks to the communist welfare body, the Rote Hilfe. On 5 April, a squad of about twenty Storm Troopers arrived at the firm and took Buber to the Parochialstrasse detention centre. Another squad, meanwhile, went to Wilfrid's office to demand that he dismiss Buber. Wilfrid refused: 'First bring back Buber.' Infuriated, the Storm Trooper shouted, 'You want to join him, then?', and marched Wilfrid, Herbert and Krentz down the street to the former Anti-War Museum. There Wilfrid tried to negotiate for Buber's freedom, but the Nazis insisted that either he dismiss Buber, or Buber would stay with them. Wilfrid would not agree, and eventually the Nazis changed their tactics: Buber was released on condition that he himself promised not to return to the firm. Wilfrid subsequently paid him a full year's salary and helped him to leave Germany.[14]

Alfred Front, the young trainee, had been admitted to the Hochschule together with a group of young men, many of whom were Jews. He was the son of a Polish immigrant and had wanted to study engineering, but at sixteen he was too old for Youth Aliya and too young for an adult 'worker's' certificate to Palestine. The job of apprentice at N. Israel was to enable him to fill in time. Wilfrid had befriended all the young Jews admitted to keep them employed in this transitory phase, and Front, who had graduated from the messenger boys' department to the curtain buyers' section, had been lulled, by Wilfrid's friendship and the liberal curriculum of the Hochschule, into thinking himself safe from the outside world. At one of the school debates, he got up and attacked Nazi ideology. The same afternoon he was called to Wilfrid's office.

'How could a friend have behaved like this?' Wilfrid asked him, pale with anger. 'Don't you realize that you're endangering other Jews, perhaps the whole firm?' Then he explained, painfully, that Front would have to go. But the friendship survived; Wilfrid continued to help Front, and arranged for his younger brother to enter Ben Shemen. Front himself left for Palestine the following year.[15]

Meanwhile, at the family's insistence, Wilfrid left Berlin for ten days in Baden Baden, to keep away from further trouble with the Nazi squads. It was only then, in enforced tranquillity, that he realized how close he had come to death at the hands of the Wecke group. His letters to a close friend indicate how vivid, as a consequence, the physical world suddenly became to him: 'The peach trees are surrounded by a halo of blue vapour, reminding me of Japan ... the effect of winter damp in the breathing earth.' Now, almost apologetically, he admitted fear: 'Yesterday there was the feeling of a storm approaching ... the wood was dark ... the hillslopes dark by day ... I couldn't help being affected. Today I'm not so afraid; I've thrown off the ghosts eager to devour me ... damned scowls of an over-lively imagination.' Even ten years later, writing to Reissner of that spring in Baden, he was to associate the flowering of cherry blossom in the English countryside with the days of fear in that other April.

Violence had already driven many of Wilfrid's friends from Germany. Einstein had left to spend the winter lecturing in California, and never returned; in April, he wrote to a physicist friend, Paul Ehrenfest:

> ... a small group of pathological demagogues has been able to capture and exploit a population which is completely uneducated politically. The lack of courage on the part of the educated classes in Germany has been catastrophic ... the Jews have become victims only because they occupy an exposed position both as individuals and intellectuals.[16]

Elisabeth Rotten's home was raided by the Storm Troopers in April, and she took refuge in Switzerland. Efrem Kurtz, who by Hindenburg's presidential decree had become a naturalized German citizen, was living at the Marquardt Hotel in Stuttgart, where he was resident conductor of the opera, when the Nazis came to power. One morning in March, he received an urgent telephone call from Wilfrid in Berlin: 'I've seen your name on a list; you must leave Germany immediately. Take nothing with you, just go.' Kurtz obeyed; he took only the key to his hotel room to suggest that he was still in his bedroom, and crossed the frontier at night, heading for Paris. He was convinced that Wilfrid had saved his life.[17]

Wilfrid remained. To have left would have meant abandoning responsibility not only to his employees, but to the community at large; for, imperceptibly, Wilfrid had become a man to whom hundreds of Jews now looked for help, advice and money. From this time on, the myth grew of his immunity and invulnerability and the wholly unfounded belief that he was protected by his British nationality. Even those who saw him as an effete, pampered individual assumed that only someone who could rely on British protection would behave as he did. He encouraged this belief quite consciously, as it helped people to trust him and to seek his aid. But as Wilfrid was a German citizen, the British Embassy could officially do nothing for him while he was on German soil.[18]

As Wilfrid noted in his letters, the claims of strangers increased daily. He was expected to find work for hundreds of people, either in his own firm, or in others. Writers and other intellectuals wanted introductions to influential friends abroad: Rudolf Kayser, for instance, who only four years previously had been one of the famous speakers at the Habima celebrations, now wrote to Wilfrid begging for any work he could obtain.[19] Wilfrid's family demanded that he make the operative decisions. Berthold, a gentle and now disoriented man, abdicated responsibility to his sons. Herbert looked to Wilfrid for guidance, and Amy, always the grand English lady, decided to ignore the Nazis completely, and continued to hold her usual tea parties and *soirées*.

Wilfrid had returned from Baden Baden to his books and statues, to the downcast eyes and sealed beauty of the Khmer buddhas, in the hermetic silence of his Bendlerstrasse home. He had hoped for a happier return. For during these last months, his one source of comfort was a young man he loved deeply, one of the many Jewish boys who had sought his help during that period. Imaginative and well read, he had, like so many other young Jews, left the provinces for Berlin in hope of work; originally he had hoped to study for one of the professions, but now this was impossible. For him, too, it had been comforting to be befriended by someone apparently so worldly and powerful, yet so ready to sympathize completely with the ideals and conflicts of an eighteen-year-old boy that the age difference – Wilfrid was thirty-four – was scarcely felt.

But before long, Wilfrid could not conceal the intensity of his feelings. The friendship was suspect in the eyes of the boy's contemporaries and, despite his admiration and affection for Wilfrid, and the temptation to accept his offers of an escape to study abroad, he began to avoid Wilfrid's company and eventually left Berlin. Wilfrid pursued him with letters which were alternately confessions of hope and despair. 'At the moment I'm in such misery; it increases all the time, and my steadily growing responsibilities make it hard to bear. Then I have such a longing to be sheltered by someone, and it can't be satisfied.' At this time, Wilfrid wrote to a woman friend whom he trusted, 'For people who are difficult, deep within themselves, the question of their relations with others is and remains in most cases insoluble. Lately I've had this experience again and again.' As the months passed, he became bitterly resigned. He wrote to the young man:

> I shall really have to work. But what emptiness around me! Time passes, and narrow, petty duties to work and people consume me, swallow me. You'll say that is a vague, empty complaint. I know that for someone else these duties, these many headed little monsters, would be satisfying. For me they are just troublesome and exhausting.... The struggle to reach out and touch the world is my particular burden in life.

But Wilfrid's suffering did not isolate or paralyse him. To the world he appeared the same elegant, smiling figure as before. Now he forced himself to fulfil – hesitantly at first, then with determination – those 'narrow, petty duties' which soon became his whole life.

German Jewry, from being the proudest, most assimilated and apparently most secure of all the European-Jewish communities, now became, almost overnight, a harried minority struggling for unity and dignity under almost impossible conditions. Hitler's accession unleashed a flood of anti-semitic decrees and propaganda, whose result was the expulsion of all those who, as Einstein noted, were particularly exposed in the arts and professions. Petty persecution and vilification by Nazis drove many Jews from the provinces almost at once. In April, Jews, with a few exceptions, were prohibited from government service and their children were only admitted in small quotas to German secondary schools. The younger children were exposed to cruel discrimination; Shenhabi, on his return from a visit to Germany, reported to Weizmann that Jewish children were not only deprived of school milk, but the racist cause of their deprivation was explained to the other children. Weizmann refused to believe him. 'If I didn't know you so well, I would ask you to leave my house; the Germans could not do such things,' Weizmann said.[20]

It was in vain that official spokesmen of the various Jewish organizations, such as the Central Verein and the ex-soldiers' league, reaffirmed their loyalty to Germany, their identity as Germans and their determination to contest their rights. Officially, the Nazi leadership scarcely recognized the Jews' existence. Distinguished Jews chosen at random were hauled before Goering in March and told to send messages abroad to counter 'libellous propaganda' against the Nazis. There was not even to be a dialogue of rulers and supplicants between the Nazi leaders and the Jews. The 'Jewish question' was to be handled henceforth by special offices in the ministries and by 'experts', such as Hasselbacher and Kuchmann, in the Gestapo.

Paradoxically, those Jews whose power was the ostensible object of much Nazi propaganda - the big businessmen, the bankers, the brokers - were the last to be uprooted in the pre-war years, for fear that their crash might endanger the German economy. The huge Tietz department chain, for instance, faced possible liquidation in mid-1933; it was saved by a grant of over 14,000,000 reichsmarks from the state-controlled Azkept und Garantiebank.[21]

After the first few weeks of Nazi rule, with thousands of Jews - perhaps as much as 20 per cent of the community - out of work, the various Jewish communities attempted to counter the damage by planning for social welfare, the retraining and education of youth, and, where all else failed, for emigration.

The first German-Jewish organization which attempted to grapple with these problems was the Central Bureau for Relief and Reconstruction (Zentralauschuss für Hilfe und Aufbau), set up, on 13 April 1933, on the initiative of that small group of Jews with whom Wilfrid was associated - bankers, community leaders and Zionists among them. The Central Bureau was to form the main welfare organization and, for some time, the operative nucleus of the Reichsvertretung der Deutschen Juden, the overall Jewish representative group headed by Leo Baeck, which finally took shape in September.

Wilfrid was odd man out in the Central Bureau, the only member with no tag to his name and no previous experience in any welfare or communal organization.[22] The Bureau's most dynamic member was Ludwig Tietz. Tietz's surgery, which had an unlisted telephone, was a centre of rescue activities from February 1933 onwards. He received information about imminent arrests of Jews all over Germany; it was possibly from him that Wilfrid learned that Kurtz, among others, was in danger. Couriers were despatched across Germany to warn Jewish youth leaders to leave the country. On the day of the Reichstag fire, Tietz had bluffed his way through a police cordon into the offices of the Central Verein, and removed all their papers before the Storm Troopers arrived.[23]

It was in Tietz's surgery that Wilfrid met, for the first time, the group of young men who were to found Kibbutz Hazorea. They belonged to a group called the Werkleute, the offshoot of a big German-Jewish youth movement, the Kameraden. The children of middle-class parents, they tried to reconcile German socialist ideals with a deliberately, and newly, acquired Jewish culture. They studied Jewish history and customs, but were not orthodox. They were Jewish nationalists, but not at first Zionists: they had favoured a revival of Lehmann's 'Volksheim' ideas for a proud, united Jewish community within Germany; Nazism made them Zionists. They opposed dual morality for men and women, and believed in the virtues of the commune.[24] For the first time, Wilfrid found an organized German-Jewish group he wanted to join; even if he was older than most of its members and set apart by his position and obligations. He was a strange recruit. The Werkleute had all heard of Wilfrid as a rich and important man with an interest in art. But they did not see him as an activist; he seemed altogether too frail and diffident.

On the eve of the boycott, Tietz and his young helpers decided to make a tour of eastern Berlin to check on the poorer quarters and offer help. Wilfrid went with them, bringing two cars, two secretaries and the family chauffeurs.

After that first encounter, the Werkleute began to revise their opinion. Several of them became his close friends: there was Friedrich Altmann, a tall young electrical engineer, who had worked for some months as an engine driver on the East Prussian railways and had been a student of Einstein's; Gustav Horn, who had studied Jewish history and religion and was now a member of Hehalutz, the pioneering Zionist movement; Rudi Baer, a young editor working on the art encyclopaedias produced by the Ullstein press; Ernst Bauer, a student of philosophy and Arabic; and others.

Wilfrid's friendship with the Werkleute was sealed in the second week in June, when Tietz, Friedrich Borchardt (a banker with Gebruder Arnhold and one of the mainstays of the Central Bureau), Wilfrid, and several of the Werkleute met to co-ordinate welfare plans in a hotel for young unemployed Jews from the provinces, which Tietz had founded. Late in the evening, Leopold Kuh, Tietz's right-hand man, was sent out to buy cigarettes, and on the way down the stairs passed a squad of

Storm Troopers going up. He guessed their destination, muttered a quick 'Heil Hitler', and positioned himself to watch what followed.

The squad burst into the room where Tietz and the others were sitting; several of the Nazis were drunk, and one fired a shot into the ceiling. They accused the Jews of holding an illegal meeting; cries of 'Heil Moscow', they said, had been heard outside – a standard pretext for summary arrests. The Jews were herded into trucks waiting in the street outside. Kuh, who had the keys to Tietz's car, followed at a safe distance as they were driven away. Wolf Mattesdorf, a young lawyer who consulted Wilfrid frequently for help in his defence of dismissed Jewish employees, remembered being driven along a street lined with café terraces, and seeing the amazed faces of friends among their customers. The truck finally drew up at the General-Pape-Strasse barracks, at the time one of the most notorious sites of torture and murder in Berlin. The men were hustled out and pushed down steps into a cellar. Tietz and Wilfrid, who were both tall men, had to bend almost double to get through a low door, butted forward with kicks and blows.

The Jews were held for hours, abused and beaten. Meanwhile, Kuh hurried to Alfred Wiener of the Central Verein, who alerted the state police. After some time Wilfrid was taken out, alone, and sent under escort to the Prinz Albrechtstrasse, the centre of the Prussian political police, now the Gestapo, where he was interrogated. In the early hours of the following morning, the whole group, including Wilfrid, was released.[25]

The following week, the incident was reported in the London *Times*, in its own inimitable style. Israel and Borchardt were described as 'businessmen of prominence' in a passage which ended, 'after ineffective intervention by the local regular police, word was got to the state secret police who, despite the hour, intervened, and until the order for release came the prisoners were well treated, except one who left the room and came back with a broken eardrum.'[26]

Wilfrid and his friends had clearly become the object of a tug of war between the Storm Troopers and the newly established Gestapo. Ludwig Tietz later received a letter from Rudolf Diels, head of the Prussian secret police and not yet a Nazi Party member, answering the complaint he had filed. It said that Diels had asked the police 'to take measures to prevent the recurrence of events such as those you describe'.[27] Dozens of less fortunate prisoners left the General-Pape-Strasse in coffins sealed with lead.

The 'wild actions' were coming to an end. But Wilfrid's interrogation was his first contact with the Gestapo. From this time forward, he was the subject of their constant interest, though methods of surveillance were still primitive. He had earned the respect of the Werkleute; a little later he was to ask to become a member, and was accepted. This time, however, Wilfrid did not go to a watering place to recover from his bruises; within a few days, he was on his way to London to report on the situation of German Jewry, on what was his first mission abroad on behalf of the community.

To represent German Jewry in the outside world was to prove a task of extraordinary difficulty. German Jews wanted foreign Jewry to be their spokesmen, to convey their dilemma to politicians in Britain and America, and to co-operate with German Jews in evolving a policy of self-help based not on charity, but on their own evaluation of the situation in Nazi Germany. They were to argue consistently that, inside Germany, they knew best how to counter the damage done by the Nazis. As Leo Baeck wrote to Anglo-Jewish leaders in September 1933:

> We recognize with deep gratitude the excellent work which is done for the benefit of German Jews by collecting funds and elaborating plans. But we sincerely believe that . . . the German Jews themselves should be treated as an equal partner in taking the decisions for relief and reconstruction for German Jewry in Germany as well as abroad.[28]

Rabbi Jonah Wise, a veteran fund raiser for the Joint Distribution Committee, had already taken the point: 'We cannot deal with them [German Jews] as the JDC has been accustomed to deal with our Eastern European brethren, with the masses of Jews to whom we had to dole out as best we could whatever assistance we could gather. They are stricken, but by no means defeated or beaten individuals.'[29]

The German Jews wanted financial assistance not primarily for ordinary charitable work, for which they were already well organized – the German system of taxation meant that taxes were levied on different denominational groups in each region and channelled back in the form of welfare – but for educational and retraining schemes for Jewish youth, and to help those made bankrupt by Nazi policies. They needed funds on a flexible basis and one that could be updated according to circumstances.

As far as political assistance was concerned, there were, almost immediately, differences of opinion about the foreign Jewish boycott of German goods abroad. While the Anglo-Jewish leadership, in particular, held back, most Jews (and many Gentile sympathizers) thought the boycott a demonstration of solidarity. The German Jews, threatened with reprisals by the Nazis from the outset, thought it not only ineffective, but dangerous.[30] Finally, several of the more influential German-

Jewish leaders wanted to work out a plan for the emigration of about a third of the Jewish population – first and foremost its young – financed by a new 'liquidation bank' with branches both in Germany and abroad.[31] These Jews believed from the outset that the mobilization of all German-Jewish property and capital as collateral for loans raised abroad to assist emigration was the only realistic basis for large-scale emigration of Jews from Germany, given currency restrictions, on the one hand, and world-wide economic depression, on the other. The feasibility of these plans was queried from the outset by equally influential Jews outside Germany.

From the beginning, the main obstacle to emigration was twofold. Most countries had restrictive immigration laws which dated back to the beginning of the century, when there was a large influx of refugees who travelled west. However, those who could prove that they were able to support themselves were usually able to find a haven, particularly during the early years of the Nazi period. The chief problem was the controls on the transfer of currency imposed by the Government, under Heinrich Brüning, from 1931 onwards, to prevent the collapse of the German banks; a 'flight tax' meant that 25 per cent of the emigrants' capital had to be forfeited. Moreover, the problems involved in the purchase of foreign currency after the Lausanne reparations agreements of 1932 with Britain, France and the United States, by which the chief Versailles creditors agreed to cancel German debts in return for the rigorous control of foreign currency transactions inside the Reich, meant that German 'blocked' marks could only be sold at an enormous loss. This meant, in effect, that only the wealthier Jews could hope to find refuge elsewhere. Any large-scale emigration plan had to be underwritten financially either by the Nazi Government waiving or lessening the existing restrictions on the export of capital – something which was unlikely – or by some other arrangement which would not affect the German balance of payments adversely.

The German Jews had no direct line to the Nazi leadership, but there were communications between Jews prominent in banking and business circles, and members of the administration of the Third Reich (which did not become Nazified overnight), most notably in the Reichsbank, the Economics Ministry, the Emigration Department of the Ministry of the Interior, and even inside the Ministry for Foreign Affairs. Many of these civil servants had belonged to the conservative National Party, and other Centre Party members were still active in the civil service.

Thus, while Jewish leaders officially protested their loyalty and attempted, until the Nuremberg Laws of 1935, to reclaim their rights as citizens, those Jews who had influential contacts in the administration tried to work out trial emigration schemes. The impression gained from the official Jewish publications and the declarations of Jewish bodies during the early 1930s is that they continued to struggle for the 'second emancipation' within Germany. At the same time, in conversations with leading Jews abroad, German Jews proposed different political and financial plans to assist emigration.

It is difficult to describe these proposals as representing German-Jewish 'policy'. Many were made before the establishment of the Reichsvertretung; and before the Nazi period the Jews of Germany, unlike Jewish communities abroad, had no one organization which represented them with the authorities. Even the Reichsvertretung was set up after complex discussions between the various communities in Germany; it was a representative, rather than an elected body, as its name indicates. While Rabbi Leo Baeck was accepted as the undisputed leader of German Jewry, the authority of the Reichsvertretung was often challenged, notably by the men around Heinrich Stahl, the head of the Berlin community. Max Warburg, arguably the most powerful of German Jews, and the only man who, as Werner Senator commented, had direct contact with Hjalmar Schacht, the financial expert in the Nazi leadership, was never in the foreground, although he was one of the men behind the founding of the Reichsvertretung. Yet Warburg's hand was everywhere, and his fertile financial mind evolved numerous schemes by which Jewish funds could be transferred abroad. Warburg was a much maligned figure, both for his conservative German loyalties and his influential contacts in the administration of the Third Reich. In practical terms, his contribution to emigration, both privately and as head of the Hilfsverein, was substantial.

In meetings with foreign Jewish leaders in early 1933, Warburg, Werner Senator (who travelled regularly between Jerusalem and Berlin and was in this early period, with Ludwig Tietz, in charge of relations with the Jews in Britain and the United States) and Karl Melchior, Warburg's chief colleague and one of Germany's negotiators at the Versailles conference, all emphasized the necessity for a long-range plan (usually spanning ten years) for the emigration of young people and those who could no longer be employed in the Nazi State. As early as 31 March 1933, Bernhard Kahn, the Joint representative in Berlin, informed Neville Laski, President of the Board of Deputies of British Jews, that 'German Jews had started a formation of an administration to liquidate Jewish assets' and place them '... in non-German banks'.[32] At this time, too, Max Warburg drew up a plan for the export of capital, which he submitted to leading members of the Reichsbank, and during the summer, preliminary talks were held with the Economics Ministry.[33]

But it was clearly essential to secure the support of influential Jews abroad, particularly those in financial circles, for what was an extraordinarily complex political operation. But no one outside, whether Jew or Gentile, was to fathom, without personal experience, the labyrinthine policies of the Nazi State.

In early April, Werner Senator despatched a plan of action to the Joint in New York, on whose board leading members of the American community, most of them of German origin, were represented. Senator stressed that official telegrams and messages from the community were often dictated by the Nazis; thus he suggested setting up a reliable information service from bases on German frontiers. British and American Jews, he thought, should set up a joint committee, and Jewish communities abroad should abandon their traditional reluctance to intervene on behalf of their fellow Jews elsewhere. He pointed out that the economic assault on the Jews was modified by German economic self-interest, and that this self-interest could be exploited.[34]

But American reaction was lukewarm. The report was minuted 'intelligent', but the community leaders 'should take definite exception to the idea of a political committee'. When Felix Warburg consulted with Lord Rothschild later in the month, both agreed that it would be impolitic to canvas the support of their respective governments openly.[35]

In June, Melchior and Tietz told British Jews that they were working on a plan for emigration and the setting up of a 'liquidation bank'; Melchior reiterated that the Jewish boycott was counter-productive, and that, on the contrary, foreign Jews should suggest *raising* the boycott in return for emigration with funds, thus making the Nazis believe that they had obtained an important concession.[36] Neville Laski was impressed by German-Jewish opposition to the boycott, which had appeared not only in telegrams but in private conversations; but the reluctance of the Board of Deputies of British Jews to support the boycott was seen as pusillanimity by indignant Jews who gained emotional satisfaction from refusing to buy German goods. This was understandable. On the one hand, German Jews had asked for political pressures to be applied against the Nazis, diplomatically, through foreign governments; on the other, they were asking for economic agreements which appeared to favour Germany, in the interests of emigration. This was, indeed, to be the main drift of the argument of the handful of German Jews in constant contact with foreign Jewish leaders throughout the 1930s, and it had an inner logic of its own, dictated by what they knew of the workings of the Nazi State. Very few outside could understand it, or reconcile it with their own interests.

Wilfrid was far too diffident and unsure of himself to play a leading role in the Jewish community at this period. If his plan had been, as he told Spender, that the Jews should counter Nazi harassment with open defiance, he was not the man to lead demonstrations. As Robert Weltsch, who had called publicly, in a famous article, for a display of Jewish pride shortly after the boycott day, wrote to Buber later that month: 'The responsible groups are paddling round doing petty secretarial work. I spoke to Wilfrid, who had very good proposals but doesn't seem to have the charisma to carry them out.'[37] There was only one role he could play better than the community leaders, and that was to act as German Jewry's emissary abroad.

Wilfrid arrived in London on 29 June 1933 and met with leaders of the Anglo-Jewish community in Neville Laski's Lincoln's Inn chambers. His mission was to involve the British Jews more closely in what was happening in Nazi Germany. He came on behalf of the Central Bureau and as Max Warburg's personal envoy. First, he reported on a new wave of terror which had begun ten days previously; typically making no mention of his own arrest and ill treatment, Wilfrid said that, to his own knowledge, 'at least sixteen Jews had been arrested and flogged almost to death within the last six days. . . . Dr Tietz was one of those Jews for whom it was no longer safe to sleep at home at nights.' Warburg, he said, wanted the funds of the Central Bureau transferred to the offices of the Joint, which, as an American institution, would be immune from Nazi action. Wilfrid suggested that an American Jew be sent out to take charge of the community funds, and an English Jew come 'to act as observer and intermediary between the Jewish community and the British Embassy'. Once more, he stressed German-Jewish opposition to the boycott abroad; the Nazi reaction had been to intensify the persecution of Jews in the smaller German towns.[38]

The response to his visit was to set the pattern for subsequent events. Wilfrid was promised that the atrocities he described would be immediately passed on to the British Government, and Laski, who was in contact with Sir Robert Vansittart, Permanent Under Secretary at the Foreign Office, reported Wilfrid's account the same afternoon. But the British Government had already defined its stand: non-intervention in Germany's internal affairs. The Foreign Office had ample information about dismissals of Jews and discrimination against them from the Ambassador, Sir Horace Rumbold, though less certain evidence of actual atrocities. But Vansittart assured Laski that he was 'most distressed by the helplessness of the Foreign Office', and that he would consult the Ambassador regarding the safety of any British Jew who might go out 'to establish liaison with the German Jews'.[39] The question of liaison was vital. As Jonah Wise had already noted, however, few Jews were prepared to visit Nazi Germany, even with the protection of foreign passports. 'The British Jews do not trust the continent,' he observed.[40] Nor was the Joint prepared to safeguard German-Jewish funds; Bernhard Kahn had already left Berlin for Paris, and the Joint funds were transferred there, where they remained until 1940. The Joint, the source of millions of dollars of aid, dealt with Germany from outside; others, including the Quakers, administered its funds inside Germany until 1936, after which no further Joint funds were sent into the Third Reich.[41]

The closer contacts and free flow of information, which the German Jews regarded as so important, were to depend almost entirely on the ability of the Germans to leave their country at regular intervals, something which became increasingly difficult. The role of 'observer and intermediary' between the Jewish community and the British Embassy eventually devolved on Wilfrid himself.

The 'liquidation bank' idea seems to have had no takers at all abroad, at this stage. When Warburg led a delegation to London in August to discuss the finances of German Jewry, Kahn reported that the German group 'was treated in a very aloof manner' by British Jews and its proposals were not taken into account at all at the first meetings.[42] The idea Melchior had proposed, that Hitler's concept of 'Jewish world power' should be used against him, sent a shudder down the backs of those British and American Jews who did wield financial clout: the notion that export facilities for German goods should be encouraged as a way of transferring Jewish capital (an idea which Senator had put forward in July and which was the basis of Warburg's subsequent proposals) cut straight across American Jewry's strategy of marching down Madison Avenue, urging their fellow citizens not to buy from Nazi Germany.

Wilfrid, like most German Jews, expected Britain, with its long tradition of political asylum and its role as defender of liberal values, to respond in two ways to the Nazi persecution of the Jews: firstly, by protesting through diplomatic channels, and if not by British diplomats in Berlin then through the League of Nations; and secondly, by relaxing existing restrictions in the admission of aliens to Britain. Both options were deliberately rejected despite anti-Nazi statements in the press and Parliament. At the time, the ostensible reason given for diplomatic silence was that Britain had no legal standing to make representations on behalf of German citizens; but the real reason was a fear of prejudicing Britain's relations with the German regime, which was now believed to be stable. The same thinking prevented Britain from bringing the question of Jewish refugees to the League for action under Article 11 of the League Charter, which dealt with the rights of minorities; again, the quibble that the Jews, as German citizens, did not constitute a minority, shielded the underlying fear that the Germans would interpret British action as interference, if not actual hostility.[43]

As for the immigration laws, no refugee could enter Britain as a permanent resident, unless he or she had labour permits or visible means of support – a policy buttressed by post-Depression economics and widespread unemployment.

Similar policies applied in most other European countries and in the United States, which had rigid immigration quotas. This meant that the onus fell on voluntary bodies, Jewish and other, which were remarkably active in England, or on the willingness of individuals to sponsor the refugees in person.

Unlike its American counterpart, British Jewry was prepared to commit itself to the support of Jewish refugees in Britain.[44] A remarkably open-ended commitment made by community leaders to the British Home Office in April 1933, to take responsibility for all German-Jewish refugees who immigrated with the help of refugee organizations, was made, however, on the assumption that the numbers involved would be between 3,000 and 4,000, less than a tenth of those who actually arrived. Other voluntary organizations – including the Quakers and the Academic Assistance Council, which found places in universities and research institutes for German refugee scholars – also lobbied for the refugees. But at first the main emphasis was on financial help for Jews inside Germany, and not for emigration.

The Central Bureau suffered two blows towards the end of the year: the suicide of Ludwig Tietz and the death of Karl Melchior. Tietz's death was not directly the result of persecution. He had contracted tuberculosis shortly after the First World War and, like many casualties of that period, was treated with morphine, to which he developed an addiction. The tensions of the time drove him to even greater reliance on the drug, which ultimately destroyed him.

Wilfrid mourned Tietz bitterly. He had known of his problems and blamed himself for not having tackled them more openly: 'I should have been more reckless with him,' he wrote. Tietz's death now galvanized Wilfrid into playing a far more active part in the Central Bureau. In the first months after Tietz's death in November 1933, he was travelling constantly between Berlin and London, soliciting funds from German Jewry's benefactors, the Central British Fund, and reporting on conditions in Germany. It was a task which his letters show he hated: it was painful for a man who for years had given money away tactfully, and usually anonymously, to be sent on what were essentially begging missions.

In mid-December, he told British Jews that there was now less fear of violence, but also described the slow process of expropriation of and discrimination against Jews, which was to be the more general pattern of Jewish life in Germany until the pogroms of late 1938. The greatest pressure against them in business life, he explained, was from individual firms who were using anti-Jewish feeling to suppress competitors, restrict credit, and block the issue of permits to those who wanted to open new businesses. Jews were eligible by law for social welfare relief, but in the smaller towns no longer received it. The Jews were retreating continuously into Jewish-owned firms and community organizations, a tendency Wilfrid thought all the more significant because it was developing 'unconsciously'. It was not yet, perhaps, a return to the ghetto, he said, but the search for places for emigrants abroad should be energetically pursued.[45]

That point needed to be made. By the end of 1933, concern over increasing emigration had already dampened the initial sympathy for the Nazis' victims. At a refugee conference in London, Otto Schiff, the most important member of the Central British Fund, a banker whose personal contacts with the Home Office had ensured the admission of hundreds of refugees, argued that emigration on a relief basis was 'undesirable' and produced a 'bad psychological effect' on the refugees. Only genuine political refugees, not those who left because 'business was bad', should be admitted; it would cost less, he concluded, to support German Jews back home.[46]

The Jews of the West were already torn between their traditions of charity and solidarity with distressed Jews elsewhere, and fears for their own reputation and security. Both in Britain and the United States, unemployment was widespread and there was much fear of Jewish competition, particularly among the professional and commercial middle classes to which most refugees belonged – as the British Medical Association's notorious protest against the influx of refugee doctors proved. The argument much favoured by the friends of the refugees, that the Jews were 'new Huguenots' who would contribute greatly to their host countries, did not lessen apprehension. In the United States the initial offers of work to refugees had given way to public denials, by large firms such as Macy's and Abraham and Strauss, that they had discharged American workers to give positions to refugees.[47]

Moreover, the real nature of the Nazi regime was still not understood even by liberals, as is most strikingly evident in the case of two staunch friends of Wilfrid's – Leonard Montefiore in London and Corder Catchpool, the Quaker representative in Berlin. Montefiore, joint chairman of the Anglo-Jewish Joint Foreign Committee, a lover of German culture and a totally civilized man, speaking at a protest meeting against the persecution of German Jews in October, said that

> he would not assert that the Nazi movement was only composed of hatred and prejudice and all that was evil ... there were certain good elements among the Nazis, a certain austerity and readiness for self-sacrifice, a spirit of patriotism, and a desire to see Germany take her place among the nations. That was one of the most tragic things, for were it not for the anti-semitic plank in the Nazi programme there was no doubt that a large proportion of young German Jews would be enthusiastic followers of the movement.[48]

Catchpool had voiced very similar views in a Whitsun report to the London office of the Quakers. He argued that, given slightly different circumstances in Britain, anti-semitic outbursts could take place there as well, and thought Britain should show understanding for Germany's revolutionary phase: 'Different forms of government were not a reason for hostility.'[49]

For a short time, Wilfrid, with his contacts among founder members of the League of Nations, hoped that the League could play some part in helping German Jews. The British Government had refused to refer the problem to the League, but by the end of the year, the steady flow of German refugees into Europe led to the founding of a 'High Commission for Refugees (Jewish and other) coming from Germany'. James G. McDonald, an energetic American lawyer, was appointed its head, and Norman Bentwich, an old friend of Wilfrid's, his deputy. Bentwich, an Anglo-Jewish law professor who had served as Attorney-General under the Mandate in Palestine, worked with the Central British Fund as well as with McDonald. On 22 November, he arrived in Berlin on a fact-finding mission and met the principal Jewish leaders, including Baeck and Otto Hirsch, Baeck's deputy in the Reichsvertretung, Max Warburg and Wilfrid, and had talks at the American and British Embassies.[50]

All were pessimistic about German Jewry's future and anticipated further economic pressures on Jewish businessmen. Like other foreign observers at this time, Bentwich reported general agreement among the Jewish leaders that their young people should emigrate; and, just as they had urged that German-Jewish views be taken into consideration in framing relief policy, they now argued that German Jews should be represented at meetings of the League Commission.

Dodd, the American Ambassador, was well informed and sympathetic, though the Americans demurred when the issue of visas from the German quota was raised – an ominous sign of things to come. The

British Embassy was notably unresponsive. Bentwich was received by the First Secretary, Basil Newton, who, Bentwich reported, was 'not much concerned with the persecution of the Jews'. The one British official who was active, concerned, and very well informed, was Frank Foley, the principal passport officer at the Consulate. Bentwich reported that 'Mr Foley has been in Germany since the end of the [First World] war and has a most intimate knowledge of the growth of the anti-Jewish movement. He is responsible for the issue of all the certificates for Palestine and he administers his functions most sympathetically.' This British official, with so insignificant a role in the official hierarchy, played, as it later emerged, an extraordinarily influential part on the spot. His knowledge of Nazism and German Jewry were part of his unknown official duties, for Foley was also a British intelligence agent.

He had known the Israels since 1920, the time of the death of Wilfrid's sister Viva in London. Amy Israel had been at her daughter's side when she died, but Berthold had difficulties in obtaining a visa. Foley, then a junior consular official, was sympathetic, and Berthold obtained permission to join his wife. From that time onward, Foley and Wilfrid knew each other well. Wilfrid's contacts with Foley, never mentioned in any letter written in Germany, lasted for the rest of his life; Foley's double role in Germany and his links with Wilfrid were to be of more importance for the Jews of Germany than any of the activities of his superiors in the Embassy.[51]

Baeck decided to apply for government sanction to send representatives - Wilfrid and Dr Friedrich Ollendorff, a welfare expert - to the League Commission's first meetings in Lausanne in December. This proved a mistake. A few days later, he had to write to McDonald that no German-Jewish delegate would attend, because 'obstacles prevented it at present'.[52] Germany, which had withdrawn from the League a month earlier, and had abstained from voting for the Commission, had no interest whatever in an official Jewish delegation.

It was impossible now for McDonald to renew his invitation, but Bentwich made sure that Wilfrid had notice of the meeting of the Permanent Committee of the Commission in January.[53] Wilfrid, as envoy of the Central Bureau, but probably on what he explained to the Nazis as a business visit to London, managed to be there when the Commission met. A dozen years earlier, he had given his 'reports' to the League on behalf of refugees in Eastern Europe and the victims of the Russian famine; now he was to deliver a report on his own community. His journey to London in January marked the beginning of clandestine work for German Jews.[54]

At its meeting on 30 January, the Permanent Committee called on the member governments to grant facilities for the vocational retraining of refugees, and on McDonald to negotiate with the governments involved concerning settlement and emigration schemes, the issue of work permits, and travel documents for the stateless. McDonald made several visits to Berlin himself in attempts to convince the Nazi Government to allow German Jews to export capital – to no avail.[55]

Meanwhile, Wilfrid was having trouble in convincing the British charitable organizations of the extent of German-Jewish welfare problems. The day before the Commission meeting, he wrote from his London hotel urging the adoption of a budget which would be regularly updated in accordance with events in Germany. He explained that the meagre contributions the Central Bureau was receiving forced it to cut its relief budget to a minimum, and he feared a collapse of the entire project.[56] In February, he was again back in London, expressing the Bureau's distress that the British benefactors were not prepared for a regular debate, and, on his own initiative, attempting to explain some of the handicaps under which the Bureau was functioning.[57] To his friends, he confessed his desire to be free of this impossible task; he supported the line taken by Warburg and Senator, and also by Kurt Battsek, a Jewish *émigré* resident in London and a leading member of the Central British Fund, that Jewish capital in Germany could be used as collateral (administered by international trustees) for loans, rather than that begging should continue. There was no response.[58] Wilfrid spent the 1934 Passover alone at home; his family was abroad, and he refused all invitations. Shortly after, he left on a brief visit for Palestine, which looked at the time like the only haven for German Jews, both politically and economically.

Palestinian Jewry had not hesitated to exploit the German need for increased exports in order to promote Jewish emigration. The first man to take up the idea was Chaim Arlosoroff, the brilliant but ill-fated head of the Jewish Agency's political department (he had been murdered by unknown assassins in the summer of 1933). A pilot plan was drawn up in April 1933 by the director of the Hanotea citrus groves in the coastal plain, Sam Cohen, and Heinrich Wolf, the German Consul in Jerusalem. In August the Anglo-Palestine Bank and bankers in Germany, including Warburg and Wassermann, replaced Hanotea, and the transfer scheme was later expanded after negotiation between the Jewish Agency and the German Government, though it aroused great controversy in Zionist circles outside Palestine, and was not approved by the Zionist movement as a whole until 1935.

The plan was simplicity itself. Emigrating Jews deposited their assets in blocked accounts in Germany; this paid for agricultural and other machinery which was exported to Palestine, and the emigrants were refunded in Palestine in local currency. The procedure became decreasingly profitable to emigrants in subsequent years, as they were forced to bear the loss resulting from the depreciation of the German mark: 6 per cent in 1933, the loss had increased to 26 per cent by 1936. But the arrangement aided many of the 50,000 Jews who escaped from Germany to Palestine, at a loss which was at first minimal compared with that involved in emigrating elsewhere. The funds transferred were not large; but politically speaking, the agreement indicated Nazi willingness to encourage Jewish emigration if German economic interests remained undamaged. Between the formalization of this transfer scheme and the riots of 1936 in Palestine, after which there were dramatic restrictions on immigration quotas, more German Jews were to emigrate to Palestine than to any other destination. The transfer agreement, moreover, helped not only Jews with property but students, immigrant workers, and even the Youth Aliya children, for whom there were special allocations. Furthermore, Palestine's British administration put few obstacles in its way during the first few years; the influx of capital into Palestine from Germany increased its prosperity.

The spring of 1934 thus looked brighter on the eastern horizon. Yet when Wilfrid arrived in Palestine on 20 May, he found a society far more problematic than he had expected. The Mandatory Government, which periodically issued quotas for the respective categories of immigrants, was generous with 'capitalist' certificates, for those possessing £1,000 sterling or more; but the labour schedule for 'workers', proposed by the Jewish Agency (three-quarters of which was destined for Eastern European Jews), had been cut to less than a third; buildings were left half finished and fruit rotted on the trees for lack of working hands. Though the Va'ad Leumi (Jewish National Council) had ordered all Jews out on strike in protest, this was not enough for Jabotinsky's right-wing Revisionists, who organized violent demonstrations. On the day after Wilfrid's arrival, singing 'Jabotinsky lives', they broke all the windows in the Agency building in Jerusalem. On the following day, that of the strike, the Revisionists sparked riots in Tel Aviv in which fifty-two were wounded. Some of the Revisionist supporters wore the fascist brown shirts; a nightmarish sight for a visitor from Berlin.

The press was full of the daily reports of the Arlosoroff murder trial, also a focus of bitter recriminations between Labour and the right-wingers. In orchards in the coastal plain, the lack of available Jewish labour gave some Jewish plantation owners the excuse to employ Arabs at cheaper rates. The subsequent uproar meant that British soldiers had to escort Arab workers to the orchards. Jewish labourers refused to work with them, or picketed the plantations; several went on trial and were sentenced to hard labour by British magistrates in the Jaffa courts.

On the other side of Tel Aviv, the Levant Fair, attended by Mandatory officials and foreign dignitaries in top hats, was in full swing. Tel Aviv was celebrating its twenty-fifth birthday as a centre of industry and commerce. There were so many banks that their founders ran out of sober names and began calling them after Biblical heroes like King Solomon; and there were too many Jewish doctors chasing patients (the ratio was higher than that either of Britain or Austria, which held the world record). It was not quite Wilfrid's ideal society.

The Werkleute too were in trouble. Many of those who had already emigrated were still employed as hired labourers. Despite the money their sponsors in Germany had raised to help purchase land for a kibbutz, through the Jewish National Fund, no land was yet available. They earned a meagre living picking fruit in the orchards of the prosperous Jewish farmers of Hadera, or working on roads and railways, camping out in semi-derelict buildings. Their water supply was cut off because the previous tenants had not paid the bill, and when they went into the public gardens and washed themselves from a public fountain, police were sent to arrest the 'German bolsheviks'; only the intervention of the local Labour Party bailed them out.[59]

Wilfrid went to stay with Mordechai Shenhabi in Mishmar HaEmek, one of the first kibbutzim set up by the Marxist Kibbutz Artzi Federation, founded seven years earlier. The comrades welcomed Wilfrid warmly, but deplored his lack of orthodox Marxist education. They were locked in a struggle with the main Labour kibbutz movement, the Meuhad, over educational questions. Despite their exhausting physical work in primitive conditions, they were prepared to accept new immigrants from Germany - which often meant that the minimal comforts they had achieved, such as the privacy married couples enjoyed in a shack or tent, now had to be shared with a new arrival. This sacrifice was enough; they insisted that the newcomers must belong to precisely the same socialist group as themselves.

Wilfrid was sadly confused by the ideological battles and political rivalries he now encountered for the first time, in what he had imagined to be a community united by its great task, and devoted to the idea of Jewish reform. When he returned to Germany, he wrote to Shenhabi:

> The towns are growing, the villages are growing, and so are the colonies. But not the human horizon! I see a threat that hearts and minds are closing. I also recognize - and this is surely not arrogance on my part - that an exchange of thoughts and ideas is of first importance, and will remain so, for us in the Diaspora and for you. However, so many people seem locked up in their own

> preoccupations, lacking in . . . lucidity, and create so many crises, that I don't know how it will end. I have to confess openly that despite my happy hours with you I did not return with a happy heart. The kibbutzim ought to be dealing with educational tasks of much importance, but instead, everything falls to pieces, perishes, in a morass of mutual accusations – I don't even want to know the details because it all leads nowhere. . . .[60]

He wrote to a woman friend about to emigrate, warning her that Palestine was 'more of a challenge than he had imagined', and demanded, in those who were to emigrate, 'much inner strength'.

He had not yet developed that strength. The return to Nazi Germany, after the Jewish whirlpool of Palestine, was painful. Suddenly, Wilfrid collapsed, exhausted, and was unable to function; after several weeks spent in a sanatorium, he returned to Berlin and informed his British colleagues that he would not return to 'Jewish executive work' for the time being. All his energy was to be devoted to the business, 'an exasperating and wholly unproductive affair at present'; the only reason he continued was his personal responsibility and the family tradition. 'Nevertheless, I want you to know that I am ready to undertake anything which at any time might be necessary, should an emergency arise or my friends at home or you in London make it seem feasible for me to do so.'[61]

Emergencies were soon to be the order of the day.

6
Double Lives

At the beginning of 1935, the Israels attended a concert given by Wilhelm Furtwangler with the Berlin Philharmonic; Vivian Prins, Wilfrid's young nephew, on a visit from London to see his ailing grandfather, Berthold (who was too ill to attend the concert), stared earnestly at the celebrated Goebbels and Goering, who were sitting nearby. Jewish violinists had been dismissed from the orchestra, despite Furtwangler's protests, but Jews and Nazis could still sit side by side in the audience.

During the first few years of Nazism, the Jews of Germany lived with the devil at their elbow. In Berlin and other big cities, they could still attend theatres and concerts and dine in big hotels, though Jews had been driven from the professions and, even within their own cultural groups, were forbidden to perform German classics; one of Herbert's classmates lost his job in a publishing firm because, as a Jew, he could not edit German literature. Open violence was rare in the big cities. But in the provinces, the notorious billboards proclaiming that Jews were unwanted, or that towns were 'free of Jews', multiplied. Wealthier Jews went on vacations abroad, rather than risk public eviction from hotels in German resort towns. During this period, Wilfrid travelled to Hamburg frequently on business; on one occasion, on his way back to the station, he suddenly panicked, fearing - for no particular reason - that he might be unable to return to Berlin.

The Gestapo infested Jewish life. They were at meetings of the Reichsvertretung, in synagogues listening to the sermons, and they checked the text of books written by Jews for publication, searching for evidence of subversion.[1] Jews in public life learned to speak in a code of their own. Rabbinical sermons abounded in defiant references to the Bible or the Talmud, often incomprehensible to their Nazi listeners, but which they attempted to decipher. The Gestapo brought copies of rabbinical commentaries found in communal offices to Gustav Horn, the Werkleute young Zionist, for translation.[2] Buber published an attack on the Nazi regime disguised as a philosophical discourse with Kierkegaard; the

Nazis failed to penetrate his language and passed it for publication, though he wrote, 'the last generation's intoxication with freedom has been followed by the present generation's craze for bondage; the untruth of intoxication has been followed by the untruth of hysteria'.[3]

Many German Jews who had left in haste in 1934, later returned to Germany. Outside the professions and the civil service, there was still work in the larger cities. The beginnings of the Nazi rearmament programme, the schemes to check unemployment, led to temporary prosperity and a revival of confidence in the economy, from which Jewish businessmen profited, too. In the textile industry, the department stores and the banks, Jews continued to prosper; Jewish brokers operated on the Berlin stock exchange until the late 1930s. German conservatives continued to bank with firms such as the Warburgs, Arnhold, and Bleichroder, and to buy at Wertheims and Israels, though in the provinces Jewish traders were easily bullied into selling out cheaply by local Nazis. The Gestapo were often not only enemies, but the Jews' only real court of appeal: sometimes the Reichsvertretung could work through the Gestapo to hold off the immediate persecution of Jewish businessmen.[4]

In the business world, too, Jews lived double lives. Some sought Gentile partners to protect themselves from sanctions, or to disguise the Jewish ownership of firms; others worked through Gentile intermediaries. For there were subtler ways of forcing a man out of business than plain threats of violence or public boycotts. The famous boycott of April 1933 was not renewed, as originally intended. But Jewish firms were increasingly excluded from government contracts; public institutions were forbidden to buy from Jews; and Jewish firms were suddenly denied import certificates, or found it impossible to obtain essential raw materials which were in short supply.

Alberti's 'citadel of commerce', in which Wilfrid had served with so many inner reservations, now became, for the Jewish community, a stronghold of resistance. Wolf Mattesdorf, a young lawyer who regularly consulted Wilfrid for advice as to how Jewish employers could best resist Nazi pressures, remembered the feeling of reassurance he experienced on entering Wilfrid's office. Now, for the first time, Wilfrid began to speak and write of the firm's 'tradition', and of his own duties as the last heir. For the first time, he saw a purpose in the existence of N. Israel beyond commerce and patronage; the ambivalence of the past disappeared. Daily routine might be tiresome, and Gestapo interrogations continued: one of the N. Israel lift attendants remembered Wilfrid being whisked out of the building in the spring of 1934, and returning a few hours later; and there are other, unconfirmed stories of further interrogations and even an attack on Wilfrid himself in the street – his letters refer to 'frightening experiences' throughout the mid-1930s. But Wilfrid now saw precisely what it was that he had to do: if the Israel tradition had any meaning, it was to assume responsibility not only for the lives of its own Jewish employees, but also to help those in less well-established Jewish firms.

Wilfrid and Herbert, who now ran N. Israel, now benefited from their father's conservatism; in 1934 Wilfrid became *Betriebsführer*, or managing director, of the firm. There were no mortgages on the buildings, and no debts; therefore they were not vulnerable to financial pressures from Nazi-controlled banks or institutions. The exceptional structure of the firm, and the ties they had built up with their Gentile customers, both meant that the Israels had more freedom of action than most Jewish firms. But they, too, adopted disguises: delivery vans no longer bore the Israel name, and the mail order department sent parcels which bore no senders' label. Wilfrid obtained contracts through Gentile friends, including a tender to supply the Hamburg shipping yards, from which the 'Strength through Joy' cruises set out, with thousands of yards of floor covering.[5]

The Israel building was redecorated, to convince the employees that the Israels had no intention of selling out. One visitor commented to a Gentile employee that 'since the Nazis had taken over, the firm looked much smarter'.[6]

Meanwhile, Wilfrid was slowly helping his Jewish employees to leave Germany; in 1935, Otto Heilbut, the export manager then on a visit to the United States, canvassed American Jews for affidavits. The export side of N. Israel was expanded, which provided another way of arranging for employees' funds to be transferred abroad. Fritz Ollendorff, a young trainee, was sent to open a new branch in London; he also ran a courier service to Norman Bentwich. With the Gestapo noting every journey Wilfrid made, and the Nazi works' committee acting as watchers inside the business, Wilfrid knew himself under constant surveillance. After his visit to Palestine, he wrote to his friends in the Werkleute:

> My situation is very frightening and it always costs me an effort to master my nerves. Nevertheless, Jewish work is consolidating itself. ... It seems to me that only Martin Buber and Ernst Simon do challenging work, and that the work in Palestine has some force. Besides that, the rest seems superficial ... long range plans are not clear, but I have confidence in my spiritual toughness and ability to think things out clearly.

The work of Buber and Simon, another famous Jewish teacher who had returned temporarily from Palestine, was the education of both Jewish children and adults. The 'Jewish work' was emigration and relief;

the 'work in Palestine' was Wilfrid's work for Youth Aliya, and the source of his 'spiritual toughness' was his sense of a new role he had to fulfil in the community. Everything that had been imposed on him, and which he had accepted so unwillingly, now had a meaning.

His letters indicate that he helped Buber financially where he could. As the number of Jews in universities was limited, Buber organized a teacher training programme run from Frankfurt, and lectured both at Baeck's famous Berlin Hochschule, a Jewish university in all but name, and elsewhere - notably at Quaker meetings - until he was finally prevented from teaching in 1938.

In the 1920s, only some 15 per cent of Jewish children had attended Jewish schools. Early in the Nazi period, the Reichsvertretung opened an education department and hundreds of Jewish schools were founded. They provided a German and Jewish curriculum, and also tried to prepare children, who now had little hope of a professional career, for a vocation or trade. To teach Jewish children the German classics was to prove that they had not been totally excluded from the culture of the country in which they were born, as the Nazis sought to prove; to teach them Jewish history was to show that they also had another tradition, for which they were now being persecuted. Nothing could be more humiliating than to know nothing of that tradition, yet to be damned for it.

This was the source of the success of Buber's adult education schemes. Wilfrid, too, made time to study Jewish history and Jewish thought with one of his colleagues in the Reichsvertretung, Günther Friedlander, who visited the Bendlerstrasse regularly to give him lessons. Under the impassive gaze of Wilfrid's buddhas, they read texts from the Bible and commentaries from the Talmud. In Wilfrid's view, the buddhas were not alien witnesses, for, as he wrote at this time to a Werkleute friend in Palestine, Fritz Aronstein, he now saw that, as Buber had written, the relationship of Judaism to oriental religion was 'astonishingly clear' - in particular the discipline of action, the Jewish *mitzvot*, or ritual commandments, which codify everyday life. Wilfrid was never to become an orthodox Jew, but he now began to adopt certain Jewish practices, in particular the Friday evening ritual of lighting candles and saying blessings over wine and bread, which he continued until his death.

Among the new Jewish schools set up at this time were three private boarding-schools, 'pedagogic islands in a sea of alienation and hatred', as the Jewish historian Yosef Valk has called them. One came under Wilfrid's special care; it was to survive unscathed until it closed in 1939.

In February 1935, Wilfrid was asked by Hugo Rosenthal, a teacher who had returned from Palestine for voluntary work, to serve on the board of the Landschulheim at Herrlingen, near Ulm. Until 1933, the Herrlingen School had been run by one of the 'New Era' veterans and a close friend of Elisabeth Rotten, Anna Essinger. When the Nazis came to power, she decided to emigrate with her Jewish pupils to England. Rather than leave her property to be confiscated by the Nazis, she offered the school and its grounds, in a tranquil wooded valley, to Rosenthal. At Herrlingen, the famous 'German-Jewish symbiosis', later lamented by Buber and Baeck, functioned for the last time. Hebrew was taught in place of Latin, together with the German classics; Talmud study alternated with Bach and Handel festivals. Prayers were translated and rationalized, with Rosenthal explaining to the children the differences between the Christian and Jewish manner of appealing to God. The 'New Era' ideas and Zionism also met. 'Digging was as important as Pythagoras', as Rosenthal later wrote: carpentry, mechanics and portable trades were taught to children whose parents had intended them to be doctors and lawyers. The children went out into the woods after hearing Ludwig Koch's famous recordings of birdsong, to identify the calls of the birds who nested nearby.[7]

In October 1937, when one of the children died after a short illness, Rosenthal decided to plant a tree in his memory in the school grounds, explaining to the children that the act was valid, though all of them would soon leave Germany for ever. Many did so through Youth Aliya.

The Education Department in nearby Wurtenburg placed few obstacles in Rosenthal's way. The school remained unmolested even during the 1938 pogroms, when the synagogue in Ulm was destroyed and all other Jewish schools in the region were burned down or evacuated.

In spring 1939, the school was closed when Rosenthal was warned that his licence would not now be renewed. It was later used as a home for old Jews, then as a deportation centre. When all its residents were finally taken to the concentration camps, the Nazi Government presented the Herrlingen estate, as a gift from the nation, to the victorious General Rommel. It was in the woods nearby, where the Jewish children of Herrlingen had gone birdwatching, that Rommel committed suicide in 1944, on Hitler's orders.[8]

Wilfrid's part in the administration of Youth Aliya was as circumscribed as all other Jewish work. By 1935 no public appeal for money, or propaganda work, was possible in Germany. Taxes on money sent to Palestine rose steeply, and Wilfrid joined others who negotiated with the Ministry of Economics for their reduction.[9] Mail to and from the Berlin office was censored, and the office had to renew official permission to transfer funds every two months. Those who ran Youth Aliya were summoned to the Gestapo periodically.[10]

When the capacity of the Palestinian orphanages and Ben Shemen village was exhausted, Wilfrid and his colleagues decided, together with the Zionist pioneering movement, Hehalutz, to send groups of children to the kibbutzim: sixty children left for Eyn Harod, in the Jezreel Valley, in 1934, and another group was sent to Mishmar HaEmek, Shenhabi's kibbutz, a little later. Through Shenhabi, Wilfrid was able to follow every detail of the children's experience; among their instructors were graduates from Ben Shemen; among the youth leaders who accompanied them from Germany was a Werkleute friend, Ernst Bauer;[11] and some of the children even stayed in Wilfrid's flat on their way through Germany.

Wilfrid helped set up committees in several European countries, for fund raising and propaganda, and in January 1935 he proposed that the main organization of Youth Aliya be transferred to Jerusalem, with the Berlin office remaining mainly as a consultative body;[12] in this way, he aimed at reducing the dependence of the organization on Nazi Germany as far as possible, though the selection of the children clearly had to take place there, and to speed up emigration. Delays could decide the fate of the young candidates, for the age limitation - between fourteen and sixteen - was rigid and, if certificates were not issued in time, a child who had prepared to leave Germany might suddenly be disqualified on his or her seventeenth birthday. The Mandatory authorities had no fixed policy on youth immigration and considered applications on an *ad hoc* basis; thus the Jerusalem office could make no commitments to Germany in advance.[13] To complicate matters still further, the kibbutzim refused to take any children who had not belonged to youth movements affiliated to the Palestinian Jewish organizations.[14] Only some 600 children had reached Palestine in the first three years of Hitler's rule; when Mordechai Shenhabi wrote to Wilfrid at the beginning of 1936, giving enthusiastic details of how the children had already learned Hebrew and had begun to settle into the communal way of life (and that the palm trees Wilfrid had seen as shrubs had grown six feet), he answered soberly: 'I am indeed happy that from the very beginning I was identified with Youth Aliya. If the scope of the work could only be enlarged, it would become a very important activity.'[15]

To visitors to Berlin, Wilfrid appeared to be living an elegant and successful business and social life, untouched by Nazi persecution. Such was the view of Diana Hopkinson, an English friend who, with Adam von Trott zu Solz, met Wilfrid at Lola Hahn Warburg's Wannsee home; and then at one of his mother's tea parties, 'picking his way through the furs and flowers' in an atmosphere of scent and Turkish cigarettes; and in the Bendlerstrasse, where his flat, with its stone sculptures, exquisitely lit against moss green carpets, 'suggested a compromise between the severity of his artistic tastes and the immense comfort which the customary standards of the wealthy imposed'. She was given only one glimpse of the reverse side of Wilfrid's life, at a lunch party in Schwanenwerder in March 1935:

> Half way through lunch, a man servant came in to say that there was a telephone call. ... After enquiring who it was, he told the servant to say he was not at home. A little later the man came back in obvious distress and whispered something to Wilfrid. This time Wilfrid left and then returned without saying anything. Towards the end of the meal, the whole rigmarole was repeated. Wilfrid finally returned to the table and said 'I don't think they will interrupt us again'. He then explained that the authorities had telephoned to say that Israel's was the only building in the centre of the city which had failed to put out swastika flags. As he would remember, this was an important day, so would he please give orders to have the oversight rectified. He had refused the first time. The second call had produced threats from higher quarters, but he had repeated that he preferred to take no action. I wondered how long it would be before he was arrested.

This was, she understood, 'the kind of incident with which Wilfrid had to contend almost daily'. The only sign of agitation she noted was that, although Wilfrid usually shrank from all physical contact, he took her arm as he led her through the garden to the greenhouse to pick winter roses.[16] The particular incident was not repeated; a few months later Jews were forbidden to fly the swastika, now the official flag of Germany.

Just at this time, when the Nazis were doing all they could to proscribe contacts between Jews and Gentiles – the race laws were already pending – Wilfrid became a friend of Adam von Trott zu Solz, a Prussian lawyer who had many friends among those outlawed by the regime: Social Democrats, Communists and Jews.

In character, the two friends could scarcely have been more different. Wilfrid was restrained and found it hard to formulate his thoughts; Trott was exuberant and a fluent talker. Wilfrid had a supersubtle talent for assessing the responses of people he talked to, as one friend commented, 'answering questions that had not been asked'. Trott was often recklessly unaware of the effect he had on his hearers. Trott was at heart a countryman; Wilfrid cultivated the 'weekend idea'. Trott could ignore his surroundings; Wilfrid clung to elegance as to a lifebelt.

There was some symmetry, however, in their experiences. Trott was also descended, on his mother's side, from English-speaking ancestors;

having been a Rhodes Scholar at Balliol, he was also a natural emissary. Though over a decade younger than Wilfrid, he too had admired the post-war pacifists, and developed an interest in the culture and society of the Far East. But these were probably superficial affinities. Unlike almost all Trott's English friends, Wilfrid understood why Trott chose to remain in Nazi Germany, hoping to work against the Nazis from the inside. He believed, as he was later to write frequently, that it was impossible for Germans to combat Nazism from abroad.

There was little enough time for the friendship to develop. The few surviving letters from Wilfrid to Adam von Trott suggest that Wilfrid saw little of Trott in 1935, when his father was already gravely ill, and less in the following year, in the autumn of which Trott left for two years in the Far East. When he returned, after the Kristallnacht, Wilfrid was already involved in a desperate last ditch struggle, in the firm and in the Hilfsverein. The two men exchanged ideas periodically and Trott was occasionally a house guest in the Bendlerstrasse. There is one undated note, urgently worded as if Wilfrid needed to know – perhaps as an answer for an English visitor – whether Trott believed that an increase in German commerce in the Far East could assist German, Italian and English intervention to terminate the Sino-Japanese War. (This was also an idea that Trott put to the American Institute of Pacific Relations in early 1939, and which won him a second visit to the United States in that autumn.[17])

Wilfrid and Trott had different preoccupations. The plight of the Jewish community was Wilfrid's first priority, whereas for Trott it was one of the marginal consequences of the surrender of Germany to Nazism. It was not a political friendship in the practical sense, for Wilfrid's ties with anti-Nazi groups evolved in different ways. What sustained the friendship – in the light of what Wilfrid later wrote of his views on Germany and Nazism – was Wilfrid's enduring loyalty to pre-Nazi Germany, and both men's determination that the Nazis should not decide their friendships.

The violence which lay below the surface of the Jews' continuing existence in Germany erupted again in the summer of 1935, when Nazi Party members were encouraged by the country's successful attempts to defy world opinion: first in the Saar plebiscite in January and – possibly the cause of a display of flags in Berlin in March – Hitler's rejection of the arms clauses of the Versailles Treaty that month. In conversation with his English friends in London – among them Clifford Allen, a MacDonald peer and one of his pacifist friends – Wilfrid had clearly received the impression that there were Englishmen in influential positions who were prepared to intervene on behalf of the Jews, if fresh persecution threatened. When hostile placards reappeared in the Berlin streets and Jews were openly harassed – events reported in the foreign press – Wilfrid managed to travel to Venice for a few days and took the opportunity to write both to Bentwich and to Leonard Montefiore. To Bentwich he wrote:

> This might be another decisive moment for England to state her attitude. Is this not the situation and moment, for instance, that Allen thought it might be useful to wait for? Can you get in touch with him? and Lothian? I don't want to pester you; but being in a position to write ... I could not induce myself to remain silent.[18]

The response to Wilfrid's appeal indicated that no one – whether Jew or non-Jew – outside Germany shared his sense of urgency; that routine harassment was taken for granted; and that relief bodies outside were not prepared to accept the advice of German Jews as to the action which could be taken abroad.

Bentwich was in America when Wilfrid's letter arrived, and he did not reply until 26 June, when he asked a friend visiting Germany to tell Wilfrid that he would see what could be done. The subsequent correspondence indicates that Bentwich did meet Allen a little later, and that Allen agreed to make some 'representation' to the German authorities provided that he had information about retraining and capital transfer problems put in the way of Jews wishing to emigrate. On 26 July, Bentwich wrote to Bernhard Kahn of the Joint in Paris making further enquiries, complaining that he could get 'only vague generalities' from the refugee committee in London, and that he would like to have 'definite cases of obstruction of retraining and of refusal of reasonable facilities for emigration by persons with some modest capital'.

What, however, were these 'vague generalities'? The man to whom Bentwich was referred in London was Kurt Battsek, the representative of the Hilfsverein in London. Battsek wrote to Bentwich on 16 July that, in the formal sense, training and retraining of Jewish artisans was not opposed by the German Government 'as everything promoting the emigration of Jews is welcome'. In practice, however, Jewish labour exchanges could not find openings in agriculture, Jews could work only on private farms, and the training of artisans was impossible in many cities, notably in Berlin, for lack of official permits. Battsek proposed, as the Central Bureau delegates and others had argued two years earlier, that an outside organization should negotiate with the Nazis to set up a trust fund which would gradually liquidate Jewish property in Germany, for the mutual benefit of German Jews and the German Government, as there was no hope for the Jews in Germany and 'every day's delay in reaching this goal will make it all the less attainable'.[19]

But Bentwich did not pass on this message, and Allen was concerned at this time with British domestic politics; his protests to the Nazi Government centred on the case of Hans Litten, a half-Jewish communist lawyer imprisoned by the Nazis who eventually committed suicide. Both Allen and Lord Lothian, influential members of the House of Lords, were more distressed by Nazi persecution of the Jews than were most British politicians. Yet as they had already shown on their joint visit to Berlin early that year, not only were they prepared to be duped by Hitler's promises of moderation, but, as Lothian put it, by the belief that persecution was the concomitant of the 'German revolution ... an extravagance of the rebellious spirit', and the best hope for the Jews, more appeasement. This made their protestations of distaste worthless.[20] Lothian did talk to Ribbentrop in London, at Weizmann's urging, that summer, and told him that 'if Hitler wanted to establish friendly relations with England it was essential that the persecution of individuals [*sic*] by an omnipotent government should be ended'; all he could tell Weizmann subsequently was that Ribbentrop had 'listened well'.[21]

Not only could German Jewry hope for no effective diplomatic action from Gentile friends; Jewish envoys who, in the summer of 1935, again pleaded with Jewish organizations for supplementary funding for re-training and emigration, had to contend with a reluctance to commit themselves to future contributions or to active help for large-scale emigration. As early as May 1935, Max Warburg warned of the likelihood of a large emigration from Germany and 'the part liquidation of the activities of German Jews', and stressed that 'nobody who does not continually follow the daily rush of the movement in Germany could report exactly how matters stand'.[22]

But a deputation of the Reichsvertretung to New York in the summer of 1935, in the somewhat impatient presence of James McDonald and representatives of all the great Jewish charities, met with the rejection of the pleas of Otto Hirsch and Max Kreutzberger (both speaking in German) for open-ended funding.[23] No further fund-raising campaign was contemplated for 1936, either in the United States or in Britain, where even the educational 'clearing' scheme, which had enabled several hundred young German Jews in England to pursue their studies, had run out of funds.[24]

Therefore, there was great consternation abroad when, on 15 September 1935, the Nuremberg race laws were promulgated. These laws effectively deprived all German Jews, including many who had left both the faith and the community, of what was left of their status as German citizens. Jews and Aryans could no longer marry, and the notion of 'racial pollution' meant that even sexual relations between Germans and Jews became a punishable offence. The obscenity of these edicts was equalled by the brutality with which Jews could now be removed legally from all positions of responsibility and importance. The numbers of those seeking to emigrate increased by tens of thousands who had not previously considered themselves as Jews, and the laws, by striking a further blow at the Jews' ability to support themselves, added to the burden on the organizations responsible for welfare and relief. Even before the Nuremberg laws were officially promulgated, Jewish children were banned, on 10 September, from attending classes in elementary school together with Gentiles.

On 1 October, Bentwich finally wrote to Allen: 'You will think it strange that after our talk some months ago you have heard nothing from me about the difficulties in the work of retraining and emigration which are put in the way of the Jews of Germany', and added, 'I had hoped to go to Germany myself during the summer; but it was considered inadvisable. And so far I have not been able to obtain from the organizations most concerned any definite statement of obstruction.' Since their talk, the Nuremberg laws had been passed, but, said Bentwich, 'we realize that representation about that is out of the question'. It was not until 14 October that Bentwich finally wrote to Allen saying that he had been informed by German friends that camps training 2,500 young people were threatened with closure, that the Jews were planning to leave, and that there was danger of a 'panic exodus'. It was no longer a question of specific difficulties, but of a request 'to represent to those highest in authority the call of humanity'.[25]

The Nuremberg laws were the first of the 'emergencies' for which Wilfrid had pronounced himself prepared to return to active work in the community. But by now his responsibilities to the little society in his care had increased. In mid-summer his father's condition had worsened. He had no time even for close friends. In May he wrote that Berthold's condition was 'so serious that we can't absent ourselves for more than a few hours from his sick bed. Difficult for all of us, the perspectives for me are even more difficult.' The slow decline, with crises interrupted by false recoveries – one of which allowed Wilfrid's trip to Venice – proved harder than sudden death. 'To have to confront death is part of living; but to do so continuously, over such a long period, demands strength I scarcely have.'

On 23 July, in the early morning, Berthold Israel died at the age of sixty-seven in his home in the Hildebrandstrasse; Amy had stood all night at his bedside. A memorial ceremony was held in the main hall of the firm, where a marble plinth, on which precious silks were usually displayed, was draped in black and banked with white roses. Wilfrid, Paul Krentz and Kurt Liepert, the Nazi works' foreman, spoke in Berthold's memory. The only ceremony spared the Nazi presence was Berthold's funeral, which took place three days later, in the Schoenhauser Allee cemetery, where Leo Baeck performed the ceremony. Wilfrid wrote to a friend that 'it would be egoistic to mourn my father's death'.

Wilfrid's formal role as fifth head of the firm was to last a mere four months. Two months after the Nuremberg laws were issued, their provisions were implemented in every business in Germany; on 14 November, Wilfrid was served with notice that he was officially removed from his post, now to be formally filled by Paul Krentz, former head of the Hochschule.[26] Wilfrid never in fact left his office, thanks to Krentz's loyalty and that of most of the staff. His ownership could not be challenged, and he still made all the operative decisions, working through Krentz. But, henceforth, he was his own double: the heir, but not the master, of N. Israel.

Henceforth, the Nazis did all they could to undermine the relationship between the executive and the employees. The special medical and pension schemes which the Israels had introduced, and to which employers and employees had jointly contributed, collapsed when the Nazis insisted that any voluntary contributions could only be made to the representatives of the Arbeitsfront, the Nazi trade union to which Jews could not belong. In April 1936, the trade school's licence was withdrawn. The Nazis inside the firm began to harass employees with threats of reprisals if they did not join the party. But they proved unable to shake firm friendships between Gentiles and Jews built up over long years in service, and Jews left the firm only to emigrate. Though the welfare schemes were ended, the habit of consulting Wilfrid persisted. There was a limit, however, even to his ability to hide his feelings. There were no more outings to the river or to the country, no celebrations or anniversaries, no escorting the Israel sports team to the police stadium, no more theatre groups or debating societies. When the doors closed at seven in the evening, management and employees went their separate ways.

Publicly and formally, the Reichsvertretung welcomed the Nuremberg laws as legalizing existing practice; they had little alternative. The laws had followed warnings, in April, from the Ministry of the Interior, and the official edict, in June, proscribing Jews from service in the German army – thereby setting Jewish status back to the pre-Napoleonic era. Legislation and institutionalized discrimination were seen as preferable to a return of the 'wild actions' of the Storm Troopers. But in their encounters with the outside world, German Jewry, including some of those who had, until now, backed the policy of 'second emancipation', now pleaded for help with emigration. Wilfrid was once more sent out to British Jewry, in the late autumn, on behalf of the Reichsvertretung. From now on his role as emissary was to be almost totally clandestine, and far more dangerous than it had been in the past.

One of the first unequivocal statements of the plight of German Jews to the outside world was delivered by an unexpected intermediary: Eric Mills, the Commissioner for Migration and Statistics in the Mandatory administration in Palestine, whose ostensible reason for being in Germany was to take a cure in the Black Forest. In the company of Frank Foley and Werner Senator, who – as in all emergencies – was now in Berlin, he met with diplomats, 'leading German Jews' and members of the German Economics Ministry. On 6 October, he reported to the Foreign Office: 'The policy is clearly to eliminate the Jew from German life and the Nazis do not mind how this is accomplished. Mortality and emigration provide the means.' In a significant footnote, Mills added: 'The Jewish boycott of German goods is politically unwise. Practically, its effect is no more than one-sixth of the decline of German exports. Hence it is ineffective. But Jews outside Germany will not be persuaded in this matter. The boycott is indeed infantile exhibitionism.'[27]

Mills went on to London, where he handed in a more complete report, comparing the plight of the German Jews with that of the White Russians after 1917, or the Armenians in the Turkish Empire. The only answer, he stressed, was the planned emigration of younger Jews.[28] It was Mills who, in January 1936, escorted by Bentwich, went to the leaders of Anglo-Jewry and urged them to review their decision not to make further appeals for the financial help of the German Jews.

Mills did not, of course, advocate increased emigration to Palestine; he emphasized that the exodus of German Jewry was an international responsibility. But Frank Foley, in a memorandum appended to a letter from the Ambassador and sent a little later, urged that the bulk of emigrating Jews be sent to Palestine, that a larger labour schedule be allowed, and that the transfer system be enlarged; he gave his opinion that 'the persecution was as relentless as ever though perhaps more subtle in method', and noted a 'definite disposition on the part of the Economics Ministry to do everything possible to facilitate emigration of Jews, that is to say, to find a solution of the transfer problem'. He enclosed copies of correspondence to prove his point.[29]

The Jews of Britain and America were now called on to formulate a plan of emigration and, almost immediately, the Reichsvertretung made suggestions about ways and means. The leading figure at this point was undoubtedly Max Warburg, who, working through long-established contacts in the Economics Ministry, together with Siegfried Moses, a German-Jewish solicitor, held a series of talks at the Ministry, which were reported piecemeal to his banking and industrial friends in England. These talks were clearly carried on with the knowledge of Nazi officials, but in such a manner that, as a report months later in the *New York Times* explained, it could appear that high policy was scarcely involved. This was the manner in which the Palestine transfer was handled, well into 1938, without the open opposition of Nazi Party officials. Even after Nazi intervention, it continued quietly until the outbreak of war.

At this stage, the decisive figures in England were no longer the official Anglo-Jewish leaders, such as Laski and Montefiore, but the wealthy - and far more secretive - bankers and industrialists who made up the Jewish commercial elite: Anthony and Lionel de Rothschild of the famous banking firm, with its headquarters at New Court in the City; Edward Bearsted, director of British Shell; Simon Marks, of the Marks and Spencer chain stores, who was a Zionist; and others.[30]

Wilfrid made at least one visit to London at this time; it was noted by a man who was involved in intelligence work for Foley in Berlin.[31] But all contacts between the Reichsvertretung and British Jewry, at this time, were concerned with the evolution of the so-called Warburg plan, which became the focus of debate in London. The Rothschilds and Lord Bearsted mobilized the most distinguished figure in British Jewry, Sir Herbert Samuel, an ex-Cabinet Minister soon to be a member of the House of Lords; according to his letters, Samuel was also in indirect contact with Warburg. Wilfrid was the obvious choice as go-between. Moreover, all Wilfrid's subsequent representations to the British Foreign Office on behalf of the Reichsvertretung indicate close involvement in all contacts between that organization and Jews outside Germany, and make little sense without knowledge of the following events.

Warburg's original plan was that the Jews abroad should offer to lift the boycott, thereby suggesting to the Nazis that some benefit would accrue to the Reich from the sale of German goods to be exported by emigrating Jews: a plan on the lines of the Palestine transfer, but also a manipulation of the Nazi belief in Jewish international power, just as Melchior had suggested two years earlier. Samuel, however, was convinced that no such scheme would be accepted by American Jewry, to whom the British magnates planned to appeal for assistance in raising funds, or by 'labour circles' politically opposed to increasing German exports.[32] The Rothschilds, Simon Marks, and one of Marks's close aides, a Cambridge economist named J.L. Cohen, who travelled to Berlin in November, saw quite clearly that the export of German goods, in one form or another, would have to be the principal method of extracting Jewish capital from the clutches of the Nazis, and enabling large-scale Jewish emigration.[33] The Warburg plan, as it eventually emerged, was based on a modification of the Palestine transfer scheme and envisaged the dispersion of German Jewry between Palestine, Europe and countries overseas – in particular to South America, where Jewish non-Zionist philanthropic efforts had been focussed, without much success, for many years.

The majority of Zionist leaders, both outside and inside Palestine, were fiercely opposed to Warburg's scheme. Simon Marks, who noted in his correspondence on the matter with Weizmann that the German Jews had been 'hammering away at the liquidation bank idea since 1933', wanted the transactions to be handled, as far as possible, by Gentile bankers, who had already taken an interest in the plan, in order not to involve the Zionist organizations in further recriminations such as those which had bedevilled successive international Jewish congresses over the Palestine transfer – and which had now quietened.[34] Bearsted favoured the Warburg plan. Samuel was hesistant. From the outset he had been publicly identified with the anti-Nazi boycott, which he had supported in Parliament. Until now, he had been reluctant, as he explained in his memoirs, to play any part whatever in Jewish communal affairs, and, when asked by the Rothschilds to lend his prestige to an emigration scheme, did so without enthusiasm.[35] Those who had sought to rouse Samuel to action, with accounts of Nazi atrocities, had found him too cautious to respond. His mental set was virtually indistinguishable from that of so many of his Gentile colleagues in Parliament or the London clubs, who thought Nazism deplorable but supported the policies of appeasement none the less.[36]

News of the Warburg plan reached Palestine only in December, where it raised the hackles of the entire leadership. Weizmann, in semi-retirement in Rehovot, was deeply hurt that plans had been elaborated in London without the knowledge of the man his friends there called 'the Chief'. He warned Marks against any schemes to settle Jews elsewhere than in Palestine, and attacked Warburg, 'who now poses as an expert on Palestine', for his 'arrogance': 'The Warburgs and the Rothschilds and their methods have gone for ever,' he wrote to Marks; all funds raised should go to Palestine where 'the prosperity of the past three years has been largely due to the influx of men and money from Germany'.[37] He also appealed to Samuel not to support any funds but those intended to bring emigrants to Palestine.[38] David Ben Gurion, after a meeting of the Jewish Agency Executive, declared the entire affair a reflection of the tug of war between 'philanthropic assimilationism' and Zionism, between the select circle of the rich and the large masses of the Jewish people. 'Only yesterday we were struggling with the problem of how to balance our poor budget ... and now we hear messages about projects and schemes running into millions supported by great names; Jewish lords, millionaires and cabinet ministers.' For Ben Gurion, as for Weizmann, the very notion of dispersing Jews abroad meant increasing anti-semitism: the German-Jewish question was an historical test case for Zionism.[39]

In London, meanwhile, the bankers had planned a trust there into which money raised abroad could be placed. Another, parallel trust was to be set up in Germany to handle the proceeds of the liquidation of the property of emigrating Jews, and to administer relief funds; the Berlin office, to be run by a non-Jew, Sir William McClintock, was also to explore the possibilities of extracting funds in the form of selected imports. Several Gentile merchant bankers had agreed to serve on the trust with the Rothschilds and Marks.[40] In early January, before he was due to leave for America with Marks and Bearsted, Samuel canvassed opinions at the Foreign Office on what was now renamed the 'Bearsted plan' - naturally without mentioning the opposition in Jerusalem and Rehovot.[41] Lord Cranborne, the Under Secretary of State for Foreign Affairs, consulted the Ambassador in Berlin, Sir Eric Phipps. Phipps's view was that if foreign countries agreed, through the League of Nations, to arrange for the import of additional goods over and above their normal imports, Jewish capital might be released, and that the German Government would probably co-operate, 'if it were made clear to them that the object of the scheme was not to cast reflections on their treatment of Jews but to help them to get rid of unwelcome Jewish population'.[42] The more cautious view in London, however, was that the League should not negotiate over the matter - for the reasons advanced in the past - but that if the Jewish organizations handled the affair privately, it might work.[43]

All this was communicated in conditions of the greatest secrecy; the Warburg-Bearsted plan was put on ice, made dependent on agreement with the Americans, who were to be asked to contribute an initial £500,000 sterling to the London trust. An alternative plan, to raise a joint fund of £3,000,000 - two-thirds of it from American Jews - to enable the exodus of 100,000 young Jews, half to Palestine and half elsewhere, within four years, was elaborated. With these two contingency plans, Samuel, Bearsted and Marks prepared to set sail for New York. Before they could embark, however, the Warburg plan was blasted into the open by newspaper articles in the American press, which effectively scuttled any further chances it might have had.[44] Samuel was forced to spend much of his time arguing that he was not 'a commercial traveller for German goods';[45] the American-Jewish press argued, as Stephen Wise, the American-Jewish leader, had done the year before, that 'a general must sacrifice a regiment to save an army' – German Jews being the regiment – and that 'enlightened Christian opinion' would not tolerate the Jews buying out their brothers at the price of bolstering the economy of Nazi Germany.[46] Similar arguments had been raised before against the Palestine transfer and had been shown to be empty. But the Warburg plan was dead.

Zionist opposition to the plan was understandable. Only the Jewish community in Palestine was genuinely interested in receiving Jewish immigrants – particularly those with capital, for between 1933 and 1935 the Palestine Office in Berlin had only received from Jerusalem two-thirds of the certificates needed for those who applied for the 'workers' schedule'. The plight of Eastern European Jews was seen – correctly, from the economic point of view – as more urgent.[47] James McDonald, the official who had done most to canvass support for the refugees and who resigned at the end of the 1935 trumpeting his condemnation of German barbarity, privately told Weizmann that his disappointing experiences with Jewish leaders abroad had convinced him of the Zionist case.[48] Unfortunately, only weeks after the Warburg plan was finally rejected, Arab opposition to increased Jewish immigration exploded in the longest display of organized rebellion Palestine had known. The British response was to limit the number of Jews immigrating more strictly than before.

The ambitious 'four-year plan', which replaced Warburg's, remained on paper: by the following year, American Jewry had fallen badly behind in its contributions, and in the first half of 1937 barely a third of those leaving Germany were supported by the funds raised abroad;[49] by 1938 the plan was recognized to be inadequate to the new circumstances;[50] by this time, too, the Nazi leadership had realized that expropriation and forcible expulsion were feasible alternatives to negotiations.

Norman Bentwich, who was privy to the 1935 and 1936 talks, reflected later on the failure of the Anglo-Jewish mission:

> In the light of the past experience with the Transfer agreement ... and of the ultimate confiscation of Jewish property in Germany, the abandonment was regrettable. The choice was between satisfying the emotion of the Jewish masses outside Germany and facing the economic realities of Jewry inside Germany; and German Jewry was the loser.[51]

* * *

Wilfrid's involvement in these negotiations had brought him under closer surveillance. When he left for London, he was followed by a Gestapo agent, Fritz Bartenstein (alias Dr Benender, alias Fritz Stern), a notorious figure nicknamed 'Schwarzer' by those who knew and feared him. He was German Jewry's home-grown spy, having served before the Nazi period as a plainclothes man in the service of the Prussian political police; in 1934 he was given the task of watching the movements of prominent Jewish personalities. But behind Bartenstein, on this occasion, was someone more dangerous where Wilfrid and others were concerned: Georg Kareski, the right-wing Zionist banker who, until he left Germany in 1938, attempted to insinuate himself into the Jewish leadership by every stratagem possible, including currying the support of the Gestapo. After the Nuremberg laws, he managed to get appointed as head of the Kulturbund, the organization set up to co-ordinate Jewish cultural activities. He had his own rival plan for mass emigration – to Palestine alone – and he was more than prepared to hint to the Nazis of subversive 'left-wing' activities by Jewish leaders. Wilfrid, a 'leftist' envoy of the Reichsvertretung to Jewish circles abroad, was an obvious target for suspicion; Kareski provided Bartenstein with a letter of introduction to Jewish bankers in London and paid his journey. Later, he argued that the Gestapo had pressured him into sending the man to London.

However, Scotland Yard had advance knowledge of Bartenstein's arrival. He was arrested, not at the port of entry, which might have indicated that he aroused suspicion during a routine check, but at his hotel in London; and he was brought before a magistrate, where he was charged with entering Britain under a false name, imprisoned for a fortnight and then sent back to Germany. Wilfrid thus remained unshadowed during his stay in England.[52]

But Kareski's enmity did not end there. A few weeks after Wilfrid's return to Germany, a number of left-wing Zionists, including the social welfare expert Shlomo Adler Rudel and the Palestinian envoy Yitzhak Ben Aharon, were summoned to the Gestapo and given forty-eight hours to leave Germany. Other members of the Reichsvertretung were threatened and Wilfrid's German passport was impounded.[53] J.L. Cohen, Simon Marks's aide, who now visited Berlin to elicit more details of the clandestine negotiations, urged the utmost secrecy on all the many parties now involved, and warned Weizmann in Palestine that 'the entire Reichsvertretung had narrowly escaped the concentration camp' because of careless articles published there.[54]

On 10 February 1936, the Gestapo became the supreme Reich police agency, with Himmler, the SS head, independent of the former control of Goering. The security police was now headed by Heydrich, and those who remained from the former Prussian political police and were not convinced Nazis were weeded out. Almost immediately, the Gestapo tightened its watch on Jewish organizations and their leaders. The Reichsvertretung, and in particular the Hilfsverein office dealing with emigration, informed their contacts in Jewish bodies abroad that all Jews visiting Germany on official business would henceforth have to obtain permits from the Gestapo before entering the country.[55]

Germany now prepared to host the Olympic Games, an event prefaced by a display of political brutality. On 7 March, Hitler ordered the German army into the demilitarized Rhineland, thus demonstrating his contempt for the terms of the Locarno Pact of 1925, and once more proving the impotence of the League. The Western European powers made no opposition, Lord Lothian commenting that Hitler 'had merely entered Germany's back garden'. In preparation for the Games in the late summer, however, the Nazis stopped demonstrations against Jews, which they knew might offend their visitors; the anti-semitic posters which had decorated Berlin the previous year disappeared, and *Der Sturmer*, Julius Streicher's anti-semitic journal, which incited to violence, was not distributed while foreigners thronged the capital. The Jews enjoyed a temporary respite. Not so, however, any Jewish leader suspected of exploiting the unusual presence of so many foreign visitors to communicate what the Nazis termed 'atrocity propaganda'.

The Olympic Games was a chance for Wilfrid to plead for intervention with one of the few British diplomats who had shown concern for German Jewry, definite hostility to the Nazi regime and the policy of appeasement, and who was now the guest of a British ambassador known for his anti-Nazi sentiments.

Robert Vansittart arrived in Berlin on 30 July for a two-week stay. One of his aims was to put an end to private visits to Hitler, such as that of Allen and Lothian the previous spring; another was to prepare the ground for a five-power meeting later that year, in which he hoped that Germany could be manoeuvered into a new arms control agreement, a substitute for the Locarno Pact.[56] Vansittart's impressions of the Nazi leaders, as set down on his return, reduced them to figures in drawing-room comedy. Hitler, he noted, ate only spinach and water at a state dinner; Vansittart described him as an 'amiably simple, rather shy, rotundly ascetic bourgeois, with the fine hair and thin skin that accompany extreme sensitiveness'; Goering was 'a Smith Minor suddenly possessed of unlimited tick at the school stores'; and Goebbels, 'the man with whom I got on best in Berlin ... a limping, eloquent slip of a Jacobin'.[57]

Vansittart enjoyed his Berlin stay until the day that Wilfrid Israel was smuggled in by the back door of the Embassy, 'plainly terrorized'. He told Vansittart that the visit could cost him his life, but attempted to convince him that Britain should intervene on behalf of German Jewry, who were otherwise doomed.

Vansittart was in a quandary. 'I had, in fact, been tempted to say something of this in Berlin while discussing Anglo-German relations.' Phipps, however, had discouraged him, arguing that 'any apparent intervention would do far more harm than good to the victims'. All Vansittart could suggest to Wilfrid was that, if an agreement was reached between Germany and the other European powers in the autumn, Britain, 'as a newly signed up friend', could 'put in a moderating word'. This, Vansittart noted, did not reassure Wilfrid, who warned the diplomat that another outbreak of anti-semitic violence was on its way, and left 'tremulous and dispirited' – again by the Embassy back door. 'I did not relish this interview,' Vansittart recorded.[58]

Wilfrid Israel was not the only informed observer who predicted 'further unpleasant surprises after the Olympiad'. But the others warned of a possible extension of German military service, presaging Hitler's intentions of war. This was a more serious matter than the continuing persecution of the Jews; the two matters were not – in British eyes – linked.

Once the Gestapo ruled that all foreign visitors who contacted Jews should be closely supervised, there were few visits. However, there were two important exceptions: an intrepid American lawyer who spent over two years in Germany on Jewish migration business, and an eccentric Englishwoman who arrived in 1937 to help the Christians of Jewish origin, the 'non-Aryan Christians', and the *mischling*, part-Jews whom the Nazis had outlawed from 'Aryan' society. She remained until the outbreak of war. The work of these two, which was never made public, was carried out with the consent of the Gestapo; and both worked in close co-operation with Wilfrid Israel.

Shortly after the Gestapo intensified their surveillance, Max Warburg contacted his brother Felix in New York, urging him to send out an American citizen who might work in Germany as liaison between emigrating Jews and Nazi officials – an idea proposed without success by German Jews since 1933. The man who volunteered for the job was David Glick, a Pittsburgh lawyer, who spoke German fluently and was prepared to take risks. The American-Jewish leaders were unwilling to authorize an official representative of the Joint to enter Germany, and did not believe that he could move freely inside Germany, even if he complied with Nazi regulations. But Bernhard Kahn, the Joint's man in

Paris, was impressed by Glick's personality and, after a briefing in London with Max Warburg and other German Jews, Glick arrived in Berlin in May 1936.[59] He insisted that he should present himself to the Gestapo immediately; otherwise, he argued, he would be picked up and ordered to leave within days of his arrival.[60]

He was right. To the surprise of the American Embassy staff, whose help he enlisted, Glick was received by both Himmler and Heydrich. The American Consul, Geist, explained that Glick was in Berlin at the request of American Jews, that there would be no publicity of any kind, and that Glick would say and write nothing of his experiences in Germany on return to America. His sole purpose was to help German Jews to leave 'with as much of their property as possible under the laws of Germany'. Glick, meanwhile, observed Himmler coolly: the 'feared Gestapo head,' to a practised lawyer's eye, resembled 'an experienced title searcher in the office of the Recorder of Deeds of a country seat ... with the body of a tackle on a football team'. Glick was referred to the Gestapo deputy in charge of Jewish questions, Dr Karl Hasselbacher, with whom he had several subsequent conversations on the ideology of anti-semitism, and who had his own card index, he boasted, listing all the important Jews in Germany.

During his first year in Germany, Glick visited not only the larger Jewish communities in the towns but 'hundreds of smaller towns and villages'. In the spring of 1937, he returned briefly to the United States for consultations - passing through London where he attempted, at Wilfrid's suggestion, to raise support for the Christians of Jewish origin - and was asked to return for a further year.[61]

By now, persecution had intensified, and Glick was continually intercepted and questioned by junior Gestapo agents. He met Heydrich once more with Werner Best, deputy head of the Gestapo; this time they provided him with official Gestapo papers which enabled him to work without interruption for the remainder of his stay in Germany. Glick's work was probably not limited to liaison between Jews and German government offices, or Jews and their friends and sponsors abroad: during this time, among other rescue systems, it was possible for emigrants to deposit capital in Germany and receive dollars in exchange from the Joint, outside its borders. Glick also performed more secret work. In October 1937, towards the end of his stay in Germany, Glick negotiated for the release of 120 of the 200 Jews then held at Dachau concentration camp near Munich. The Gestapo were prepared to release them on condition that they emigrated immediately to a country beyond Europe; the local British Consul, Carvell, was prepared to issue visas to Palestine on condition that a deposit of £5,000, to assist their settlement there, was paid into a bank outside Germany. At this point the Joint entered the picture. This was probably the first instance, on such a scale, of what subsequently became part of the Gestapo system of encouraging emigration after the mass arrests of 1938 and 1939.[62]

Glick's mission, from beginning to end, was kept totally secret, unrecorded – save for two telegrams setting out Jewish leaders' opposition to his mission – even in the archives of the Joint itself. He finally revealed the outline of his mission in the *Harvard Law School Bulletin* in 1960, a few years before his death. He indicated that most of those whom he had helped to leave Germany emigrated to South America, and that he had negotiated with representatives of South American states while in Germany; one contact alone, a German émigré to the Argentine, a tin mine millionaire named Don Mauricio Hochschild, financed the settlement of 3,000 refugees in Bolivia. This compares impressively with the 4,000 German Jews who, according to official reports, emigrated to South America between April 1933 and October 1935.[63] Sufficient data does not exist, however, to confirm Glick's contention that the majority of an estimated 90,000 emigrant Jews found refuge in South America between 1936 and 1938, when he worked with the Reichsvertretung.

Wilfrid Israel is one of the handful of German-Jewish leaders Glick mentions as having assisted him in his work and one of those whose courageous work remained unknown. According to colleagues who survived the war, Wilfrid began working intensively in the Hilfsverein in 1937.

During the first three years of the Nazi period, the Hilfsverein, which directed refugees to all countries apart from Palestine, was little more than a counselling centre; it was only after the Nuremberg laws that it became an efficient source of aid. The Hilfsverein had 400 correspondents abroad, who reported on the labour situation all over the world, on investment possibilities, and even on the living quarters available and their price. Its officials negotiated with German government offices, with emigration and finance officials, and with Jewish organizations abroad, and they ran language courses for emigrants. The Hilfsverein obtained visas and permits, chartered ships, and arranged for group settlement with the help of organizations such as the Jewish Colonial Association (ICA). It even provided loans and arranged the transportation of household goods; from 1936 onwards, it had fifteen branches in Germany.[64]

When Wilfrid began to work there, he firstly reorganized the reception procedure for applicants; secondly, he instructed those who worked

TOP LEFT Nathan Marcus Adler, Wilfrid Israel's maternal great-grandfather, first Chief Rabbi of Great Britain
TOP RIGHT Jacob Israel, Wilfrid's paternal grandfather

ABOVE Early nineteenth-century water colour of the Israel firm in the Berlin Molkenmarkt

ABOVE LEFT Berthold Israel, Wilfrid's father
ABOVE RIGHT Amy Israel, *née* Solomon, Wilfrid's mother
LEFT Wilfrid Israel, aged about five years old, ready for his dancing class in a blue and white sailor suit. He refers to this photograph in a letter, describing these as his 'most militant and successful days'.

ABOVE The Israel firm, Berlin, during the 1920s
BELOW LEFT The central stairwell and linen department of N. Israel, 1920s
BELOW RIGHT The dress fabrics department

TOP Viva Israel's wedding. Wilfrid is second from right in the second row.
ABOVE Julius Salinger's sixtieth Jubilee celebration with the Israel firm, 1926. In the front row: Berthold Israel (centre); Julius Salinger (with white beard) on his right; Paul Krentz, head of the Hochschule and from November 1935 managing director, on Salinger's right; Otto Heilbut (far right), Wilfrid's cousin and exports manager. Wilfrid is in the centre of the third row.

TOP The N. Israel sports team, with Wilfrid (seated, wearing jacket, front centre), at the Berlin police stadium, September 1928
LEFT Wilfrid at Schwanenwerder about 1932
ABOVE The head of the buddha in the gloriole; this is in sandstone from Angkor Wat, Cambodia, 12th century AD

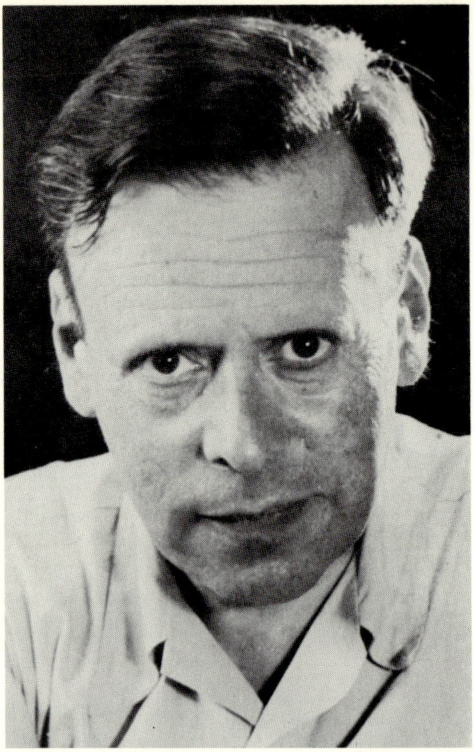

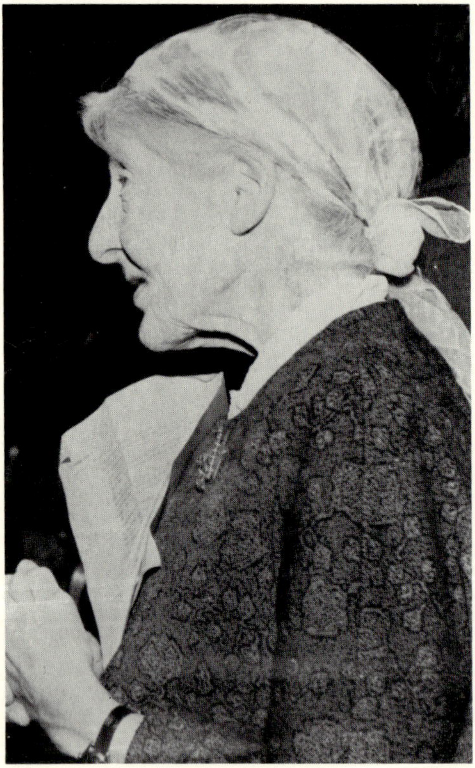

ABOVE Hazorea, 1936: the settlers wait for the arrival of the Mandatory authorities after seizing several acres of the land promised them; Friedrich Altmann, wearing a cloth cap, is in the centre
RIGHT Hazorea, 1940, as Wilfrid Israel saw it on his last visit

OPPOSITE
ABOVE LEFT Wilfrid, Amy and Herbert Israel, mid-1930s
ABOVE RIGHT Hubert Pollack, Israel's aide from 1937 and his intermediary with the Gestapo and with other 'political agents'; Pollack also worked for British Intelligence
BELOW LEFT Adam von Trott, Japan 1938
BELOW RIGHT Laura Livingstone, who went to Germany in 1937 to work for the rescue of the Christians of Jewish birth or origin

LEFT Wilfrid Israel, 1942
BELOW The last photograph of Wilfrid Israel, Lisbon, spring 1943, probably at a dinner given by the Jewish community

under him that the Hilfsverein should extend its services, not only to Jews registered with the Jewish community organizations, but also to the Christians of Jewish birth and other 'non-Aryans'.[65]

'Non-Aryan' was a blanket term for ex-Jews or part-Jews affected by the Nuremberg laws. This was such an amorphous group, and so far removed from the organized Jewish community, that many of them did not know whom to turn to for help. Some had left the Jewish community after intermarriage; some had been Christians for generations; some had deliberately rejected their Jewish background, while others knew nothing of it: many 'non-Aryans' only discovered their Jewish origins when, in order to qualify for a job, they had to present their baptismal certificates or other records to their employer. They were Jews to the Nazis; to the Jews, strangers. Even their numbers were unknown; some assessed them at 500,000 or more; the Nazis thought the number of *mischling*, those with two or more Jewish grandparents, was over 300,000.[66]

Because of the danger of exposure to Nazi scrutiny, only a small minority – 30,000 – registered with the Paulusbund, an officially recognized body which attempted, with pathetically meagre results, to imitate the Jewish self-help organizations. The only active groups functioned in Berlin and Hamburg. Individual Protestant and Catholic pastors helped, but the official church organizations, whose leaders never spoke out against racism, did little for the converts.[67]

It was obviously as necessary to appeal to Christians abroad, on behalf of the Christians of Jewish birth or origin, as it had been for the Jews to appeal to their co-religionists abroad. In May 1936, Wilfrid's friend, Corder Catchpool of the Quakers, called together all those interested and actively concerned to meet Sir Wyndham Deedes, a well-known British social worker who had come out to investigate the persecution of German Jews, at a clandestine meeting at the Swedish church in Wilmersdorf, Berlin.[68] On his return to England, Deedes alerted George Bell, Bishop of Chichester, the British churchman most closely involved in German church affairs.

Until Deedes's visit to Berlin, Bell had known nothing of the fate of the 'non-Aryans'. In the initial stages of Nazi rule, Bell had shared the widely accepted view, in ecclesiastical circles, that German Christians supported Hitler as a defence against communism, and accepted the diplomatic commonplace that any public expression of opposition to the regime – prayers and sympathy apart – would be detrimental to the oppressed. He was finally shocked into speech by the Nuremberg laws, which extended the full machinery of persecution to Jewish converts to Christianity. On 20 November 1935, he moved a resolution in the Church of England Assembly condemning Hitler's racial persecution.[69]

The national Christian appeal launched a fund-raising campaign in early 1936; but it met with a dishearteningly feeble response. In January 1937, nearly a year after Deedes had reported to him on the plight of the 'non-Aryans', Bell visited Germany himself with a Church of England delegation and, at a meeting with the heads of the Paulusbund, was handed a report outlining the situation: most professions were closed to non-Aryans, as to Jews; they were being asked for baptismal certificates going back to 1800; they had no international help; state examinations were closed to them and few schools would accept their children, and – when they died – their corpses remained unburied while police checked documents to decide whether they should be given Jewish or Christian burial.[70]

In March 1937, their situation worsened; the Nazis now ordered the Paulusbund to confine its membership and activities to those with no more than 50 per cent 'Jewish blood'. At this stage, Wilfrid, who had been in close touch with Deedes and had sent Glick to Bell with further evidence of persecution, took the opportunity of a journey to Zurich to appeal to Bell to act more vigorously on behalf of the part-Jews. The Paulusbund, he told Bell, was now inadequate. He informed him that Glick had news of an American-Christian delegation even now on its way to Germany. Could he not despatch 'an equally important British delegation, acting on the same lines'?[71]

Bell had already fulminated against the apparent inability of Christians to help their converted brothers; now his national pride was also challenged. He approached a number of public figures, including Lothian and Arnold Toynbee. Those who had already made their anti-Nazi stand clear argued that they were *personae non gratae* with the Nazi Government; the others pleaded previous engagements. After some weeks, having found no other envoy, Bell sent his own sister-in-law.[72]

Laura Livingstone, who left for Berlin in July 1937 as the representative of the International Christian Committee for German Refugees, and set up shop in the Quaker offices, was a woman of splendid eccentricity, with the courage of a Victorian explorer. During the First World War she had worked as a Land Army girl; she later lived at home with her mother, keeping goats to whom she gave Greek names, and – when her mother died – had her own room near her brother-in-law in the Bishop's Palace at Chichester, accompanied by a grey cat called Agrippina.

In the early years of what the Anglicans called the 'German church struggle', Laura Livingstone, a fluent linguist, translated much of Bell's correspondence.[73] In Berlin, she was received by the Gestapo as politely as Glick had been; she, too, received Werner Best's visiting card and an invitation to consult him at all times.[74] Wilfrid deputed one of his juniors, Arnold Horwitz, to explain to her the mechanisms for helping prospective emigrants; the following year he was to explain the procedure for getting detainees out of concentration camps. But there the resemblance to the Glick affair ended.

Laura Livingstone had no powerful charitable body behind her. While Glick enjoyed the support of Dodd, the American Ambassador and a staunch anti-Nazi, the British Embassy was clearly unhappy with Miss Livingstone's presence in Berlin and did little to make it easier, refusing her even the use of the diplomatic bag.[75] Clearly Laura Livingstone was not the easiest person to work with, being either unaware of the dangers menacing her Quaker co-workers or indifferent to them. Her carelessness in dropping compromising documents into the Quakers' waste-paper basket was of much help to the Gestapo.[76] But in Germany, she was the frail, lone symbol of international Christian concern, and she was never arrested; Horwitz recalled her confronting Eichmann over exit permits for her clients with complete self-confidence.

Without the help of the Hilfsverein, and the contact between the Quakers and the Joint, it is doubtful whether she could have continued with her work. Christian organizations in England and elsewhere, though well meaning, had no experience in arranging emigration and resettlement – something which Jewish organizations had coped with since the turn of the century. Glick introduced Laura Livingstone to Dr Paul Klemperer of Mendelssohns Bank, to Max Warburg, and to the Hamburg Quakers. She wrote to her brother-in-law that she wanted the help of the Embassy, and that she was trying to work on the lines of the Jewish organizations.[77]

When Anglican and Quaker backers in England attempted to imitate the Zionist experiment of settling townsmen on the land, the adventure ended in farce. Some sixty ill-equipped settlers were selected at random and were already at odds on the voyage out; the land, which had been purchased in Bolivia by an agent of doubtful political affiliations, was worthless, and most of the crops planted were destroyed immediately by pests, though the emigrants worked long and exhausting hours. The adventure ended in violence and bankruptcy, and even the Foreign Office could not persuade the Bolivian Government to buy back the land.[78]

Bell's personal efforts were no more successful. In August 1937, he wrote to the Colonial Secretary, Malcolm MacDonald, asking for help in settling young people of good Christian background in the Dominions. MacDonald took informal soundings, with no result; the Dominions were as uninterested in absorbing penniless young Christians as they were in absorbing penniless young Jews.[79]

The attitude of the Gestapo to Glick, Laura Livingstone, and the Jews who worked with them was double-edged. On the one hand, they were satisfied to stand by while Jewish emigration proceeded, which, after all, was the Nazi aim; the work had to be secret because it could not appear that Nazis were actually assisting the Jews in any way at home, or that they were encouraging the dissemination of anti-Nazi propaganda abroad. On the other hand, the risks these people ran were genuine. All Jews having financial dealings abroad were under suspicion; emigration involved the most intricate financial negotiations, and the death penalty could be exacted for any infringement, real or imaginary, of the currency regulations. No one was exempt from the possibility of trumped-up charges and summary execution.[80] And if the visitors might claim some protection from their embassies, those who helped them, in Germany, had no such defence.

Wilfrid's links with German Christian organizations, which apparently began with the meeting at the Wilmersdorf Church, were widely extended. According to the papers he wrote for the Foreign Office during the war, he was in touch with an underground network set up by Catholic Action, which covered all parts of Germany. He was also in contact with at least one Catholic-led group of socialists in southern Germany, which included local industrialists – possibly his business friends – and civil service officials who were ostensibly members of the SS.[81] He worked with Protestant clergymen in Berlin and Jena. The meeting Hans Reissner describes between Hans Schönfeld, a leading anti-Nazi Protestant, 'in or around 1937' fits the general picture Wilfrid sketched to Tom Marshall in 1942. As, by this time, these were totally forbidden contacts, no written record remains; but after Wilfrid's death, Laura Livingstone wrote to Horwitz of the 'hundreds of people scattered over the world' who owed their lives to him.[82] These hundreds, apart from his 'Jewish work', were the Christian lives he saved.

1937 was the last year during which the casual visitor to Berlin would not have detected the fact that the Jews were being eliminated, not only from the professions and the civil service, but from the business world as well. An American rabbi, who had last visited Germany in the summer of 1933, found that to his surprise the streets were safe even for Jews dressed in orthodox style. It appeared that Jewish businesses were open as usual. 'The name of Wertheim floats on a banner over the largest department store in Berlin. N. Israel's name is flashed in electric lights over the entrance of another great establishment.' But he soon discovered that Wertheims, like most firms who still kept their Jewish names, had in fact been 'Aryanized'.[83]

Jews now rarely attended theatres and concerts. Social clubs evicted 'non-Aryans': in December 1936, Wilfrid was expelled from the Berlin Industrialists Bruderverein; Herbert Israel from the Golf and Land Club of the Wannsee. As the Jewish owners of Schwanenwerder moved out, Nazi leaders moved in: Goebbels, Dr Morell (Hitler's physician) and Albert Speer.[84]

Wilfrid continued to travel abroad for the Hilfsverein; among the recorded destinations were Warsaw in 1936, Italy in 1937, and many visits to Zurich. He later told friends that all these journeys were connected with emigration, but he gave no details. Whatever he did, it seemed to him too little. As he wrote to Diana Hopkinson on his way out of Zurich in 1937, he felt no better in or out of Germany. 'One feels very small and rather at a loss ... and at "home" one must always play the game and show no faltering on the surface.' Germany was no longer a real home. To Shenhabi and his friends in the Werkleute, he wrote that 'Palestine represents a home to me'. He was in fact a disorientated man by now, as his letters to Friedrich Altmann reveal. 'Perhaps I am too much in my thoughts with those who are far away, the negative result of my having remained alone here. ... What has happened to the centre of my life? I must remain here, however, and show the world little of my confusion ... for despite everything, I have to be a power centre.' This was in 1936, when he was twice hospitalized. The following March, he wrote again to Friedrich:

> You will scarcely believe it's possible that I am still here! I have had to call upon my last reserves of strength, patience and my very easily hurt self-confidence to stop myself running on to the rocks. ... I'm ground to pieces by the hard-edged objects of my everyday life, members of the family, people who claim they depend on you.

Yet what gave him strength was his conviction, however far he belittled his own contribution, that it was still possible to rescue most of German Jewry. Werner Senator and Mordechai Shenhabi continually appealed to him to leave; he refused, always assuring them that, eventually, he would join them in Palestine. But Palestine, for Wilfrid, was Mishmar HaEmek and the kibbutz the Werkleute had now set up, Hazorea; and Ben Shemen, the children's village. The towns scarcely existed in his mind, and in more than one sense he was afraid of the test of pioneering Palestine. To Alfred Front, he wrote: 'It seems to me important to form solid relationships with people while in Europe, before emigration. Over there the land demands everything from you, and your relations to human beings are easily pushed into the background.' For a man who worked so patiently at his friendships – which were everything to him – and who believed that to reach out to another human being was a process as elaborate as lacemaking, the pioneers' life was daunting, threatening to shatter all his frail defences. In Germany, moreover, he knew exactly what his task was; in Palestine, it was still uncertain what he could contribute.

Moreover, he was increasingly worried by events in Palestine. Anti-Jewish riots had broken out in the spring of 1936, developing into a full-scale Arab revolt. The disturbances had affected Ben Shemen, where only a handful of adults protected hundreds of children; Lehmann cabled Wilfrid and Lola Hahn Warburg in Berlin for emergency funds to strengthen the village's defences.[85] In Hazorea, the settlers traded shots with armed marauders from the day the kibbutz was established. The dangers of life in Palestine discouraged many parents from sending their children there, and made many German Jews seek other havens.

The British Peel Commission, set up after the Arab Revolt, was followed by one of the most important documents of this stormy time, the Partition Plan of 1937, designed by Reginald Coupland, an Oxford professor of political science, who envisaged statehood for the Jews, drawing frontiers between Arabs and Jews in Palestine for the first time. While the plan was still being debated, Wilfrid wrote to Robert Weltsch, editor of the *Judische Rundschau*: 'Do we have the moral and historical right to reject it [partition] as a mere proposal of despair?' And he asked:

> Should we not take into account that this plan may become a reality, i.e. lead to the partition of Palestine, on the one hand an autonomous Jewish entity similar to a British dominion, and on the other an Arab entity consisting of the rest of Palestine . . . which could come under Trans Jordanian sovereignty? And would that inevitably bring about the end of the realization of the Zionist idea?

This was what many Zionists were now predicting. Wilfrid argued that it would not.

> For the first time since the first congress at Basle, the Zionist idea would take concrete shape. Though obviously these new realities would limit, condense and intensify the dimensions of Jewish Palestine, they would consolidate intellectual, social, economic and political forces, a process which has been necessary for years.

Wilfrid believed that the wish for expansion at all costs had been disastrous, and, as Coupland himself believed at the time, that co-operation with Britain could produce an agreement on the lines of British and Afrikaner relations in South Africa.[86]

In the event, the Arabs rejected the plan out of hand, the Jews accepted it with reservations, and the British Government eventually disowned it. In August 1937, a new White Paper restricted Jewish emigration still further, a crushing blow to those working for the rescue of German Jewry, and one more step towards confrontation between the British Government and the Jews. Wilfrid knew quite well that his counsels of moderation and co-operation with England could already 'be regarded as treason by my friends in Palestine', as he wrote to Shenhabi. But he was still convinced that reason and compromise could defuse conflicts, even as he fought an enemy who knew no reason and saw compromise in opponents as a sign of weakness.

7
Flood Warnings

At the beginning of 1938, Friedrich Altmann wrote to Wilfrid with news of the birth of his first son. The little community now settled in Hazorea was living in shacks, and crates with the Berlin despatchers' names still housed most of their possessions. But the kibbutz children's house was the first permanent building.

It took time for Wilfrid to send his congratulations; the news had intensified his own loneliness. 'My thoughts are often with you, because when I am weary I am conscious of the emptiness of my life. Then I seek you, to overcome my loneliness, and long for you, for all of you, for the Land,' he wrote.

Martin Buber was now leaving Germany. In February, Wilfrid wrote to Heppenheim sending birthday wishes, and enclosing, as a parting gift, copies of the sketches he had made at the Wetzlar Congress in 1919. Buber replied: 'I wish to tell you how much your words meant to me. You recall common memories which at this hour of parting ... are particularly vivid for me. We have created, in the Jewish context, an element which ... defies ordinary definition ... a quiet, almost impalpable community.'[1]

The Anschluss, the Nazi annexation of Austria in March 1938, accelerated the persecution of the Jews under Nazi rule, first in Austria, and, weeks later, in the Old Reich.

Everything that had taken the Nazis five years to implement in Germany was carried out and bypassed overnight in Austria. The brutality which had been sporadic in Germany since 1933 became daily routine in Austria. Foreign observers like Eric Gedye, the London *Times* Vienna correspondent, who in earlier years had seen anti-Jewish rioting as part of the local colour of the city, was now hard put to convince his readers that the Nazis' new sadism was unprecedented. 'When I say that one's Jewish friends spoke to one of their intention to commit suicide with no more emotion than they had formerly talked of making an hour's journey by train, I cannot expect to be believed,' he wrote.[2]

Gedye witnessed scenes of horror: rabbis were forced to dance in their synagogues for Nazi amusement, as the sacred scrolls were destroyed in front of them. Jewish women were pushed on to their knees in the street, their winter coats drenched with dirty water from buckets, and forced to scrub pavements with hydrochloric acid; they returned home with the skin hanging from their hands.[3] Unseen and unreported, thousands of Jewish men and women disappeared off the streets and from their homes, first in Austria and then in Germany, and were consigned to separate barracks in concentration camps.

Shortly after the Anschluss, trainloads of Jews left Austria under guard for Dachau, near Munich, and for the recently opened Buchenwald camp near Weimar.

Until this date, the Jews in the concentration camps had been a minority, imprisoned either for their left-wing politics, or as the result of personal vendettas; they were not generally segregated from the other prisoners. Apart from one particular category – Jews accused of *Rassenschande*, or racial (sexual) pollution, from August 1935 onwards – and returning emigrants sometimes jailed before being forced to leave Germany again, the concentration camp was a threat in the back of their minds, not an immediate danger.[4]

In Buchenwald, opened in July 1937, there were no Jews among the prisoners until May the next year when 400 Jews, either unemployed or with police dossiers (a parking offence sufficed), were rounded up in Berlin and sent to Buchenwald, where they joined others brought from Vienna. In June, hundreds of Jewish shops, including N. Israel, were daubed with swastikas, and their windows broken.[5] Mass arrests were so overt that they were reported in foreign papers. According to Foley's consular report for the month of June:

> In Berlin as well as in other parts of Germany there were systematic house to house searches for, and arrests of Jews; cafés were raided and even cinema halls were emptied of Jews so that they could be arrested in concentration camps. In Berlin the methods of persecution were particularly severe ... it is no exaggeration to say that Jews have been hunted like rats in their homes, and for fear of arrest many of them sleep at a different address overnight.[6]

However, few people – including most German Jews – knew exactly what happened inside the camps; those who were released, on condition that they left the country within two weeks, were forced to sign a document saying that they had been well treated, and warned not to talk of their experiences; Gestapo agents, they were told, were now planted in every country in the world, and the long arm of the SS would find and punish them, even in the Far East. The vast majority of eye-witness accounts emerged from Germany only after the Kristallnacht in November; none was signed.[7]

The news of what was happening to Jews inside the camps reached Wilfrid almost immediately. On 28 June, a week after the first mass arrests in Berlin, he wrote a letter to Lord Samuel which, by unknown means, he smuggled out of Germany. It arrived in an unstamped envelope on Samuel's desk some time later, delivered by Maurice Stephany of the Council for German Jewry. The spelling alone reveals Wilfrid's distress:

> You will no doubt have heard of the plight of many of our co-religionists since their arrest in the past weeks (they may number 2–3000). They are now suffering the tortures of hell in one of the new concentration camps, in the so-called stone quaries [*sic*] of death. They are mostly made to slave for 14–16 hours a day by hawling [*sic*] or carrying stones. Their supervisors use their whips only too willingly under this or that pretext. Discipline is enforced by slashing [*sic*] old and young to tree trunks and beating them while others are made to be eye witnesses of their misery. Old men up to seventy and young men are heaped together. Medical aid is only offered when wounds are open or manifest to the eye. For many the only way of escaping this torture is to run into wire entaglement [*sic*] loaded with high tensioned electricity. Deaths are frequent for this and other reasons.
>
> I make the following earnest request and appeal. Have a British troop transport ship chartered for Hamburg without lack of time and deport these lost souls under British escort and supervision of the Red Cross to Islands if necessary, semi military camps, for instance, to the Isle of Man. Let an English general of repute undertake this task and organize the deportation without loss of time. The lack of liberties of prisoners of war, regardless of all rigours this status may include, would mean to these unfortunate wretches the exchange from their present life of horror to that of semi paradise. A redistribution of the deported could be organized within a period of 2–3 years without disturbing and counteracting the necessary regulated emigration work and without complicating the future decisions of the Evian [refugee] conference. Please, dear Lord Samuel, do all in your power to assist and make this plan possible. Please inform the PM and the members of the Cabinet. Action must be taken!

The letter was signed clearly in Wilfrid's bold script.[8]

Negotiations for the release of these people, through appeals from their families to the refugee committees in England and, thence, to the Home Office, was to drag on until after November.[9] Many of the prisoners went mad or died during the first days of imprisonment and torture, and hundreds died in the subsequent winter. According to Wilfrid's account of the stone quarries and tree lashings (a method of torture also used in Dachau, but where there were no stone quarries), the camp was Buchenwald.[10] In this camp and in Sachsenhausen, the nearest to Berlin, there were in June 1938 between 2,000 and 3,000 Jewish prisoners, as Wilfrid noted.[11]

The notion of sending a troop ship may have occurred to Wilfrid because a similar measure had been adopted by the British Government, to evacuate the White Russian General Wrangel's men, twenty years earlier. He knew that the Nazis were prepared to negotiate for the release of Jews if they left the country; there was already the precedent of Glick's negotiations, through the British Consul in Munich, in the previous year. Within a few months, the proposal for temporary camps was to become one of the main themes of German-Jewish representations to the outside world, and a camp set up in January 1939, for which Wilfrid and others negotiated, was to accommodate thousands of young men released from concentration camps.[12]

Samuel was not the only man in England to whom Wilfrid appealed for help. He sent another detailed report to Norman Bentwich, who passed it on to George Bell. In July, Bentwich wrote to Bell asking whether he had found it possible to approach 'any persons of goodwill and of some little influence with the German government about the slavery camps of which Wilfrid Israel wrote. Our German friends think that private intervention could help. I think, as I told Laura, that it would be best to keep out Wilfrid Israel's name in communicating his letter to anybody.'[13] The mention of Laura Livingstone may indicate that it was this doughty lady who brought the letter out of Germany. Bentwich, for his part, had attempted to visit Austria, but was turned back at the frontier.

Another prominent Englishman, Sir Robert Lindsay, Master of Balliol, who visited Germany that autumn, was handed a report on the concentration camps and immediately forwarded it to the Foreign Minister, Lord Halifax. Oliver Harvey, Halifax's private secretary, sent it back to Berlin enquiring of the Embassy counsellor, George Ogilvie Forbes, whether the Ambassador had any observations to offer. Forbes replied: 'While of course it is not possible for us in the Embassy here to obtain definite proof, still less to visit a concentration camp, I am afraid that a great deal of what is stated in the paper enclosed ... tallies with what we are told by Jews here and I consider it to be good *prima facie* evidence.' Referring to a specific visit to the Embassy by someone who was by now a frequent caller, Forbes added: 'Mr Israel in moderate language enlarged on the brutality with which Jews were treated on lines very similar to several statements in Lindsay's document.'[14] Another document dated four days later, submitted by 'Herr X', a member of a charitable organization in Germany, and including a report on 1,500 Jews in Buchenwald, sounds like a sequel to the appeal to Samuel:

Herr X entreats that some way may be found by which these men could be reached *en bloc* and placed in some kind of humane concentration camp in another country while their ultimate destination and fate were decided. He realizes that such a proposal is beyond the scope of any private refugee committees and needs international planning, but begs that it may at least receive careful and sympathetic consideration.[15]

Ogilvie Forbes's view was that there were only two ways to put an end to the persecution, since direct intervention was out of the question. One was to help the work of the Evian Committee, the refugee body formed in July; the other, to

put the Nazis into Coventry . . . in other words to decline to have cultural or social relations on the ground that their cruelties to Jews and political opponents make them unfit for decent international society. The Nazis would be most sensitive to this, which I presume is out of the question in view of the matters of high policy and the political repercussions which would be involved.[16]

Forbes presumed correctly. The correspondence was later minuted: 'To put the Germans in Coventry would be simply playing into the hands of the Nazi propaganda machine which would once more be able to raise a yowl about the wicked outside world under the thumb of World Jewry. It is a pity, because they deserve it.'[17]

But there were practical measures to be taken, and people prepared to take them. From this time onwards, the word went round among Berlin Jews that Wilfrid was the man who could get prisoners released from concentration camps and ensure that they left Germany within the two weeks demanded by the Gestapo, and that this was somehow connected with his British background.

Even for the ordinary emigrant, the bureaucratic procedures involved were formidable: to receive a passport the applicant had to prove that he or she had paid all taxes owing. For those wanting to leave Germany with more than the clothes on their backs, there were other papers governing the transfer of moveable property, which took three months to obtain. To obtain release from the camps, moreover, they had to prove that they had a valid visa for a foreign country: something which, in its turn, demanded proof of funds, and could be denied to anyone with a suspicious political background, the ostensible reason for many Jews' detention, or with a criminal record, often fabricated by the Nazis.

While the diplomats and foreign friends dithered, lesser people were patiently evolving a routine. In the British consulates throughout Germany, there were people who not only collected evidence from those who escaped from the camps, but who, knowing Germany far more closely than their superiors in the Embassy and familiar – as all consular officials are – with the local police system, were not deterred by considerations of high policy from dealing with Nazi officials. The British Consul in Munich, Carvell, had played a part in releasing Jews from Dachau the previous year; the British Consul in Frankfurt, R.T. Smallbones, was to do the same in November. But by far the most important figure was Frank Foley.

In a book written by one of those who owed their life to him, Foley is described as a 'small, pleasant man with white hair and red cheeks', who 'in his heart' was with the Jews.[18] Letters he wrote to German Jews, with whom he formed a strong bond during the period, like his reports to London, suggest an emotional, peppery man who at no time doubted the evil of Nazism or the truth of the stories he was told by his Jewish clients. Towards the end of the war, when the death camps were liberated, he wrote to Werner Senator:

> We are now reading about and seeing photographs of those places the names of which were so well known to us in the years before the war. Now the people here really and finally believe that the stories of 1938–9 were not exaggerated. Looking back, I feel grateful that our little office in Tiergartenstrasse was able to assist some – far too few – to escape in time.[19]

A German Jew working for British Intelligence, Hubert Pollack, who was closely associated both with Wilfrid and with Foley at this time, in a testimony written in 1944, the year after Wilfrid's death, stated that German Jews owed an unrecognized debt to Wilfrid Israel, and that 'the number of Jews saved from Germany would have been tens of thousands less had Captain Foley not sat in the consular office in the Tiergartenstrasse', a judgement – where Foley was concerned – confirmed at the Eichmann trial.[20] There were undoubtedly others who worked to release Jews from the camps, but the system evolved by Wilfrid, Pollack and Foley can be reconstructed; each was an essential link in the chain. Pollack had contacts in the Gestapo; Wilfrid had money, and direct links with sponsors abroad; Foley was the man in charge of issuing visas.

Hubert Pollack was a descendant of an old Prussian-Jewish family with English connections, and a classmate of Herbert Israel's in the Mommsen Gymnasium. He was employed as a correspondence clerk while studying law, as his family had been impoverished by post-war inflation. A specialist in public finance, he began working with the statistical office of the Reich in 1927. Subsequently, with a Berlin economics professor, he set up a statistical office for the Berlin Jewish Gemeinde (community organization) to enable the community to distribute its charity on a scientific basis. He had scarcely completed this job when Hitler took power and the community abolished the office, to reduce expenses, in April 1933. Pollack then opened an advisory office of his own for Jewish emigrants, and, after it was closed by the Gestapo in 1937, worked under Wilfrid at the Hilfsverein.

Pollack was a statistician, but, by his own account, one who carried a Mauser pistol and made clandestine appointments with Gestapo officials – not in the Prinz Albrechtstrasse headquarters, to which the leading Jewish officials were publicly summoned, but in cafés and back-streets where money could change hands smoothly. His contacts with the Gestapo went back to 1933, when he was asked by a Zionist colleague to investigate the arrest of her brother, a Polish-born communist, who had been taken to the notorious 'Columbia House' Storm Troopers' centre, and whose horribly mutilated body was later delivered to the family. As Pollack commented, to be a communist and an *Ostjude* together meant sure death. Beginning with an old acquaintance in the political police, Pollack swiftly built up a network of contacts among policemen and officials who, he later discovered, would produce virtually any document for suitable payment, either in cash or in valuables. The prices were surprisingly low. It was Pollack who knew of 'Schwarzer's' tailing of Wilfrid to England in 1935, and probably Foley who engineered his arrest until Wilfrid's work in London was finished.[21]

In his post-war testimony, Pollack makes no mention of his work for British Intelligence; nor does he suggest that Foley was other than a helpful consular official. He kept this information for a letter written to a leading member of Israeli Military Intelligence after Foley's death, asking for his help in inviting Foley's wife and daughter to a tree-planting ceremony in Foley's memory in the Judean Hills.[22]

'My work was mainly secret and brought me into contact with political agents of various types,' Pollack explained in his 1944 memoir. 'Besides my superior and friend, Wilfrid Israel, no one knew of my activities.' Wilfrid had not released him from his 'vow of silence', he wrote, and thus his account would be only partial. However, it is clear that Pollack was the essential intermediary between Wilfrid, Foley and the Gestapo, and in addition had contacts with other 'political agents' – whose identity becomes clearer at a later stage.

Wilfrid had at least two other sources of information about Nazi Party activities and police actions: Kurt Liepert, and an unnamed source in police headquarters who, according to British records, warned him of impending attacks on the firm. But it was clearly Pollack who was the go-between with the SS, together with a young Gentile communist who had a personal vendetta against the Nazis, as Pollack explains, and is probably identical with the young man (unnamed) mentioned in the

Reissner monograph who acted as intermediary between Wilfrid and the Sachsenhausen camp commander later in the year.[23]

People came to Wilfrid pleading for his help in releasing their relations from the camps; Wilfrid gave the necessary funds to Pollack; Pollack obtained the documents; and Foley granted visas to those who Wilfrid and Pollack told him were honest people whose name had been blackened by the Gestapo. This appears to have become standard procedure well before the Kristallnacht pogroms of November that year.

The relationship with Foley, moreover, was not entirely one-sided. Foley obtained information from the few well-placed Jewish businessmen in Berlin who still had contacts with Nazi administrators. One was Dolf Michaelis, a banker who took messages from leading anti-Nazis to their colleagues in exile, and gave information to MI5 agents in London; another was Wilfrid himself.[24] Pollack also suggests that he and Wilfrid kept Foley informed of any agents planted by the Gestapo in the lines of applicants for visas; this was probably the most dangerous aspect of their work.[25]

If Wilfrid had any British source of protection in Berlin, it was Foley. When Werner Behr was taken to a concentration camp, Wilfrid had him swiftly released; in late 1938, it was Foley who warned Behr's wife to leave Germany. When Friedrich Altmann arrived in Berlin, in early 1938, for several months' stay, ostensibly to buy machinery for the kibbutz, but in fact to help other Werkleute members and their parents leave Germany, and to smuggle out funds (inside a large doll), Foley provided him with a British passport, replacing his Palestinian one, which suggested he was a Jew, with one which enabled him to cross frontiers repeatedly without trouble. When Altmann was asked to report to the Gestapo on arrival in Germany, Foley told him to contact the Consulate within a few hours, promising that if he did not, he would personally take action. He also told him of a special compartment in trains leaving Berlin which he could enter if he was in danger.[26]

From the evidence of Wilfrid's private letters, it is clear that he remained in close contact with Foley until his death. He knew when Foley was posted to Oslo in 1940, and of Foley's intelligence activities in 1941. It was assuredly Foley's connection with Wilfrid which most satisfactorily explains the answer given to Ian Colvin, in 1954, by an unnamed intelligence source, who had worked with the British consulate in Berlin (possibly Foley himself): 'I am not going to tell you about Wilfrid Israel.'

From the Anschluss onwards, even in Berlin and Hamburg, Jewish businessmen were forced out of their offices. On 22 April 1938, Aryan firms were forbidden to help Jewish businessmen – thus closing one of the loopholes N. Israel, among others, had used. At the end of May, Schacht invited Max Warburg to a meeting and told him that Warburg could no longer remain a member of the German banking union, the Reichsanleihe Konsortium; Warburg resigned his position as director.[27] On 14 June, Jewish firms were ordered to register their holdings with a special office, a clear warning that further repression was in store. Street violence accompanied the message.

At a family council of war, the Israels decided to sell. Amy left Germany. She returned to England no longer the grand lady, but an ageing widow and a fugitive.

On 16 June, the Israels' London solicitors, Adler and Perowne, advised the Foreign Office that the firm was to be sold and requested that the Berlin Embassy oversee negotiations and the transfer of the proceeds of the sale to Britain. They were 'authorized to mention connections with Lord Samuel, particularly with regard to work which Mr Israel has done for the Jewish community in Germany'.[28]

But despite the diplomats' past attendance at Amy's birthday parties and 'Sundays' – 'Mrs Israel is well known to the embassy' was the comment from Berlin, with the 'well' crossed out on someone's second thought – and Samuel's 'connections', the Foreign Office refused to take the matter up with the German authorities since Wilfrid, as a German citizen, was not entitled to British protection.[29] Only subsequent proddings by the solicitors on Amy's behalf, after she had renounced German citizenship, extracted the promise of a watching brief.[30]

Meanwhile, Wilfrid had notice of an impending full-scale attack on the business. On 21 June, Ivone Kirkpatrick, Third Secretary at the Embassy, on a routine visit to Otto Furst von Bismarck, an official at the German Foreign Ministry, issued a guarded warning. Though the Embassy had no intention of intervening in German affairs, he said, it had come to the Ambassador's attention that an attack on N. Israel was contemplated; as the firm was heavily insured at Lloyds, such an action would cause 'tremors in the City', and might prove damaging to Anglo-German relations. After Kirkpatrick had left, Bismarck contacted the Gestapo and, according to the official record, the attack was averted.[31]

In July, Wilfrid and Herbert concluded negotiations with a well-known rival, Koester's 'Family Emporium'. Believing that his part was done, Herbert left Germany. But though the contract was signed on the day after Herbert's departure, the Economics Ministry withheld its agreement to the sale; though Wilfrid negotiated with two other firms, these sales, too, were blocked – despite the belated intervention of the

British Embassy's economic counsellor. The Nazis now clearly intended to take their revenge.[32]

N. Israel was foundering. In 1936, the number of those working at the firm had fallen to 1,300 employees; now it stood at less than 1,000. Wilfrid had evacuated some two-thirds of his Jewish employees, and many of the Gentile employees had left of their own accord, afraid of continuing to work for a Jewish firm. The *Daily Telegraph*, commenting on the proposed sale of the business, which had 'held out' longer than any other of the big Jewish firms, noted that 'a great part of the proceeds of the sale of the business will be devoted to a pension fund for the firm's Jewish employees'.[33]

The Nazis increased their pressures on the non-Nazi staff. Employees who had not joined the Nazi Party were threatened, and those married to Jews were systematically harassed. In August 1938, *Der Stürmer*, Streicher's obscene journal, devoted a whole page to a violent attack on the Israels and, in an article which was a black parody of Alberti's essays of forty years earlier, described how it had developed from 'a little pedlar's shop' 120 years before, as a result of the Israels' 'typically Jewish fraud and trickery'. Wilfrid and Herbert were described as Jewish 'extortioners' and 'exploiters of their Gentile employees'; the famous façade was photographed with the closing sales posters in its windows, with the *Stürmer*'s comment: 'This is how the Jew sucks his profits from the public.' The names and addresses of all the executives, Jews and non-Jews alike, were given in full: an open invitation to personal violence.[34]

By the autumn, there was still no official agreement to the sale; all Wilfrid's family, and most of his friends, were gone. Meanwhile, after the failure of the Evian conference the outlook for German Jewry at large looked blacker than ever.

The Evian conference, which took place in the second week of July 1938, had been eagerly awaited by the leaders of German Jewry, to whom it appeared to signal the first combined effort, with America taking the lead, to find a solution to the problem of German-Jewish refugees. But the conference took four months to organize, during which time the first mass assaults on German and Austrian Jews took place. Roosevelt's initial proposal for the international meeting had been little more than a public relations exercise, which did not even disguise the fact that the American administration had no intention of extending the immigration quotas.[35]

Before the conference even began, those most closely involved knew quite well that it was unlikely to produce results. The week before it opened, Lord Winterton, head of the British delegation, wrote to Lord

Halifax, the British Foreign Secretary: 'The more I go into the question, the more convinced I am that no emigration solution is possible unless the German government is prepared to relax the restrictions placed upon their Jewish nationals in the matter of taking their property out of Germany and Austria.'[36] On the day the conference opened, when Henderson, the British Ambassador, read a telegram to this effect from Halifax to Ribbentrop, the German Foreign Minister, Ribbentrop's answer was an uncompromising refusal: there would be no discussion of the export of Jewish capital. Moreover, he threatened that any anti-German propaganda at the conference would result in reprisals against the Jews in Germany.[37]

The British Foreign Office, which had initially criticized what it saw as an amateur approach to the entire problem by the United States, gradually warmed to the idea that aiding German Jews to emigrate to the Dominions might simultaneously, as Roger Makins, a young official, later put it, 'increase the prosperity of the colonial empire ... discharge such moral obligation as we might be thought to have towards the Jews, and ... take the pressure off Palestine'.[38] All this, however, depended on available financing; Winterton had dismissed the idea of an international loan at the outset, and knew that the refugee organizations could not possibly raise the necessary funds.[39] Where the Jewish organizations were concerned, the syndrome of late 1935 repeated itself. Disagreements between Zionists and non-Zionists prevented the appearance of a united Jewish delegation, Winterton having made it clear to Weizmann that he would have no special standing.[40] The Anglo-American organization, the Council for German Jewry, sent the mild-mannered, academic Bentwich; Samuel, with his usual caution, had consulted the Foreign Office as to whether leading members of the Council should attend, lest their presence indicate that the conference 'was being run by international Jews' and was accordingly advised to follow his instincts.[41] Thirty-nine refugee organizations competed for the attention of the sub-committees; they had ten minutes each to outline their plans. The result was chaos.[42]

At the Evian conference, country after country refused to admit persecuted German and Austrian Jews, a refusal which, seen retroactively, condemned most of them to death. But only those inside Germany knew the meaning of Nazi terror, and even those sympathetic to the Jews and their sufferings thought mass emigration impossible without financial concessions on the part of Germany; the *Manchester Guardian*, for instance, wrote, during the conference: 'It is obvious that Germany must relax the severity of her laws on the export of capital; that she should expect the rest of the world to receive and settle thousands of paupers in the next few years is carrying international co-operation to the limits of lunacy.'[43]

However, only the German Jews knew that the Nazis were prepared to bargain over their fate with the West. Their official appearance at the conference was deliberately low key, their official memorandum no more than a polite cough to draw attention to their presence; in public they had to keep up this act, for fear of reprisals on their return. But behind the scenes they tried to convince the sceptical diplomats that Ribbentrop's was not the last word, and that German Jews could be silent partners in an economic arrangement between the Third Reich and the democratic countries outside.

Contacts between the Economics Ministry and the German-Jewish leadership had clearly been renewed, and the idea of combining forced Jewish emigration with a boost for German exports was once more circulating in Nazi financial circles. This process probably began towards the end of 1937, but halted temporarily with the dismissal of Schacht from the Ministry in November. This would explain a curious letter, signed by Otto Hirsch of the Reichsvertretung and Wilfrid Israel in February 1938, and addressed to the Council of German Jewry, asking for a new fund-raising campaign to be launched to help emigration, since foreign funds were necessary to supplement funds sanctioned by the 'authorities' – details of which could not be revealed until 'the authorities had spoken'. The letter, unlike official Reichsvertretung correspondence, is written on unheaded paper.[44]

The attitude of the Council for German Jewry before the Evian conference, however, was that they had done enough for German Jewry and that, henceforth, German-Jewish property should be mobilized to pay for emigration and settlement. Voluntary contributions could not assist large-scale emigration, and any financial plans would have to be supported by governments.[45]

Two days after the conference had formally ended, Otto Hirsch and Siegfried Moses, heading the German-Jewish delegation, told Lord Winterton and Sir Michael Palairet, the British delegates, at a private meeting, that they believed the German Government would allow 200,000 German Jews and 100,000 Austrians to leave with a third of their financial resources. The emigrants, they said, would be prepared to share whatever sums the authorities agreed to; a new departure in terms of German-Jewish plans. Other funds could be provided by foreign currency obtained from returning German immigrants and the expansion of the transfer agreement.[46] Other German-Jewish delegates also put various financial schemes before the British and American representatives; but there was no confirmation yet of German willingness to open talks.

All that emerged from Evian was the creation of the Inter Governmental Committee for Refugees,[47] whose appointed head was a seventy-year-old American corporation lawyer brought back from retirement, George Rublee. German Jewry's hopes now centred on this rather nebulous figure, and they pursued him eagerly with proposals for ways and means of extracting their money from the Nazis' hands. But it was to take several more months before he was invited to Berlin.

Wilfrid had not joined the delegation; but the post-Evian period marked the beginning of his own efforts, on behalf of his community, with the British Government. His first approach was made to Halifax through his old Quaker friend, Corder Catchpool, who accompanied the dying Clifford Allen to Berlin in the late summer of 1938. On his return to London, Catchpool sent an appeal from 'Wilfrid Israel ... the principal director of the Jewish Hilfsverein in Berlin', to Halifax, to the Board of Deputies of British Jews, and – yet again – to Samuel.[48]

The ability of the Hilfsverein to cope with the predicament of German Jewry, Wilfrid told Catchpool, had been maintained until that spring, but the last six months had seen 'a savage tightening of the screw', with Nazi edicts 'disabling' nearly 50 per cent of the remaining Jews in Germany. High hopes, he said, had been entertained

> that Evian conference might regularize relief measures ... might achieve by direct negotiations with the Reich government some agreement for controlling and humanizing the application of a policy aimed at driving ultimately the whole Jewish population from Germany. There was never any real prospect of modifying the policy itself.

But the result of the conference had been, Wilfrid said, 'a catastrophic setback'. This was not because he or others had estimated that the West would accept destitute Jews. He thought neither overseas countries, nor the 'saturated' states of Europe, had any desire to contribute, but had made a token gesture to please Roosevelt. What the German Jews had hoped for, he stressed, was an approach regarding the financing of emigration. Instead, he said, 'some circles in the Reich experienced malicious enjoyment at the spectacle of others attempting ... to deal with the problems ... and a satisfaction at their failure'. Only a fresh approach, 'both idealistic and practical', could save German Jewry. Wilfrid suggested that one form such help might take was 'the addition of clauses to existing trade agreements between the various nations and Germany [Brazil, Argentina, the USA, Great Britain and South Africa were mentioned] whereby a certain percentage of foreign exchange accruing to the Reich would be earmarked for the use overseas of Jewish refugees' – roughly what Eric Phipps had suggested three years earlier. He concluded by arguing that

> there is a close relation between Jewish persecution and the wider international situation, including the imminent danger of war over Czechoslovakia. The extent to which the treatment of the Jews and other excesses of National Socialism have set up a barrier preventing genuine friendship between the British and German people ... can hardly be overestimated.

But at this stage German-Jewish warnings were not taken seriously. Ribbentrop's outright refusal to discuss the export of Jewish capital was taken as the Nazis' last word. Moreover, the Foreign Office view was not that the Germans intended to expel their Jews, but that they wished to despoil them and keep them 'as a helot class'. The friction the Jewish question caused between Britain and Germany was soon to be dramatically demonstrated; but for the moment, the policy of non-involvement appeared to be paying off.

Two weeks later, on his way to the United States, Max Warburg confirmed the desperate situation of German Jewry. While he agreed, during a visit to the Foreign Office, that Rublee would not gain a hearing in Berlin while the Czech crisis was unresolved, like the others, he thought that a possible solution to the problem of Jewish funds could be an expanded German exports scheme, and he met, to discuss this, with Rublee and Myron Taylor, Roosevelt's delegate to the Evian Committee. Warburg added that on a recent visit to the German Foreign Ministry, he had warned officials there that violent expulsion would be counterproductive, and that they should aim at an exodus of not more than 50,000 Jews a year.[49]

Whatever surreptitious talks had been held were frozen during the Czechoslovakian crisis, culminating in the Munich agreement signed on 30 September 1938. But after Chamberlain's triumphant return to London, the Nazi Government put out feelers regarding the export of German-Jewish capital. The approach was still not official; and the method aroused great suspicion among the diplomats. For Rublee, however, they confirmed what he had already been told by Warburg and other German Jews. Before long, the link between German trade and Jewish emigration again became the focus of rescue plans, as it had been in late 1935, though it was not openly stated Nazi policy until December.

The ideas, which, as the Foreign Office commented, were transferred through 'dubious sources', clearly originated once more with Schacht at the Reichsbank. According to what Dr Puhl, Schacht's deputy, told Frederick Leith Ross of the British Treasury in late November, the Reichsbank, after Munich, put up financial proposals to the Nazi leadership for the reduction of armaments expenditure and a renewed exports drive, which also involved a plan for relaxation of exchange control restrictions. The plan had gone up to Hitler, Puhl said, was returned 'with quite a good instruction from him', and this encouraged Puhl to reconsider a plan he had prepared 'long ago'. It was based on putting the property of German Jews under a holding company in Germany, the transfer of which could be carried out if the Jewish community abroad would raise a loan, in foreign exchange, on the security of Reichsmark assets in Germany; the rate at which it could be transferred would depend on the possibility of securing additional exports to foreign countries.[50]

In October, all this was unknown in London and Washington; Rublee had not been invited to Berlin. But some German-Jewish leaders had word, at least, of what the Nazis were planning. Nothing else explains the background to Wilfrid's talk to Roger Makins, the Evian Committee secretary, in Berlin in mid-October and the proposals framed by Rublee later that month.[51]

Makins was literally the only young and energetic man involved in the Evian Committee's deliberations. He thought Myron Taylor, Roosevelt's envoy, naïve and inexperienced, and Winterton, Rublee and Bérenger, the French delegate, a herd of 'pachyderms', cumbersome and slow moving.[52] In theory, he understood the German Jews' impatience; but in practice, he had no answer to make to Wilfrid's plea for urgent action.

Wilfrid once more described the camps, the suicides, the impending collapse of relief projects. But the remedies he suggested went beyond anything that had been proposed so far, and all Makins could do was to protest that Wilfrid's suggestions 'presented difficulties', and to refer them back to his superiors in London.

Makins could not have known the background to Wilfrid's first proposals, that 100,000 Jews a year should emigrate (twice the number Warburg had put to Winterton in London barely a month earlier), and that 'Jewish bankers' would find part of the finance required. In fact, it was the Gestapo that was now insisting on the figure of 100,000 – which Wilfrid could hardly tell Makins[53] – and even when the Foreign Office had news, a little later, of three Jewish bankers who were conferring in Amsterdam with Fishboeck of the Economics Ministry, the information came to them in such a roundabout manner as to cast doubts on its veracity.[54]

Wilfrid's most specific proposals related to the American quota. The quota could be filled retroactively and future quotas could be anticipated, he suggested, and other countries should transfer their unfilled balance to German refugees. Makins parried the first two requests 'for the United States', and he was no more optimistic about the acceptance of Wilfrid's repeated request for labour camps to be set up in the Isle of Man.

In the light of Ribbentrop's official refusal to co-operate, Wilfrid's insistence that an 'energetic personality' sent out to Berlin could, with the help of German Jews, produce results, must have appeared far-fetched to Makins at this stage. In addition, Wilfrid's warnings that the Nazis were even now preparing to expel half the Polish-Jewish population could only have reinforced the British apprehension that whatever they proposed, the Nazis would do precisely what they wished.

Wilfrid's suggestions, regarding the American quota and the idea of temporary camps, were temporarily shelved; both were to be revived after the events of the following month.[55] But his hints that the German authorities were ready for discussions were confirmed, from an odd source, as soon as Makins returned to London.

There he was told that Rublee had been approached by a British fascist and 'ex-master mariner', named Commander Godman, who advised him that the best chance of doing business with the Nazis over the Jews was to deal directly with Goering or his 'entourage'.[56] But other rumours spread by this unsavoury go-between were to increase British scepticism that any plan put forward by the Nazis was to be taken at its face value. Distaste for the Nazis' style of negotiations had not prevented the pursuit of the policy of appeasement; where the exodus of Jews was concerned, it was to prove a formidable obstacle.

Rublee, the corporation lawyer, was less deterred by shady informants than the diplomats. He now came up with a proposal which was considered in several capitals by financial and political experts – who looked at it sceptically – and somehow reached Berlin, where it was enthusiastically approved.

Rublee's plan was strongly reminiscent of all the ideas which had been circulated, through Warburg and others, since 1933. The Jewish boycott of German goods would be withdrawn if the Germans agreed to transfer emigrant capital to the value of half the foreign exchange proceeds of increased exports. Jewish emigrants would receive dollar bonds in exchange for their property in Germany, the money to be raised by a corporation outside.[57]

This plan was strongly criticized in London and Washington, though not dismissed entirely as a basis for negotiations. The British experts thought that the Nazis would wish for additional and hidden benefits;[58] the boycott was an unknown quantity and no one knew if the Jews would, or could, 'withdraw' it.[59] Cordell Hull, the American Secretary of State, suspected that the plan would create the impression, 'though not based on fair reasoning or controlled feeling', that the Jews were responsible for unfair competition.[60] But now a debate had been launched on whether foreign governments could make any trade concessions, however small, to Germany, as a means of releasing the German Jews.[61] The details of the Rublee plan reached Berlin on 14 November, together with a similar proposal by Sir Otto Niemeyer, English representative at the Bank of International Settlements, and it was warmly approved by the Nazis, as well it might have been.[62]

This debate, which might have produced results three years earlier, ended almost as soon as it began. For barely three weeks after the Rublee plan appeared on the desks of treasuries in several countries, and just before it was approved in Berlin, the situation in Germany suddenly changed.

For while German bureaucrats and Jewish bankers were exchanging financial proposals, and while Rublee, somewhat out of his depth in a world of hypothetical funds and concrete threats, was working on the Nazis' own proposals, other men in the Nazi leadership were drawing up plans for a campaign of destruction which would make rescue work more urgent and turn the negotiations into a barely veiled plan of blackmail and ransom: the November pogroms.

8
Command Performance

Wilfrid's prediction to Makins that the Nazis would shortly expel Polish-born Jews from Germany was borne out ten days later, on 24 October, when 15,000 people were rounded up and driven over the frontier into Poland: the first mass deportation of Jews in the Nazi era. German Jews, too, were menaced, according to a rumour circulating in Berlin, which reached Jews with official contacts, warning of a 'terrible outbreak' in the offing.[1]

On 7 November, a young Polish Jew living in Paris, Herszel Grynszpan, whose family was among those deported to Poland, entered the German Embassy and shot the First Secretary, Ernst vom Rath. Rath's death, two days later, triggered the Kristallnacht pogrom, and the subsequent decrees aimed at the total social and economic destruction of German Jewry. Grynszpan's act has generally been represented as a desperate deed. The Jewish leadership in Berlin believed otherwise; they told a visitor that 'the course now taken by the German Government was prepared and planned many months ago, and after all the preparations were completed, Grynszpan gave the starting shot'.[2]

On the morning of 8 November, therefore, Wilfrid called at the British Embassy in Berlin as representative of German Jewry to repudiate Grynszpan's act and to warn of imminent reprisals against the Jewish population.[3]

On the afternoon of the following day, Wilfrid received a warning from Kurt Liepert, the N. Israel Nazi works' foreman, who advised him not to open the business on the following day. Shortly afterwards, Chaim Weizmann, in London, received a telephone call from Germany, asking him to inform the Foreign Office that 'the situation had changed dangerously during the last twenty-four hours', and that, in the opinion of German Jews, the only way to save the situation was for some 'prominent non-Jewish Englishman' to go to Berlin immediately. Weizmann phoned William Strang at the Foreign Office – who noticed his obvious distress – and a cable was sent by Halifax to Ogilvie Forbes, *chargé d'affaires* in Berlin. Meanwhile, Weizmann had also contacted Lord Lothian, who was prepared to go to Berlin, but was rapidly discouraged by Chamberlain and Halifax.[4]

Ogilvie Forbes's answer was only received after midday on 10 November, when the pogrom was at its height, and although Forbes had already confirmed that morning that 'anti-Jewish rioting on an unprecedented scale' had broken out late the previous night in Berlin and all over Germany, he advised Strang that it was neither in British nor in Jewish interests to intervene. That evening, Strang telephoned the Embassy in Berlin and was told by Ivone Kirkpatrick that the pogrom had been a 'deliberately organized operation' which was now lessening; Goebbels had issued a statement that the demonstrations were to stop, and the Jewish question be regulated by law. Kirkpatrick added that, for Berliners, 'It is rather like watching a sideshow at an exhibition, where you pay so much to break as much crockery as you like.'[5]

During the night of 9 November and on into the next day, ninety-one Jews were killed, and synagogues all over Germany were burned to the ground; fire brigades stood by only in order to stop the flames from spreading. By the time Kirkpatrick spoke to Strang, the mass arrests of Jews had begun; over the next few days, 30,000 men were taken from their homes and from streets, offices and shops, to the concentration camps of Dachau, Buchenwald and Sachsenhausen. Ernst Cramer was one of a trainload of Jews in 'protective custody', taken to Weimar Station,

> exhausted, hungry and dazed. There all the passengers, men between eighteen and seventy, were herded in great confusion by the guards into the station subway, where members of the SS Deaths Head formations hit us for about twenty minutes with sticks, steel rods and rifle butts.

They were driven in trucks to a parade ground at Buchenwald, where they had to stand without moving until dusk.

> The whole day long men were dragged out of the ranks at random and beaten before our eyes, hung up with their hands handcuffed behind their backs, or strapped on to the dreaded 'horse' and beaten with rubber truncheons. Others had to pick up the old and the weak who had collapsed and carry them into the washhouse, which became a mortuary ... during the course of that first night many went mad ... some were driven against the electrified wire fence and during the night, two were also drowned in the latrine. But officially they all died a 'natural death'.[6]

In Kirkpatrick's 'sideshow', Jewish shops and stores were methodically vandalized and looted and their windows smashed. Thousands of men, who had evaded arrest, feared to return to their homes and hid in the woods which surrounded Berlin, in what was recorded as one of the coldest winters of the century. The Nazis twisted the knife; on the night following the pogrom, the actors in the Jewish theatre were ordered to play to a completely empty house.[7]

Despite Wilfrid's warnings to the outside world, he had not taken Liepert's advice where his own business was concerned. The heavy iron shutters were opened on the morning of 10 November, despite the havoc of the previous night and the continuing assaults on Jewish property. Since 1933, Wilfrid had refused to compromise with Liepert, and he clearly believed that he could count on promises from highly placed police officials. During the morning, N. Israel was the only Jewish establishment in Berlin around which a protective cordon of policemen was deployed.[8] When he saw that this was done, Wilfrid left to help his colleagues in the Reichsvertretung. But at about two in the afternoon, the police guard was suddenly withdrawn. The assault began soon afterwards.

Young men in work clothes, armed with sticks and iron bars, followed by SS men in uniform, pushed their way past the commissionaires; they had been assembled from their places of work all over Berlin. Bruno Wolff, who had worked for N. Israel as interior decorator and was now employed by their rivals, Hertzog, noticed that one of his fellow employees went out in the morning and complained, on his return about midday, that the Israel firm was still intact. After lunch he returned to the attack.

Irmgard Smurka, a cashier on the ground floor, heard shouts of 'Jews out! All Jews out!' Frieda Grimm, the staff nurse, a Gentile employee known for her anti-Nazi politics, ran, together with some tens of employees, out of a side door, across a courtyard, to the sanctuary of the priests' lodge of the nearby Nikolaikirche. As she went, she heard an architect, who had been working on repairs to the building, stammer to an SS man, 'But I'm a party member!' 'So much the worse for you – working for a Jew!' was the answer.

The young wreckers set to work as the SS guards rounded up the Jewish staff. They smashed display cases, tore down lengths of silk from the stands and trampled clothes and materials underfoot. They went up, floor by floor, scattering the frightened employees, and hurled furniture into the main stairwell from the galleries. They took typewriters from the administrative offices on the second floor and pitched them through the windows. Hans Reissner, in the secretary's office next to the directors' suite, noticed that their faces were completely expressionless. Rita Luedecke, Wilfrid's young half-Jewish secretary, hurried ahead of the SS detachment to his office, took all his personal papers and files and hid them. When the wreckers finally reached the directors' suite, they smashed the chandeliers and slashed the oil paintings of Nathan, Jacob and Berthold, ignoring two women employees, one of whom had fainted, in a corner.

The SS men clearly had a quota, for not all the Jews in the firm were arrested; the SS left first, while the wreckers continued. Someone had called the state police, and soon a fresh detachment arrived, but it was soon clear to the staff that this was to keep the crowds back from the pavements, now covered with debris and glass, and not to protect the firm. By now, winter darkness was falling, and the wreckers tired. Bruno Wolff's Nazi colleague returned to work well satisfied: 'Now we've finished that one off as well; another Jew's done for,' he reported.

Meanwhile, Wilfrid had been reached. He hurried back, calmed the employees and immediately checked the names of the Jews arrested. Then he drove back to the Bendlerstrasse with Rita Luedecke; she recalled that he was totally calm and controlled. He quickly found out that the men had been taken to Sachsenhausen and began negotiating for their release. The procedure was familiar to him. According to Reissner, the camp commander of Sachsenhausen, Hermann Baranowski, was assured by an intermediary of unlimited credit at the Israel store, in return for the release of the men arrested.[9] During the Air Ministry conference of 12 November, Goering, totting up the damage, complained that it would have been better to kill more Jews and waste less foreign currency on imported glass. He was asked whether the big Jewish department stores should be left open over Christmas. Certainly, Goering replied, 'otherwise we'd be in a fine mess'.[10] Baranowski did all his Christmas shopping at N. Israel and no bill was sent. Nor were Wilfrid's employees the only Jews he released. Hans Reichmann, one of the leaders of the liberal organization Central Verein, told his wife that Wilfrid's name was a legend at this time among the prisoners at Sachsenhausen, and his office was besieged by families asking for his intervention.

Wilfrid opened an office in the empty mansion in the Hildebrandstrasse to deal with the emigration of the remaining 200 Jews in the firm; they were also given the equivalent of two years' salary in cash. Among the friends who helped him find jobs for his employees abroad was a young Australian constitutional lawyer from Oxford, Richard Latham. Latham caused a diplomatic incident a few months later by vouching for the entrance into Holland of 2,000 Czech refugees, and was to become an energetic champion of the refugees in his wartime role as clerk in the Foreign Office. But he knew no German. A young secretary on the Israel staff, Ursula Borchard, went with him to interpret. It took some time to find a café on the Kurfurstendamm which would allow Jews inside, and where he could interview the women candidates.[11]

The only employee who did not take advantage of his help was Irmgard Smurka, the young cashier married to a Gentile. Wilfrid offered both a passage to England, but Herr Smurka thought he could do better, in Sweden. When the war broke out, the Smurkas were trapped.

There was little time left to salvage the Israel family inheritance. The Nazis now decreed that all Jewish firms were to be 'Aryanized' by the end of the year, and Wilfrid received little support from the British Embassy. When the damage to the firm was reported to London, the official view was that, as Amy's interest was in the ground the building stood on, it could not have been said to have been affected by the attack. Official protests rang hollow, since, as a Foreign Office minute makes clear, the complaints regarding the property of British subjects to the German Foreign Ministry were worded in such a way 'that the Wilhelmstrasse should not be obliged to make any reply beyond a formal acknowledgement'.[12]

The British press, however, took an interest in the Israel case. In a Reuters' interview with Goebbels the week after the pogrom, he was asked how German-Jewish firms in which British capital was invested – N. Israel, for instance – would be affected by the new economic laws. Goebbels replied that foreign interests would be respected.[13] When, on 6 December, the German Government issued an order sequestering all Jewish real and personal property, Ogilvie Forbes immediately enquired whether the order applied to British subjects. When advised that it did, he reminded the German official of Goebbels's statement and was blandly told that this 'had no legal basis'.[14]

There was nothing, now, that could be done to prevent the forced sale of the firm at a fraction of its worth – the Economics Ministry now having withdrawn its previous objections to the sale. Wilfrid saved what he could of the family's personal possessions and investments; but the Israel fortune was lost.[15]

On 6 February 1939, a parting message was handed to all the N. Israel employees: 'At this moment of parting, after generations of work together, I wish to express once more my deepest appreciation and personal thanks to all my co-workers, men and women, who together with us have served the firm of N. Israel so loyally and for so long – Wilfrid Israel.'[16]

Five days later, a poster appeared all over Berlin, headed: 'What all Berlin is talking about! The N. Israel takeover!' It concluded: 'All are cordially invited to the inauguration of the renamed "Das Haus in

Centrum". We shall do our best to gain your sympathy and goodwill and to satisfy the most demanding customers. Heil Hitler!'[17]

German Jewry now faced total destitution. All but a handful of Jews employed in Jewish organizations were deprived of the ability to earn their living. A huge fine was imposed on the community; the Nazis began confiscating their possessions and even their homes. Their children were banned from state schools, making their segregation complete. Even their self-sufficient Jewish world was smashed: the training camps were closed; the young Zionists were in concentration camps, and the Jewish press was closed down, as were all Jewish offices – except for those in charge of emigration, which were soon reopened. An envoy from Palestine wrote: 'German Jewry are panic-stricken. They know that they are lost,' and added, 'They are not sure that other countries will take them out of Germany, and so far, they are not yet convinced that world Jewry will maintain them in Germany or pay the ransom hoped for by the German Government. Therefore, there are Jews in Germany who think that the intention is to arrange for a second plot and then to make short work of the Jews in Germany, or a considerable part of them.'[18]

Most Jewish leaders were in the camps or in hiding. Appeals to the Nazis by Baeck and Otto Hirsch after the Kristallnacht were fruitless; no one in authority would even speak to them and, before long, Hirsch too was in detention.

This was Wilfrid Israel's hour. With the help of the Quakers and leading British Jews, he launched the exodus of 10,000 children to England; he kept up pressure for the establishment of a transit camp to accommodate the young men in the concentration camps – which saved another 8,000 lives; in the Hilfsverein, with his colleagues, he worked to transport Jews to every corner of the world; and he urged on the British Foreign Office two further plans of rescue.

In London, all kinds of rumours were reaching the Council for German Jewry; the British press had carried graphic accounts of the pogrom and its aftermath, their correspondents briefed by Leo Baeck in his apartment at Frank Foley's home, and by Wilfrid and his Hilfsverein aide Arnold Horwitz, who talked to correspondents in the streets.[19] But there was no direct contact. On 15 November, Wilfrid cabled the Council details of the problems facing the community, and proposed the immediate rescue of German-Jewish children and young people up to the age of seventeen;[20] an Anglo-Jewish deputation led by Lord Samuel, and which included Chaim Weizmann, Lionel de Rothschild and the Chief Rabbi, hastily put together a petition incorporating his cable and went to see the Prime Minister, Neville Chamberlain. Chamberlain's initial response was non-committal, but the proposals were debated at a cabinet meeting on the following day.[21]

Meanwhile, the Council appealed to the Quakers for their help; no Jew was prepared to go to Germany. The Quakers selected five people to go to Berlin and make contact with Wilfrid. They travelled via Amsterdam, where Wilfrid was supposed to contact them; but receiving no word, they went on to Berlin where he met them and explained exactly what they were to do. Under his direction, they set out for Jewish communities all over Germany: to East Prussia, Saxony, Silesia, Central Germany and the Rhineland. In each community, they made contact with the Jewish women leaders of the Frauenbund, who – their men being imprisoned – were now running all the relief organizations, and with the Protestant pastors who were involved in helping the non-Aryans. The Quakers handed out urgent financial help, where possible; one of them returned to London within days. His report made it clear that German Jewry wanted immediate help for emigration, not relief on the spot.[22]

On 21 November, Samuel led another delegation – this time made up both of Jewish and non-Jewish representatives of groups concerned with refugees – to the Home Secretary, Samuel Hoare. Samuel was accompanied by Lola Hahn Warburg, Wilfrid's colleague in Youth Aliya, who had left Germany in the autumn, and was henceforth to be one of the chief workers for child rescue in England, and Bertha Bracey, of the British Quakers, who brought Ben Greene, the Quaker who had returned to deliver first-hand evidence. Greene testified to the plea of the German parents and their readiness to part with their children.[23]

Speaking in the House of Commons that evening, Hoare announced that the Government had agreed to the admission of refugee children, quoting Greene's evidence; he added that the Government had extended its consular machinery in Germany and facilitated immigration procedures; passports and visa requirements were waived, and 1,000 applications a day were being received at the Home Office.[24]

This was the beginning of the exodus of German children, both Jewish and 'non-Aryan'. Professor Dennis Cohen, head of the Emigration Department of the Council for German Jewry, was sent to Berlin, where he worked with Wilfrid, organizing the first transport of children to Britain.[25] Meanwhile, the other Quaker envoys were reporting on their meetings with Wilfrid, their man in Berlin, Roger Carter, Laura Livingstone, and Hanna Karminski of the Jewish Frauenbund, who headed the new German-Jewish committee, organized to speed the children's emigration. Their account mentions that Wilfrid 'was evidently suffering under a great burden of responsibility and work', and praised the 'speed and efficiency with which the work of the children's emigration was tackled on the German side, in spite of the difficulties'. The mothers in each region of Germany 'leapt unanimously at the chance.' Fathers 'could generally not be consulted': they were still in the camps.[26] Ben Greene, returning from a second visit to Germany, reported in December that the Jewish suicide rate was now so heavy that 'the Mainz town authorities have turned off the gas in every Jewish house'; the Jews were threatened by starvation, but they had begged him not to allow promises of relief to postpone emigration. Local relief was pointless, Greene insisted; to keep up the physical contact with Germany was essential.[27]

The first party of children from Germany – 200 in all – arrived in Harwich from the Hook of Holland on 2 December. Half were from an orphanage in Berlin, 'which was burnt down', as the London *Times* put it; they had left at twenty-four hours' notice, bringing one mark and two bags of clothing with them. Most of the children were bewildered, though reporters said that 'a dozen of the youths surprised the staff [of the hostel] by appearing from their huts in bathing costumes and plunging into the open air swimming-pool before they had breakfast'.[28] The hostel 'New Herrlingen' was run by Elisabeth Rotten's friend, Anna Essinger.[29]

The Home Office, at this stage, had agreed to admit 5,000 children as a first batch; but by mid-December, the Colonial Secretary reported to the Government that the Jewish Agency had asked for 21,000 additional certificates to be issued, 10,000 of them for German child refugees. The Government rejected the request, but decided that the 10,000 children could be admitted to England if the refugee organizations would guarantee their maintenance.[30] No limit was ever placed on the number of children who could enter England, which depended on the speed at which the refugee organizations submitted the thousands of applications and the Home Office processed them.[31] Regulations which changed frequently, arguments over financing, and the chaotic disorganization in the refugee offices in London, meant that many sponsors began to suspect deliberate obstruction.[32]

At the Berlin end, the pace seemed maddeningly slow, and by mid-December, the Quaker envoys reported bitterness following the first gratitude and elation.[33] There were many stops and starts: on 1 January, the transports were stopped completely for lack of funds but for 150 urgent cases of adolescent boys in concentration camps;[34] at the end of that month, children from Danzig were held up for two months while the authorities in London bickered over financing;[35] and in March there were fresh delays when the Government issued new regulations – among them, a guarantee from sponsors to cover the children's post-war re-migration.[36] To add to the confusion, German parents who received visas sometimes fled taking children whose names were already on the lists, forgetting to tell the organizers.

Josiah Wedgwood, a British MP who personally sponsored 222 refugees, argued bitterly, in the summer, that the poor and friendless would be left behind;[37] only the success of a broadcast appeal for funds on 8 December 1938 by the former British Prime Minister, Stanley Baldwin, which brought in funds from Jews and non-Jews alike, and the many English volunteers who came forward to offer homes to strange children, kept the scheme alive.[38]

The scenes of arrival were often tragic: sometimes the children were herded together in large halls where sponsors would pick out the children they found attractive, leaving the others to institutions. Most observers noted the children's unnatural calm; one described how the sponsor's first act was to tear the labels off the children before taking them away – the adults were in tears, the children dry-eyed. Youth Aliya children came with the rest, and many were dispersed. When a group did stay together, it found an incongruous home on the Scottish estate of the Balfour family, their classroom a ballroom with gold-framed mirrors from ceiling to floor.

Few of the children, whether in foster homes or groups, were to see their parents again, and many were haunted by the feeling that they had deserted them.[39] About half the 60,000 Jewish children in the Third Reich escaped from Germany; of those, nearly one-third reached England on the children's transports.[40]

The admission of children to Britain was both a humanitarian gesture and a political move designed to lessen pressure on Palestine. But if the British Government hoped that the United States would follow its example, it hoped in vain. American Quakers who also visited Germany and were briefed by Wilfrid and his colleagues in the Frauenbund – and who won a promise of support from Heydrich for their emigration work – also attested to the children's plight when they returned home;[41] but the Wagner Rogers Bill for the admission of 20,000 children was defeated before it could reach Congress. While nearly 10,000 German children had reached Britain by the outbreak of war, only 433 children who left without their families, many of whom had emigrated before the pogroms of November 1938, reached the United States under various voluntary schemes.[42]

Meanwhile, Wilfrid's proposal to allot unused places from the British immigrant quota to America to German refugees was reconsidered at a meeting of British ministers on 14 November. On the following day, Halifax told the American Ambassador, Joseph P. Kennedy, that he had instructed the British Ambassador in Washington, Sir Ronald Lindsay, to 'put the point to the State Department'. Though Kennedy informed Halifax that legislation would be required for the diversion of a portion of the quota for Jewish use, as for any other change in the German quota, the proposal was not withdrawn; but Lindsay sabotaged the plan, apparently on his own initiative, in a conversation with Sumner Welles, the American Secretary of State. Welles's account of the meeting makes it clear that he accepted Lindsay's personal repudiation of the British proposal with relief, reminding the envoy that Roosevelt had no intention of increasing the German quota and adding that it was 'his very strong impression that the responsible leaders among American Jews would be the first to urge that no change in the present quota for German Jews be made'. Lindsay's own account of the meeting made no mention of his own part in suppressing the proposal, but stressed Welles's argument about Jewish opposition, expressed because increased Jewish immigration 'would have the effect of increasing anti-semitic feeling in America'. Thus Wilfrid's proposal was revived, only to be defeated by a diplomatic exercise using the arguments of his fellow Jews.[43]

American Jewry had failed to press for a relaxation of the immigration laws, or to argue that unfilled quotas from previous years be filled retroactively. They had made no gesture comparable to that of British Jewry's offer of financial guarantees. Their silence on the immigration question contrasted markedly with their loud protests over the boycott. For whatever reason – local anti-semitism and the economic depression were obvious factors – they had been reluctant to provide affidavits to enable the quota to be filled by those Jews who could not prove they would not become public charges.[44] Now, despite the Kristallnacht reports, there was no change in their attitude. Welles's remarks to Lindsay came four days after Samuel Rosenman, a member of Roosevelt's circle and leader of the American-Jewish Congress, was approached on the question of the quota. His answer was: 'I do not believe it either desirable or practicable to recommend any change in the quota provision of our immigration law.'[45] American Jewry took its lead loyally from the American administration. No better proof could have been adduced that the existence of a world Jewish conspiracy was a product of the anti-semitic imagination.

Wilfrid's repeated proposals for temporary camps had more success. The pogroms and the incarceration of many more young Jews sent Wilfrid back to the British Embassy on 17 November, on behalf of the Reichsvertretung, to ask formally that Britain do all possible 'to accelerate the emigration of Jews from Germany, and particularly those who had been driven from their homes – about ten to fifteen thousand – and install them in temporary camps whence they could be evacuated in due course to their country of destination.'[46]

At first the Foreign Office made no response, save to argue that the question of large-scale settlement was already under consideration by the Evian Committee, and that temporary measures for 'relief' were minor issues.[47]

But two weeks later, Wilfrid's appeal was reinforced by the return to England of an odd emissary, whom the Council for German Jewry had sent out to Berlin after the Kristallnacht, and who now impressed everyone in London with his first-hand knowledge and heroism. This was Sir Michael Bruce, the Scottish soldier of fortune, who was now working as a stunt man. He had been introduced by the Jewish Odeon cinema chain owner, Oscar Deutsch, to Samuel, the Rothschilds, and Laski, who sent him to contact Wilfrid in Berlin and bring back first-hand information.

Bruce's swashbuckling account of his mission, complete with secret meetings, car chases across Berlin, and howling German crowds slavering for Jewish blood during the Kristallnacht, was largely invented, as was his preposterous claim to the Foreign Office, on his return, that he had 'more or less had to take control' of Jewish affairs in Berlin.[48] The record shows that he arrived in Berlin well after the pogrom ended, and his 'eye-witness' account, quoted in several histories of the period, was second-hand.[49] But he undoubtedly contacted Wilfrid (in Bruce's account, through a beautiful young girl wearing a Campbell tartan scarf), and through him, other Jewish leaders still at liberty, took their messages back to London, and picked up scraps of information which he faithfully relayed – nonsense jumbled with fact – to Patrick Reilly at the Foreign Office, who was impressed by his 'obviously knowing a great deal about the position of German Jewry'. The most important message he brought was that German Jews 'thought it essential that a large camp or camps should be set up rapidly in this country, possibly in the Isle of Man, to which refugees could be sent at once, and where they could be confined pending consideration of their applications to enter the UK or other countries'.

Roger Makins minuted: 'I am not particularly impressed by Sir M Bruce's observations, more especially as I recognize in para 3 and 4 proposals made to me by Mr Israel when I was in Berlin. I was also confronted with criticism of Mr Rublee and with the suggestion that someone else should be sent to Berlin.' Makins recommended action only on Bruce's suggestion that the Consulate should issue papers to Jewish would-be emigrants testifying that their requests for visas were being considered. Foley, when contacted, responded drily: 'We have of course tried Sir Michael's suggestion long before he heard of refugees.'[50] Reilly told Bruce that the matter of camps in Britain for evacuees was for the Home Office to consider, that no proposal had yet been made to them by the refugee organizations, and that Bruce should discuss it first with the latter. A few days later, Lord Samuel led another deputation to Lord Winterton, to whom the Government had now handed over responsibility for the refugees. Samuel now declared that the Council was convinced the Jews were in immediate danger of physical destruction, and that camps should be set up in Britain and elsewhere. Winterton answered that the Home Office had no objection in principle, but that the Government could not provide the finance.[51] Over the next three weeks, the Government and the refugee organizations argued over who was to foot the bill, until the Council for German Jewry capitulated; by now Leo Baeck, Otto Hirsch and Paul Eppstein of the Reichsvertretung had all visited London to argue the urgency of evacuation.[52] Despite the fact that they were subsequently offered visas and the chance to leave Germany, they all returned to their posts.

In January 1939, seven months after Wilfrid had first suggested the opening of a camp for evacuees, an old army camp at Richborough in Kent was refurbished to accommodate 3,000 at a time. Passport and visa formalities were waived, as they had been for the children. The Reichsvertretung had the task of allocating the first 2,500 permits sent to Foley in Berlin among 10,000 applicants, most of them from the concentration camps.[53] In all, nearly 8,000 young men had passed through the camp by the outbreak of war; many joined the Pioneer Corps as volunteers in the British army. The camp chief was Leopold (Poldi) Kuh, formerly Ludwig Tietz's aide, the resourceful young man who had followed the Storm Troopers' truck in Tietz's little car in June five years earlier.

The camp idea was developed further. Shlomo Adler Rudel, who had been expelled from Germany in 1935, now combed Europe for new sites for training camps for Jewish youth, henceforth banned in Germany.[54] Youth Aliya sent hundreds of its wards to camps in Holland and Belgium. As well as these, 2,500 young agricultural workers were brought over to work in English fields and farms, pending their re-migration to Palestine. When the war broke out, some 50,000 German refugees, most of them Jews, had found at least temporary shelter in Britain.

One month after the Kristallnacht, Wilfrid put another rescue proposal to the British Government; though it was made in his own name, and not, like most of his other representations, on behalf of the Reichsvertretung, it was clearly a reworking of many of the ideas circulating among German-Jewish leaders since 1933.

Wilfrid's own position was more precarious than ever. Since the Kristallnacht, he had not slept in his own bed; he was closely watched by the Gestapo, and was now told that he was not to visit the Embassy without a special permit. It was at night, on 7 December, therefore, that he appeared at Ogilvie Forbes's private residence to propose his plan. He told the *chargé d'affaires* – Henderson was still in London on sick leave – that if the persecution of Jews continued at the present rate, their position within a month would be desperate. They feared more pogroms and knew that more concentration camps were under construction. More men, he told Forbes, would be taken from their families and consigned to treatment which would be 'either a living death, or make them totally unfit for a new life'. Five thousand men had been arrested, in addition to those taken the previous month.

His proposal was that the Germans should 'suspend further aggression, relax regulations, and release some prisoners – in other words "call an armistice" and agree to earmark a proportion of the remittances from Germans abroad for emigration'. The armistice, he said, would cause a favourable reaction abroad and result in the easing of the boycott and an increase of German exports. The resulting increase in foreign exchange would provide 10 per cent free exchange for Germany, with the rest going to a central office not in Germany for use for emigration. Its equivalent would be paid by the German-Jewish community in marks to the German exporters.[55]

The origins of this plan were complex, but it was clearly not a wild improvisation. Whether Wilfrid knew that a week later Schacht, with Hitler's approval, was to put forward a scheme, by which foreign Jews would indirectly underwrite German exports, cannot be established; but he undoubtedly knew some such plan was under consideration. The proposal to earmark remittances from *Rückswanderern* (returning emigrants) funds had been discussed between German officials and the German-Jewish leaders before Evian; and the first Rublee plan, offering to raise the boycott, had been approved in Berlin. Wilfrid knew that the prisoners in the camps were hostages, their release dependent on speedy emigration – and this was to be one of the conditions of the plan subsequently worked out between Rublee and Schacht.

Ogilvie Forbes was sympathetic. He told the Foreign Office, to whom he cabled the plan, that the position of the Jews was so serious that Britain should 'explore every possible avenue'. In London the response was more hesitant. There was still no sign, officials commented, that the Germans were prepared to co-operate in a financial plan of this kind;

Mr Rublee's visit to Germany had again been postponed. The Foreign Office was understandably puzzled by the contradictory signals they were getting from Germany: on the one hand, warnings of fresh outrages; on the other, rumours of imminent concessions. Their conclusion was that 'there were two factions in the Nazi party, one in favour of negotiations, and one out for another and worse pogrom, and the latter might well act on its own'. That the Nazis were capable of using both terror and diplomacy simultaneously, and for the same end – the expulsion of the Jews – had as yet occurred to no one.

The Israel plan was given careful consideration. It went up to Alexander Cadogan, the chief diplomatic adviser at the Foreign Office, and to Halifax, and was vetted by the Treasury, which argued that, 'useful as an argument or offer', it could not be made part of a detailed scheme 'because it is not possible to fix accurately what proportion of increased exports, if any, is due to the raising of the boycott, and what to other possible factors'. Patrick Reilly of the Foreign Office pointed out that if anyone was to make an offer on the lines indicated, it would have to be the representatives of 'world Jewry'.[56]

The two problems were linked. The boycott did not exist as a serious and quantifiable factor; the Treasury officials were correct. But it was a psychological card in negotiations; the Nazis believed in its force, and what they wanted was for foreign Jews either to buy out the German Jews, or to convince others to help them do so.

Meanwhile, for the first time, the Foreign Office speculated on whether Britain should threaten sanctions. 'The only possibility of bringing pressure to bear on the German government is by retaliation, expulsion of German citizens, denunciation of payments agreement, and by a clear indication that until persecution or spoilation of the Jews ceases, the policy of appeasement is at an end,' Roger Makins minuted Israel's proposal. 'Are we prepared to take these strong measures on behalf of the Jews? And if we did take them, would they in fact bring the Germans to their senses?' Makins concluded they would not. Orme Sargent, chief opponent of appeasement, asked, 'Has the policy of retaliation ever been considered?' The question remained unanswered.

Five days after Wilfrid had proposed his plan, the Foreign Office cabled Berlin enquiring as to a possible German response, and – as if in answer to that query, and to Wilfrid's night-time foray in Berlin – Schacht appeared in London in broad daylight, with a fully fledged plan of his own.

The negotiations that began with Schacht's arrival – ostensibly for discussions on trade, but on a visit which rapidly centred on the problem of Jewish emigration – meant that the ideas which had been exchanged secretly for five years were now out in the open. From the diplomatic point of view, it was all highly irregular. The Nazi Government did not recognize the Evian Committee; Schacht was bargaining over what Ribbentrop had argued to be a purely internal issue; the policy of terror and expulsion continued in the background – policy decisions by Goering and Heydrich (which Schacht argued later he knew nothing of) were to drive thousands over the border by force within weeks. But the Nazis' intentions were now clear.

The first plan, which Schacht presented to Rublee's committee, strongly resembled that of the Warburg plan of 1935. He offered German Jews the chance of removing about 25 per cent of their pooled and impounded capital, to be administered from Berlin in a trust fund, one of whose trustees was to be a Jew. The capital thus raised would serve as collateral for a bond issue, to be financed by an international corporation representing 'international Jewry'. Germany would gain no foreign exchange – a surprise to the Treasury officials who had suspected Germany's intention was to reap hidden benefits – but would also not lose by the departure of German Jews. The funds advanced to emigrants would be repaid by the international corporation, and the servicing of the loan made dependent on an increase in German exports.[57]

Schacht showed his shrewdness, in shifting the previous emphasis on the lifting of the 'Jewish boycott' – whose benefits could not be clearly assessed – to a clear financial commitment by 'foreign Jewry'. Thus, at one swoop, he had placed the central responsibility on the Jews abroad and also ensured, as he thought, the departure of Germany's poorer Jews. It was not surprising that, as Schacht later claimed, he had obtained Hitler's approval for the plan in early December, before leaving for London.[58]

However, in refurbishing the 1935 plans, he had overlooked one point. Whereas in 1935, despite the Nuremberg laws, Jewish property in Germany was still an economic asset on which financial plans could be soundly based (particularly if administered by non-Jews from abroad), the terror of 1938 and the new economic laws, aimed at total dispossession of the Jews, meant that bonds, based on the collateral of Jewish property in Nazi hands, were simply not marketable. This was probably an opening gambit, however, as Schacht swiftly agreed to abandon the bond scheme and replaced it with a near replica of the Palestine transfer agreement.

The plan was not Schacht's alone. A few weeks later, he was to resign from the Reichsbank on a totally unrelated issue, but Nazi commitment to the plan was underlined by the fact that negotiations continued under

Helmut Wohlthat, one of the senior officials in the Economics Ministry. The agreement finally drawn up in February 1939, between Rublee and Wohlthat,[59] provided for the emigration of 150,000 young German and Austrian Jews, with 25 per cent of Jewish capital, in German goods, over a period of three to five years; the old flight tax was cancelled, and the Palestine transfer incorporated into the new agreement. A corporation to be established abroad would ensure the settlement of Jews in foreign countries and the sale of German goods. It was clear from the outset that this would have to be funded by Jews.

But among the stipulations in the preamble to the agreement was an all-important clause: Berlin would not move to implement its part of the bargain until it was sure that the countries of resettlement would admit the Jews leaving Germany. This had not been demanded by Schacht, and signified a hardening of the Nazi position after his resignation. Moreover, Rublee had signed a document whose implementation depended on the co-operation of 'world Jewry', which had signed nothing and resented being held to a ransom agreement by the Nazis. The two factors were closely linked, and together were enough to have scuttled the agreement even had war not broken out eight months later.

Meanwhile, the number of applicants at the Hilfsverein increased ten fold; over 2,000 candidates for emigration a day now flooded into its offices, where the staff had been tripled. Senator, on a visit to Berlin, noted that Wilfrid was 'amazingly controlled and self-possessed, running the entire work of the Hilfsverein',[60] and this despite the fact that he was still involved in the liquidation of the firm. Four days after his visit to Ogilvie Forbes, Wilfrid's contacts in the police warned him of another large-scale attack pending on the firm, only averted at the last moment.[61]

During 1938 and 1939, 120,000 refugees left Germany, more than in all the previous five years combined, most of them during the six months following the Kristallnacht.[62] Fear of the camps was the greatest spur.

The most urgent task was to get the men out of the camps. By the end of the year, half the Jews in detention in Sachsenhausen had been released, and immediately left Germany. According to Pollack, during the pogrom itself, Foley sent a 'strongly worded' telegram to Eric Mills, the immigration head in Palestine, asking for a number of blank certificates, which arrived promptly.[63] Pollack's evidence was confirmed by the testimony of Benno Cohn, one of the German-Zionist heads, during the Eichmann trial.[64] At this time, a handful of Zionist envoys organized shiploads of 'illegal' immigrants to Palestine. According to Pollack, Foley knew of the despatch of hundreds of young men from posts in Italy and Yugoslavia, and did not inform the Mandatory authorities. Additional visas were also obtained by Foley for a number of British colonies. In November 1938 alone, 1,000 Youth Aliya certificates were issued, and, from then on, more young people reached Palestine than at any other time. Those in the camps had priority.

At the same time, another British official, R.T. Smallbones, the British Consul in Frankfurt, held 'difficult negotiations' with the local head of the Gestapo to ensure that, if visas came from abroad, 8,000 men in Buchenwald would be released.[65]

The Hilfsverein checked out many cases where the police records established by the Gestapo had to be demolished. There were some the SS would not agree to release, even in exchange for emigration. Pollack contacted an old school acquaintance, now a Wehrmacht general, who twice drove into Sachsenhausen and returned with Jewish prisoners in the back of his car.[66]

Such measures succeeded in reducing the number of those in the camps dramatically; at the beginning of 1939, 12,000 of the 30,000 Jews arrested during and after the pogrom remained in the camps.[67]

But the situation of the Jewish population was grim. Two-thirds of the community were now living on their reserves, and the rest on charity, an envoy from Palestine was told. Jews who did not sell their houses or land risked eviction by Nazi officials.[68] A fresh threat now appeared: expulsion from Germany by force. In late January, Heydrich took control of the Jewish emigration office in the Ministry of Interior, with Goering's approval. Wohlthat, negotiating with the Evian Committee, was now to work alongside him. Early in the year, officials of the Reichsvertretung were taken to Vienna and shown the system of robbery and expulsion perfected by Adolf Eichmann, formerly a minor Gestapo official in Berlin and now a bullying, powerful 'expert' on the Jewish emigration scene. Eichmann's methods had provoked an exodus of thousands of Austrian Jews within months. In Berlin, Eichmann called in several Jews, including Paul Eppstein, of the Reichsvertretung, who had to visit the Gestapo weekly to report on 'progress', hurled obscene insults at them, and told them that henceforth they would have to hand over emigration 'quotas' to be filled to a new emigration office, which would function on the Vienna model. Benno Cohn, one of those present, remembered that each time the Jewish leaders presented themselves at Gestapo headquarters, they did not know whether they would leave as free men, or in a truck bound for Sachsenhausen.

The Jews stood up bravely to Eichmann, arguing that it was not in their power to decide the policy of host countries, and that they would not be agents of the Gestapo.[69]

Henceforth, however, the Gestapo was at their backs. Hitherto,

German-Jewish emigration work had been orderly and independent. But now, under pressure from the emigrants themselves, and with the Gestapo threatening them at every turn, those who worked in the Hilfsverein had only one aim: to get as many Jews out of Germany as fast as possible.

Money was suddenly available for the emigration of tens of thousands. Whereas the Hilfsverein had been deeply in debt at the time of the Kristallnacht, unable even to pay off what it owed to the German steamship companies, by the spring of 1939 it was in funds.[70] The picture is not complete, but at least two major factors contributed to this sudden flood of money. The first was that funds held back until now – communal assets unsold in the hope that something could be salvaged in Germany – were now being used for emigration; the second, that the Nazis themselves, in imposing a special emigration tax – graded progressively from between half a percentage to 10 per cent of the Jew's property – used the money raised through the central Reichsvertretung to finance Jewish emigration, and did not, as has previously been thought, simply appropriate it.[71] Meanwhile, funds sent into Germany for maintenance purposes were diminished, by passing through various Nazi offices, a practice which meant an increasing reluctance of Jews outside to send money into Germany.[72]

There were many ways in which those who still possessed funds could obtain visas. Some bought land they were never to see in Brazil, because 'landowners' could enter the country. Others bought documents, attesting to their status as 'farmers', from German peasants. Baptisms were performed to order at the French Travel Agency in Unter den Linden to enable 'Catholics' to emigrate elsewhere. Thousands left with tourist visas.[73]

From the beginning of 1939, Wilfrid and his colleagues packed boats leaving Germany for Shanghai, an enclave where no formalities were demanded and which was administered by a posse of foreign consuls – British, American, French and others. Frank Foley, after conversations at the Hilfsverein, wrote: 'It might be considered humane on our part not to interfere officially to prevent the Jews from choosing their own graveyards. They would rather die as free men in Shanghai than as slaves in Dachau.'[74]

At this stage, Wilfrid probably had a hand in the purchase of passports, visas and residence permits, which were now freely on sale in Berlin by the 'political agents' Pollack mentions in his testimony. These people knew that the Hilfsverein had money, and a Cuban diplomat is known to have called on the Hilfsverein offering 1,000 passports at $100 each; there were probably many others. Dr Arthur Prinz, one of Wilfrid's colleagues at the Hilfsverein, maintained later that he had 'dissociated himself' from this traffic.[75] It is more than probable, however, that the South Americans were among the 'political agents' whom Wilfrid had forbidden Pollack to name. Wilfrid was known to have ransomed hundreds of Jews from the Gestapo and it is unlikely that he would have hesitated to rescue thousands of others at this stage, whatever the means; he would equally have sought to prevent his actions from being known – hence his insistence on Pollack's secrecy. Wealthy Jews could buy their way out without the help of the Hilfsverein.

The work of this body now entered a new and terrible phase. As the Gestapo increased its pressure, countries of emigration tightened their immigration restrictions. The Rublee-Wohlthat agreement remained bogged down while American Jews pondered the problem of setting up a financial corporation. Jews could be imprisoned for illegal emigration, but the Gestapo escorted transports to the frontiers of Western Europe and drove the Jews across; many were sent back – the word *réfoulement* entered refugee vocabulary. From September 1938, the German shipping companies, too, had connived at the transport of emigrants without regular visas; shiploads of Jews wandered from port to port, forbidden to land. Jewish relief agencies were forced to guarantee maintenance or risk the return of the refugees to the Nazi camps.

Wilfrid and his colleagues now faced an open clash with refugee organizations abroad. The Jewish welfare body, HICEM, called a conference on 10 March 1939, in Paris, at which, together with the Council for German Jewry and the Joint, they warned all international carriers that they would take no responsibility for the illegal refugees.[76] Then they attempted to put pressure on the Hilfsverein and its Austrian counterpart, the Kultusgemeinde.[77] All this was of no avail. The traffic continued.

Perhaps most serious was the fact that the Gestapo policy produced a complete change of attitude abroad. Persecution in November had aroused sympathy; eviction in February aroused hostility towards the Jews. Ivone Kirkpatrick, at the British Embassy in Berlin, commenting on the refugee ships, now thought it should be made clear to the Germans that these tricks would not work:

> I gather that ... the Baldwin fund feel they are being blackmailed by the threat that if they do not take over this or that individual he will be beaten to death in a camp. Certain Nazis have explained that this is part of a policy to plant undesirables on us and so arouse anti-semitism. In the face of this sort of thing mere protests are useless.[78]

Once the cry of blackmail was out, German Jews began to appear as accomplices in Nazi plans. It was in this atmosphere that Wilfrid was to make his last appeal on behalf of German Jewry, to British diplomats and members of the Evian Committee.

When the firm was sold, Wilfrid's few free hours from Hilfsverein work were spent in a twilight life in the deserted homes of his family, or with his remaining friends – either Gentiles, or Jewish friends who had foreign nationality and thus had not yet left Berlin. He distributed the contents of the Israel wine cellar among women friends; played host to Adam von Trott in the Bendlerstrasse; and supervised the crating of the furniture and paintings at Schwanenwerder.

In February, he heard from Hazorea that his friends had decided to dedicate a newly planted grove to Nathan Israel, the founder of the firm. 'Here, his name and work no longer exist,' he wrote to Friedrich, asking him to thank the kibbutz. 'It was my task to see all this to its end and I think I did so with dignity. It was a very personal and therefore a very painful task, like so many other worldly things that were a part of our generation's life.'

In early May, Siegfried Lehmann, the director of Ben Shemen, came to see Wilfrid in Schwanenwerder. Lehmann thought him 'a tired and sick man, who had fought to the last moment, had fulfilled his duty to his family and people and who had now earned the right to seek a rest'.[79] This was not how Wilfrid saw himself, though he told Lehmann, with great bitterness, that political interests had proved stronger than the human feelings he thought he might arouse in the diplomats and politicians. He did not go to London to rest, as Lehmann learned a short time later.

Wilfrid left for London on 15 May 1939, with a few reichsmarks in his pocket, as the law prescribed.[80] He arrived in London, in uncertain spring weather, as the King and Queen arrived in Canada on a state visit, Eights Week began on the Thames, and the newspapers reported that Herr Hitler was touring his western fortifications: finding the level crossings in the Saar dangerous, he ordered them torn down. Two days after Wilfrid's arrival, the White Paper on Palestine was published: it announced Britain's final opposition to partition, and the limitation of Jewish immigrants, pending the establishment of a Palestinian state in which the Jews would be a permanent minority, to a mere 10,000 a year; after five years there would be no more Jewish immigration without Arab assent. The only reference to the plight of Jewish refugees was the remark that the Government was 'conscious of the unhappy plight of large numbers of Jews who seek refuge from certain European countries'.[81]

On 18 May, Wilfrid began the most difficult mission he had yet undertaken. The Gestapo had once more presented the Reichsvertretung, through Eppstein, with an ultimatum: they were to extract a definite commitment from the countries of refuge as to the number of Jews they would accept under the Rublee plan. If not, the Nazis would increase terror tactics.

Abroad, there was no sense of urgency. Britain was examining a plan for sending the Jews to British Guiana. Leading bankers in the United States were prepared to back large-scale settlement. On 26 April, Roosevelt's refugee consultant, Myron Taylor, had phoned Robert Pell, then the Evian Committee's man in Berlin, to assure him that American-Jewish bankers – Kuhn-Loeb and Warburg were mentioned – were ready to guarantee financial backing of all settlement projects and that Rublee's successor as head of the Committee, Sir Herbert Emerson, knew the financing was ensured. Pell told Wohlthat that the emigration plan would have to be carried out without publicity, however, regarding both the trust fund and the exports stipulated in the Rublee plan.[82] By a strange irony, whereas in 1935 it was the Germans who had insisted on secrecy, it was now the financiers abroad who did so, for the entire project was anathema to official Jewish leaders. On 16 May, the day after Wilfrid's arrival in London, Schumburg of the German Foreign Ministry wrote to Ribbentrop, explaining that negotiations with 'American-Jewish bankers' had advanced so far that the regulations of the projected corporation were now being drawn up.[83] But there was still no plan of settlement.

Two days later, in London, Wilfrid and Eppstein met Winterton, Emerson – an ex-governor of the Punjab who had the disconcerting habit of stuffing his pipe still alight into his pocket – Pell, and other British and American officials. Wilfrid was the spokesman, and his impossible task was to present the brutal threats of the Nazis, in his own civilized terms, to the assembled officials.[84]

Goering and Wohlthat, he told the sceptical company, were 'relatively reasonable', but they were being pressed by the Gestapo, who argued that 'shock tactics' worked better than diplomacy. The German Jews could not fill the Nazi quotas, and 'something more was needed in the immediate future to convince the German Government of the honesty of the intentions of the receiving countries'. In short, he said, 'he needed technical, financial and diplomatic assistance at once, and would like to be able to take back to Germany to show the secret police, with whom Mr Eppstein was in weekly contact, some document showing the intentions of the Evian Committee to procure an outflow of sixty thousand a year for three years'. If the Evian Committee could not do this, he warned them, and if the corporation was not founded soon, the German authorities would return to shock tactics and brutal attacks on the Jewish community.

The officials present were clearly taken aback by Wilfrid's vehemence. Winterton replied that the British Government and the Committee 'did not propose to have the German police dictate what it was and was not to do'. The Committee had shown 'great patience' with the Germans. It was doing all in its power to find places of refuge and settlement. Financial plans were in preparation. However, he warned Wilfrid, there was a limit to the absorption of immigrants because of 'anti-semitism and anti-alienism' beyond which 'it was dangerous to go'. The Germans would have to understand this. If they continued to threaten the outside world, neither refuge nor money would be forthcoming. He personally did not doubt the Germans' good faith, said Winterton, but matters should proceed '*pari passu*'.

Wilfrid told Winterton that Goering and Wohlthat were fighting a losing battle. Hitler was losing patience; when Wohlthat had been received recently by Hitler to report on the progress of negotiations over the Jews, Hitler was 'not impressed', and would not allow Wohlthat to proceed further until the Evian Committee had come up with concrete proposals.

But all that Winterton would concede was that, on the following day, Emerson and Pell should look at the specific emigration plan the German Jews had brought with them. Pell explained that in any case the United States could not commit the other governments to any course of action.

Wilfrid and Eppstein left the meeting shaken, as Pell observed. Eichmann had insulted the German Jews, but they had confronted him with dignity. Now the foreign diplomats treated them as Eichmann's henchmen. Thus one of the rare occasions on which Western diplomats decided to stand up to Nazi pressures was at the expense of the German Jews.

But they had to continue; the prospects for rescue had never been worse. The White Paper just published had effectively closed the one exit route for large numbers of emigrants. All they could hope for now was a piece of paper with some indication of the helpful intentions of the Evian Committee, something Eppstein could hand Eichmann on his return.

On the following day, however, the atmosphere worsened. Winterton, at least, had a diplomat's respect for forms. Emerson, however, was a colonial administrator with a patronizing view of the 'Eastern peoples', among whom he counted European Jews.[85]

When Wilfrid asked for a statement of the countries prepared to receive emigrants during the following year, Emerson reacted as though he had been asked to participate in a fraud. Pell noted that 'Emerson was adamant in his refusal to give them either a plan or a programme. ... He would not be a party to a dishonest statement, and any statement which would convey an impression to the German authorities that governments would follow this course or that.'[86]

In fact, Wilfrid's request was merely a repetition of what Cordell Hull, the American Secretary of State, had proposed six months earlier.[87] In February, moreover, Patrick Reilly of the Foreign Office had minuted the Rublee-Wohlthat agreement that the German Government would have to be satisfied that the countries of immigration were ready to do their part ... 'I suppose through statements which the Director might communicate to the Germans, showing what other countries are doing'.[88]

Emerson, however, refused to respond to the Jews' appeal. He had 'the greatest sympathy for the plight of the Jewish community in Germany', but would not submit to blackmail.

The emissaries were 'very distressed', Pell noted, and begged Emerson at least to write a letter to Lord Reading, one of the British-Jewish leaders, saying that the Committee would try to take out a specific number of people in the current year; a copy of this could be taken back to Berlin as proof of the Committee's intentions. Emerson 'declined'.

Wilfrid now made one final suggestion. Emerson had read out to the deputation a memorandum which Pell had presented to Wohlthat on 6 April, saying that this was the extreme limit to which the Committee would go. Wilfrid proposed that Emerson write to Reading, stating that the Committee 'was proceeding along the lines of the memorandum of 6 April, and expressing a hope that it would succeed in carrying it out'. But, as Pell ended his report, 'Emerson refused even to consider this minimum plea.'

Eppstein returned to his appointment with the Gestapo empty-handed. Wilfrid remained, for the moment, in London. One of the first letters he wrote was to Einstein: 'For fourteen days now I have been on the other side of the border, but for many years now I have wished to let you know with what feelings of nearness I have thought of you.... I have tried to live according to my principles and I have tried to make a supportive contribution with all my power.'[89]

But even on 'the other side', knowing what was happening in Berlin, Wilfrid was unable to rest. As Diana Hopkinson wrote: 'He felt that he had no place amongst his English relations however welcoming they were. Although he was half English he thought of himself that summer as wholly a German refugee.'[90] He made no attempt to find a home, staying with Werner Behr and his wife in a little house they had found in a London suburb. He soon found that his fellow Jews had no more sense of the urgency of the German-Jewish plight than the diplomats and officials of the Evian Committee. Samuel had retired from Jewish work in February; the refugee organizations decided, in late summer, that they had no further funds and must thus limit all further emigration from Germany.[91] Wilfrid turned to a wealthier organization, the Jewish Colonization Organization (ICA), which, German Jews now hoped, might, under Wilfrid's influence, become a solid source of help. Within a few weeks, he was elected to the board of directors; the word now went round that, with the ICA as his ally, he would return and renew his work in Berlin.[92]

In mid-August, telling his friends only of another trip to the Continent – he had visited Zurich again in June – Wilfrid went back to Berlin. He immediately set to work with Hanna Karminski and Cora Berliner, of the German-Jewish women's organizations, who were despatching what were to be the last of the children's transports across Holland to England.[93] Meanwhile, through Foley, he arranged for the departure of some of his friends' parents.

On 23 August, Germany and the Soviet Union signed a non-aggression pact; the last barrier to world war was now down, and Hitler could turn his guns on the Poles. Three days later, German breaches of the Polish frontier were reported, and Agnes Schneider, the Israels' old friend at the American Embassy in Berlin, heard rumours from the Consul, Geist, that all dual nationals were about to be interned; she warned Wilfrid that if he wanted to avoid imprisonment he must leave Germany immediately.[94] It was only now, when he knew that he could no longer help his fellow Jews, that he left Germany and his colleagues for good. In Paris, he parted with Otto Hirsch, who was attending a conference of the Joint, for the last time.

Hirsch returned to Berlin. Like Leo Baeck, Paul Eppstein and his wife Hedwig, and Wilfrid's colleagues in the Reichsvertretung office for child emigration, Cora Berliner and Hanna Karminski, Hirsch had been offered a visa to England, but, like the other community leaders, preferred to remain in Germany with those whose chances of escape were now minimal. None of the plans for a large, planned exodus was finally realized; the odds against their success had been overwhelming, not least because the warnings and proposals of Wilfrid Israel and his colleagues had been so often played down or put aside. These proposals were based on the assumption that the aim of 'humanizing' expulsion, in fact of making it practicable, could be meshed with Nazi perceptions of the viability of anti-semitic policies during the mid-1930s, and the drive to expel the Jews at all costs towards the outbreak of war. This was not an attempt to seek an accommodation with the Nazis, as it has sometimes been represented.

German Jews were frequently blamed, in the years that followed, for their excessive loyalty to their homeland and blindness to the threat of Nazism. The Holocaust casts its monstrous shadow in both directions, obscuring both the options open to the Jews of Germany during the 1930s and the fact that the decision to massacre European Jewry was taken only when the policy of expulsion was exhausted. Little attention, therefore, has been paid to the efforts the German Jews did make to preserve their lives, and Wilfrid realized this even in the early years of the war. As George Bell was to write after his death: 'There was a fire burning in his soul all the time, and few things stirred him more than the blindness of those who failed to see not only what the Jews of Germany suffered, but what they dared and did.'[95]

9
'Merely Transitional'

The outbreak of war did not mean that all options for refuge and rescue for the Jews under Nazi rule were closed. The Nazis were still concerned with expelling Jews, by methods at first haphazard and unco-ordinated, and not with killing them. Hitler had more urgent objectives.

The last few hundred children thus slipped out of Germany unnoticed. On the last day of peace, sixty children and their escort travelled on trains crowded with soldiers from Cologne to Kleve, the only point on the Dutch border to which trains were still running, and arrived in Harwich to hear that Hitler had attacked Poland. The rescue of others continued throughout the first week of the war; Youth Aliya certificates deposited in Foley's office were traced to the American Embassy, and hundreds of children left for Scandinavia and, through Trieste, for Palestine.[1] Even when this legal rescue work came to an end, a Youth Aliya executive in London said confidently, in late September: 'Sooner or later, there is sure to be a movement of the saving of the children of the two million Jews now under the Nazi regime; but not by Youth Aliya, which has other tasks.'[2]

The Nazis made it clear that, war or no war, they were still interested in German-Jewish emigration. On 27 September, the American Embassy in London told Washington that Berlin wished to continue negotiating with the Evian Committee, and that the trust fund could still be set up in Germany. The Hilfsverein, too, continued to appeal for the acceptance of emigrants with valid visas and passages on neutral ships.[3]

There was only one sign of the terrible alternative. In mid-October, deportations of Polish Jews in Germany began. By November, some 5,000 had been deported from Germany and several hundreds of others from Prague and Vienna, sent under armed guard, without food or water, to the bombed ruins of Lublin, where epidemics raged in the overcrowded city; the Nazis now threatened to deport all the Jews of Germany.

Once more, Wilfrid was isolated in his concern and appeal for immediate action. He knew that with the drawbridge to Britain now raised, America was the Jews' only hope; Roosevelt had begun talking of a vast new refugee plan, including a 'supplemental national home' for the Jews, which would not cut across Britain's Palestine policy - an idea equally unpopular with the British Foreign Office and the Jewish Agency. But Wilfrid had few contacts with America; he appealed to the Zionists.

Hearing that Weizmann was shortly to visit the United States, Wilfrid approached Moshe Shertok, head of the Political Department of the Jewish Agency, who was visiting London. Shertok lunched with Wilfrid on 14 November and recorded that Wilfrid Israel, who had left Berlin just before the war,

> was entirely and deeply worried about the fate of the Jews who remained in Germany and who are threatened with deportation to Lublin. Should not the help of America be enlisted? He wants to talk to Chaim [Weizmann] about this. I said I doubted whether Chaim could help. Any effort on the part of the US to bring pressure to bear on Germany in order to moderate its cruelty towards the Jews must, in the event that it succeeded, put the US in Germany's debt. Such a sense of obligation could only mean less identification on the part of the US Government with England. Chaim would not be able to suggest such a course. Israel disagreed with my approach to the question. There was no danger of burdening America with obligations towards the Nazis.... America would only have to make the entrance of Jews easier; the question of its policy towards Germany would not be affected at all.[4]

Shertok's tortuous justification of inaction disguised the real reason for his refusal to pass on Wilfrid's plea. The main purpose of Weizmann's visit was to ensure American support against the May 1939 White Paper; and to rally both Zionist and non-Zionist Jews to contribute all possible funds to Palestine. An appeal for a change in the immigration policy of the United States, by the Zionists, was no part of this policy. But Shertok could scarcely explain this to a man whose one aim was to rescue Jews from Germany, whatever the destination.

Wilfrid's occupation was gone. In letters to Palestine, he wrote that he was 'lonely and isolated'. He grasped at straws, hoping against hope that the German anti-Nazis he had known might yet spark a rebellion against Hitler's regime. When an attempt on Hitler's life was made in Munich in November, he wanted to believe this was a sign of some wider plot. And when he heard that Adam von Trott was in America, he saw this, too, as a sign that the opposition had some plan of action.

Wilfrid and Trott had not met since May. Trott was now in the United States as a semi-official envoy of the German Foreign Office, and used his visit to appeal secretly to the State Department, together with other anti-Nazis, on behalf of the German opposition; their message was that the United States could bring pressure on Britain and France to offer lenient peace terms to Germany, in the hope that this might encourage an overthrow of the Nazi regime – an ambivalent message which was received with suspicion. Wilfrid, meanwhile, clearly assumed that Trott had left Germany for good. He wrote, 'How grateful I am to know that you are in the USA. I pray to God you will be prompted to stay there. I am absolutely convinced that you will be constructive in your present surroundings. It is essential to carry on and be ready to strike at the critical moment.' At another time, he said, he might have urged Trott to remain in Germany; but now, 'You are an ambassador of all those within who are of good will and at the present moment ... they need a permanent intermediary and interpreter of their attitude and motives.' He did not write only as a friend: 'You know I feel responsibility towards the future; that is the reason I have a clear conscience in writing you this letter.'[5]

But Trott returned to Germany and the opposition did not strike. In London, meanwhile, the politicians floundered as Hitler rested on his eastern conquests and planned further moves to the West.

In September 1939, Britain had been catapulted from appeasement into belligerence. For six years, the British people had been told that peace was the supreme aim and that Britain had no real quarrel with Germany. The aims of the new war, and the new peace which was to follow it, were improvised as rapidly as the distribution of gas masks during the period between the end of Hitler's Polish *blitzkrieg* and the Nazi offensive which followed in May 1940. George Bell, with whom Wilfrid remained in touch, suggested that forming an international committee of thinkers would be a way of getting 'informed Christian opinion', about the peace which might now be negotiated, to the Government. Wilfrid was apparently an honorary member of this odd club, for an open letter of his survives in Bell's 'Peace Aim Conference' papers from the end of 1939. There were no 'patent solutions', Wilfrid wrote. 'The New Order will never appear to us as a tidy and well-groomed *deus ex machina* to be produced at Round Table Conferences.' That said, however, he let loose an avalanche of ideas, calculated to warm the hearts but puzzle the minds of the assembled professors and bishops: European federalism; a world drive for adult education; a Christian revival; the decentralization of industry; Zionist agrarianism as a model for new rural economies; a plan for the ex-territorial control of European electricity, and planned migration from the over-populated areas of Europe.[6] After his experience in Nazi Germany, he wrote, he now opposed all radical creeds. The letter was an explosion of the old reforming spirit he had kept under control since the 1920s, a levitation into intellectual fantasy, since his plans for practical action were frustrated.

For despite all his efforts, no one would sponsor his visit to America. Two weeks after his 'peace aims' letter to Bell, Wilfrid wrote to relations in New York: 'I was hoping to come over to the USA on Jewish affairs, but there are too many difficulties to surmount ... my Jewish work has come to a tragic standstill.'

At the beginning of 1940, Wilfrid wrote to all his friends that he saw his life in England as 'merely transitional'. He thought of himself as a refugee, knowing that he did not belong in London.

> I am installed in a little flat of my own again for the time being with a few of my belongings round me. I feel happy in these surroundings ... but it is not home. I am still thinking a good deal about Palestine, still conceive that is the aim. It won't be easy for me in that part of the world, but perhaps I belong there, if anywhere, after all we passed through during these latter years.

Wilfrid was unlike the other German-Jewish refugees in Britain. He could not resume life as a businessman, like the fur merchants of Leipzig or the Berlin bankers, who had managed to transfer money to England; he was not one of the refugee professionals, who were quickly placed in teaching or advisory jobs. Though no longer a millionaire, he was financially independent, unlike most German and Austrian refugees, who lived in rented rooms with a gas ring, and queued for their weekly handout at the refugee centre, Bloomsbury House; the men were usually unemployed, spending days in London's public libraries, while the women worked in domestic service or doing odd jobs at home – a situation which continued until the mobilization orders in 1940 made room for them in factories and workshops throughout Britain. They had become England's *Ostjuden*.[7]

Wilfrid did not go to live near his relatives in fashionable Kensington or Mayfair. He chose to remain near other German Jews in north-west London, in Riverside Drive, an ugly block of flats like a stranded ocean liner which stood near the Great North Way, an arterial road along which lorries thundered between suburban factories. The 'river', which he soon discovered on weekend walks, was the Brent stream, which meandered through one of the narrow bands of parkland which remained in the outer city.

Wilfrid stored the furniture from the Hildebrandstrasse, with the gold plate and crown china, in a small house nearby, which remained locked and dark, with Wilfrid as its caretaker. Amy soon appeared on the scene. She had been staying in the country with Lady Samuel, as an unhappy duenna, but as the house filled up with close relations leaving London, she had to leave. Wilfrid planned to send her to California, though in the meantime he took her in to Riverside Drive. He wrote glumly: 'I hope to be able to give her the feeling of being at home again. She has felt uprooted for a long time and is going through a psychological crisis.' Living at such close quarters with a querulous and difficult mother soon sent Wilfrid on his travels again.

In the early spring, Wilfrid was able to arrange a visit to Palestine, through his connections with the Jewish Colonization Association. He had joined the directorate in the autumn of 1939 in the hope of helping German Jews; now, as he told the Zionist writer Leib Jaffe in 1941, he was also attempting to 'breathe a new spirit of Zionism' into a philanthropic organization, which had, until now, done little in Palestine.[8] At the beginning of 1940, he visited Paris and discussed the development of the Huleh Valley, a swampy area in Northern Galilee which drainage would make suitable for cultivation.[9] Both the British Government and the ICA had originally committed themselves to the project in 1935, but after the outbreak of war, British participation was postponed indefinitely. When a new British colonial development was tabled in February, the scheme was reconsidered, and Wilfrid's offer to investigate conditions on the spot was accepted.

He left London on 2 April for Zurich, where he posted a last message to Adam von Trott, now back in Germany, 'an inadequate sign of an old and constant friendship';[10] it was a sign that he knew Trott had returned, and did not condemn him. On 12 April, he sailed for Palestine from Trieste.

As in 1934, Wilfrid arrived during a period of high political tension. In February, the Mandatory Government had announced restrictions on land purchases by Jews, and hostility between the Jewish Yishuv and the Government was kept alive by the British refusal to allow the formation of a Jewish fighting force; Jewish preparations for defence went underground. When Wilfrid arrived in Haifa, he was met by a friend who told him Siegfried Lehmann was on trial, on charges of concealing arms.

On 22 January, a police raid on Ben Shemen, the children's village Wilfrid had helped to found, had uncovered bombs, rifles and machine guns under the floor of one of the office buildings. Lehmann and ten other administrators were arrested. Lehmann had recently asked for extra defences for the village; the office where the arms were found had been repaired recently, with his approval, and the weapons had been newly oiled. Though he argued that his pacifism was well known, and despite the testimony of both British and Jewish friends, who maintained that he had always been 'a man of peace', he and several others were sentenced a few days after Wilfrid's arrival, to the maximum penalty of seven years' imprisonment.[11]

Wilfrid kept his visit to Hazorea to the last; first he made his official tour to the Huleh, held meetings with the head of Youth Aliya, Henrietta Szold, in Jerusalem, and only then made for the place he had for so long thought of as home.

The young men of the Werkleute had changed. Their first few years in Palestine had not been easy. They had been buffeted between the powerful Land Development Corporation, which favoured private farmers over kibbutzim, the Mandatory authorities, who policed the land, and the Arab absentee landowners, who sold the land to the Jews but would not compensate the tenant farmers from the nearby villages who remained resentful and potentially hostile. At first, the Werkleute had lived among Arab watchmen and cultivated the meagre strips of land they had been given, until, in desperation, they had gone out one night and fenced off a few more acres of the land they had been promised, and confronted the Mandatory police on the following day. They had only put down roots two years earlier in the autumn of 1938, after a series of appeals to the bureaucrats in Jerusalem – and to Wilfrid, in Berlin, who, on the same day he wrote to Samuel about the prisoners in Buchenwald, had fired off a batch of angry letters to all his influential contacts in Palestine and abroad. A few weeks later, the Werkleute had their land.[12]

Thus, when Wilfrid arrived in 1940, he saw stone buildings among the wooden shacks and tents, cultivated fields, vines in the wadis, grazing cattle and a young forest on the hills.

Relations between Hazorea and its Arab neighbours now seemed peaceful; the Arabs brought tools to be soldered at the kibbutz smithy and the Hazorea cattle pastured on Arab land. Wilfrid's intellectual young Berlin friends were now weather-beaten farmers; many of them had changed their names – Friedrich Altmann was Yosef Amir; Rudi Baer was Uri; Ernst Bauer was Eliezer Be'eri. Politically they had linked up with the Marxist Hashomer Hatsair group to which Mordechai Shenhabi's kibbutz, Mishmar HaEmek, down the road in the same valley, also belonged. They had taken their place in Jewish politics. There was another change, too. Most of the young men were married, and many of them had children.

The little community was everything Wilfrid had always imagined as a perfect society: money never changed hands, for the farmers shared all they earned; the children roamed barefoot, as free as any 'New Era' teacher in the 1920s could have wished; and the rhythm of his friends' lives now followed that of the changing seasons. Despite the physical hardships, the young men were content, because they had lived out their ideals; and Wilfrid envied them.

It was now, possibly for the first time, that Wilfrid must have realized how homeless he really was. He made a double decision: to build a house for himself in Haifa, on the heights of Mount Carmel, where he went with Shenhabi to look at plots of land; and to keep at least a corner of Hazorea in his mind for the future. He saw that the life of the kibbutz, experimental commune though it was, centred as firmly on the family as any Jewish community. Nor could even Wilfrid's closest friends in the kibbutz imagine this restless, worldly man living permanently in their village. They were all the more surprised at the request he now made of them.

They had talked of the artist's life on the kibbutz of the future – the chance he or she would have to share routine duties, yet be free to paint or write, for example, without financial cares. Wilfrid now asked, rather diffidently, whether he might build a bungalow somewhere in the kibbutz grounds where, after the war, he might once more take up his abandoned career as a sculptor. He knew, he hastened to add, that he was not a suitable candidate for membership of the kibbutz. But would they allow him to spend some of his time with them, and to work beside them? After some hesitation, the young men agreed. In terms of their ideology, the request was outrageous; the commune was so preoccupied with the concept of absolute and perfect equality that members had even suggested that the many nursing mothers should divide their milk equally among the new-born babies. It said a great deal for their feelings towards Wilfrid that the founding members agreed to his proposal.

But another, darker thought occurred to Wilfrid on one of his last walks round the kibbutz perimeter with Friedrich and Gustav Horn. High above the kibbutz, on the southernmost of the hills which sheltered it, the founders had, rather romantically, set aside an area for a forest cemetery. Later it was abandoned, too difficult a climb for elderly mourners; at the time, it seemed a place fit for pioneers to rest, overlooking the whole Jezreel Valley. Here, Wilfrid said, was where he would like to be buried.

A few days later, the news came that Hitler had invaded the Low Countries, and Wilfrid hastily made preparations for his return to Europe, where, he told his friends, he was sure that he was most urgently needed. When he was at sea again, he wrote to his friends in Hazorea: 'I know that my path is laid down by necessity. I also know that the security of Hazorea gives me a feeling of being at home. I go out again with renewed strength. And whatever the future may hold in store, my stay within the country will greatly soften in my heart all that may come, however painful it may be.'

Wilfrid returned to London to find the refugee community, which had just begun to find its feet, once more disrupted, this time by the threat of internment. Hitler's rapid advance through Europe had ended the false sense of security and the British Government's hopes of a possible accommodation with the Nazis. Chamberlain finally stood down and was succeeded by Winston Churchill, and Britain braced itself for a possible invasion. The roadsigns came down, civil defence units were mobilized, and fear of fifth columnists and plain xenophobia led to the internment of 'aliens' – a measure which put two-thirds of the male refugees from Hitler, and many of the women, behind barbed wire in weeks.

Tribunals set up early in the war had already classified three-quarters of the refugees as fugitives from Nazi oppression, who could not possibly be 'security risks' in wartime Britain. But the tribunals had not been staffed by experts, because the Home Office had rejected the suggestion that a panel of 'reliable refugees' should assist the officials in weeding out the Nazis from the rest. At the end of May, first the aliens in coastal areas, and then nearly half the refugees in Britain were arrested; Wilfrid's friend Richard Latham, now a temporary clerk at the Foreign Office, again renewed the suggestion for a refugee committee, which could work anonymously. But again the proposal was rejected.[13]

The policy of mass internment evolved by an inter-departmental committee, whose deliberations were secret, was absurd as well as inhumane. In a scathing attack on internment policy, written days after the mass round-up, Eleanor Rathbone, the refugees' chief defender in Parliament, showed that it was, in fact, counter-productive. Expelling aliens from the coast had dispersed those under supervision; interning useful employees damaged the industrial war effort; hundreds of soldiers, policemen and civil servants were wasting their time on a futile exercise.[14] But it had its own mad momentum. Under War Office orders, 27,000 aliens were rounded up and herded into improvised camps; one of the first batches was marched off by Grenadier Guards with fixed bayonets. The refugees were taken from offices and workshops, homes and libraries, young Zionist trainees snatched from farmers' fields, and many men were threatened with deportation to the Dominions; families were separated, children left without care. All this was at a time when invasion seemed imminent, and the Jews were, as they knew, far more vulnerable if the Nazis came than their English neighbours.[15]

Once more Wilfrid was to play a unique and near-anonymous role on behalf of the refugees: as the main link between the refugees, the refugee organizations at Bloomsbury House, the Home and War Offices, and the various committees who came to the help of the internees – among them the 200-strong Parliamentary Committee for Refugees. It was a unique role, because Wilfrid was more closely involved with the internees than any Englishman, yet understood the mentality of British officials better than the Germans.[16] Again, his position was delicate: the official Jewish leadership, afraid of being branded as disloyal, kept its distance; in Parliament, Gentile MPs, it was agreed, should put the internees' case; while as representative of Bloomsbury House in the camps, Wilfrid was the easiest target for the refugees' bitterness. His letters indicate that his task was more thankless, and more painful, than anything he had undertaken hitherto.

Wilfrid and his Quaker friend, William Hughes, who had worked with him in Berlin, were the first relief workers to be admitted to the camps near Liverpool and on the Isle of Man, appointed by the inter-denominational Edinburgh Committee in June.[17] Their first visit took place in early July – before any British MP had visited the internees. Wilfrid's first report described the sufferings of old men forced to lie on damp ground, the insufficiency of rations and, above all, the isolation and anxiety of the internees; this account clearly contributed to the initial attack on internment policy launched by Eleanor Rathbone, which took place in the House of Commons on 10 July.[18]

A few days later, Wilfrid paid a second visit to the camps on the Isle of Man – to which, ironically, he himself had recommended transferring the camp victims two years earlier. The internees, he reported, were being treated as enemies of the country; they were pathetically grateful to be allowed a first meeting with their wives, a month after internment. Young men had been threatened with deportation to Australia if they did not volunteer for service with the Pioneer Corps; three weeks or more passed before letters posted in England were received; telegrams could only be answered in cases of life and death, and – unable to reach the outside world – the internees were victims of every rumour. Food was still inadequate and medical care urgently needed. 'If one wishes to maintain morale amongst the internees and the prestige of those dealing with their problems,' Wilfrid concluded bitterly, 'no day may be lost in rectifying the existing problems.'[19]

Permission was granted for interned doctors to practise, together with the residential medical officers, and the regular visits of Wilfrid and Hughes were now punctuated by the occasional visits of MPs, heads of committees and members of the clergy; George Bell, in particular, campaigned vigorously for improvements in the camps and the release of Jews and anti-Nazi Germans. But more than one day was lost.

Wilfrid intervened personally in hundreds of cases, for Jews and non-Jews alike. Early in his work, he asked an acquaintance with influential contacts 'how he did his conjuring tricks', and soon performed them himself, never telling those released of his own intervention. Marion Schreiber (Alward), who worked as his secretary at Bloomsbury House, remembered that he often followed up his applications for release with personal visits to the official involved, and that he vouched personally for the anti-Nazi past of non-Jewish refugees. One sign of the stress under which he worked was that he insisted on destroying every note she had taken for the letters he sent, or that they be made illegible, as if the Gestapo were liable to raid his office – a practice which had clearly become second nature during his work in Berlin.

Wilfrid became one of the most important advisers – acting informally and without publicity – to the circle of MPs who were lobbying for a change in government policy; to the public opinion council set up to counter anti-refugee propaganda, and to the curiously named Friendly Aliens' Protection Committee.[20] Lady Reading, one of Wilfrid's first foreign collaborators in Youth Aliya, served with Rathbone and Lord Winterton on the Asquith internment committee; and in the Foreign Office, Richard Latham was to be both a persistent and effective critic of the brutality and frequent incompetence of MI5. Wilfrid provided much of the essential information and advice the committees needed when they proposed additional categories for release to the Home Office, after the issue of two White Papers on 31 July and 26 August, which were the first official attempts to repair the damage.[21] By the end of 1940, Wilfrid was able to hint to the internees that they would shortly be released, because of chronic labour shortages, and that the census of skilled labour in the camps was not merely another barren statistical exercise. Overcrowding was now ended, most invalids had been released, and the menace of deportation lessened.

No detail of the prisoners' lives was too small for Wilfrid's attention, from the need for spectacles or trusses, to the fact that the white bread provided was 'very moist indeed', and the clothing and shoes supplied by Bloomsbury House, for some odd reason, came in small sizes only. But his repeated message was that Bloomsbury House, and the official organizations behind it, should take action on policy, particularly regarding the internees' future: 'The fundamental feeling that the great majority of men interned have been wronged, and that, whatever the outside world maintains, they are looked on with suspicion, is the conviction of all ... the fear of a permanent stigma on those interned for so many months.'[22] By the end of 1940, 10,000 of the internees had been released.

By early 1941, all but one of the categories recommended by the Parliamentary Committee for Refugees had been adopted, and among the new categories were persons who had been in concentration camps or who had suffered other forms of persecution, persons known as anti-Nazis, and young people in agricultural jobs – particularly the Zionist pioneer groups, Hehalutz (socialist) and Bachad (orthodox). However, the problem of a future stigma was only solved in August 1941, when the Home Office finally agreed, under pressure from a committee headed by Norman Bentwich, that aliens claiming to be refugees from Nazi oppression could apply for recognition as such and have their claim formally inscribed in the documents they needed to show employers.[23]

Although Wilfrid battled for the refugees' rights, in the camps he was vulnerable to their anger. He was not an MP, or a bishop; one camp newspaper singled him out in an attack on Bloomsbury House, and he could not explain the silence of the Jewish Refugee Committee and the Chief Rabbi, who had not raised a voice in public on the internees' behalf. Hermann Berlak, Leo Baeck's son-in-law, interned between July and November 1940, compared this timidity with the stand of Baeck and the Reichsvertretung in Berlin: 'There was much less oportunity to get in touch with the Gestapo and German Jews were not frightened by the danger . . . to ask for help for the interned men.'[24]

Wilfrid fought the injustice of the policy, but he grew tired of hearing the British compared with Nazis. He did all he could to obtain releases; he even urged one of his ex-aides in the Hilfsverein, Arnold Horwitz, to perform a 'chivalrous gesture' and marry a woman internee to get her released. But when a distinguished internee wrote a pamphlet on 'spiritual resistance' to internment and the possibility of transferring this into 'productive experience', Wilfrid commented:

> I do not like his propagating the 'strength through suffering' idea. When one thinks of the misery and terrible ordeal of the majority of Jews today I do not feel that the lamenting overrules everything . . . we over here have little to suffer in comparison to the majority of Jews, and I feel that it is embarrassing to develop a philosophy of human suffering which is . . . beyond our ability to comprehend.[25]

At the beginning of 1941, Wilfrid began to receive news of the arrest and imprisonment of his colleagues in the Reichsvertretung, and he knew their lives were in danger. He received regular information from Germany, probably from Hans Schäffer, an anti-Nazi civil servant from the Ministry of Economics, who now lived in Stockholm and corresponded regularly with the women leaders of the Frauenbund. Since communication with Germany was a wartime offence, Wilfrid passed the news on to Hans Reissner, now in Bombay, in a coded language which strangely resembled his own restrained, 'English' style: 'Paul had to contend with great difficulties. He was away for some time, thank goodness has now returned home. But I hear that Jules is now in the same unfortunate position.'[26]

'Paul' was Paul Eppstein, who had been arrested for the first time; he was to be deported to Theresienstadt and die there two years later. 'Jules' Seligsohn was arrested on 12 December 1940, and never released; he died in Sachsenhausen in the spring of 1942. Wilfrid knew almost immediately, later on, of the death of Otto Hirsch, and the deportation of Cora Berliner and Leo Baeck.

His chief concern became the Jewish children in the countries now overrun by the Nazis; in particular, for those Youth Aliya wards whose names were kept on lists in the offices in London. He wrote to Werner Senator, in March 1941: 'I maintain that Jewish organizations should be working in Portugal saving as many youngsters as possible from Central Europe and France, in close touch with the Joint and Hadassah.'[27]

From the summer of 1940, when Wilfrid had rejoined Youth Aliya in London as its honorary treasurer, he had urged moving children out of Europe, whatever the destination. He had met with very little success. Eva Michaelis, his colleague from Berlin days, had managed to get 300 children into Denmark from Holland, by simply signing documents promising they would be admitted to Palestine after the war – though she had no guarantee of this.[28] That summer, all Jewish children in Europe seemed at risk, no less in Britain than elsewhere. But moving them had to be weighed against the dangers of wartime transportation. On 18 September, seventy-seven children were drowned when the evacuee ship *City of Benares* was torpedoed. Several hundred children were transported from Sweden to Palestine through the Soviet Union and, at Wilfrid's suggestion, the children's journey to Odessa was monitored by the Joint, which still had representatives in Moscow – the last year this was possible.[29]

From early 1941, Wilfrid proposed evacuating children from Vichy France. From the mid-1930s, Youth Aliya had been partly financed by the Hadassah women's organization of America, and Wilfrid's first proposal was that Hadassah should work for the children's admission to the United States, where they would be safe for the duration of the war and could train for ultimate emigration.[30] But London Youth Aliya raised two objections: the children would be going in the wrong direction, and proper selection would be difficult. Wilfrid, they said, could appeal privately to Hadassah if he so wished. When he did so, the woman responsible answered, explaining that there was an 'immigration block' against Jewish children, which Hadassah was powerless to breach.[31]

Two weeks later, he returned to the charge, appealing to the executive to 'resume the old spirit of Youth Aliya' and to try to widen the scope of its work. He wanted 'more initiative with regard to countries where there was an urgent need of help, such as, for instance, the Balkans and unoccupied France.'[32] Like Richard Lichtheim in Geneva, who constantly urged action on his Jewish colleagues in Jerusalem and the capitals of the West, and was disregarded until it was too late, Wilfrid pleaded constantly to evacuate the children. But the final decision remained in the hands of the Political Department of the Zionist organization in Great Russell Street, and with Jerusalem. Youth Aliya had no money to launch rescue operations on its own, though Wilfrid continually cut funds to all but essential welfare work and insisted on transferring every penny possible to Jerusalem. But there Henrietta Szold argued for caution in rescue operations, seeing more danger in wartime transport than in Nazi expansion. The rescue of a group of twenty-five children in Vichy France, in the care of a Mrs Karafiol, was debated by telegram for months without action being taken.[33] The fate of the Jews of Western Europe was still not clear and, until late 1942, no one in the Zionist offices, either in Jerusalem or in London, was prepared to launch rescue activities through the neutral countries, or to listen to Wilfrid's pleas for action.

In September 1940, Wilfrid wrote to Diana Hopkinson admitting his depression over the slow pace of release of the internees, and regretting that he had not stayed on in Palestine:

> There is a lull at present which reminds me that I am rather tired out and literally a little dishevelled in mind. Previously, one's own private and public *weltanschauung* was seemingly so well established, and now I flounder about; so much seems to be frustrated. I suppose one wants a superstructure for the mind as one needs a protective tin hat against shrapnel from the air. . . .

This was no metaphor. To Gustav Horn in Hazorea, Wilfrid wrote: 'At nights I quite often have to lead a so-called fire bomb fighting squad – funny, isn't it?'; and to Friedrich Altmann, 'One is not always a hero when the whistling bombs come and shrapnel flies around one; but after all, this experience does not burden one as all the much more frightening experiences we lived through three, four, five and seven years ago.'

Wilfrid had seen his mother off to California in September, and his brother was in Haiti. He never thought of leaving England. When he received descriptions of life in New York from relatives, he wrote:

> It all sounds extraordinarily odd and reminds me of a vision one sometimes has in medieval paintings of angels in the heavens, trumpeting the triumph of celestial security to all the sinners of the underworld (I suppose that is rather our position over here). I rather fancy the idea of . . . and a few others floating about the skies in long pre-Raphaelite draperies.

But his letters give the impression he preferred the dangers of London during the Blitz to the 'celestial' circles of his old business friends in New York. For the first time, he was free of family obligations and had escaped from the 'vicious circle of stability'. But between his visits to the internment camps and his fire-fighting duties in the Blitz, he had so little time for his own affairs that his library and his art collection remained unclaimed in their crates in the London docks, where they were badly damaged during the first heavy raids of the autumn.

In November, he wrote to Hans Reissner that the crates had been 'more or less demolished. I am sad about it, because it meant much to me and was to be something of importance to me in future; but I must take it with my last reserve of grace and equanimity of mind.'[34] By the spring of 1941, he had salvaged what he could, 'sorting and restoring my poor art collection'. Among the survivors were the Khmer Buddhas; they took up residence in Riverside Drive.

Socially, Wilfrid was almost completely isolated. He cared deeply for his fellow refugees. He wrote to Arthur Ruppin, the German-born Zionist leader who kept him informed of progress at Hazorea, that the social and legal status of the refugees worried him, and he deplored the fact that the German-language newspaper, *Die Zeitung*, on which so many were dependent for their day-to-day information, encouraged the idea of a 'return to Germany' after the war, a thing 'even in theory quite beyond reason'.[35] In order to help them adjust to life in England, Wilfrid helped the other refugees set up their own association, effected all the necessary introductions to British Jews, and retired from the scene: 'I played the part of a rather unnecessary and baroque appendix,' he wrote. But the refugees, he knew, did not regard him as one of themselves; to them, he was a privileged Englishman.

Wilfrid looked, in England, for a parallel to the intellectual Jewish tradition which had flourished in Germany, and found 'no spiritual strength'. He was unable to find a common language with the businessmen who handled the financial side of Zionist affairs. As for the more assimilated English Jews, he was equally unhappy in their company. He wrote of Herbert Samuel, 'I was asked to his home in Oxford more than once, but I am a snob, I suppose, and did not have time for celebrities', and he felt out of place in any middle-class family. He wrote of his relatives, 'My worldliness certainly perturbs them, and so I keep away from their cramping, fuggy influence'; and when invited to a country weekend: 'I could not live up to family life atmosphere, and made a fool of myself.'

His friends were thus mostly exiles like himself, foreigners, or people who lived on the fringes of wartime London: artists, booksellers, writers. He found the atmosphere of Bloomsbury House, the refugee centre, so oppressive that sometimes, with his secretary, he escaped from the office to daytime concerts or plays and worked later, long into the night. He sketched, walked in London's parks, and spent hours contemplating the few paintings displayed in the galleries, whose contents had been removed and stored in the Welsh caves for the duration of the war. Contemporary English painting, by artists much praised at the time, annoyed him by its blandness.

> Picasso was moved by the shelling of Guernica to create a study of fear, but Piper sees only an excuse for pseudo-romantic abstractions, and Sutherland sees the desolation of suburbia through the eyes of the common man, or else the aesthetic effect of twisted girders. The elements of reality are passed by, because England is a quiet gentle country unimpressed by fanaticism.

After noting that 'the Romantic tradition is blossoming out into strange unsteady blossoms', and that the older English painters were finding it difficult to adjust to the war, Wilfrid added: 'The war artists have merely changed their cows and carts to men and tanks if they were landscape painters and dressed their men in uniform if they were figure painters.'[36]

Until the end of 1941, Wilfrid planned to play a more active part in the war. As soon as his intensive work for the internees was done, he volunteered for service in the RAF, despite his age - he was now over forty - and despite his ill-health. While he waited for a final answer, he took on only temporary work - at the Ministry of Information, and commuting to Oxford between the German exiles and the Balliol team of researchers who were working for the Foreign Office. He also contacted Frank Foley, who was now in charge of Rudolf Hess, the Nazi leader who had parachuted into Scotland in May 1941; he wrote to relations in America: 'Foley is doing a job which has quite an historical background; one day, when my hair has whitened (there is anyway not much of it left) I shall give you some further particulars.' It was only when the RAF finally turned him down, towards the end of the year, that he accepted his first regular job.

He would soon be moving on, he wrote to friends. Nothing was permanent; even his friendships were 'transitional'. Yet one thing remained unchanged: his role as counsellor and protector to much younger men, not all of whom recognized his own emotional need for their company.

He befriended the lonely young Germans in the Youth Aliya camps in the countryside, against whose 'loveless treatment' by their English supervisors he protested; he took into his care a young son of refugee parents, Hans Neumann, whom he helped to adjust to life in England, and he acted the great European connoisseur to a group of students evacuated to Oxford from London's Slade School of Art. He played uncle to the nephew of an old schoolfriend, whose mother was in South America and whose holidays from school in Scotland were often spent in Wilfrid's company. Wilfrid's reports to the boy's mother showed him trying hard to act as a substitute parent: 'Mathias has grown a good deal and is therefore much better proportioned than he used to be. We spoke about his headaches and concluded that he should not read late at night. Teeth, feet, etc. seemed to be in quite a good condition.' He noticed, too, that the boy was precociously independent for his age. 'One must try to avoid his growing up too rapidly.'

Wilfrid soon found a regular companion in a nineteen-year-old teacher and writer, Peter Vansittart, whom he met while on one of his lonely walks on Hampstead Heath. Wilfrid stopped to ask the time, and Vansittart, with a copy of the recently published *Goodbye to Berlin* in his pocket, discovered, to his astonishment, that he was talking to one of its characters. In Wilfrid's home, he recognized the statuettes, books and even the atmosphere Isherwood had described, and was mesmerized by this strange foreigner who had walked out of literature and history. Later he wrote: 'Wilfrid was to haunt my imagination; ironical, elusive, obliquely powerful, Merlin without the malice. His first gift, Rilke's poems, hitherto unknown to me, transformed the flowers, the rooms, the Heath.'[37]

Vansittart wrote his first book in Wilfrid's flat, casting his host as the blue-eyed Herr Oberfelt, nicknamed 'Herr Perfekt', a middle European magician, a quiet benefactor dispensing gentle advice to a young admirer.[38] Vansittart kept Wilfrid company and was treated with teasing affection. He would invite the young man to an 'unusual foreign film', and Vansittart would find himself watching Mickey Rooney. If he pretended, rashly, to any expertise on music or architecture, Wilfrid would introduce him solemnly to friends as 'the authority on Glinka, you know', or would remark that, in his own view, Selfridge's department store was the finest building in London. Vansittart puzzled over Wilfrid's bookshelves, on which Rilke sat beside P.G. Wodehouse, *Great Bibles of the World* beside Burnham's *Managerial Revolution*, and Mann's *Magic Mountain* beside Vachell's classic novel of the English public schools, *The Hill*. These juxtapositions were not evidence of esoteric taste, however, but more the result of the destruction of most of his books, of his upbringing by an English governess, and the fact that he was not educated to cull his library. But Wilfrid seldom talked of himself, or of his past life; he preferred to remain a mystery.

Vansittart was not entirely comfortable in Wilfrid's flat, which was too hot and stuffy for a young Englishman, and where yogurt and muesli for breakfast were a poor substitute for bacon and eggs. He was bored and mystified by Wilfrid's German friends, and, despite Isherwood's introduction, he never learned much about the Nazis, whom Wilfrid regarded as 'deranged and uninteresting'. But Wilfrid provided Vansittart's European education, and Vansittart relieved Wilfrid's loneliness.

For, as the camps now emptied, and the raids became steadily less frequent, Wilfrid's life was briefly becalmed. 'I become a modest recluse with the fleeting years,' he wrote to an old friend at this time. But the conflict of his life as German and as Jew had pursued him beyond the borders of Nazi Germany, and was soon to resurface in a new role, from the summer of 1941.

10
A German Patriot

On 17 November 1941, after working on a trial basis since the summer, Wilfrid Israel was formally appointed to his 'little research job' as consultant to the German section of the Foreign Research and Press Service of the Royal Institution of International Affairs, at a 'subsistence allowance' of £5 a week.[1] 'I have a legitimate income at last; I contend, for the first time in my life,' he wrote to relations in New York.

Arnold Toynbee's famous Institution, which canvassed the opinions of men of affairs, politicians and distinguished foreigners as well as those of university professors, was well suited to Wilfrid's intellectual convalescence. He had imagined himself at Oxford twenty years earlier and now wrote enthusiastically of its 'monastic atmosphere', though in fact it was packed with evacuees from London ministries, art students and wounded soldiers. The Oxford brahmins, with whom he now worked and at whose high tables he dined, never learned that the man Harold Beeley called 'an unaffectedly civilized European' (in Oxford no one thought him oriental) had not even completed his formal schooling.

'Chatham House at Balliol' was remote from practical politics at the beginning of the war. Though the Royal Institution had put its services at the disposal of the Foreign Office in 1939, at first the FRPS was little more than a monitoring service for the foreign press, though even the papers rarely arrived on time. Post-war planning was limited, initially, to documenting public statements on peace aims, a job 'to keep the professors quiet',[2] while, in Chatham House in London, the Reconstruction Committee sounded out delegates of exile governments for their views on Britain's role in the post-war era.

The Foreign Office wariness of 'the professors' was the result of their post-First World War experience, when technical experts with what often proved too narrow a field of knowledge were bracketed to every British delegate at Versailles.[3] Chatham House also had a professional rival in the Political Intelligence Department of the Foreign Office. The 'professors' were regarded with no less scepticism in Parliament; when the FRPS Treasury grant was debated in the Supply Committee in November 1940, a Conservative MP asked whether 'this money is to provide us with a better understanding of those who are dropping bombs on us?'[4]

The FRPS's most important task was to answer specific queries put to them by government departments, but, in the view of Political Intelligence, they were 'to concentrate on past history, to deal with a very small extent with the present, and not at all with the future';[5] odd advice to those planning for the post-war world.

'Everyone is talking about reconstruction,' wrote E.M. Forster in 1941, blandly advocating tolerance all round rather than a new ideology.[6] But it was premature to speak of reconstruction while Britain faced Germany alone, and the defeat of the Nazis was far from a certainty. Churchill himself had little interest in the subject at this stage of the war. Central Department noted that a ministerial committee under Clement Attlee had produced a mild general statement, 'was sat on by the PM', and closed down.[7] In the Commons, Churchill told the Minister in charge of reconstruction, Sir George Chrystal (whose small staff were known as the 'crystal gazers'), that 'it was not his task to make a new world but to plan, in advance, a number of practical steps'.[8] These included assessments of the post-war supply of stocks of food and raw materials necessary after a war which had at first been expected to last three years. Thus the first practical work the FRPS was given concerned information about the industrial and economic state of Europe; by the beginning of 1942, the Ministry of Economic Warfare had become uneasy about what it called 'the absolute dependence of the Foreign Office on FRPS information' in this field.[9]

In the first two years of the war, the only two political groups in London who took the FRPS and its work seriously were those who had no official recognition, but were deeply concerned with British policy in the immediate post-war era: the Zionists and the exiled German politicians. Wilfrid's role in the German and – unofficially – the Jewish Departments evoked interest, and no little apprehension, in both groups.

Most of the 50,000 German refugees in Britain were Jews who had no further interest in post-war Germany, but the Social Democrats and other opposition groups in exile had initially been given reason to hope that both the Foreign Office and the British Labour Party would lend a willing ear to their informed views.[10] By mid-1941, when Wilfrid began his work, they were totally disillusioned.

By this time, after the Nazi conquest of Western Europe, and the Blitz, the national mood had swung from confused support for the policy of appeasement, to total Germanophobia. Speaking on the BBC in June

1941, Churchill spoke of 70,000,000 'malignant Huns' who were 'curable or killable'.[11] Only a handful of pre-war pacifists demurred, among them Wilfrid's friend Corder Catchpool. Robert Vansittart's 'Black Record' broadcasts tarred all Germans with the Nazi brush, and was opposed even by Churchill as too extreme.[12] By the end of the year, Geoffrey Harrison of the FO Central Department, invited to answer 'woolly minded' questions from Roosevelt's aide Myron Taylor regarding post-war policy, commented learnedly: 'Herder developed the idea of the Volk, Fichte that of Autarchie, Jahn that of the racial superiority of the Germans and Hegel of the paramount importance of the Staat nearly 150 years ago. Hitler has collated all these ideas and called them Nazism. To that extent Nazism is indestructible.'[13]

It was not the best time to discuss Germany's place in the reconstruction of post-war Europe. Yet, in the summer of 1941, this was what Wilfrid began to do with his superior, T.H. Marshall, head of German research in the Foreign Office, in the cloistered calm of Balliol.

Tom Marshall was a sociologist, a man of original views and a modest manner, whose knowledge of Germany had been acquired during student days terminated by internment in the Ruhleben camp, where he remained throughout the First World War. Since that time, he had visited Germany only once, with a deputation of university teachers. 'Research was rather a grand word for what we were doing,' he said of his work at the FRPS. He 'leaned heavily' on the expertise of German scholars in exile, initially hindered by the absurd restrictions applied to 'enemy aliens', who at first were not even allowed to cross the Balliol portals. But even beyond these formal barriers, there was a further ban. The attitude of the Foreign Office to German exiles, whether political or not, was clear: their knowledge was valuable, and where points of German administration and law were in question, essential to intelligent post-war planning. But they were under no circumstances to advise on policy.

Nominally, Wilfrid was neither a refugee nor an exile. None of the restrictions applying to enemy aliens applied to him. What was more important to Marshall, however, was that though Wilfrid was, to all intents and purposes, a German refugee, he had 'a total lack of rancour against the Germans', and possessed an encyclopaedic knowledge of the economy and politics of pre-war Germany. Wilfrid's detachment made their discussions of the major planning issues much easier than talks with the Poles or Czechs, whose emotions, Marshall thought, dominated their ideas. His personal diffidence was also an advantage, for, as Marshall noticed, 'his power to influence in debate was balanced by his complete lack of desire for office'. What capped his qualifications was his absence of a politically active past in Germany; he had no 'axe to grind' for any party and was thus, in British eyes, totally reliable.[14]

Wilfrid had been working with Marshall for several months when the Foreign Office began to have second thoughts on the wisdom of denying 'the professors' a part in consideration of the future of Germany. The catalyst was the realization that both the Soviet Union and the United States had very specific contingency plans for post-war Europe – while Britain had not.

By the end of 1941, the only specific commitment to post-war policy was the Atlantic Charter, drawn up in August by Churchill and Roosevelt, which was, as Marshall was to note, 'a declaration of faith and not a political programme'. In December, the British Foreign Minister, Anthony Eden, returned from a visit to the Soviet Union with the alarming news that Stalin had proposed a formal military alliance and an agreement on post-war reconstruction, including a secret protocol regarding post-war frontiers. The Foreign Office commented: 'It has become apparent that the Soviet Union has made much more progress than we have on the question of European frontier rectifications.' A battery of queries were now fired at the FRPS, not only on the history of European frontiers, but on the viability of various plans for their readjustment.[15]

Britain's other major ally, a few months later, was also applying pressure. In July 1942, as Gladwyn Jebb recalled in his memoirs, 'The United States had only been in the war for six months, but already they seemed to have a much more powerful machine than we had for formulating post-war policy.' American policy contemplated a military occupation of Germany and its possible dismemberment; parts would associate themselves with the West, and the rest with an Eastern European confederation under Soviet influence.[16]

The Foreign Office was divided on the possible British response. Some, such as Jebb, favoured backing the American view; others, including Frank Roberts, head of the Central Department, and Orme Sargent, a veteran anti-appeaser, opposed dismemberment.[17] By the end of 1942, the FRPS was supplying not only background material but, in answer to requests for assessments, its own distinct suggestions as to policy.

It was finally recognized that intelligence, planning and operative decisions could not be totally separated, and that 'sooner or later the really operative members of the FRPS will have to be absorbed into the executive body, where they will make their contribution, not as planners, but as experts.'[18] Richard Law, the Parliamentary Under Secretary of State, argued forcefully that three or four officials in the Economic and Reconstruction Department, established in 1942, could not possibly carry out all the work involved; the United States, he pointed out, had a parallel body to the FRPS inside the State Department.[19] Anthony Eden agreed: in a letter to Chatham House, proposing a takeover at the end of 1942, he wrote: 'The work of the FRPS, with changing circumstances ... has insensibly shifted from the periphery of our activities towards their centre.'[20]

Wilfrid, meanwhile, had shifted - invisibly as far as the Central Department was concerned - from the periphery of the FRPS to its centre. In the summer of 1941, he had been little more than the *geeignete mittelsmann* between the German specialist exiles and the Oxford professors - Eric Dodds, Norman Baynes (both classical scholars, the latter with a remarkable knowledge of the Weimar constitution) and Marshall. By February 1942, Wilfrid had so impressed Marshall with his knowledge of German affairs and his assessment of Germany's post-war role in Europe, that Marshall proposed to Toynbee that Wilfrid, together with himself, should become a member of the Political Group of the Committee for Reconstruction in London.[21] When Wilfrid left a year later for Portugal, it was agreed that he was to be one of the twenty-five 'really operative' members of the 160-strong FRPS, who were to join the newly constituted Foreign Office Research Department as full-time civil servants.[22]

'I work happily and ceaselessly, diving into past phases of history, excavating knowledge accumulated in my mind during the last twenty years and more,' Wilfrid wrote to relations in New York in April 1942. 'We are all planning ahead, once again building in our minds, rebuilding and refashioning the world, dreaming and working. We did so twenty years ago and more. This time it must be more real, more stable, more constructive,' he wrote to an old friend from Russia, Elsa Hirschberg, who had known him since his youth.

He worked, for the most part, at home. Marshall put questions to him, which he answered in informal drafts; his name was never appended to a Foreign Office document, and, where his views were clearly incorporated in memoranda, they appear in Marshall's own papers. Marshall was the crucial link between the German exiles and the Central Department, where, according to Frank Roberts, his views were regularly sought and discussed.[23] Wilfrid was the only one among the German exiles whose views were canvassed by Marshall, not only for his detailed knowledge, but also for his overall view of Germany and Europe; he was probably the only exile who had access to such news as the approaches to Britain by opposition groups inside Germany, on which his views were sought.[24]

His first task had been to widen the FRPS reservoir of *émigré* consultants, and to make his own suggestions for the further use of their knowledge. He surveyed the political groups represented in London, gave his own evaluation of their leaders and other 'individuals of significance', both political and non-political. His conclusion was that 'it is more than doubtful whether they have any "background" at all in Germany today'. Most of the political groups, he added, 'had no more than a very transitory ... or even archaeological significance ... though their accumulated knowledge and experience are of some weight and consequence'.[25]

This expert opinion would have confirmed the prevailing view in the Foreign Office, which believed the exiles to be unrepresentative and out of touch with Germany.

The other question of whether the exiles might, through the formation of a Free German movement, have a part to play in post-war Germany was widely discussed in May 1941, and Foreign Office officials were at first divided on whether it should be encouraged. The famous publicist, Henry Wickham Steed, writing in the German exile paper *Die Zeitung* in the spring of 1941, asked, 'Who will undertake the reform and re-education of the German people...?' In the first instance, the German political emigrants, who had remained 'good Germans'. Wilfrid disagreed. Emigration in itself, he thought, was not a creative force, and though individual leaders might have a role to play in post-war Germany (he praised Erich Ollenhauer), *émigrés* as a group would not. He was confident that the younger generation in Germany would cast off Nazism and its dogmas, but to lead it from abroad would be destructive. Meanwhile, he thought, 'the political emigration is a caricature of yesterday'.[26] Again, this coincided with the decisive Foreign Office view which was 'that it would be foolish to hope that any group of refugees now here, after whatever tutoring, could take over'.[27]

In the autumn of 1941, Wilfrid accompanied the SPD leaders, Erich Ollenhauer and Hans Vogel, to Oxford and participated in Marshall's briefings – Vogel knew no English – after having transmitted to them questionnaires on the anti-Nazi opposition.[28] Wilfrid's own views of the Social Democrats, his papers show, were highly critical; he put the blame for Hitler's early successes firmly on the political opposition, together with the failure of the West to assess the threat of Nazism, and the inability of the early political *émigrés* to put their case convincingly to the outside world.[29]

He was not to be drawn into the exile controversies regarding the SPD's past record, unlike another very well-known Jewish exile, Walter Loeb, a former SPD leader and banker, who had noisily adopted the views of Robert Vansittart. With Kurt Geyer, a former political editor of the Social Democrat paper *Vorwaerts*, Loeb violently attacked the German working class, claiming that the German worker was as aggressive a nationalist as any Nazi.

Ollenhauer and Vogel sprang to the defence of German workers and their own party, on whom, they said, Geyer and Loeb had passed a death sentence, 'from the safety of an English fireside'. Vogel attempted to elicit Wilfrid's views; but all he would answer was that 'the basic questions which are the centre of the controversy can be discussed endlessly. . . . I nevertheless fear sometimes that too much energy is being used on clarifying the pros and cons of the past.'[30] He saved his own views on the German working class and the SPD for Marshall. These were that the industrial working class had constituted a strong potential source of opposition to Nazism, which, if it had been recruited to an active militia, might have combated the SS and the SA by force. He believed that the SPD and the trade unions were jointly responsible for this failure.[31]

Thus, through his reports, Wilfrid could only have strengthened the prevailing Foreign Office rejection of the political exiles, either as partners in debate or as the nucleus of a British-sponsored future government in post-war Germany.

However, many of the views that Wilfrid expressed, both in his papers and in debate in Oxford and London, were those of a German patriot. He placed the failures of Weimar in the widest European perspective; he pleaded for the post-war unity of Germany, opposing dismemberment, and for federalism as a solution to the problem of German government, within a new European confederation of states; he proposed socialist reforms inside Germany itself, and warned of the dangers of the country becoming an ideological battleground between the Allies and Soviet Russia.

In the reconstruction debates at Chatham House, he reminded his colleagues constantly of the existence of a 'hard core of resistance in Germany', which they admitted they tended to overlook, and argued that, once liberated, the Germans would be perfectly capable of re-educating themselves.

But when he argued that Britain could co-operate in this process at any earlier stage by stating its own ideological principles more clearly, he was rebuffed by British academics who shied away from too open an involvement in political debate.

Wilfrid grasped at any event which indicated a radical change in the political climate that had made the war possible. He thought he saw one such spark in Churchill's offer, in June 1940, of an interchange of citizenship between Britain and France, which he saw as 'one of the few great climacterics of the war'. European citizenship, he argued at Chatham House, should be conferred on Britain's allies, to be extended at each phase of liberation; but if this was to be more than a mere gesture, it would have to be backed by detailed post-war planning for a European economy in which a uniform currency, employment, welfare and other projects would be worked out on a supranational basis.

For this, he thought, all the 'moral and intellectual reserves of Britain should be mobilized, stage by stage', and the ground should be prepared even while the war continued. At the end of 1941 he wrote to Sir Alfred Zimmern, one of the Oxford brahmins, urging a total ideological battle on Nazism by the British universities, as the war was being waged against 'a great spiritual void', and thus 'even the most shrewd propaganda campaign cannot but prove to be a failure'. Zimmern did not agree. The 'moral authority' of Oxford could not, he thought, be mobilized and set down in the form of doctrine, nor had the critical moment been reached, as Wilfrid suggested. 'We are all at sixes and sevens – not simply in our opinions but in our intellectual make up and our philosophies. Indeed we rather glory in keeping the Oxford mixture in solution.'

Wilfrid replied that he had not suggested the adoption of a rigid doctrine, but that British intellectuals should attempt to explain how the new socialism which he believed was now emerging in Britain was consistent with Britain's tradition of individual liberty. 'This eagerness and insistence of mine may seem to verge on mental crudeness. But experience in the past has too often shown that intellectual laxity can very often deteriorate into a disinclination to show any initiative or to give any intellectual lead at all – a danger which, I maintain, is still facing the world at this juncture.' Oxford had a responsibility, having remained the only free centre of learning, and while it might be hard to reduce his proposal to practical terms, 'practical terms can only be effective if the idea involved is regarded to be a vital one'.

When the two intellectual giants of that time, the British historians E.L. Woodward and Sir Charles Webster, came to discuss Britain's contribution to the re-education process in late 1943 (Webster, as Zimmern told Wilfrid, was thinking along 'slightly less ambitious lines' regarding an Anglo-American brains trust), it was the problem of insufficient intellectual manpower that troubled them, rather than the redefinition of first principles. Britain was not to play the role Wilfrid had hoped for, though the exiled Germans were greatly influenced by their association with British socialists.[32]

The first papers Wilfrid prepared were purely research background documents on the political parties of Weimar, the trade unions and the anti-semitic legislation of the Third Reich. He collated material assembled, with the help of his refugee friends, on the German universities, and added his own comments to papers on the SS and the SA. In this way, he added to British knowledge of Germany just like many other exiles, who, from the time of their release from internment, were employed by the press, the BBC and in other institutions where background knowledge was useful.

He helped Marshall, Baynes and others brief German-Jewish professors, such as the jurists Ernst Wolff and Ernst Kohn, whose knowledge of the German system and the extent to which it could be repaired after the Nazi excesses, was vitally important to informed policy after the war. He discussed detailed proposals for administrative reform with Dietrich Mende, an anti-Nazi civil servant of many years' experience, whose knowledge was encapsulated in many of Marshall's papers.[33]

But with Marshall, Wilfrid also discussed the reasons for the failure of democracy in Germany; the Nazis' appeal to different sectors of the German people; the partial disillusionment with Nazi promises, which he believed had set in before the beginning of the war; the chances of an anti-Nazi uprising inside Germany, and the policies he thought should be followed by Britain immediately after the war.

He argued that the absence of a democratic tradition, the effects of rapid industrialization unaccompanied by radical social reform, as well as the psychological and economic dislocation caused by punitive treatment at Versailles, had prevented the stabilization of Weimar democracy, which he contended had been undermined as much from without as from within. Wilfrid's own experience in Eastern Europe in the early 1920s, and his work for the League, had convinced him that Nazism was not a peculiarly German growth, but had been at least partly inspired by the counter-revolutionary movements in Eastern Europe, which the Allies, 'obsessed by Sovietophobia', had supported. He did not deny an irrational element in German idealism, what he called 'the Gothic urge', but he denied that this, too, was uniquely German, and thought that only its subservience to a militarist tradition made it dangerous. In the Committee for Reconstruction in London, he argued doggedly against all proposals for reforms enforced by the Allies; restitution, he argued, was to be demanded of Germany, but only in kind, and within a new 'economic masterplan' for Europe; re-education should be carried out by the Germans themselves.[34]

In the spring of 1942, these were fighting words. German armies were deep in Russia. The prevailing view was that Germany should be dismembered, vigorously punished and totally reindoctrinated. But Wilfrid found an ally in Marshall for most of his views.

Tom Marshall had been strongly influenced by his own experiences. While he did not share the prevailing view that German philosophy and Prussian domination were permanent obstacles to a future democracy in Germany, the revolutionary scenes he had witnessed in 1918 seemed, to him, a sign that the Germans were politically volatile by nature. He felt that the Germans might once more refuse to accept responsibility for the destruction they had caused. Unlike most of his Foreign Office colleagues, he thought that the Germans would have a strong reaction against war and would not soon constitute a menace; but he feared that change would not be stable.[35]

Despite his qualms about the permanence of post-war change, however, Marshall was convinced by many of Wilfrid's arguments. In May 1942, he submitted what he called a 'deliberately provocative' staff paper for internal distribution in Central Department, tackling all the leading policy questions head on. Where Wilfrid's defence of a future democratic Germany had been impassioned and idealistic, Marshall's arguments rested on a wholly English pragmatism. He suggested that the British Government adopt a lenient policy towards Germany in the general interest, as there was no clear moral balance dividing that country from the rest of the world; Germany would have to pay for its war crimes, but peace aims needed their collaboration, and the German issue could not be isolated from Europe as a whole. He followed Wilfrid's arguments closely in analysing the Nazi regime throughout the 1930s, and echoed his opinion that, by 1942, the Nazi Party was once more 'an army of occupation' within Germany. Marshall ended his memorandum with specific suggestions for action, among them opposition to dismemberment, the reconstruction of a federal republic and a recommendation to leave re-education to the Germans themselves. The new Germany, he thought, 'would have to work out its own salvation through socialism'. Marshall later remembered that the paper provoked reassessments.[36]

In mid-1942, Wilfrid's loyalty to the 'core of opposition', which, he continued to argue, remained in Nazi Germany, and who he believed would form the nucleus of a future democratic Germany, was put to the test. His friend Adam von Trott, and one of the clergymen with whom he had worked during the 1930s, Hans Schönfeld, were among those who now attempted to contact the British Government, asking for support for a projected uprising against Hitler. Wilfrid, in England, was among those consulted by Marshall for his views on the credibility and viability of such plans.

In April 1942, Adam von Trott, on a visit to Geneva for the German Foreign Office, handed the Dutch Protestant clergyman W.A. Visser 'T Hooft a memorandum, setting out the broad outlines of an uprising and the political programme of the prospective rebels. Visser T'Hooft gave this document personally to Sir Stafford Cripps, recently returned to London from the British Embassy in Moscow and, since February 1942, Lord Privy Seal in the British Cabinet. In June, Hans Schönfeld and Dietrich Bonhoeffer, both German Lutherans, separately contacted George Bell, the Bishop of Chichester, in Stockholm, where he was on a lecture tour for the Ministry of Information. They eventually drew up a programme for submission to Anthony Eden, naming Trott as a possible intermediary. At the same time, a memorandum reached the Foreign Office from the German nationalist leader in exile and formerly a leading Nazi, Hermann Rauschning, the central thesis of which was that organized Christian groups would replace the Nazis after a military coup. The Trott and Rauschning memoranda were sent to Marshall, among others, for evaluation. Bell visited Oxford and gave a small group, including Marshall and Wilfrid, the outline of the Schönfeld-Bonhoeffer plan; and, subsequently, Wilfrid made a special appeal to Stafford Cripps, urging the recognition of these groups within an overall drive to topple Hitler.[37]

According to David Astor, Trott's closest English friend, Wilfrid had waited anxiously, during the early war period, for news of an anti-Nazi coup, in which he was convinced Trott would be involved; Wilfrid had telephoned Astor and urged him to approach Cripps, as soon as the latter returned from Moscow, on Trott's behalf. As Astor recalled, Wilfrid was sure that Trott 'would not have altered his attitude after Hitler's victories, and that it was of the highest importance that Britain should try and help him and his fellow conspirators'.[38]

However, Wilfrid's view of the various opposition forces inside Germany, on the evidence of his own papers, was very complex, and not dictated by his loyalty to any one friend. He never told Marshall of his personal friendship with Trott, or of his acquaintance with Schonfeld, and his view of the potential opposition was guided primarily by his absolute hostility towards the German army, and his very hard-headed assessments of the abilities of the other German dissidents.[39]

The opposition inside Germany, in 1942, was not one united group. There were army officers, such as the generals Beck and Hammerstein; administrators, including Karl Goerdeler, Mayor of Leipzig; trade unionists; clergymen, and others. The 'Trott' memorandum (written by members of the Kreisau circle) suggested two possible ways in which the Nazi regime might be overthrown: one, as a result of a Soviet victory and possible military revolution; the other, by the efforts of different anti-Nazi forces in Germany, including sections of the working classes, the army, and militant groups from the churches. They proposed to stage a *coup d'état* in the autumn of 1942, if Allied support were forthcoming. The memorandum warned that if this was not given, the 'bolshevization' of Germany was likely. The rebels' success, on the other hand, would ensure Germany's incorporation into a reorganized Europe, from which German military forces would be withdrawn – though the terms for that withdrawal were not made entirely clear.[40]

The message Bishop Bell brought back from Stockholm was very similar. Schönfeld had told him that, in German opposition circles, there were reports of an impending SS revolution inside the Nazi Party, to be carried out by Himmler and his followers, after which the army would take control. If the opposition were to overthrow the Nazis, would the Allies promise that there would be no second Versailles? The dissidents wanted private encouragement and some public statement to mobilize popular support, otherwise they could see no point in incurring the terrible dangers of a coup.

The approaches of 1942, originating in so many separate groups, were clearly different to peace feelers to Britain made earlier in the war, which came primarily from army sources and were invariably suspect.[41] To the extent that they indicated a weakening of support for Hitler's policies, they were welcomed; and the people involved were not thought intent on deliberate deception. Much was subsequently written about the importance, or otherwise, of Trott's credibility. Eden and Cripps exchanged irritated letters on the question of his alleged deviousness, with Cripps defending the man who had been his own son's friend.[42] But the leading question was neither the *bona fides* of the intermediaries, nor the existence of opposition groups inside Germany; it was whether they would in fact act, given encouragement; and it was connected with the larger debate concerning the 'two-stage revolution', the possibility that another group might succeed Hitler before the end of the war, or during a final débâcle, and when, and how, it could be replaced.

Dominating all other considerations, moreover, was the problem of Soviet Russia. In September 1941, the Soviet Government had sent an *aide-mémoire* to London, stating its absolute rejection of all further peace feelers aimed at weakening the alliance, while, as Vyshinsky the Soviet Foreign Minister told Cripps, the Soviet Union 'continued to bear the whole brunt of the blows of the Hitlerite war machine'.[43] By mid-1942, the British Government was particularly anxious not to raise Soviet suspicions as, despite pressures, the War Cabinet and Chiefs of Staff saw no way of launching an effective Second Front in Europe that year. There was at least a suspicion that the conspirators were being used, perhaps without their knowledge, by Nazi sources. While the Bell report was under consideration, Elisabeth Wiskemann reported from Berne that, according to reliable sources, Theo Kordt, of the German Legation, had been called to Berlin in mid-June to receive instructions from Hitler 'to use all opportunities to discuss peace with the Anglo-Saxon powers'. The Fuehrer 'regarded the Anglo-Saxons as more dangerous to him than the Russians, whom he thinks he can wear down, and hoped to achieve a breach between the Western Allies and the Soviet Union'.[44] Under these circumstances, the conspirators' insistence on the threat of 'bolshevization' was clearly a major error.

The predominant view in the Foreign Office was, according to an unnamed source, that, 'The group Adam represents really does exist, is of some importance for our political warfare, and could be misdirected by us in ways useful for HMG.'[45] Geoffrey Harrison of the Central Department thought it 'more than probable' that the opposition groups existed. But those capable of liquidating the Nazi regime, he thought, were already compromised; the 'Christian groups' or others who might rebuild Germany could only take over later. Thus, he minuted the Rauschning report, the Foreign Office faced two dilemmas:

> The first is to offer to the groups capable of overthrowing the regime sufficient encouragement, but without committing ourselves to anything, to make it worth their while to act. The second is, when and if they do act, how to dispose of them after their period of usefulness has ended, and to build up and get substituted elements which hold out the hope of leading the new Germany in the right direction.

When Wiskemann, who had contacts with Trott, whom she admired, asked if she might 'cool him off', Harrison responded: 'I do not think it is in our interest to do so, since his value to us as a "martyr" is likely to exceed his value to us in post-war Germany.'[46]

Marshall and Wilfrid were far from sharing such views. But it is clear that both were sceptical as to whether the Christian groups, mentioned so prominently in both the Trott and the Rauschning memoranda (which were jointly considered, though Rauschning was not in Germany), could replace the Hitler regime.

Wilfrid noted that, in his experience, the confessional church opposition consisted only of small groups of intellectuals, and that in Berlin itself even they had functioned in very few districts. Apart from the various groups he could personally vouch for, he stressed that the church rebels were not backed by the Church as a whole, which 'had no moral strength or authority and was totally subservient to the state'. He singled out several leaders in the Catholic Church – Preysing and Faulhaber among them – but, again, advised Marshall that, apart from Catholic socialists involved in resistance work, who had unofficial contacts with the Catholic Church outside, there was no 'institutional strength'.[47]

Marshall thus reported that Rauschning's theory was 'a highly dubious' one, and that though the Trott memorandum showed the possible involvement of church circles in dissident groups, it was improbable that religious opposition circles would be the determining force. He concluded that 'the foundations of a new order in Germany must be sought elsewhere. When a new Germany ultimately emerges, it is bound to be a socialist Germany.' 'The anti capitalist urge in the working class has been exploited, not killed by the Nazis ...' he wrote, 'it is clearly realized by peace-loving Germans that some socialization of heavy industry and of Junker estates is essential if Germany's aggressive spirit is to be quelled.' This was, almost word for word, the view Wilfrid had put forward in a paper for the Political Group for Reconstruction in London some time earlier. The Trott and Rauschning memoranda, treated together, suggested to Marshall and to Wilfrid only the last gasp of the old order – not the breath of the new.[48]

Cripps himself told Visser 'T Hooft that the Trott memorandum could serve as a useful basis for talks only after the defeat of Germany. 'After consulting the Foreign Office and the secret services', Eden reports in his memoirs, he wrote to Bell on 17 July to say that, though he did not question the honesty of the two pastors, he had come to the conclusion that 'it would not be in Britain's national interest to reply'.[49]

Meanwhile, however, Bell had visited Oxford, and Wilfrid now knew more of the details of the proposed uprising. After the proposal was rejected, Wilfrid decided to approach Cripps himself, and did so through Diana Hopkinson – who wrote to Isobel Cripps. Her answer was the only personal letter which, by chance, remained in Wilfrid Israel's files when all others were removed – perhaps because detailed pencilled notes for a conversation were written on the other side. Isobel Cripps's letter is dated 24 July, a week after Eden's rejection of the proposal to Bell.[50]

The notes, expanded on an accompanying paper, indicate that Wilfrid, excited by the detailed news brought by Bell, thought that if the Western Allies and the Soviet Union were to launch a concerted attack in Europe against Germany – something which in July 1942 still appeared possible – then the opposition might rise from within. The first draft begins: 'Do we want to win in '42? Then encourage united front of opposition. Policy of mutual liquidation of Third Reich. Create German Allies – only way to stamp out regime. Later – too late.' As he developed his notes he made three separate points: Britain should 'come to the aid of the besieged opposition' with a 'call to German patriots'; the aim was the social reconstruction of all Europe, and the dangers of missing the opportunity were legion. He refers to the danger of an SS coup, of which the conspirators had warned Bell, leading to the 'consolidation of tyranny

... the dangers of retarding stimulating gestures ... fear of vengeance strengthening resistance of population. Attack from within and without. Russian-British-US synchronization.' And again he repeated, 'Later – too late.'

The summer of 1942 marked the zenith of Anglo-Soviet relations. Britain had signed a twenty-year treaty of alliance with the Soviet Union, in June 1942, and the Second Front appeared near; on 27 July, a demonstration was held in Trafalgar Square, advocating 'Second Front – Now!' But while continuing to send massive military aid to Russia, Churchill and Roosevelt had already agreed on the North African campaign, and, in August, Churchill was to take the unwelcome news to Stalin that there would be no European invasion that year.

Wilfrid probably knew, through Bell, that the anti-Nazis' overtures had been rejected; but there may well have been another reason for the sudden passion of his appeal, and the repeated 'Later – too late'. Wilfrid had been monitoring, week by week, the deportation of Jews from every country in Europe to the East.[51] He was receiving, week by week, news of the disappearance and death of his friends in Germany. The only hope for the Jews of Europe was the Second Front. 'Victories would hasten end,' Wilfrid wrote.

Once it became clear that there was no chance of an 'attack from within and without', Wilfrid's interest in the German opposition waned. He had never regarded the German army, or any of its members, as possible participants in an uprising. The Third Reich was, in his view, 'a coalition of the army and the Nazis', as he wrote in 'Notes on the Opposition' in late 1942. While he had confidence in the integrity of small opposition groups inside Germany, and in the personal integrity of his friends, he believed that only a total defeat of the German army could bring peace. Early in the Nazi period, Wilfrid observed, the army had proved a refuge for many young Germans, but this had not strengthened the opposition. 'It is significant', he wrote, 'in regard to 1933/4 and 1935 that many sought their "salvation" in the army, where they were safe from the Gestapo. Of course they were safe, just where the Third Reich wanted them, among the soldiers, at war! The "Reichswehr illusion" was fostered by the army itself: "the Reichswehr is better than the Nazis – the grey uniform is better than the brown".' But all this, Wilfrid argued, was disastrous for Germany both at home and abroad. He now wrote:

> There is no mass opposition in the Third Reich. Not one opposition, and not different groups. The working class is like all other large groups, neither uniform, nor, in the great majority, either anti-Nazi or anti-military. The socialist workers' revolution is just as much of an illusion as any other

> revolution. Without a complete military defeat, not one like 1918 with the generals undefeated in the field, no overthrow of the system is possible. An overthrow of National Socialism would not mean the fall of the whole system because the nucleus, the enemy, are the generals – the NSDAP merely one brigade. Militarism is the main enemy.

There were two possibilities, he thought, of creating such an opposition:

> one, not through the communist party but through the USSR, which might use propaganda and infiltration through central Europe. The role of the communist party is unforeseen at present, nor can one see whether Russia will be supported by other forces, perhaps even by the generals; this is one possibility;[52] the second possibility is to gather and strengthen the support of all democratic forces in different regions and also attracting the younger generation. This depends on Western Europe and the real help it can give to the splintered forces within. Left to themselves they can do nothing. It is impossible to reap where one has not sown.

Those 'splintered forces' were, in his view, neither the old political centres of power in the army nor the Church, but groups in industry, among the rural communities, and among groups of young Christians. But all this could only follow a total military defeat of Hitler.

Thus, Trott and Wilfrid, pulled apart by the currents of war, were now working almost at cross-purposes. For though Wilfrid believed the opposition should be encouraged, by promising a better future for Germany after the war, he supported the principle of 'unconditional surrender', which was to be spelled out by Churchill and Roosevelt in Casablanca in January 1943. There was to be no quarter now for those anti-Nazis who had remained in Germany.

At the end of 1942, Wilfrid made his most important contributions to Foreign Office research to date on an issue affecting policy. He was the only German involved in the composition of two important FRPS papers, one on the proposal to dismember Germany in the post-war period, and the other, an assessment of the probable situation in Germany at the end of the year. Together, the two papers formed the major section of a War Cabinet paper at the beginning of 1943. The dismemberment paper was the basis of subsequent Foreign Office opposition to punitive post-war measures against Germany, a policy which, had it been carried out, would have driven Germany back into the pre-Bismarck era. First recommended by American policy-makers in 1942, supported subsequently by the Soviet Union and favoured at different times by Churchill and Eden, it was only finally rejected at the 1945 Potsdam conference. The Foreign

Office always opposed it, overtly or covertly, and the 1943 paper was the basis of their opposition.[53]

Dismemberment was a fundamental issue in post-war planning and one that clearly demanded the most expert consideration; yet, as Frank Roberts, head of Central Department, pointed out later, until 1944 the debate was restricted to a small circle 'of about ten persons' and the difficulties involved were not widely known. These difficulties, and the destructiveness of the entire proposal, were fully set out in the FRPS paper written in late 1942.

From October 1941, FRPS had supplied various papers on frontier questions and the possible division of Germany. The most detailed and comprehensive treatment, however, was submitted on 12 January 1943. Initially prepared as a background paper, as Marshall pointed out in forwarding it to the Central Department, 'it differs somewhat from the other Handbook papers in that it discusses policy'.

The paper made out a devastating case against both the dismemberment of Germany and 'truncation', or the detachment of large frontier areas, though it did not rule out transfers of territory in the interests of security; for example, that of East Prussia to Poland. Marshall's team examined this thesis from the historical and contemporary political viewpoints, arguing that all efforts to divide Germany would meet with a strong counter-reaction from all the former German states, despite local loyalties and 'particularism'; for 150 years, Germany had developed as a single economic unit, which could not be split without destroying the possibility of the future economic prosperity envisaged in the Atlantic Charter, even though it might facilitate control of Germany's war potential. The paper queried the 'dubious validity' of the popular theory that German militarism was still fundamentally Prussian, and recommended destroying the institutional foundations of Prussianism by eliminating the military caste, reforming the bureaucracy and breaking up the great estates, rather than detaching all of Prussia from Germany. It queried whether the victorious powers would have either the will or the practical means of preventing a German move towards reunion, particularly since this would be supported 'by the very men whose influence the victor powers wish to see increased' – in other words, the anti-Nazi Germans who survived the war. Geoffrey Harrison of the Central Department minuted this as 'an extremely good paper which will serve as the basis for an examination of the problem of the future of Germany', querying only its form and its length. He rewrote it, eliminating one third entitled 'the history of Germany unity', reordering many of the paragraphs and summarizing others, but retaining the basic argument and its supporting evidence.[54]

In July 1942, at Chatham House in London, commenting on reconstruction, from the viewpoint of security and the prevalent view that 'the Nazi Government would not collapse without civil strife', Wilfrid asked, 'would it not be wise to envisage the various aspects of a collapse of the Nazi regime and to venture to analyse Great Britain's attitude towards Germany, in the case of the Nazi regime being overthrown from within?' He suggested three groups who might achieve this – among them, the army and the heads of administration and industry.[55] At the beginning of January 1943, Frank Roberts asked for Marshall's views on internal developments immediately preceding to and following an armistice. Marshall answered the first question 'after discussions with some of my colleagues', who included Wilfrid, and declined to answer the second, which, he argued, could not be answered 'without considering what our policy (Russia included) was going to be'. The view Marshall and his colleagues put forward was that, while a *coup d'état* by the generals, the single most important force in Germany, together with the Nazis, could not be ruled out, the difficulties involved were enormous. It was very likely, they thought, that the generals, like the people, would fight on to the bitter end, and until further resistance became impossible.

> When that happens, the Nazi clique is almost certain to break up. Some may attempt to escape, others will fight one another, and Hitler may commit suicide. Then the storm will break over Germany. What kind of regime, if any, will then emerge is another question, but it is unlikely that a government will be established soon enough to do anything but capitulate.[56]

This was, of course, an accurate prediction.

The resulting Foreign Office paper reproduced the analysis Marshall had given of the forces operating inside Germany, word for word and paragraph by paragraph.[57] However, the Central Department of the Foreign Office did not accept his conclusion, and substituted another, based on papers prepared in the Foreign Office Library on the situation in 1918; these suggested that, after eliminating the Nazi leaders, the German army might seek terms on a purely military basis with one or other of the Allied powers, or support the establishment of a 'conservative' government, headed 'by someone like Schacht or von Papen'. In other words, the prevalent opinion in the Foreign Office was that the Second World War would end like the first, with an intact German military establishment and a strong central government in Berlin. At this stage, the officials underestimated both Nazi fanaticism and the military power of the Soviet Union.

The FRPS dismemberment paper, and the memorandum on conditions preceding the armistice (minus its important conclusion), constituted two of three parts of a War Cabinet paper circulated by Eden to all service departments and chiefs of staff; the dismemberment paper, in summarized form, was one of the briefs prepared for Eden's visit to America in April 1943.[58] It convinced neither the generals, who remained in favour of dismemberment; nor the Americans, who subsequently, under the Morgenthau plan, proposed moreover to destroy Germany's industrial potential completely. But the Foreign Office remained persuaded that dismemberment would be fatal to post-war security.

The last paper to which Wilfrid contributed was typical of his thinking, in that it stressed the need to co-ordinate Allied policy on post-war Germany, in order to avoid turning the country into an ideological battleground. In February, Marshall wrote a paper on federalism in Germany, in answer to a request by Gladwyn Jebb of the Economic and Reconstruction Department. This was not concerned primarily with security, but showed how federalism 'might in the long run contribute to security through its value as political education', and might be based on the tradition of local self-government in various parts of Germany. It bore Wilfrid's imprint, not only in its analysis of the Weimar democracy, which is almost identical with summaries in his papers, but in the final section, which, as Marshall stated, opened up 'a larger question than that he had been asked to answer'. This was the prospect of a post-war clash between Western democracy and Russian communism, and the possibility that 'Germany would become its battle ground'.[59] The closing section of Marshall's paper was taken, almost word for word, from a paper Wilfrid wrote for him at exactly this time.

Wilfrid's paper suggested two alternative post-war policies which the Allies might adopt: one, punitive and repressive, the other, a policy calculated to reintegrate Germany into Europe – in the light of what he saw as the lessons of Weimar. Marshall concluded his paper:

> The Weimar Social Democrats are often condemned because they did not make a social revolution. They put democracy before socialism, because the alternative was to give rein to those who put socialism (or communism) before democracy. But the countries to which their critics belong were then actively promoting counter-revolution in Russia and elsewhere.

This prevented the Germans from finding a synthesis, for

> The Germans are by nature neither democrats nor communists; they have tried both . . . and neither has struck deep enough roots to stand without the aid of coercive power. . . . If by harmonizing their differences, [the Allies] can solve the German problem, they may in the process find the synthesis which will bridge the gap between west and east. If they fail, their failure will not be felt by Germany alone; it will rebound upon themselves.[60]

* * *

Thus some of Wilfrid's ideas did reach the eyes of those who framed British policy, though they scarcely knew his name. Shortly before his death, he was to defend German anti-Nazis publicly; but only one man knew this.

The Bishop of Chichester had continued to press Eden for some statement, if not to the opposition, then to the world at large, promising that Germany would be treated generously after the war. No statement was made; but the argument that the German will to fight would only be strengthened by dire threats of indiscriminate retribution had not been lost on the propagandists in the Political Warfare Executive, which had also seen the opposition's memoranda. In early July, leaflets were dropped over Germany making the distinction they had asked for, between the Nazis and the mass of the German people. Bell learned that this had been done.

On 19 December 1942, during the Christmas recess, he wrote to Wilfrid telling him that he had tried to discuss the leaflets publicly in the House of Lords, but was being prevented from doing so by Lord Cranborne and Anthony Eden. They had, however, agreed to his sponsoring a debate in the Lords when Parliament resumed, in order to elicit public support for that distinction. Bell told Wilfrid that he wanted to use the occasion to appeal strongly to the German opposition, and to do it carefully, but he was prepared to be told that all Germans were responsible for the Nazi actions. Could Wilfrid provide him with arguments?[61]

Wilfrid did not reply immediately. These were days of horror: the massacres of European Jewry were at their height, there was no sign of the European Second Front, and no hope of rescue by military action. Two days before Bell wrote his letter, the House of Commons had stood in silent tribute to the Jewish victims in the death camps; with others, Wilfrid was trying to translate that tribute into terms of action.

There were also signs that Wilfrid was somewhat impatient with Bell. The Bishop, as head of a relief committee, had sent him a letter in October, enclosing a 'Resolution' urging Britons to economize on food and drink, in view of the sufferings of those under Nazi rule. Wilfrid had answered,

> is there not perhaps too great a discrepancy between the form of sacrifice you suggest and the great tragedy on the Continent? It demands such vigour and staunchness of spirit not to have one's faith dwarfed and thwarted by the ferocity and enormity of the crimes committed by the Nazis against all European peoples, including their own countrymen.[62]

When he finally did reply to Bell's appeal, the struggle in Wilfrid's mind was clear:

> My conflict of conscience is often most acute when thinking of the trend of events in Europe, and sometimes my sense of justice towards the Germans seems to be on the wane. Then I attempt to rediscover the essential facts and thus the essential truth.... I still remain true to my basic conviction that the Nazi party and its affiliated formations commenced their great war of conquest in the first instance by occupying and subjugating Germany and the German people in 1933.... The simple but significant fact that the German people - not only the Jews - were the first victims of Nazi oppression is still too often ignored. This historical fact is not accepted, possibly just because it is something beyond comprehension, beyond simple logic.

The method of Nazi infiltration, the process of *Gleichschaltung*, had a dislocating and paralyzing effect in Germany, psychologically and morally, Wilfrid continued. He thought many 'Aryan' Germans had revolted against the regime, and that Germany was in the midst of a civil war, 'invisible only because of the raging world war'. According to his own study of German propaganda, he told Bell, he was convinced that the policy of terror and extermination had never been accepted by a majority of the Germans. The degree of secrecy maintained over the massacres, the fact that the Allied Declaration had also been kept from the people, and that the deportation of German Jews had never been explained to the Germans, were further proof that the Nazis wished to hide the annihilation of the Jews from the people. Nor, he maintained, was the persecution of the Jews ever popular in Germany. 'Nowhere could the Nazis instigate a really spontaneous and popular rising against the Jews, in not one town, district or village.' He knew personally, he said, of individuals who had shown sympathy and help even at the risk of their own lives, and told Bell that German Jews who had escaped from Germany to a neutral country during the previous few months had also emphasized the help they had received. 'To stay in Germany as an active or even passive anti-Nazi was certainly much more risky, and demanded far greater courage, than to take shelter in a foreign country as a refugee.' There was no way, Wilfrid wrote, in which this could be proved. Nevertheless, it should not be difficult 'to make a marked distinction between the German people and the Nazi dictatorship'.[63]

Wilfrid had recognized the threat of Nazism at an early stage; he had fought it with courage; yet he refused to condemn the German people at large for their tolerance of the regime - the charge against them in the court of history. Perhaps this was because Wilfrid felt a debt to those anti-Nazis who had helped him. Glick, too, in his memoir, recalled 'humble and poor Christian families who risked all to provide food for their Jewish neighbours under cover of night in the small villages'.[64] But for most witnesses, as indeed for Glick, the bravery of such people was overshadowed by the silence of the vast majority of Germans and their passive tolerance of brutality.

But Wilfrid's experiences alone do not account for his reaction. It was not in his nature to hate, and still less to hate any nation or group, and it was in his nature to seek for the tolerance in others which he had within himself. Despite all that had happened to him, moreover, and though he had left Germany forever and saw the return of Jews to Germany as 'beyond reason', he was still, at heart, a loyal German; there is no other way to explain the ardour with which he defended pre-Nazi Germany against its critics.

After several postponements – for the Government was intensely wary of the difficult bishop – Bell rose in the House of Lords on 10 March 1943, to put his motion. He began by quoting Stalin's recent statement that 'it was ridiculous to identify Hitler's clique with the German people and the German state'. Bell asked whether the British Government could not draw the same distinction in the interests of the German opposition and the future of post-war Europe.

Bell's speech elicited from the Lord Chancellor, Lord Simon, who spoke on behalf of the Government, a restatement of the unconditional surrender formula, but also the promise that the German people as a whole would not then, as Goebbels had maintained, be destroyed. The Foreign Office cabled the British Ambassador in Moscow to assure him that the speech had been in no way inspired by the Government.[65] But the Political Warfare Executive noted, with relief, that the debate had been a success; R.H.S. Crossman termed it 'the best and most objective to date'.[66] Goebbels had not made capital out of it.

But the most remarkable aspect of the debate was unknown.

In delivering his plea for understanding for the German people, as distinct from the Nazis, Bell had quoted directly from Wilfrid's letter in the most dramatic section of the speech, which Bell was to term, years later, 'evidence of the reality of an opposition in Germany'.

> It is no mere myth that hundreds of thousands of Aryans were sent to concentration camps, that thousands were executed, that the prisons were overcrowded; it is no mere myth that many hundreds, many thousands, of so-called Aryan families had the ashes of their nearest relatives cynically sent to them from prison and concentration camps; it is no mere myth that hundreds of thousands, nay probably millions of Aryans are now living in Nazi Germany as permanent suspects, untouchable from the Nazi point of view, trembling in face of the direct and indirect persecution of the Gestapo . . . it is a simple matter of fact that Germany was the first country in Europe to be occupied by the Nazis.[67]

Thus, in a speech by an English bishop, in the British House of Lords, and at the height of the Nazi massacres of the Jews, a Jew spoke out for the 'other Germany'.

11
The Adviser

'I still – in my best days and hours – possess a restrained idealism which most likely is unreal and unworldly, but something I cannot cure myself of. It is a kind of mysticism, which I know most of you distrust profoundly.'

In letters written in the spring of 1941 to a young Zionist friend, who was ploughing English fields, Wilfrid sketched his growing alienation from the policies of the Zionist leadership. He did not want 'capitalist' Jews to become too involved in the economy of Jewish Palestine; he wanted to see agrarian socialism as the basis of the new homeland; and he shrank from the prospect of conflict with the Arabs, which mass immigration would inevitably entail. The fate of German and Polish Jews, the growing rumours of mass deportations and arbitrary murder of Jews in Eastern European towns and villages, had underlined the defencelessness of the Jews in hostile countries, and the appeal of political Zionism grew daily. But Wilfrid did not see the rescue of Jewish survivors and the need for the early establishment of a Jewish state as one and the same question. It was this which made it possible for him to work closely with the anti-Zionist Harold Beeley in the 'Jewish Department' of Chatham House, while at the same time planning for his own emigration to Palestine after the war.

By early 1941, Wilfrid was already longing to return to Palestine. 'To be away from you and all other friends from Eretz just at this critical time is very depressing,' he wrote to Friedrich. 'My thoughts are very much with you all, and I trust you know how much I feel I belong to the Palestine world,' he wrote to Arthur Ruppin. In the middle of a heavy raid on London in March, he wrote to Gustav Horn at Hazorea, 'I realize that any day Palestine can be in the centre of active warfare. I trust you are all prepared,' and asked for details of kibbutz housekeeping: 'What about the price of water? The new five hundred dunams of land? Has anyone been transferred to you in the meantime? Did the forest fruit trees bear fruit this year?' By the summer, he wrote of his relief that

Palestine was still safe, and his hope that the Soviet entry into the war would stabilize things, 'if you take a wide view of the future'. He hoped for a new revival of socialism in Palestine and rejection of the 'capitalist intentions of our so-called Jewish friends'. By the autumn, when he began working in Oxford, he was even beginning to learn Hebrew and, in November, he wrote to Friedrich that he wished 'to proceed to Palestine' whenever possible; he had already received his immigration certificate from the Colonial Office.

Wilfrid's work for Beeley began as an offshoot of his much greater involvement with the German section of the FRPS. He knew that it was not approved of by his friends in Great Russell Street: 'I fear many of my Zionist friends believe me to be a lost soul – Chatham House being looked upon generally by them with much suspicion. However, I believe that I have remained unchanged, and my loyalty will not waver.'

Wilfrid's collaboration with Beeley was a curious alliance between a shrewd political mind and one dominated by obstinate idealism. Both men were opposed to mass immigration to Palestine in the post-war period – for totally different reasons: Beeley, because British interests in the Middle East, as he saw them, meant supporting Arabs against Jews; Wilfrid, because he believed that a 'panic exodus' from Europe would destroy the social and ethical basis of the young Jewish community. Beeley realized that the resettlement of Eastern European Jews after the war was the necessary corollary of Britain's Palestine policy. Wilfrid, haunted by the memories of his youth, hoped that in a socialist post-war Europe, Jewish minorities would be accepted as equal citizens. This, and his past experience of the co-operation between Jewish and other relief organizations in the wake of the First World War, convinced him that Britain would play an important role in post-war Jewish rehabilitation; this belief was encouraged by the fact that the British officials with whom he came in contact were – in theory at least – obsessed by the problem of what was to be done with the Jews of Eastern Europe after the war.

The danger that the expulsion of Eastern European Jews by their governments would put pressure on Palestine as a country of refuge had disturbed the Foreign Office long before the war. That the political leaders of Eastern Europe would follow Hitler's example was evident during the Evian conference – when the Polish and Romanian Governments enquired whether, while the Jewish question was on the agenda, substantial numbers of their 'surplus Jewish population' could be transferred elsewhere. The subsequent negotiations had stimulated the Polish Foreign Minister, Colonel Beck, to sound out Lord Halifax, who was warned by the Warsaw Embassy that all Polish Jews – from the 'westernized' business and professional middle class to the 'oriental' masses, with their kaftans and sidelocks, in the urban ghettoes and the village 'middlemen' – were all 'equally resented by the average Pole', and that many laws were already enacted 'in an anti-Jewish sense'. Roger Makins advised Halifax that no country wanted Polish Jews and that he should 'avoid confusion of Polish emigration questions with refugee questions'.[1]

A similar pessimism prevailed at Chatham House. Leonard Stein of the Anglo-Jewish Joint Foreign Committee (JFC), attending a conference with Toynbee and some of the Oxford pundits in 1940, found them 'well informed about the Jewish situation in Poland and Romania ... and ... highly pessimistic about the Jewish future'. One participant was 'anxious to have from us some account of the principal Jewish organizations in the USA; this arose, I think, out of a question as to whether there was any likelihood of a united Jewish approach to the Jewish problems which might arise in connection with a peace settlement'.[2] This was Harold Beeley, who continued to cultivate links with the Anglo-Jewish organizations and to inform himself about their degree of unity – or disunity – on post-war Jewish affairs; and on the importance of Jewish opinion in the United States. Through Toynbee, he lobbied successfully for fresh sources of information, notably from Isaiah Berlin, working in Washington for the Ministry of Information, in 'monitoring the Jewish press'.

Beeley complained that his work was impaired because he had too few contacts in other government departments, but he had no reason to complain of a lack of co-operation from the Jewish organizations. On 25 August 1941, he was invited to sit in on the JFC's meetings, discussing the future of the Jews in Europe and elsewhere. The Foreign Office noted that his knowledge of Jewish questions 'could be useful', and Toynbee supported his continuing surveys of Jewish opinion.[3]

The conservative Jewish bodies, such as the JFC, and the Zionist organization in Great Russell Street, did not constitute a united force; many British Jews did not sympathize with Zionism. But Wilfrid's 1928 observation that 'the world does not know Zionists or non-Zionists, the world knows only Jews' had never been more apposite. As far as the Foreign Office was concerned, all Jewish organizations were likely to exert pressure on the British Government for increased Jewish emigration after the war, and it was duly concerned to keep them at bay.

Zionist suspicion of Chatham House, whose influence on Middle East policy was substantial, had long predated Wilfrid's appearance there.[4] In November 1939, Weizmann had written to Reginald Coupland, the architect of the 1937 partition plan, asking his help in connection with the newly founded 'Jewish Department', which was to deal with Palestine. At Chatham House, Arnold Toynbee, the Arabist Professor H.A.R. Gibb, Albert Hourani, a Christian Syrian, were all anti-Zionists. Now Beeley had been put in charge of the Jewish section. 'The dice are loaded against us,' Weizmann complained, and appealed for Coupland's mediation.[5]

The letter, unfortunately, was sent at the same time as another Zionist envoy whose tactlessness knew no bounds. As Shertok noted, 'He succeeded in making the impression that the Jewish Agency claimed to have the right to interfere in the running of the Institute.'[6] Professor Alfred Zimmern announced that if the Zionists did not 'co-operate with Beeley', he would resign and the whole idea of a Jewish section would be dropped. But he also promised that there would be a 'Zionist' in the section, while Beeley 'would do everything to prove that he was free of prejudice and wanted to co-operate with us'.[7]

But Reginald Coupland was increasingly distracted by the much larger issue of Indian self-rule, and the idea of a 'Zionist' was forgotten until Wilfrid, imperceptible as always in official memoirs, strolled into Balliol.

He could not have been under any illusion as to the political purpose of Beeley's work. Among his papers is the FRPS programme initialled by Beeley, from September 1941, which explained that all work for the section was to elucidate for government departments, during and after the war, the connection between the problems of the Jews of Eastern Europe and the Jewish situation in Palestine. The views of American Jewry were to be monitored for this purpose.

Beeley explained that the work would proceed on the hypothesis 'that the problems faced and presented by a large concentration of Jews in this region can be approached without any demand for a large-scale emigration as a condition precedent to their solution'. To this end, the queries were to focus on the causes of anti-semitism since 1919, the effect of post-war reconstruction on these causes, and the state of mind of Jewish communities in that area and throughout the world as to the measures to be taken to improve their position. The 'working hypotheses' were that: 'The Jewish National Home cannot be securely built against the Arabs; that the Arabs would only come to terms with it if it is somehow integrated into the Arab world; and that Zionism cannot accept such a policy of integration unless it provides the Jewish national home for some scope for immigration and development.'[8]

Wilfrid had no quarrel with any of these hypotheses. His problem was – as he himself knew – that despite his long experience in international relief work, he had very little first-hand knowledge of Jewish politics in Palestine, and none, save that acquired on hasty journeys over the previous decade, of the situation of the Jews in Eastern Europe. He complained to his friends in Palestine that 'nobody seems to give a clear concise report of developments; the Executive is silent and all friends of Zionist affairs are kept in the dark', and he was certainly not in the confidence of the Zionist functionaries who came and went in the offices of Great Russell Street. He attended an informal 'study group' of Zionist businessmen, which met at Rebecca Sieff's house in Park Lane, but, as Walter Zander, a jurist and ex-internee who kept the minutes, remembered, he was silent and withdrawn, except on one occasion when Mrs Sieff exclaimed, 'An Arab! We must have an Arab at these discussions. Who knows one?' and Wilfrid alone raised his hand.[9]

The 'Arab' was Albert Hourani, the young Syrian scholar, who was Wilfrid's fellow worker at Chatham House. At that time Hourani thought the fundamental cause of the abnormal Jewish political situation was the Jews' 'sense of mission', and did not believe that nationalism would solve the problem. Nor did he think that economic 'restratification' – of which Wilfrid approved – would change the Jews' social nature. He was convinced, however, that mass immigration to Palestine would endanger the established Jewish community because of radical and widespread Arab opposition. Hourani, who, after a few meetings with Wilfrid, was sent on a six-month tour of the Middle East, could only have increased Wilfrid's sense of the vulnerability of the Zionist enterprise.[10]

Hourani noted accurately that Wilfrid had little experience of daily life in Palestine and that he was remote from the Zionist main-stream. Beeley, however, ten years younger than Wilfrid and deeply impressed by his personality, thought him a detached and authoritative adviser on Jewish affairs. Immediately after Wilfrid's death, he wrote to Norman Bentwich that he had 'admired him more than almost anyone else I knew'.[11] He was not to know that most of the background information which Wilfrid provided in his memoranda came from a seventeen-year-old Youth Aliya instructor, whose daily task it was to drive a tractor on a farm near Shrewsbury.

Eric Lucas had begun his studies in Germany, had sat at Buber's feet, together with most of the young Zionists of his generation, and had already heard much of Wilfrid when he came to pay Youth Aliya a first visit in 1940. When Lucas was interned, Wilfrid arranged for his early release, encouraged him to attend study courses, and debated German and Zionist politics with him by letter. Lucas's ideological training in the Werkleute meant that he knew most of the available literature and sent knowledgeable answers to Beeley's questions.[12]

The first questions Wilfrid put to Lucas related to a paper on Jewish emancipation he was asked to prepare. Where, he asked, could he find material on Jewish assimilation and anti-semitism? He needed 'some clues' as to what 'specific Jewish characteristics could be sacrificed without exterminating basic forms of belief (kaftans, beards, certain customs of everyday life which cause alienation)'.

Two weeks later he wrote with fresh questions – 'how far obstacles to assimilation could be broken down by Jewish action, how far German anti-semitism resembled that of the old Russian Pale', and whether assimilation was possible 'without violating the feelings of large masses of Jews, especially in Eastern Europe, and which would at the same time help in a marked manner to improve the attitude of the non-Jews to their Jewish fellow citizens'. As if realizing how grotesque these questions were, he explained, 'You will realize that the origins of these questions is a non-Jewish one.' When he received Lucas's answers he wrote, 'My hair stands on end when I think of the knowledge I should possess to set out to do this piece of work. I feel rather humble and helpless. Your guidance means a lot to me.'

The long paper Wilfrid finally produced in which, as he wrote to Lucas, 'the independent contribution of my learned mind can be summed up in a very few sentences', showed how uneasy he was with the proposition that Jewish conformism, the shedding of 'kaftans and beards', would protect Jews from anti-semitism; he pointed out that this had not helped the Jews of Germany.[13]

Two subsequent papers produced by the Jewish section indicate how the partnership between Beeley and Wilfrid developed. In November 1941, Beeley submitted a detailed paper on Great Britain and Palestine in which he predicted that the devastation of European Jewry would give rise to a strong current of feeling in America and elsewhere, unless positive measures were taken to improve their situation in Eastern Europe, or provide homes for them in other parts of the world, and that 'Jewish spokesmen were sceptical regarding the chances of improvement between Eastern European states and their Jews'. He predicted possible violence in Palestine unless there was a reconciliation between British and Jewish aims. There were, however, factors which might lead to a reconciliation:

> The first of these is the cultural as distinct from the 'political' wing of Zionism, working for the development of the National Home not into a state but into a spiritual centre for Western Jewry. Although this group is today negligible as an effective force, it has played a considerable part in the history of Zionism, and might in favourable circumstances recover its importance. The efforts which the leaders of cultural Jewry might be expected to make to persuade the Palestine Jewish community to renounce its political aspirations

> would have more chance of success if it were possible to induce the Arabs to permit the continuance, even on a greatly reduced scale, of Jewish immigration.[14]

These were precisely Wilfrid's views at the time, as all his letters indicate. But 'cultural Jewry' scarcely existed by now; the ideas of Ahad HaAm, the Jewish writer who had developed the idea of a 'spiritual centre' decades earlier through classics of Zionist literature, no longer influenced Zionist politics.[15]

In January 1942, the Jewish section submitted a longer and more detailed paper on world Jewry and Eastern Europe. After a detailed and accurate analysis of past developments, it noted that anti-semitism predated Nazism and could be expected to survive it. Despite the 'setback' in Germany, however, assimilation was recommended, particularly in 'external characteristics' (the Foreign Office was by now acquiring an obsessive interest in kaftans and sidelocks). The most important measure to be taken was to improve the general economic situation of the region, given a reasonable measure of financial assistance and commercial co-operation from the Western powers. Moreover, the writer added, in the case of the formation of a government by the workers and peasants parties, Jews and Gentiles might reach 'harmonious relations'.[16]

As this paper was submitted, Wilfrid wrote frankly to his friends in Palestine about his views on the future of European Jewry and his relationship with Zionism. 'I fear I am drifting away from the official interpretation of Zionism,' he wrote. A 'stampede' from Eastern Europe would mean 'a transfer of disaster from Europe to Palestine'. The Jews who survived the war would have to have new opportunities, and, for the masses, Eastern European socialism 'would be a greater reality than Zionist ideas and ideals'. Even the Orthodox Jews would have to face 'the scientific facts of our days and reinterpret rigid orthodox ritual'. At the same time, under the pressure of co-operation with peasant and labour organizations, a united trend for professional stratification would set in. 'Then for the first time in history there might be a hope of a decent solution ... for the masses of Jews without breaking up community life as a whole.' Young people would prepare for life in Palestine as the result of 'a true conflict of conscience and part of the fundamental urge ... not the result of a disastrous process of mass immigration of a disintegrated people. I still have faith in Socialism, most people have lost theirs. When I spoke to Ben Gurion I had the feeling that he was one of those fanatics without true faith.' Wilfrid had probably met Ben Gurion when the Zionist leader visited London in the autumn of 1941; his letters indicate that the two men found no common language: 'Since I met him and had a talk with him,' Wilfrid wrote in October 1942 to Rudi Baer, 'I feel that his trend of mind and tendencies have dangerously much in common with an ideology intensely opposed to mine.' For Wilfrid saw Ben Gurion not as a socialist leader but as a fervent nationalist.

Wilfrid's views, as filtered through Beeley, were precisely what the Foreign Office wanted to hear, though the Colonial Office had dissociated itself from Beeley's modest proposal for the continuance, even on 'a greatly reduced scale', of Jewish immigration.[17] However, the Eastern Department had already received opinions, from the most authoritative sources available in London, that Eastern European socialists did not share Wilfrid's gently optimistic view of the future of emancipated Jews in plans for their own post-war policies.

The cheerfully romantic beliefs Wilfrid cherished about Russia dovetailed with ideas which lingered on in the Foreign Office until 1941; there was continuing interest in the work of the AgroJoint and in any news that Jewish refugees from Eastern Europe might migrate eastwards. In February 1941, Wilfrid's friend in the Refugee Department, Richard Latham, minuted a report that 1,000 more Jewish families were to settle in collective farms in Birobidzhan, the Jewish Soviet Republic: 'Refugees section would be most interested if it should appear that the USSR would absorb any of the capitalist world's surplus of Jewish refugees'; it took a far better informed observer, Donald McLean, of the Eastern Department, later unmasked as a Soviet agent, to minute, 'These families were just from another part of the Soviet Union, and have probably been deported.' He informed Latham that 'the Joint institutions had now been liquidated by the Soviet Union, who confiscated its funds and shot most of the Jews'.[18]

Subsequently, Polish Jews who had fled to Russia were suspect, both to the Poles and to the British Government, which suspected them of staking out Russian claims to post-war Poland.

In exile in London, meanwhile, there was one man at least who was in the position to disillusion both Wilfrid and Beeley, at this early stage, as to post-war Polish attitudes to the Jews. This was Dr Ignaczy Schwarzbart, a Zionist member of the Polish Parliament in 1939, and in 1941 the only Jewish member of the Polish government in exile, the Polish National Council. As his wartime diary shows, Schwarzbart was deeply ambivalent about both Poland and Zionism, bitter about the overt anti-semitism of many of his colleagues on the Council, and desperate about the fate of Polish Jews. Schwarzbart's London exile was very different from Wilfrid's.

He had a sick wife at home and spent most of his spare time with fellow Poles at the Cumberland Hotel; he admired British behaviour in the Blitz and the honesty of the British press, but he also hated national phlegm (visiting Oxford, he saw only its 'aloofness from war; aloofness means indifference'), and he trusted no one. He hated his fellow Poles, including, later, his fellow Jew on the Council, the socialist Zygielbojm – the two were not on speaking terms; he disliked his fellow Zionists (Weizmann was a 'pro-British opportunist'); where the English were concerned, he had a good word only for Eleanor Rathbone, the 'pigeon-hearted lady' (a Polish term for courage). Schwarzbart knew that the right-wing Poles supported the idea of mass Jewish emigration, though the Council had pronounced its opposition to anti-semitism. He had, however, hopes of the Socialist and Peasant Parties. These hopes were dashed when, on 31 August 1941, he received information about the replies given by three Polish leaders in London – Ciolcocz of the Socialists, Micolajczyk of the Peasant Party (who was to become the leader of the exiles after Sikorski's death in 1943) and Professor Gurka of the Democratic Party – to a Chatham House questionnaire. Ciolcocz thought Jewish assimilation impossible and supported partial emigration; Mikolajczyk thought the Jews a separate nation and advocated their emigration to Palestine and other countries; Gurka noted approvingly that Jewish emigration was exceeding natural increase.

Schwarzbart commented bitterly, 'It was very enlightening for me to be acquainted with these views, for two reasons.' One was his surprise at Ciolcocz's views, and the other 'to see the deep interest of the Royal Institute of International Affairs, which has probably been very dissatisfied with the replies, as Mr Beeley in charge of all these problems is an anti-Zionist, and would like the Jews to stay put in Poland and not emigrate'.[19]

Two days later, Schwarzbart met Wilfrid for the first time to discuss the situation of the Jews in Europe. He noted that Wilfrid was 'leaning to assimilation, though it is not his ideology – it is the old Jewish problem'. Next day, he lunched with Beeley and Wilfrid together. This was the chance for Schwarzbart to explain his conviction that the Poles were not interested in the Jews as partners in their post-war world, and that all groups supported Jewish emigration. But his pride prevented him from doing so. Schwarzbart was, after all, an ex-member of the Polish Parliament; he was serving an exile government despite what he describes as daily insults from its right-wing members. For the sake of his own dignity, he could not tell Beeley and Wilfrid any of this. Thus he recorded:

> The fox [Beeley] was of course interested in getting some information from

me about and around the Jewish problem. I took it seriously and analysed the economic and structural plans of the government meant to check emigration. He listened but was visibly not convinced.... Beeley did not ... stress the problems around the crisis because his question would decamouflage his intentions and I was not willing to begin myself with any confessions. So we parted without having achieved what we set out to do.[20]

Wilfrid and Schwarzbart continued to meet at intervals. Wilfrid mollified the testy Schwarzbart, who described him as 'a very likeable man with very attractive manners' – for Schwarzbart an extraordinary accolade – and who tried to convince Wilfrid that socialism was not the solution to the Jewish problem in Eastern Europe: 'I pointed to tens of examples proving that a socialist has applied competitive anti-semitism in the economic field.'[21] But the underlying resentment towards what he suspected was contempt for the *Ostjuden* by all Western Jews soon soured the relationship. When Wilfrid communicated to Schwarzbart an offer from the ICA to help Polish Jews in Spain, he immediately took offence at the terms: 'It is for me quite clear that for the ICA one German Jew is more precious than ten Polish ones ... we should have more respect for ourselves, rely more on self-help, and be more arrogant ... the German Jews know it better.'[22]

Wilfrid did not know the daily agony Schwarzbart went through in the Council, but he perceived Schwarzbart's intense bitterness, as one of his notes on a conversation indicates, and thought it distorted his sense of reality.[23] Thus, though on the evidence of the diary, Schwarzbart's views were remarkably close to those of Wilfrid where the rights of Jews in post-war Europe were concerned, the two men never spoke frankly to one another. And though Beeley had already begun to realize, as Schwarzbart noted, that resettling Jews in Poland was not a practical proposition,[24] neither he, nor any other British official, was to face the issue realistically until after the war.

In the spring of 1942, one of Wilfrid's tasks was to piece together information, and to report, on the deportations to the East of the Jewish populations of European countries. Evidence surviving in his private papers shows that he was among the first to evaluate the significance of these deportations, to link the news with what he knew of the massacres in Eastern Europe, and to convey these assessments to those who were in touch with the Ministry of Economic Warfare.

Wilfrid's evidence is contained in a series of reports, entitled 'Movements of Jewish Population in Europe since the Outbreak of Hostilities', dated March 1942 and updated subsequently to May and July.[25] According to other documents in his papers and the evidence of Jewish colleagues, his sources of information included those available to people in London who were concerned with the fate of the Jews of Europe at that time:[26] among them the Jewish Telegraphic Agency reports and the publications of the World Jewish Congress. But they also included a contact in Stockholm who was in direct communication with the Frauenbund women in Berlin. The fact that Wilfrid also knew promptly of the fate of his colleagues indicates that he may have had other sources of information inside Germany.

A striking aspect of Wilfrid's reports is the fact that he realized almost immediately the ultimate Nazi objective and the significance of the pattern of deportations, and accurately predicted what was about to happen. Scarcely less striking is the attempt to convince the recipients of these reports of the objectivity and caution with which he treats the information conveyed. Neither Marshall nor Beeley credited these stories at the time.[27] Many Foreign Office minutes show that British officials were intensely wary of what they saw as Jewish hysteria and atrocity propaganda. Wilfrid wrote his reports from inside the British Establishment itself, as a consultant at Chatham House; and he must have been aware that their credibility would, once more, depend on his ability to present the terrible facts in what Ogilvie Forbes had called in 1938 'Mr Israel's restrained terms'.

As early as March 1942, Wilfrid wrote of Germany:

> Nazi rule is aiming at the extermination of the Jews. As they are still at present required to slave for war production, wholesale deportation to the East has been held up. They are outcasts, neither receiving average food rations nor normal wages, nor sufficient clothing or heating. They are merely existing under the control of the Gestapo, constantly menaced with concentration camps, punitive forced labour or deportation.

In this same document of March 1942, Wilfrid reported mass deportations from Belgium and Czechoslovakia, the annihilation of the Jews of Bessarabia, 250,000 Jews murdered in occupied Poland. In Austria, where 'strong anti-semitism has always been prevailing, certainly within the ranks of the middle class', the remaining 40,000 Jews were 'probably only waiting for their deportation to Poland'.

Also in March, Wilfrid reported on the lack of direct Nazi initiative in Italy, on the 'determined resistance of the government and King' in Denmark, but insisted that most of the Dutch Jews sent to concentration camps in 1941 had died and that only the lack of transport prevented the deportation of the rest. In Romania, he wrote, 'the official anti-Jewish policy doubtlessly aims at the entire extermination of the Jews'; meanwhile, they were concentrated in ghettoes and camps. 'The aim may be to concentrate them all in the forced labour camps of Transnistria (Bug Valley annihilation area).' The only glimpse of light came from Russia, where Wilfrid estimated that the refugees would be rehabilitated, and Portugal, 'a vital centre of transmigration which has, in fact, been the only outlet of importance to overseas from the West European area under Nazi rule or influence.' Spain, he reported, was hostile to refugees from France.

In another section, dated May 1942, it is again clear that Wilfrid was trying to present the picture of Jewish deportations objectively, in order that it should be accepted as genuine. He distinguished between the murderous response to the Nazi initiative in traditionally anti-semitic countries and those which had no such tradition; he noted that the Lublin resettlement scheme had failed, attributing it to a 'change of methods'. 'It seems that considerations of a military and strategic nature have, for some time, dislocated the Nazi plans aiming at rapid annihilation of the entire Jewish population', and pointed out that forced labour in some of the camps was 'an indirect method employed to hasten the process of extermination'. He emphasized that the forced labour camps, planned for the entire Jewish population of Europe, meant plans for Jewish annihilation.

> These plans, should the Nazis be given opportunity of enforcing them systematically, will eventually result in the evacuation of all urban Ghettoes [where the Jews were now concentrated] and in the concentration of the entire European Jewish Population in 'annihilation areas' of Eastern Europe.

This assessment of Wilfrid's was made three months before Gerhard Riegner, the World Jewish Congress observer in Geneva, sent a telegram to Jewish leaders in America and Britain about a plan to exterminate the Jews of Europe 'at one blow', and seven months before the Allied Declaration of 17 December 1942 publicly acknowledged the fact that the Nazis were systematically murdering all the Jews in the countries under their control.

In Wilfrid's later report, dated July 1942, he described the large-scale deportations from Germany that were renewed in the spring, anticipating the deportation of all German Jews by the end of July; he reported a fundamental change in Italy since 'the Italians have quite obviously given way to Nazi pressure', though there were 'no deportations yet'; and that official anti-semitism in Holland was intensifying daily 'and now clearly aims at the entire segregation and ultimate deportation of all Jews as rapidly as possible'. The same was true, he said, of France.

In his report of July 1942, Wilfrid appeared to be quite deliberately subordinating the emphasis on numbers, which he insisted could not be authoritatively checked, in order to stress the Nazi aim of extermination. To Hans Reissner, whose parents he was trying to extricate from Germany through appeals to the Red Cross and neutral embassies, he wrote at the end of the year, when the news was generally accepted, 'I am afraid the trend of that which is being published is true and real, though I do not believe the figures, which have been compiled hastily, superficially, and without the possibility to check up on them.'

Who was reading Wilfrid's reports, and what use was made of them? One government committee which was openly engaged in monitoring Jewish deportations in Europe was the Allied Post-War Requirements Bureau (APWRB), established during the early war period as the nucleus of an economic intelligence service, which assessed Allied needs and sources of supply, and was preparing a programme of the Allies' requirements in the post-war period. The Bureau was staffed chiefly by officials seconded from the Board of Trade Post-War Commodity and Relief Department to the Relief Section of the Ministry of Economic Warfare.[28] One of these officials, J.H. Gorvin, an expert on relief supplies who had worked with the Allied Commission in Paris after the First World War, had been in contact with Nansen over Russian relief and probably knew Wilfrid from that period. A three-page document among Wilfrid's papers, dated 9 June 1942, indicates that he was consulted by Gorvin on post-war relief measures in Europe. Headed 'Mr Gorvin', it answers questions about the tasks of a post-war relief force whose aim would be to handle the rehabilitation of the surviving displaced persons and refugees in various parts of the Continent.

As another source makes clear, Wilfrid was proposed by Beeley for this task at a FRPS meeting in late May, after several of his deportation reports (to which no reference is made) had already been submitted;[29] the Bureau had undoubtedly received those reports. For Foreign Office files record that, from the beginning of 1942, the Bureau received most of its information on population movements from the Chatham House Committee on Reconstruction – on which Wilfrid was serving. Sir Frederick Leith Ross, head of the Bureau and, until 1942, of the Ministry of Economic Warfare (MEW), thought these reports so important that he suggested giving them a wider circulation. But Nigel Ronald, of the Economic and Reconstruction Department, and Roger Makins, head of the Central Department, were both uneasy about a government department of 'temporaries', such as the staff of the Bureau, being in touch with an 'unofficial body', such as Chatham House, though contact with the FRPS under Foreign Office supervision was approved. All this suggests that Wilfrid's reports, which were unconnected with his work for

Harold Beeley, were commissioned in the first instance by the Bureau, a body which dealt with post-war problems. And they were almost certainly seen by the heads of the Ministry of Economic Warfare, most of whose work was connected with Intelligence.[30]

Jewish deportations are mentioned, very briefly, in the MEW weekly intelligence bulletins which refer to 'expatriation ... on a scale new in history ... including the deportation of Jews', from March 1942. This was precisely the period of Wilfrid's first reports. Specific mentions of 'strikingly inadequate' rations for the Jews in Germany and 'anti-semitic measures', including deportations from Holland to Germany, are echoes of the information he relayed.[31] Foreign Office documents refer to their reception of APWRB reports on deportations, and to the source as Chatham House, between February and November 1942 – by which time the numbers of those deported to Poland were given as 2,350,000.[32] Central Department officials were thus less than candid in maintaining at the time of the Riegner report in August that they had 'no information from other sources confirming this assertion' – that is, that the deportations meant the extermination of the Jews of Europe.[33] All the indications are that Wilfrid's reports, with his analysis of the deportation patterns, were indeed seen by Foreign Office officials as well as those of the Ministry of Economic Warfare. They did not, of course, bear his name.

The reports themselves are carbon copies, and reaction to the originals is unknown. Wilfrid was debarred from discussing his work for government offices and Jewish colleagues never learned what his work comprised. He did not even tell David Astor, whom he knew he could trust, of the messages George Bell had brought back from Stockholm from the German opposition, or that he had been asked to assess the strength of the opposition and its chances of overthrowing the Nazi regime. Nor did he tell his Jewish colleagues of his attempts to convince British officials of the threat to all the Jews of Europe. He was therefore doubly bound to repress his feelings. With his official superiors, he had to appear as detached and objective as possible; it was this, as has been seen, which won him golden opinions, this for which he was consulted. With his Jewish colleagues, he could say nothing of official response to his reports – if, indeed, he learned it. By the end of the year, his Jewish friends noticed that he was desperate for any move, however small, on behalf of potential deportees, and found himself unable any longer to limit his work to 'reports' alone, which, as he had noted in a different context twenty years earlier, could do so little to change reality.

'Deportation', 'annihilation' and 'extermination'. These were the three words in which Wilfrid described the fate of the Jews at a time when the news was not generally accepted. At the same time, he was attempting, through Youth Aliya, to move the Zionist bodies to action. Joseph Linton, Weizmann's secretary in London, remembered Wilfrid asking to be sent to Portugal from the autumn of 1942.[34] He kept Eleanor Rathbone informed of what he knew; she was to tell Churchill that she knew more about the refugee problem than almost anyone else in London, and was to press for the admission of refugees to England, from the time the news of the massacres became public.[35] But, meanwhile, what preoccupied the various departments of the Foreign Office, and the Colonial Office, regarding the fate of the Jews of Eastern Europe, and what was increasingly to perturb members of the Government, was what was to be done with the 'millions' of Jews in that area after the end of the war.

From August 1941, in meetings with the Colonial Secretary, Lord Moyne, both Weizmann and Ben Gurion stressed that, during the post-war period, the aim of the Zionists was for mass immigration to Palestine; the Jewish people, they argued, would never accept the restrictions of the 1939 White Paper. Weizmann told Moyne, at the beginning of August, that it was proposed to emigrate 1,500,000 Jews within twenty years; barely three weeks later, Ben Gurion spoke of 3,000,000 within ten years; this startling escalation, coming from the two men who represented Zionist diplomacy abroad and the grass roots movement in Palestine, caused alarm in Whitehall.[36] If any further confirmation were needed of Zionist plans (though in fact Weizmann and Ben Gurion worked not only independently of one another but without any formal decisions having been taken in Palestine), documents taken from Ben Gurion's luggage when he left for the United States in November 1941, which included the protocols of meetings with leading British 'non-Zionist' Jews, confirmed there was a consensus that large numbers of Jewish refugees would have to be resettled in Palestine in the post-war period, that Weizmann was also now speaking of numbers between 2,500,000 and 3,000,000, and that a Jewish state was the immediate post-war aim.[37] The battleground for Jewish statehood had long since shifted to the United States. The Biltmore programme, announced by Ben Gurion publicly in a New York hotel of that name in May 1942, postulated, for the first time, the foundation of a state, and called for millions of Jews to emigrate there as soon as the war was over. This was a challenge to Britain rather than a plan of action, as was Weizmann's letter to Churchill in September 1941, circulated to the War Cabinet, arguing that the power of 5,000,000 American Jews would affect the American war effort, but could only be ensured by Britain's support for a Jewish fighting force.[38] Churchill himself consistently supported the idea of a post-war Jewish state, in accordance with the terms of the Balfour Declaration – to the consternation of the Foreign and Colonial Offices – and reiterated his opposition to the White Paper. The rationale of this paper steadily eroded and, in response to pressure from the Prime Minister, its timetable was suspended entirely; its March 1944 deadline was allowed to pass without the Arab majority being fixed or an Arab veto on further Jewish immigration being put into force. Churchill encouraged Weizmann's parlays with Roosevelt in 1942, apparently in the hope of drawing the American President into a joint Anglo-American Middle East settlement after the war.[39]

The Zionist leaders' proposals stimulated a flurry of proposals for an alternative territory for the post-war refugees, at Cabinet level. In September 1941, after his meetings with Weizmann and Ben Gurion, Moyne proposed large-scale resettlement in 'devastated areas of Europe', following the example set by the Nazis in transferring German populations into Poland and the Baltic provinces;[40] South America and Madagascar were also reviewed. Lord Cherwell, quoting Churchill's suggestion after talks with Orde Wingate, approved of Eritrea or Tripolitania.[41] Discussions on these proposals never took place in the Cabinet; but the issue of Jewish resettlement remained the constant concern of the Foreign Office. Officials there realized that the best way to block American support for Zionism would be 'to put forward some constructive plan for the future disposal of Jewish refugees generally, combined with a plan for the settlement of the Palestine question'.[42] This, though the subject of many memoranda, was regarded as impracticable while the war lasted and while Churchill remained Prime Minister. But the vision of an army of dispossessed refugees advancing on Palestine intensified British officials' insistence that Jews should not be separately represented, or separately treated, where humanitarian measures, rescue, or relief were concerned, from any other groups under Nazi rule, and their equally obdurate refusal to allow Jewish organizations to play any part in planning for the rehabilitation of European Jews after the war.

'Palestine must not become a dumping ground for the dispossessed masses of Europe.' Wilfrid was to repeat this phrase incessantly in his letters towards the end of 1942. He could understand the call for mass immigration, in the psychological sense, he wrote to Rudi Baer in October 1942, but he believed it was unwise and dangerous to the Zionist cause. 'I feel that I have got to take a stand on the matter of the after war situation.... I cannot any more flounder about. I have got to take responsibility for my views and face the issues, even if I am not only discouraged by my friends but even have to sever relations with people that I have co-operated with so far,' he wrote to Werner Senator.

To David Hopkinson, a friend seconded by the British army to the Mandate education authorities in Palestine, he wrote in November 1942:

> Ben Gurion's influence I feel is most unwholesome and he and many others are beginning to lose their balance. Many friends of mine will be opposing this attitude of mind. Once again they will represent a very small minority; they will be looked upon as defeatists. I'm afraid I am rather up against the same kind of difficulties over here.

When Ben Gurion returned to Palestine and announced plans for the immigration of 2,000,000 Jews in the post-war period, Wilfrid wrote to Lucas, in October 1942, 'What is that mad hatter, that maniac march hare, your beloved leader Ben Gurion doing in Eretz? I wished they would put his tongue in shackles! My undemocratic spirit is growing in the course of time and events. Sorry!'

In February 1943, he wrote to Friedrich Altmann

> Ben Gurion and his interpretation of the situation I consider to be extremely wild and ecstatic and altogether out of proportion to realities.... One cannot desire co-operation with the Arabs, proclaim a bi-national situation, and in fact assume that unlimited immigration is a natural right and the 'basic political necessity'. I am afraid understanding with the Arabs ... excludes the right of unlimited immigration.... My personal, perhaps very simple-minded attitude is that we should go on trying to build up Palestine for the next fifty years without too many pretensions and with faith in our hearts. Unfortunately there will be many less Jews living in the world ... and many of those who have survived will come under the Soviet sphere of interest.... Immigration must in the main be that of children and youth and be dominated by pioneering traditions. If we believe in the aims of the United Nations, however diluted they may become, post-war Europe will offer an asylum for many.... I say that for our sake, for the sake of a true social development of Zionism, we should not endorse a maximalist and expansionist programme.

At the same time, however, Wilfrid did not dismiss the dangers to Jewish survival of a post-war nationalist revival in Eastern Europe. But he thought of a repetition of the post-First World War situation, of a choice between reactionary nationalism and the revolutionary socialism he believed would be favourable for Jewish development. If the first occurred,

> a new wave of militant aggressive antagonism towards all 'alien' entities, including the remnant Jewish communities, might be the result. Vehement nationalism would imply that the constructive co-operation and guidance of Great Britain would be withheld, and the British Empire and the USA would

> become once more semi-isolationist in their attitude towards the Continent and above all, Eastern Europe. Then ... Jewish mass migration ... would develop into open conflict in the Near East.

He recognized that the Jews might be an anomaly in the Soviet Union; but, he argued, 'there was not sufficient proof to state definitely that continuity of Jewish life in Russia has been or necessarily will be severed altogether' – the very wording indicating his growing uncertainty. Despite all these objections, however, he still thought the socialist option 'the only realistic vision which may lead the Jews, in fact all the peoples of Europe, out of this present state of agony and chaos'.[43]

At this time, Wilfrid's views were being canvassed by the Allied Post-War Requirements Bureau regarding the immediate post-war measures to be taken for the relief of Jewish survivors. But the Foreign Office was increasingly suspicious of any joint Jewish effort to plan for post-war relief. In January 1942, Jewish organizations in England approached the Bureau to discuss problems connected with the rehabilitation of European Jews. Though the secretary of the Board of Deputies, A.G. Brotman, made it clear that he thought in terms of relief and resettlement, rather than emigration – with the exception of Germany – the Foreign Office regarded all contacts of this kind with deep alarm, and warned the official responsible, J.H. Gorvin, to steer clear of all Jewish approaches.[44] In October, a joint delegation of Zionist and non-Zionist organizations visited Richard Law, Under-Secretary of State at the Foreign Office, and suggested that an autonomous Jewish body, including American Jews, be set up for post-war and rescue work. The Central Department minuted the report that 'this looked like the thin end of the wedge for separate Jewish participation in the peace'. Though another official noted that the Jewish desire for liaison was reasonable enough, Frank Roberts, the head of Central Department, added: 'The Jewish organizations have been angling for some time to be placed, so to speak, on the same footing as the Allied governments and be allowed to speak for Jews, for example in regard to atrocities. It is, I submit, most important not to fall in with these ideas.'[45]

Wilfrid had hoped, as he told several colleagues, that there would be wide British support for rehabilitation work in Eastern Europe. In 1942, he told Ernst Lowenthal, a former Berlin colleague and co-worker for German refugees in Britain, that he would have to be prepared to return to Germany to work with the survivors of the camps after the war. Wilfrid envisaged a large-scale relief operation shared by Jews and non-Jews alike, the kind of partnership he himself had known after the

First World War. But British officials were now wary of every Jewish proposal for relief. Even the Board of Deputies of British Jews and the Chief Rabbi's Emergency Committee – neither of them Zionist bodies – were suspect, when they asked whether Jewish units could work in the liberated territories. Gorvin sent these innocuous appeals to the Foreign Office asking whether there was not 'any hidden snag'.[46]

In early 1942, Beeley, primed by his Washington reports, warned the Foreign Office that American-Jewish support for post-war Jewish emigration was growing, but that American Jews were reluctant to endanger their own position by the admission of Jewish refugees. Thus, those Jews who identified themselves as such were going over to the Zionist cause. The warnings were taken seriously.[47]

The Foreign Office subsequently consulted Herbert Emerson, League High Commissioner for Refugees as well as head of the still dormant Evian Committee, as to proposals for post-war relief and resettlement projects. He too warned of an exodus of Jews from Europe unless formal guarantees of civil rights for persecuted Jewish minorities were provided. Since the Jewish organizations were to have no separate role in post-war resettlement, the Foreign Office considered working out a joint policy with the United States, concerned by American statements 'raising hopes in the breasts of refugees ... which can only be fulfilled through a modification of British policy'.[48]

In March 1942, Emerson submitted an informal memorandum on refugee resettlement to Eden; both he and John Winant, the American Ambassador, later approved it and thought it a basis for Anglo-American discussions.[49] Emerson's main argument was that the refugees should be assisted to return to their original homes. He recognized that compulsory repatriation of the victims of 'appalling persecution, torture and humiliation' might cancel any 'homing instinct' in the Jews of Central and Eastern Europe. But acting once more as an ex-administrator in colonial territory, Emerson argued that Allied guarantees to repatriated refugees would be part of a peace treaty 'backed by the necessary sanctions'. Tolerance was to be enforced at the point of the gun. Emerson implied, in his memorandum, that the Jews themselves would have to change, in order to be accepted as equal citizens, by 'a broadening of the economic foundations of the community ... and a healthier distribution of the population between urban and rural areas ... much thought is being given by Jews themselves to measures designed to this end'. This was true: organizations such as the Central Council for Jewish Refugees and vocational training groups, such as ORT, which supported reconstruction rather than emigration, were advancing similar ideas, but not in the same spirit as British officials.

Wilfrid suggested to Gorvin, for instance, that the refugee organizations to be set up after the war should come under the overall administration of a body like the Hoover American relief administration which functioned after the First World War, 'readapted to present circumstances and necessities', but that repatriation would have to depend on the social and economic conditions in the receiving areas. Relief officials should be trained in advance, and have a thorough knowledge of the refugees' background and problems; waiting periods in transit should be used for training and retraining activities. British officials, more concerned with high policy, were scarcely sympathetic to such plans.

Nigel Ronald, a Foreign Office official in the Economic and Reconstruction Department, agreed with Emerson that Britain 'had no obligations other than eliminating the causes which led to 'the Jews being persecuted'. But he also showed that he did not think anti-semitism unjustified. The Germans, he wrote in a minute to Emerson's report, had behaved unfairly to their neighbours in evicting Jewish 'undesirables'. Moreover, 'it cannot be denied that persons belonging to the Jewish fraternity seem to have an even greater propensity than Gentiles to disregard the long-term interests of society where they see prospects of short-term profits for themselves'.[50] Emerson and Ronald were scarcely promising partners in a Jewish post-war rehabilitation scheme in Eastern Europe.

Moreover, it soon became clear that the grand plans for Anglo-American patronage of Jewish resettlement in post-war Europe would never get off the ground. At a top-level inter-departmental meeting in December, the Home Office representative argued that the United States would want to know what the Dominions intended to contribute; Roberts argued that Britain could not demand restitution of Jewish property 'while Germany herself might have to accommodate anything up to five million Germans expelled from other countries'. The Colonial Office made it clear that the colonies would neither undertake financial commitments nor take in refugees.[51] Thus, at the beginning of 1943, after the Parliamentary Committee for Refugees had told the Cabinet that, in their view, the Jews could not be treated separately from other refugees, the entire issue was handed over to the United Nations. Thirty-four allied governments finally met in Washington in November 1943 and agreed to establish UNRRA (The United Nations Relief and Rehabilitation Administration) to provide food, clothing and relief to displaced persons on their liberation from Nazi rule. The Allied Post-War Requirements Bureau was eventually merged with UNRRA.[52]

Meanwhile, the seeds of conflict between the Jews of Palestine and Britain, and the collapse of British policy in the Middle East, were already sown. The first and decisive post-war clash took place over the destination not of millions – who were dead – but of 100,000 Jewish refugees fleeing the devastation of post-war Europe. There was to be no representation of the persecuted Jews, either where reparations were concerned or at the war crimes trials, in the immediate post-war period. Vague proposals to make Europe safe for Jews, in which – according to Beeley – the new Labour Foreign Secretary, Ernest Bevin, believed, evaporated; force was employed against Jewish survivors, and not on their behalf, as Emerson had proposed. The post-war Labour Government endorsed the moribund 1939 White Paper and all its restrictions on emigration. Even Churchill did not see Palestine as a 'dumping ground' for Jewish refugees. The post-war search for alternative havens was as fruitless as it had been at Evian; no country wanted the destitute survivors. Britain made frantic efforts to keep the 'displaced persons' in Europe by turning back the refugee ships, confining those who wanted to go to Palestine to camps, and even threatening to deprive them of their welfare allowances as refugees.[53]

Wilfrid's faith in an Eastern European solution, as his last papers show, had begun to wane by the beginning of 1943. Beeley was sceptical about the possibility of resettlement there, even before Wilfrid's death. While he argued, at a meeting with Schwarzbart after Wilfrid's death, that the scale of the massacres had put an end to the plan for statehood, he clearly underestimated the determination and desperation of the Jews in Palestine and in post-war Europe.[54] How far the gentleness and moderation of the man whom he admired so greatly had influenced these miscalculations can only be surmised.

The nationalist revival Wilfrid had feared in Eastern Europe, but which he hoped against hope would not recur, was to be decisive. Even before the particularly brutal pogrom in Kielce, in July 1946, when forty Jews (on their way to Palestine) were murdered, what was left of Polish Jewry fled 'illegally' to Palestine. Over 300,000 refugees from Eastern Europe found their way to Palestine immediately before and after the establishment of the state in 1948; more were to flee later, after the communist revolutions. The gates closed on Soviet Jewry, most of whom renounced their Jewish identity; others who wished to leave were exposed to renewed persecution. Most Western European survivors returned home.

The Jewish community in Palestine fought a long and bloody war of independence, the price of statehood. It was a country which was to prove radically different from anything Wilfrid Israel, or the few Jews who thought as he did, could have envisaged.

Wilfrid was not alone in his fears for the future of the achievements of the pioneering Zionists in the post-war period. Other Zionist officials, Eliahu Dobkin and Berl Locker among them, knew how far an influx of destitue and ill-prepared refugees could threaten the stability of the Jewish community; Richard Lichtheim, one of the first to warn the Jewish leadership abroad of the impending destruction of European Jewry, wrote in September 1942 to Nahum Goldmann that there would be no prospect of mass immigration to Palestine after the war, that 'political or cultural Zionism, as it was understood and preached during the last fifty years, has gone', and that the majority of the survivors would need 'clinics and asylums'.[55] Goldmann had suggested that the Zionist masses would come from the Soviet Union and the United States; Lichtheim saw that this was unrealistic. Unable to foresee the exodus of Oriental Jewry (whose existence was outside his consciousness as it was outside that of all Western Jews) or the flight of the Palestinian Arabs, he saw no future for the Jewish state.

Wilfrid, to whom Lichtheim sent a copy of this letter while he was in Lisbon, never succumbed to such despair, because the visionary faith which had sustained him throughout the 1930s remained with him even through the darkest period of the war.

12
Last Call

Wilfrid was working at home in Riverside Drive on the afternoon of 12 January 1943, when Joseph Linton, the secretary of the Jewish Agency's office in London, telephoned him to say that the Agency finally had work for him. Wilfrid sighed: he was so busy, he said, that he feared he had no time to spare. 'This isn't ordinary work,' said Linton. 'It's what you wanted. There may be a chance to save children.'[1]

As Linton recalled, Wilfrid cried, 'What! I'm coming straight away.' Within an hour, he had agreed to go to Portugal. That evening, he wrote to Diana Hopkinson: 'The Jewish Agency want me to proceed to Lisbon without delay to help in salvage work, refugee selection, or something on that line. They enquired just today. I cannot, dare not say no. I *must* just make myself physically strong enough to tackle it.'

Despite Wilfrid's appeals in 1941, the relief work of Youth Aliya had been minimal until the autumn of 1942. The organization had neither funds, nor the ability to make policy decisions, which rested entirely with the Agency. In April 1942, Wilfrid wrote to Hans Reissner in Bombay: 'We still pretend to be a world organization and still get certificates permitting refugee children from the Continent to infiltrate to Palestine, which is a relatively trivial satisfaction in the face of the devastating news that reaches us constantly.'[2] In September, he wrote, 'In individual cases and in small groups we are successful. That is not much in the face of the great tragedy, but certainly better than nothing at all.'[3]

Youth Aliya had its first chance to contribute to rescue in October. In late August 1942, the Soviet Government allowed 5,000 Polish Jews, including some 800 orphaned children, the survivors of families who had fled from Poland, to leave for Iran. They received permission to enter Palestine. The 'Teheran children' constituted the largest contingent to leave Europe during the war, and the first batch of children of all ages to come under the care of Youth Aliya. These children had not experienced the camps; but their physical and mental condition was so serious that

Wilfrid, who played a part in their transfer to Palestine, was more alarmed than relieved.

Some children had reached the Ukraine, only to be attacked by antisemitic peasants. Others had seen their parents killed by German soldiers. There were children who had worked cutting wood in Siberian forests; children who had eaten mushrooms, wood berries and grass for months to stay alive; others who had buried their parents, brothers and sisters in the open countryside by night. One girl, who had escaped from the Warsaw ghetto, had three brothers: one was murdered by a Nazi soldier who pulled him out of a bread queue and pushed him in front of a moving tank; another was sent to a Jewish hospital, from which all the patients were deported; and the eldest brother, who escaped with his sister to Khazakstan, died of hunger.[4] A Zionist envoy reported, in October, that most of the adult refugees were men and women whose spirit had been broken, adding, 'They are lost souls not only to Palestine, but to human society as a whole. Our only comfort is that they constitute a minority.'[5] No one in Palestine yet realized that these people were the fortunate ones. The awakening only came when the first Jews to be released from the concentration camps under exchange schemes arrived in Palestine the following month.

When the reports of the children's condition reached London, Youth Aliya was asked to help in their maintenance and transport. Wilfrid's role in the ICA was decisive. He pleaded the children's case and received a large grant, which covered a major part of the costs.[6] But the children's ordeal was not over. Iraq vetoed the British proposal to transfer them by an overland route, taking a few days, on the grounds that small children would in time grow into adult enemies.

The children eventually were sent on a three-month journey through the Persian Gulf to India, then back to the Middle East via Aden, the Red Sea and the Suez Canal. Wilfrid monitored their journey through letters and telegrams to Hans Reissner in Bombay, where one group stopped on the way. He asked for personal impressions of the children, telling Reissner of his concern at the terrible reports he had heard, and asking, wistfully, whether the 'kiddies' were at all prepared for 'the spirit of their coming kibbutz life'?[7] In fact, many children were placed in mental hospitals on arrival and others, obsessed by fears, hoarded food and were afraid to remain alone in the dark.

The news from France was little better. During the summer, the Nazis had chosen to deport adults; in Paris, in July, 4,000 children were abandoned in the streets when their parents were rounded up and sent east in sealed trains. In unoccupied France, too, parents were given the choice by the Vichy police either of abandoning their children or taking them to an unknown fate in the east. Hearing that orphans would be saved, a few mothers committed suicide. Families were torn apart by force. Officials of the Vichy regime, which had launched an anti-semitic campaign of its own, co-operated with the Nazis; but many church leaders protested the deportations, and hundreds of French families and religious institutions helped to conceal Jewish children.

The mass roundups of July and August were widely reported in the British and American press, and now, for the first time, schemes were improvised for the rescue of Jewish children in Vichy France which, despite the hostility of the Vichy regime, was the only area in Western Europe from which escape now seemed possible. The American Joint Distribution Committee planned the rescue of 1,000 children, who were granted visas to the United States. After prolonged negotiations, the children were finally selected, and twenty-five escorts set sail from America to accompany them. But hours before they were to leave, the German armies, after the Allied invasion of North Africa three days earlier, occupied Vichy France on 11 November. The children were trapped, as were another 1,000 children in the same area, for whom certificates requested by the Agency had been issued by the Palestine Government, just too late for action to be taken.

After this happened, Wilfrid telephoned his Youth Aliya colleague Eva Michaelis almost daily, begging her to intervene with Shertok, then due to arrive in London, to have him sent abroad. In mid-November, he wrote to a friend that he was perhaps to be sent to Russia;[8] there was discussion at this time of evacuating a group of Russian Jews to Palestine; but this too was dropped when the Colonial Office received an official Soviet refusal at the end of December.[9]

The Jewish Agency had appealed repeatedly to the Foreign Office to help them arrange the escape of Jews from three countries which were not yet entirely under Nazi rule: Hungary, Bulgaria and Romania (where, despite the deportations of 1941, hundreds of thousands of Jews still remained). Chaim Barlas, the Agency envoy in Istanbul, negotiated tirelessly on their behalf. But apart from the 1,200 certificates requested for the children from Vichy France and their escorts, there was no plan for the children of Western Europe and no Agency envoy in what Wilfrid regarded as the most important potential focus of rescue in this area: Portugal.

The children trapped in Belgium, Holland and France were not just figures in Wilfrid's head. He had helped set up Youth Aliya camps in those countries, and the Youth Aliya office received constant appeals from relations of the children, to which they were unable to respond. He badgered the Agency endlessly, and finally Shertok, who had thought

Wilfrid too delicate for such a difficult assignment, gave in. Wilfrid obtained a two-month leave of absence from the FRPS, and Toynbee wrote to Ronald in the Economic and Reconstruction Department asking for further official backing for Wilfrid's journey, stressing his important role in the FRPS and the fact that his mission was approved by the Refugee Department.[10]

It was not easy for Wilfrid to leave the security of his home and his work. On 21 December, he had written:

> My work keeps me going, but the machine of my mind creaks and should be overhauled fundamentally. I would like to forget, as I suppose all of us would, the facts of this despicable world, and get rid of this continual pressure and anxiety ... the refuge of my home, which I am still permitted to enjoy, is something of a compensation, and above all the realization that I took decisions in the past at the right moment and just within the time limits which fate had set. This makes me feel serene, as responsibility was on the point of dislocating my very being.

The Jewish Agency decided to send Wilfrid to Portugal, and his friend Shlomo Adler Rudel to Sweden, in the spring of 1943.

Wilfrid had long desired to play a more active role in the rescue of children, and his acceptance of the mission was impetuous. But any individual mission had to wait on a favourable conjunction of events.

On the British side, there were several factors which made Wilfrid's journey possible: a tactical change in the policy of the Colonial Office regarding the fate of the 33,000-odd immigration certificates which still remained under the White Paper provisions of May 1939; the pressures exerted on the Government by the Jews and their Gentile friends in England after the news of the Nazi massacres became common knowledge at the end of 1942; Foreign Office wariness of American involvement in the refugee question; and the problem of the thousands of refugees accumulating in camps in Spain and Portugal.

Richard Latham, Wilfrid's friend in the Refugee Department, commented wrily, in February 1941, that 'the Middle East department of the Colonial Office does rather regard the Jewish world as a kind of secondary enemy'.[11] British policy towards Jewish refugees from Hitler's Europe was governed, throughout the first three years of the war, by the determination to limit Jewish immigration to Palestine, both for fear of an Arab reaction, and in order to block militant Jewish nationalism in the post-war period. Some 'illegal' refugee ships were turned back to Nazi Europe; the passengers on others were deported to places like Mauritius. 'Legal' immigration was strictly controlled in six-monthly quotas, for which the Jewish Agency had to make applications. There was an overall ban on refugees coming from Nazi-occupied countries, on the absurd pretext that there might be 'enemy agents' among them.

Almost the only exceptions, from the outset, were for children. As Wilfrid remarked in his letters to Reissner, children were admitted to Palestine: 169 from Germany in late 1939, 312 from Denmark in April 1940, and the meagre numbers who managed to escape thereafter.[12] A few hundred Palestinian Jews, 'veteran Zionists' and rabbis in occupied Europe were also admitted in exchange for German civilians in Palestine. On 26 January 1943, Wilfrid applied to have Paul and Hedwig Eppstein's names included in these lists, but it was too late; on the next day they were sent to Theresienstadt.[13]

The concession for children was not particularly significant, since it was unlikely that children on their own would manage to escape from Nazi-held territory. But, as the news of the massacres was publicly acknowledged, the overall ban on refugees from Europe was relaxed to include 'escorts' of children and Agency appeals (usually made to the Foreign Office, as the attitude of the Colonial Office was well known) were more favourably reviewed. This was not only because of the pressure of public opinion. The Colonial Office and the Foreign Office both realized now that Nazi policy was no longer to expel the unwanted Jews, but to murder them. While, as late as the autumn of 1941, sealed trainloads of German Jews were still being sent westwards to Vichy France, by mid-1942 the Nazis were proving obdurate to appeals made through the 'protecting powers', Switzerland and Sweden, for the release even of children. Thus it was possible to relax stringent sanctions on the entry of refugees to Palestine, in the knowledge that very few would in fact escape.

Once the news of the massacres of Jews became public, the issue could no longer be ignored. On 17 December, in the House of Commons, Anthony Eden promised that the guilty men would be brought to account at the war's end. There was little that could be done while Nazi arms still controlled Europe; Jewish spokesmen suggested that the Axis satellites should be warned not to co-operate in deportations, and that neutral countries should be assured that escaping refugees would be supported financially and re-emigrated at the war's end. The delegations which had visited government offices from the late autumn argued principally for Britain's help for those who managed to escape: Britain itself should revise its immigration regulations and admit a few thousand Jewish children, if they could be rescued from Europe.

Herbert Morrison, the Labour Home Secretary, was pressed by deputations demanding the admission of children to Britain from October; the most persistent members were Eleanor Rathbone and the Archbishop of Canterbury, William Temple.[14] But Morrison refused to admit more than a few hundred children who already had relations in Britain, arguing that the arrival of thousands of Jewish children would cause an upsurge of anti-semitism.

At a Youth Aliya meeting in January 1943, Wilfrid suggested returning to the tactics of 1938 and canvassing individual sponsors for 1,000 refugee children who might be brought to England from the Continent. For a short time in the spring of that year, the Jewish organizations, their sympathizers and the Archbishops of Canterbury and York considered making a new financial appeal in aid of children from Nazi Europe, on the lines of the Baldwin appeal of 1938. But there was no official encouragement for this scheme; the Archbishop of Canterbury told the British Zionist, Professor Brodetsky, that Churchill had advised him not to pursue the matter of the children's scheme, and the bogey of an anti-semitic reaction to any appeal for Jewish children alarmed Jewish leaders like Anthony de Rothschild as much as it did Morrison.[15]

With Pierre Laval and the Vichy administration determined to deport Jews, with or without children, to the East, it was difficult enough to negotiate for the release of children before the German occupation of Vichy France. After that date, the situation was desperate. But the deputations continued.

After meeting one group in December, Richard Law of the Foreign Office said:

> I feel very doubtful whether we shall be able to stand much longer on the very strict line that the Home Office is adopting. It has always seemed to me that the apprehension of the Home Office has been exaggerated and it would be very difficult for us to go on confining ourselves to denunciation of the German action while refusing to take any alleviating action ourselves.[16]

At the same time, the Colonial Office now attempted to forestall pressures on the White Paper policy at the war's end, by making all certificates immediately available, in theory, to children from Nazi Europe. In a surprise move, the Chief Secretary of the Palestine Government, C.S. McPherson, acting on orders from London, summoned Bernard Joseph of the Jewish Agency and asked him to state the number of child refugees they wished to enter as candidates for certificates of immigration to Palestine, within the overall number still available – approximately 33,000.

On Sunday, 13 December, at an Agency meeting in Jerusalem, Bernard Joseph reported that the Colonial Office wanted a rapid decision. The request caused consternation, Ben Gurion remarking that the Youth Aliya needed overhauling and reorganizing for mass work. But the offer had to be grasped. Ben Gurion suggested, with the Agency executive backing him, that 25,000 certificates be reserved for the refugee children.[17] The message was conveyed to McPherson by Bernard Joseph, who added that the number would be increased if the children could be rescued.[18]

Meanwhile, in London, to the amazement of a top-level Jewish delegation to the Foreign Secretary, Eden reported that the British Government now looked favourably on the chances of the Jewish refugees in Spain and Portugal being sent to Palestine.[19] Eleanor Rathbone's appeals to the Foreign Office on the same issue were also minuted, to the effect that 'she was knocking at an open door'.[20]

This last development was not directly linked with Palestine policy. What was more important was that, during the closing months of 1942, it appeared that the German army was likely to invade Spain, as part of the response to the Allied campaign in North Africa. The Franco Government, under Nazi pressure, threatened to send all those who escaped over the Pyrenees back across the frontier into occupied France. This meant that the escape routes, which were essential both to British intelligence agents and to escaping prisoners of war, might be blocked.[21] The refugee camps were overflowing and the British Ambassador, Sir Samuel Hoare, complained bitterly to London that the Franco regime was threatening to close the frontiers.

The Foreign Office was planning yet another refugee conference together with the United States – this time in Bermuda – and one of the proposals on the agenda was to evacuate the refugees in Portugal and Spain to North Africa.[22] In Spain, there was a chronic shortage of experienced relief workers; the stateless Jews, moreover, were no one's responsibility. It was thus not surprising that the Refugee Department actively welcomed the Agency's subsequent proposal to send an envoy who would select immigrants to Palestine from among the refugees.

On 3 February 1943, Oliver Stanley, the new Colonial Secretary, announced in the House of Commons that apart from 4,000 children from Bulgaria with 500 adult escorts, whose immigration to Palestine had already been sanctioned, a further 500 children from Romania and Hungary would be accepted, and – provided transport became available – larger numbers of children with accompanying adults up to the maximum quota still available under the White Paper, 29,000, would be admitted to Palestine. Significantly, no public mention was made of the 1,000 children in Vichy France with their 200 escorts. Although the Government's willingness to admit them to Palestine had already been announced in the House of Lords in November, this was now deliberately omitted from Stanley's statement, at the suggestion of the Home Office, which feared that it would be urged to admit the children to Britain – a much closer destination.[23]

What had happened was, in fact, the reverse of the situation in 1938. Then, children were admitted to England in order to compensate for the refusal to allow them to go to Palestine. But, this time, it was clear that the concessions were regarded as a convenient gesture, which would not, in all probability, result in practical action. Boyd of the Colonial Office minuted the Commons' debate which followed Stanley's statement: 'The difficulties which the Agency is likely to find in getting in the 29,000 refugee immigrants within the five-year period would make any request purely theoretical.'[24] The Foreign Office was to comment a short time later, 'We understand that the State Department were in agreement with us over the futility of an appeal to Hitler to release Jews.... But you may soften the blow by emphasizing the great efforts His Majesty's Government is making over the transport of Jewish children to Palestine.'[25]

When Wilfrid volunteered to go to Portugal, a Nazi invasion seemed imminent. On 14 December, Sir Herbert Emerson submitted a memorandum warning 'that if the Jews were not soon evacuated from Portugal and Spain they would be caught in a trap as they were in Belgium, Holland and France'.[26] In an accompanying letter, he pointed out that 'it is no longer a question of dealing with masses of persons whom the Nazis may try to unload on other countries, but a matter of saving a few thousands who have escaped or may be able to do so.' The Refugee Department, in April, put it differently:

> We need to clear Spain and Portugal of the present accumulation [of refugees] and keep them clear – a consideration applying with special force to Spain because we want to keep the Spanish Government sweet in order that refugees of all categories (prisoners of war, escapees, etc.) many of whom are of value for the war effort, may not be turned back across the Franco-Spanish frontier.[27]

The stage was set for Wilfrid's mission. The odds had never been so heavily against him or against the rescue of Jewish children. He was taking up an extraordinary challenge; for, had he and his colleagues succeeded in getting large numbers of children out of Nazi territory, it would have been difficult for either the Foreign Office or the Colonial Office to plead *non possumus*. But the Zionist executive was caught unawares by the sheer scope of the challenge. No word of McPherson's approach reached Shertok, who was not informed of the invitation either by the Colonial Office in London, with whom he held talks early in the year, or by his own office in Jerusalem. He was to learn of it only on his return to Palestine in April. There were only a handful of men with the necessary experience and knowledge in the field, like Barlas in Istanbul, Lichtheim in Geneva, and now Adler Rudel and Wilfrid Israel.

Shlomo Adler Rudel found, on arrival in Sweden, that the Swedish Government was no longer as apprehensive as it had been during earlier stages of the war, that the Germans would regard intervention on behalf of the persecuted as an infringement of neutrality, and that – affected by the fate of Norwegian Jews – the Government was now prepared to accept 20,000 Jewish children if they could be emigrated at the end of the war. The scheme eventually failed for a number of reasons: the Germans did not immediately reject the appeal for the release of the children, but transportation was the main problem. Adler Rudel negotiated for the charter of a ship, the SS *Drottingholm* of the Karlsen Line at Gothenburg, and found that the Foreign Office was also bidding for the same ship to transport refugees from Eastern Europe, at lower insurance premiums. A greater problem was that the Foreign Office, still unable or unwilling to grasp the scale of Jewish annihilation, objected that the children they might promise to emigrate at the war's end would be reclaimed by parents, who would object to such migration plans.[28]

Wilfrid's brief was threefold: he was to distribute 200 certificates among the thousands of Jewish refugees in Portugal and Spain; to plan their route and means of transportation to Palestine; and to examine the possibilities of further rescue, including that of the 1,000 children trapped in Vichy France.

The question of shipping alone was sufficient to defeat any effort at rescue, for even before Wilfrid accepted the mission, Eleanor Rathbone had approached another old colleague, Philip Noel Baker, now in the Ministry of Shipping, for help, without results. No Allied ship was available, at the height of the war, for the transport of refugees. There was also the problem of the route, since, with the North African campaign at its zenith, a journey through the Mediterranean was a desperate risk. But the greatest challenge was how to find a way out of Nazi Europe for the children, whether by diplomatic or by illegal means.

It is clear that from the outset Wilfrid was determined to exceed the vague and limited brief he had been given; the memorandum handed him by the Agency in London, which he gave the Joint in Lisbon and sent to Lichtheim in Geneva, made no mention of rescue from Western Europe.[29] Yet it is clear that he knew, before leaving London, of the Colonial Office's challenge and was determined to exploit it. He already knew the representatives of Allied embassies in London, and arranged for introductions to the Dutch, French, Belgian and Swiss representatives in Lisbon; he discussed his diplomatic plans with Herbert Kullman, Emerson's deputy, and talked to the Spanish *chargé d'affaires*.[30] Both the Belgians and the Dutch in exile were now under great pressure to encourage the escape of their own Jewish nationals to the Belgian Congo and the Dutch East Indies.[31] Moreover, a small group of Dutch Jews had already managed to obtain 500 certificates to Palestine on their own initiative; the ship Adler Rudel intended to charter was for the transport of both the Dutch and the other refugee children from Europe.[32]

But Wilfrid had no illusions as to his chances of success. He did not even wish to commit himself on the allocation of certificates. He cabled the Joint in Lisbon: 'On no account give any binding undertaking to individuals concerned. Do not wish to face any *faits accomplis* or raise false hopes.'[33] He wrote to relations in New York, some of whose Dutch relatives were still in Portugal: 'Please do not expect me to be able to go into cases when out in Portugal, because I must deal specifically with the subject I am engaged with.' On 12 February, he had what was to be his last meeting with Schwarzbart, and noted:

> Schwarzbart emphasizes that the last reports which he had received indicated that, all in all, including the deportees, there would not be more than 800,000 Jews left in Poland. This means, he added, that the Jewish question does not exist any more. Schwarzbart criticized both the Gentiles and the Jews still not touched by the present disaster ... his attitude on the whole was bitter, unconstructive. He made the impression of being utterly worn out and labouring towards wearing himself out.[34]

It was to Max Warburg, his old colleague in rescue work, that Wilfrid wrote the most candid and complete of his last letters.

He had agreed to go, he wrote, as 'there did not seem to be anyone on the spot'. The Joint, HICEM and the Quakers were all functioning in Lisbon, and 'as the subtle and fragile structure of the interrelation of these organizations is rather well known to me, I do not fear being tripped up. The transport bottleneck is complicating the situation, I understand, and my coming to the Iberian peninsula as a *deus ex machina* will hardly save the situation.' He was not optimistic about the plans for refugee camps, whether in North Africa, the Belgian Congo or South Africa, and the planned refugee conference reminded him dismally of pre-war conferences.

However, he was not without allies. 'Many non-Jewish friends, many people linked with the Church and with political parties are eager to help', though there was much 'wishful thinking, not always wisely propagated'. Wilfrid was sceptical as to Nazi co-operation. 'I am personally under the impression that it is childish to think that the Nazi regime would permit even children to leave the Continent at this juncture. I fear that even the attempt to get children out of the Balkans might be frustrated. But we must show confidence and go ahead with all wisdom and ingenuity to promote the children's scheme.' He thought there were several points at which 'infiltration' was possible – into Hungary from Poland, into Spain, and Switzerland. But the numbers would remain small.

> Military operations naturally will alone be decisive and perhaps save some hundreds of thousands. Those who may be alive when hostilities have ceased will, apart from the Hungarian Jewish community, most likely be living under Russian sway. In the Western sphere of Europe, there will hardly be great numbers of the Jewish people which have to be cared for. The disaster itself is solving the problem which a year ago was doubtless of great magnitude.

'You know that I believe in the vital necessity of a Jewish renascence in Palestine,' he continued; he thought that while 'a small, vigorous, selective Jewish immigration' would be 'pivotal for the future', it would not, alone, solve the global situation. The mass of Jews would remain in the United States and the Soviet Union, where he believed assimilation and intermarriage would increase.

> But Jewish tradition in some form will no doubt keep alive and will find some new mode of expression. It would be reckless pessimism to believe that the Jewish heritage can be wiped out in a generation. If we begin as Jews to think merely in secular terms, merely in terms of power politics and numbers, we shall certainly crumble to dust.

Moreover, he wrote, the Jewish problem was only one of many crises which were 'dislocating the world'.

> We as Jews, I feel, are merely *a part of* the human race and not *apart from* the human race. Humanity has to re-educate itself to realize this simple truth which has been questioned so long, and we ourselves should begin to re-educate ourselves likewise. We have been stampeded into reacting as a separatist body all over the world since 1933. This must lead up to a destructive solution in the 20th century. I think we must serve the cause in persevering to save every one child and every one adult we can get hold of during this disaster. But only a great humanist revival (which I believe must associate itself and merge with a wide socialist endeavour, at least on the continent of Europe) will be able to find a true global situation.

Wilfrid concluded:

> We should tremble for the lives of our people but not for the Jewish heritage.

> The overawing tragedy is the fact that community after community is being wiped out. From the point of view of Jewish heritage, however, we should remember that in 1815, it is said, no more than two million Jews were living in the entire world, and we should bear in mind that true spiritual fervour and ardour is never wiped out by transitory phases of war and revolution. I think this holds good for Jews in Russia likewise.[35]

Wilfrid prepared his departure with extraordinary care. In 1939, he had agreed to take the silver candlesticks and other ritual objects of the family of Arnold Horwitz, who had worked with him at the Hilfsverein; they had been sent in an ordinary suitcase on a train from Germany. Now he asked Horwitz to remove them from his flat. He returned to friends an antique pistol, which he had taken into his care when 'enemy aliens' were forbidden to own 'firearms' during the invasion scare of 1940. A week before his departure, he wrote to Hans Reissner, offering help in settling Reissner's financial affairs in London. 'I am in the state of mind of wishing to tidy up all the fringes of my existence and responsibilities. . . . I am leaving on my trip rather heavy-heartedly. Whatever I shall try to do will, I am afraid, be sidetracked by the vital impediment and great disaster of a world at war.'[36]

On the day before he left for Lisbon, 25 March, Wilfrid made his will, detailing the recipient of almost every item of his remaining possessions. He left his art collection to Hazorea; to one member, who had decorated his hut with a photograph of a painting torn from an illustrated magazine, he left a twelfth-century Madonna and Child by Bernardo Daddi. Diana Hopkinson had admired the figurine of a dancing girl on his Berlin mantelpiece in 1935; he put it down by her name. To Rita Luedecke, who had spent the last days with Wilfrid and Trott in Berlin, drinking wines from his cellar, he left an Egyptian scarab; to Eric Lucas, his Youth Aliya protégé, who visited him that afternoon, one of his own drawings.

In the evening, he went to visit Agnes Schneider, his sister Viva's old friend, who, when the United States entered the war, had been transferred to the Embassy in London. He asked her to make him a cake on his return; but after the door was shut behind him, the bell rang again. When she opened it, he was standing there, the light from the flat shining into his blue eyes, the blackout of wartime London behind him. 'I thought I'd just say goodbye again,' he said, smiling, 'because planes have funny ways.'

From the airport near Bristol, he telephoned his old friend Rosi Reiss. She had no premonitions. For years, Wilfrid had telephoned her from stations and airports on his trips abroad. She thought he needed someone to say goodbye to.

* * *

When Wilfrid flew into Lisbon on 26 March, he was seized on immediately by the local Jewish community and by the relief agencies, who saw a chance of reducing the numbers of those dependent on their funds. The news of his arrival soon reached the windswept fishing villages, where many refugees were held. His first objective was to get a passage for Spain, where the Jews were in greater danger; but, as he wryly wrote to Richard Lichtheim in Geneva, 'my employer doesn't count as a good entrée and those on Olympus [the professional diplomats] who are willing to help are apparently, despite everything, in too weak a position'.[37]

Lisbon was one of the few cities in Europe where lights burned at night and the shop windows were packed with luxuries; still prosperous under the Salazar regime, it accommodated two shadowy groups who occasionally made contact – the refugees, and the intelligence and counter-intelligence agents of the Axis and the Allies. Despite the fact that open frontiers were important to both groups, Allied Intelligence usually gave the refugees a wide berth. British MI9, the organization in charge of escape and evasion, operating with MI6 agents in Spain and Portugal, had strict instructions to avoid contacts with the refugees, among whose escape parties they feared there might be Gestapo agents, whose high payments to guides they resented, and among whom there was little chance of recruiting men for the war effort.[38] The American attitude was the same. The American Ambassador in Spain, Carleton J.H. Hayes, was interested mainly in the rescue of American prisoners of war, and believed Jewish refugees to be a hindrance.[39]

Among the Jewish refugees in Lisbon there was one man, Isaac Weissmann, who had attempted to outflank official and bureaucratic obstacles and who had been responsible, through his contacts with the Portuguese police, for getting many Jewish refugees out of prisons and into the *résidence forcée* refugee villages. He had also organized courier services into occupied territories, until the man he was using was exposed as a double agent by British Intelligence. Unfortunately, Weissmann's relations with the Joint were at their lowest ebb when Wilfrid arrived. The Joint, the most powerful relief organization in the area, was headed by Joseph Schwartz, a determined director steering a difficult course between head office officials in New York, who, far from the scene, were opposed to any but strictly legal activities, and his knowledge that more dynamism was necessary to save Jewish lives in occupied Europe. He had channelled funds into Vichy France to help the hidden Jews. The local Jewish community, which distributed Joint funds among the refugees, was on equally bad terms with Weissmann and other Zionists.[40] Wilfrid, however, while wishing for a more dynamic policy of escape, knew that the Joint was an essential ally.

With the much-coveted certificates in his pocket, Wilfrid was immediately the centre of controversy. Letters of complaint flew from Weissman and his Zionist friends to the World Jewish Congress, complaining of Wilfrid's co-operation with the Joint and HICEM, the other Jewish relief body, in the selection of candidates.[41] Wilfrid had sized up the situation immediately, and knew perfectly well of the attacks behind his back and the hostility of Weissmann. He wrote to Lichtheim, 'I have acted independently, more than I would have done otherwise, ignoring co-operation and the influence of others regarding the work of selection.'[42] Ironically, he also appealed to Jerusalem to do precisely what Weissmann wanted: to set up a Zionist office in Lisbon to organize rescue. To Eliahu Dobkin, the immigration head in Jerusalem, he cabled: 'consider establishing Palestine office in Lisbon morally and technically vital must however be staffed with your own most efficient and routined expert for first period of at least six months.'[43] But in Jerusalem, escape from Western Europe was not seen as a priority. It was only over a year later, in June 1944, that Dobkin finally arrived in Lisbon and reported that he found 'a shameful situation in which quarrels between the World Jewish Congress and Joint representatives had hampered all ... activities'.[44]

Wilfrid thus worked alone. Within the first week of his stay, he visited Caldas da Rainha and Ericeira, the two refugee villages on the coast, and decided almost immediately to keep the largest number of his certificates for Jews in more danger in Spain. Meanwhile, he was gathering information about escape routes, by patient and long questioning of all the refugees who had recently arrived from Spain. Almost immediately after his arrival, he met one of them, a young German Jew named Heinz Wisla, who came to his hotel in Lisbon asking for an interview.

Wisla was living with 150 other 'illegal' refugees in Ericeira. He had heard that Wilfrid had arrived, and recognized the name of the man who had brought many Jews out of Germany during the last years before the war. They met in the hall of Wilfrid's hotel between two of his first meetings with the refugee bodies; Wilfrid immediately asked him of his experiences and what his fellow refugees thought of going to Palestine. Wisla told him that they hoped only to escape to England or America, as they were sure no shipping was available to Palestine, and were despondent and sceptical about Palestine, of which they knew little, and which had sent no envoys to the Portuguese villages the entire time the refugees had lived there.[45]

Soon afterwards, Wilfrid visited the village and took long walks with groups of boys along the beaches. Most of them had wandered from country to country in Europe; their families were dead, and they had no hope for the future. But these were the young people Wilfrid thought could help form the vanguard of the new state. He wrote to Lichtheim that in Ericeira he had found 'a most satisfactory group who should be right for Eretz', and asked Linton in London to send them out books and journals about life in Palestine. The stories he heard of those left behind under Nazi rule tormented him. 'Every day I'm followed by visions connected with Henrietta Szold's work [Youth Aliya]. If one could carry on the work with some kind of obstinate willpower, something could be achieved, I believe. Surely, during the first stage of consultations, one wants to tear the world to pieces.'[46]

Though his first selections gave priority to young people he felt were needed in Palestine, he could not ignore the older refugees. Minna Koss, a young Belgian Jew, who had escaped with her Czech husband in late 1941 by exchanging a diamond engagement ring for two visas to Nicaragua, remembered that he distributed many certificates to the old and infirm, who had no other chance of a refuge.[47]

Meanwhile, he made the round of the embassies to which he had brought letters of introduction from London. Despite the doubts of which he had written to Warburg, every official channel was explored. The plan he repeatedly proposed was set out in a letter to the Swiss Legation after his discussion with the First Secretary there on 17 April. After outlining his official role in Lisbon, he added that his purpose was not simply to distribute certificates:

> This plan is linked up with the widest scheme of rescuing Jewish children up to the age of 16 from the German occupied territories of France, Belgium and Holland. The Government of Palestine, in conjunction with the Colonial Office in London, is willing to allocate special immigration certificates for the category of children specially between the ages of 14–16. This scheme obviously requires discretion in discussion and handling but at the same time may perhaps ... save a great number of the young generation.

He appealed to the Swiss Federal Government to try once more to promote these plans, as it had done before the German invasion of Vichy France. The scope of the scheme, he said, envisaged the evacuation of about 500 children from Holland, about the same number from Belgium, about 1,000 from France, 'numbers which could be doubled or perhaps tripled, should the scheme be regarded as ... feasible'.[48]

This was Wilfrid's own initiative; he had received no brief to negotiate for children other than those in Vichy France. Wilfrid was in touch however, separately, with Jerusalem; for on 12 April he had received a cable from Szold, 'Hope for encouraging report regarding possible rescue children Spain Portugal France Holland Belgium Switzerland stop certs available.'[49] In a further cable to Szold, which clearly refers not to official cables but to clandestine plans, he said: 'Possibilities still most vague but very faint outline which might develop lifeline of future work discernible stop this is one reason why permanent Palestine office Lisbon so essential.'[50]

But whatever his plans, Wilfrid was moving too fast for the bureaucrats. In appealing to the Swiss to negotiate the release of the 1,000 children in France, Wilfrid had actually bypassed the Foreign Office and its procrastinations. In December, the Refugee Department had minuted a report that 'The Swiss Government are – or ought to be – consulting with the German Government about them.'[51] Yet on 14 April, with deportations continuing week by week, with more than 30,000 Jews packed in trains leaving Holland, Greece and Belgium in that month alone, another official minuted: 'We decided to approach the Swiss Government about the exit of children once the negotiations about the German Palestinian exchange was concluded, but seem never to have done so or to have forwarded the text suggested by the Swiss.'[52] Wilfrid's request was passed on to Berne immediately, and a reply from there, saying that the Swiss Government were now contacting the Germans about the question of the children's release, arrived while Wilfrid was still in Lisbon.[53] Yet when he left Portugal on 1 June, the Germans had still not replied; they never gave their consent.

On 28 April, he met Carl Burckhardt, head of the International Red Cross.[54] But Burckhardt, after investigating the matter back in Geneva, told Lichtheim that he was powerless to act, as Lichtheim reported to Wilfrid by letter on 19 May.[55]

Meanwhile, with all the shipping routes blocked, and the Portuguese refusing to allow refugees to land at Lorenço Marques in Portuguese East Africa, Wilfrid determined to find an overland route for the refugees in Portugal and Spain. He wrote to Lichtheim:

> I have decided to find a new way across Central Africa. This would lead to the Congo, up the river to Stanleyville, from there across Juba to the Nile. I am consulting with doctors, the Tropical Institute, and through the Federation of South Africa to get a clear view. This way would exclude certain dangers but invite other uncertain factors. As the group would include women, children and elderly people, one would have to be careful.[56]

He persuaded Emma Wohlwill, the wife of a Portuguese Jewish professor, to accompany the party through the jungle; 'Henrietta Szold will meet you at the Quai!' he told her.[57] This was the least extravagant part of his plan. Miss Szold, though in her seventies, always met the children's boats at Haifa.

On the day of his talk with Burckhardt, Wilfrid finally received his visa for Spain, and left for Madrid on 29 April. The situation which he saw in the camps and prisons of Spain was incomparably worse than anything he had seen in Portugal. If there the refugees were apathetic, in Spain they lived in fear, being within miles of enemy territory. Most of the refugees he now met had survived a perilous climb over the Pyrenees; they all knew of cases of smugglers who took the Jews' money and then handed them over to German patrols.

In Miranda del Ebro, the largest refugee camp, there were 500 stateless refugees who were no embassy's responsibility. The camp, originally built to hold prisoners taken in the Civil War, housed refugees in barracks where they were divided according to nationalities, and the refugees claimed whichever nationality seemed to promise the best treatment. Most French-speakers claimed to be Canadians, and a wit had chalked on the Canadian building, which was overcrowded, 'Canadians of all nations unite'. The prisoners slept on stone floors, washing facilities were so primitive that most had skin diseases, and there were many cases of tuberculosis. There was a black market in bread and the extras provided by the consulates and relief bodies. Two months earlier, the Quaker David Blickenstaff had begun work, with funds from the Joint, caring for Jewish internees; and repeated hunger strikes caused the Spaniards to begin, slowly, to release those who were helped by their consulates. With no Jewish organization, or even non-Catholic organization, allowed in Spain, Wilfrid thus worked out of Blickenstaff's office.[58]

Wilfrid had not proved, as he foretold, a *deus ex machina* for the refugees; he was, however, precisely this for the top officials of the British Embassy. Since January, the Ambassador, Sir Samuel Hoare, had been bombarding the Foreign Office with requests to clear the Spanish camps of refugees. Over 600 prisoners of war had been evacuated from these camps, only one Jew among them. 'Only a small proportion', Hoare reported, 'could be regarded of genuine military interest; they present however a humanitarian problem of urgent importance which should be properly dealt with by a specially formed organization financed, staffed, and equipped on an appropriate scale with expert personnel.'[59]

Blickenstaff's arrival in March, to administer the Joint funds, afforded relief; but by now the Spaniards were threatening to close the frontiers, which they did briefly at the end of March, until Churchill threatened diplomatic reprisals. Just before Wilfrid arrived in Spain, Hoare had written to Eleanor Rathbone:

The problem of refugees in Spain is inextricably connected with the problem

> of escaped prisoners of war, and with many of the secret activities of this Mission. The Gestapo is around us at every turn, complicating and attempting to frustrate our efforts, and the Spanish government, even when they wish to show good will, are terrified of the Germany army on the Pyrenees frontier.[60]

The Bermuda conference on refugees, which had been held while Wilfrid was in Portugal, had produced no concrete results; and on 19 May, Eden cabled Churchill, who was visiting Washington, that he was 'dismayed and depressed' that the American chiefs of staff had turned down the recommendation of a camp in North Africa, to which refugees from Spain could be transferred. Thus, probably for the first time in his life, Wilfrid enjoyed the complete co-operation of British officials in his attempts, not only to distribute the certificates which remained, and to propose the allocation of more (which was part of his brief), but also to assess the prospects of the evacuation of all the 1,500 stateless Jewish refugees in Spain. After a first meeting with Hoare, Wilfrid set out to establish the exact scale of the problem and propose solutions, visiting every Jewish refugee he could identify in the camps and prisons. At the same time, he was pleading continually in cables for more certificates, and attempted to contact those who could bring more Jewish children across the frontiers.

He must soon have ascertained, through the refugees he met, that there were two possible routes. One led through the southern foothills, the other over the steep Pyrenees. The second route was virtually impassable for all but the young and strong; by the time Wilfrid reached Spain, however, this was the only way by which it was possible to avoid frontier patrols.

Among the refugees Wilfrid questioned were Siegmund Dispeker and Rudolf Jonas. Dispeker was a journalist and SPD man from Kassel, who had been on the refugee roads since 1933. Imprisoned in October 1942 in Les Milles, the assembly point for deportations in southern France, he had escaped and, with his wife and young son, had crossed the border with a smuggler between Perpignan and Figueras, one of the shorter and lower crossing points between France and Spain. The family was caught by Spanish patrols and separated. Dispecker was sent to Miranda, his wife to a women's prison, and their young son to an orphanage. After a couple of months, the boy joined his mother in the prison. Dispeker claimed Belgian nationality, but his real status was soon confirmed. Released by Blickenstaff, he was reunited with his family and, though they had thought of travelling to the Belgian Congo or to America, Wilfrid persuaded them to go to Palestine.

Rudolf Jonas, a writer, and his wife crossed the Pyrenees in midwinter. They heard of a guide but were suspicious. Jonas's wife took the Frenchman to a bistro in Toulouse, made him drunk, and asked him outright whether he intended to betray them. Puzzled and tipsy, the guide was indignant; they decided to trust him. Wearing several layers of clothing, the couple climbed to a point 9,000 feet up in the mountains. The guide knew where caches of food were hidden, and the frontier was marked with stones left by earlier escapers. The slopes were gentler on the Spanish side of the frontier, and Jonas, exhausted, made part of the descent by rolling downhill. Immediately apprehended, like most escapers, he and his wife were imprisoned twice; the Gestapo had the run of Miranda, and Jonas saw several refugees identified and sent back by the Spaniards into the hands of the German patrols. But by spring, the Spaniards were searching for pretexts to release prisoners who were unfit for military service or over age. Jonas, too, was released by Blickenstaff and met Wilfrid in May; he thought him all-powerful, 'a monastic figure', the only man who could comfort the refugees in a city where no one was responsible for their fate.[61]

By mid-May, Wilfrid knew that young children could not be taken over the mountain route. But young men and women could make the journey if he could only contact some organization inside France and assure them of his help and support. At exactly this time, two men, Shlomo Steinhorn and Joseph Croustillon, were sent over the frontier by a Jewish underground group, l'Armée Juive, to try and make contact with Jewish organizations which might help them. They reached Spain within days of Wilfrid's departure.

Steinhorn was a Romanian Jew who had been studying law in France when the war broke out. In March 1943, he was warned by l'Armée Juive, an organization which planned to get young men to Palestine, that he was in danger of deportation, and moved to Toulouse; there he contacted a Maquis guide and crossed into Spain over the Pyrenees at St Godard with a party of twenty, the oldest a French officer in his forties on his way to join General Giraud's army in Algeria. They had studied Spanish for two weeks and were well prepared physically for the journey. They climbed from ten at night until twelve the following day, were immediately captured by a patrol and brought before the local magistrate. The Spaniards released only those under eighteen or over forty, having promised the Germans to arrest all men of military age. Both men were therefore imprisoned before they could leave Lérida. Steinhorn was released towards the end of July and went straight to the unofficial Joint Office in Barcelona. It was only then that he heard of Wilfrid and his mission. But by then it was too late.[62]

On 23 May, before leaving Spain, Wilfrid submitted a detailed memorandum to Hoare on the refugee problem in Spain. A third of the refugees, he estimated, were eligible for immigration to Palestine; others, he thought, might join the Pioneer Corps to emigrate to North or South America. He suggested transferring the remainder, for whom no visas were available, to transit camps in the Azores or England until the end of the war, and asked for British protection to be extended to those who already held Palestine visas – a policy he also urged on Linton and the historian Lewis Namier in London, and which they took to the Foreign Office. Despite all the risks, he proposed that, if all else failed, the refugees should be transported to Palestine through the Mediterranean. Most of his recommendations were eventually adopted.[63]

Meanwhile, he worked at the Embassy preparing detailed lists of those eligible for certificates and also reserve lists; but his hopes of co-operation with Jerusalem were now dashed. On 10 May, he had cabled Henrietta Szold asking for twenty-five Youth Aliya certificates so that he should have a reserve for candidates he soon expected to locate.[64] But despite the talk of the rescue of thousands, and the assurance he had received from Szold a month earlier by cable, only ten certificates were transferred to Madrid, and no more were received before he left. Three days later, he cabled Linton from Barcelona, in one of the two messages he sent from Spain: 'Slow investigations new route Congo. Am terminating selection work as no further certificates available my mission thus sadly handicapped.'[65] On the eve of leaving Madrid, he again cabled Jerusalem, stressing that his work had come to a standstill because of their lack of response.

Throughout April, contacts had continued in Jerusalem between the Government of Palestine and the Jewish Agency over the rescue of children and the allocation of certificates. By 2 April, the Colonial Office had clearly had second thoughts about its earlier commitment, and Stanley told Jerusalem to tell the Jews that, 'although the scheme was not limited to the Balkans and South-East Europe, the practical difficulties of bringing Jewish emigrants out of Holland, Belgium and Denmark are likely to be so formidable that ... it would be unwise to make the attempt.'[66] Bernard Joseph, of the Agency, answered that, while he agreed that efforts should be concentrated on saving refugees from countries 'within easier reach of Palestine', a Swedish ship might be chartered to take 1,000 refugees from Holland, Belgium and France to Palestine. 'We propose pursuing this possibility as we would not wish to leave any stone unturned to save such Jews as can be saved from any of the Nazi-dominated countries.'[67]

But while Adler Rudel and Wilfrid were pursuing their joint attempts at mass rescue, Shertok returned to Jerusalem from America in April and heard, for the first time, of the Colonial Office's earlier proposals. He was immediately suspicious. The Foreign Office and Herbert Morrison, he noted, were 'playing football' with the refugee rescue question; it was ironical that after the Zionists had been asked so often not to bring Palestine into the rescue debate, it was now the Foreign Office that had done so. As for the Colonial Office, the entire project, he told the Executive, was probably a trap, intended to 'cheat the Jews out of certificates for adults'.[68]

The Agency Executive now also had second thoughts. Henrietta Szold had always been cautious in granting certificates, and it could not have been difficult to persuade her to drop the issue. By the third week in May, Wilfrid had many more candidates for Youth Aliya than certificates; he had Hoare's backing; he even, according to those who spoke to him, had the co-operation of the Spanish authorities, and he knew that the more visas he obtained the more lenient the authorities would be about admitting Jewish refugees – some of whom were even sent back across the frontier while he was in Spain. But the organization which had sent him to Portugal and Spain now reined him in.

On 25 May, Wilfrid returned to Lisbon. The only letter he sent from Spain was to his mother, reassuring her that he was pleased with the results of his work and that his health had stood the journey well. It was not a candid letter, and he did not mention the one real hour of pleasure he had allowed himself, between visiting prisons and transit camps: he had been to the Prado.[69]

Back in Lisbon, Wilfrid had another disappointment. The university committee, which had met to discuss the Congo route, was told by a Portuguese physician just back from Luanda that the route would be impassable at this time of year because of heavy rains. Only after November, six months later, he was told, would it be possible to send a party through the jungle.[70]

Wilfrid was now besieged by refugees to whom he had no more certificates to offer. All he could do was promise that once back in London, he would press for the largest allocation. His remaining few days in Lisbon were spent dictating the names and numbers of scores of friends in German concentration camps to Emma Wohlwill – including that of Leo Baeck – and arranging for her to send parcels and letters, which he could not mail from England.[71] He cabled Linton in London, explaining that he had left one of the refugees, Dr Paul Block, in charge of a 'provisionary [*sic*] office' under Blickenstaff;[72] his instructions were to continue exploring rescue routes. But he told no one of his own ideas for rescue; he left that for London. Although he made it clear to

Schwartz of the Joint that this was now the only way out for the young people in France, it was far too dangerous to commit detailed plans to paper.

Wilfrid was sitting in his hotel with Heinz Wisla, the young German who had come to say goodbye, when he was told that a place had been found for him on a plane leaving the next morning, just in time for him to return, within the two months' deadline, to his new work in the Foreign Office. After Wisla had left, he briefed Robert Dexter, the American Unitarian who was to be active in the War Refugee Board set up the following year, on the situation in Spain. Then he escorted Emma Wohlwill home; the last evening of his life was one of the long, sunny evenings of a Portuguese summer. He gave Mrs Wohlwill a Baedeker that he told her he had borrowed from a Lisbon bookseller in the Avenida da Liberdade, an ex-Berliner whom he had recognized from the 1930s, and asked her to return it for him. As they parted, he apologized ruefully that all their talk had been of war and rescue. 'How much I would have liked to talk with you about other things,' he said.

That morning, an army officer seconded to British Intelligence, Captain James Langley, prepared to return to England from Lisbon. Langley was second in command to Norman Crockatt, head of MI9, the branch of Intelligence which supervised the escape and evasion of British prisoners of war and agents in the field; he also provided liaison between Crockatt and the Secret Intelligence Service, headed by Claude Dansey. Langley was visiting Lisbon under the name of Mr Lewis, an architect checking on the maintenance of British buildings. According to Langley's recollection thirty-nine years later, shortly before he was due to leave he met Donald Darling, another MI9 official, code-named Sunday, who had flown in from Gibraltar. Darling had chilling news for him. He warned Langley that a German pilot, whom he had known since pre-war days, had told him that the Luftwaffe had plans to attack every plane flying the route between Portugal and Britain within the next few days, in the hope of shooting down the plane which was carrying Churchill back from North Africa, through Gibraltar, and across the Bay of Biscay.[73]

The route between Lisbon and Bristol had never been safe for civilian planes. There had been at least two previous attacks, in November 1942 and in April that year. But for Langley, a concerted plan was more alarming, and he was so preoccupied with his thoughts, as he waited for the flight to be called, that he did not recognize his cover name when a tall, fair man, who introduced himself as Leslie Howard – a name Langley did not know – addressed him as Mr Lewis. Howard asked

Langley whether he was taking his seat that day; he was anxious to return to England and hoped to substitute for anyone who had second thoughts. The actor was unsuccessful: Langley would use his seat. Howard remained behind.

When Langley's plane was a couple of hours out of Lisbon, he noticed an enemy fighter approaching; so did the pilot, who immediately dived for cover. Providentially, a storm broke at that moment, and the pilot managed to escape into thick cloud, where he circled until the danger was past, and reached England with no further incident.

At 9.30 the next morning, 1 June, a plane, which its Dutch crew had nicknamed the 'Ibis', prepared for take-off. Leslie Howard had finally obtained a seat. Another passenger, Tyrrell Shervington, confided to a friend who escorted him to the airport that, although he had made this journey so many times, he was oddly nervous.[74]

Instead of seeking the cover of the low cloud over the Bay of Biscay, Quirinas Tepas, the Dutch pilot, flew high above it. It was midday, more than three hours out of Lisbon, and the 'Ibis' was an easy target for the first Messerschmidt of the eight-plane patrol which suddenly veered towards him. Tepas radioed to Whitchurch control station that he was being followed, and, almost immediately afterwards, that he was being attacked by enemy aircraft. But there was no chance of escape; he had flown too high. A few bursts from the first Messerschmidt's guns set the 'Ibis' alight and wrecked its controls, and the plane plunged through the cloud towards the sea. The German fighters followed it down, but after a few minutes not even wreckage was to be seen.[75] Wilfrid had wished to be buried on a mountain; his death was recorded: 'lost at sea'.

That night, the Luftwaffe recorded shooting down two Wellington bombers, a Douglas Boston and a Liberator in the Bay of Biscay area.[76] The attacks continued for several days, then ceased entirely. On 4 June, Churchill was back in England.

A week after Wilfrid's death, his memorandum on the refugees in Spain was forwarded to the Foreign Office. Randall of the Refugee Department, who had known Wilfrid since 1939, minuted: 'It is a disaster from our point of view that we should have lost the benefit of his advice (apart from this one document) in the future.'[77] But the real disaster was that of the young Jews he might have helped escape from France. He was the one man with the determination and ability, at that stage of the war, to organize rescue through Spain. The Jewish Agency in Jerusalem did not send the 'efficient and routined expert' from Palestine Wilfrid had asked to replace him. Steinhorn and Croustillon failed to impress the Joint representatives with the urgency of their mission. Five precious months passed before Fritz Lichtenstein, one of Wilfrid's colleagues from England, arrived in Portugal. Working from Wilfrid's lists, he despatched the first of four boatloads of refugees to Palestine. The *Nyassa* sailed calmly through the Mediterranean after the end of the North African campaign and arrived in Haifa in January, the first rescue ship from Western Europe to reach Palestine during the war. Among its passengers were Heinz Wisla and BenZion Kalisher of the Ericeira group, the Dispekers, Steinhorn and Paul Block, who had vainly tried, with no experience or help, to organize the rescue of a group of Italians from southern France towards the end of 1943. Lichtenstein was not concerned with illegal rescue. It was only in the winter of 1944 that another brave man, Jules Jefroykin, with the help of Schwartz of the Joint, succeeded in bringing a few hundred children across the Pyrenees; several died on the dangerous journeys.[78]

Yet the fate of the children in Vichy France was not sealed by Wilfrid's death. Many of the Dutch children, in a country whose topography made hiding almost impossible, were deported and murdered. But in Vichy France, the children in the Jewish orphanages, who had been the subject of negotiations with the Joint, were dispersed among French villages, and in private homes and convents, a little later. All survived the war.[79] So did many of the Belgians. Though Adler Rudel's grand plans also failed, young refugees in Denmark, Youth Aliya members, rescued several hundred Jews.[80] The courage of ordinary people saved many Jewish lives.

The fate of the 'Ibis' attracted attention all over the world, but the story was never told in full. Wilfrid Israel's presence on the plane was almost certainly known to German Intelligence. When Emma Wohlwill went to return the Baedeker to the bookseller from Berlin, she learned that he was in touch with German Intelligence in Lisbon.[81] Yet Wilfrid was no more likely to have been the precise target of the attack than Howard, Howard's accountant, or Tyrrell Shervington.

Despite the subsequent declarations in Parliament, the attack on the civilian 'Ibis' was not regarded as an offence against the Geneva Convention. When the Luftwaffe squadron leader responsible was taken prisoner later in the war, it was decided not to prosecute him as a war criminal[82] – an indication perhaps that a plan to kill Churchill, if such it was, was regarded by the British, as well as by the Germans, as a legitimate wartime objective.

In November 1943, the N. Israel building in the Koenigstrasse and Spandauerstrasse crumpled in one of the mass bombing raids launched on Berlin that winter; only the ground floor remained. Paul Krentz, the personnel manager, survived the war and lived to administer pensions to all the old employees of the firm; the money was sent by the Israel family abroad. Because the firm had stood in what was to become East Berlin, no reparations were ever paid to Wilfrid's heirs.

Following the failure of the 'officers' plot' to kill Hitler, Adam von Trott was arrested, tried for treason and hanged in the Plotzensee jail on 26 August 1944. The last relic of his friendship with Wilfrid, a rustic rocking-chair his wife remembered him calling 'Wilfrid's chair' – a gift from the 1930s – went up in flames when the Russians reached Berlin in the following year.

Of Wilfrid's leading colleagues in the Reichsvertretung, only Leo Baeck survived the war. Wilfrid's uncle, Richard Israel, Hindenburg's old aide, died in Theresienstadt on the day after his arrival, having been given a fatal injection. To the last, he maintained, to a young member of the Baum resistance group who met him just before his deportation, that the Nazis would not touch him. His wife, Bianca, survived the war, and his grandson still lives in Munich.

The only employee not to take advantage of Wilfrid's offers of help, Irmgard Smurka, the little cashier from the ground floor, remained in Berlin throughout the war. When she became pregnant in 1942, her husband left her, afraid of fathering a Jewish child. Mother and child survived the bombings, but the child died of diphtheria shortly after the war's end. Baptized in 1943 by Pastor Heinrich Gruber to save her life, she was buried, at her mother's request, in a Jewish cemetery.[83] Laura Livingstone was the first woman relief worker to enter the Belsen concentration camp.[84]

Each of Wilfrid's friends mourned a slightly different man, for each envisaged a different post-war future for him. Some of his non-Jewish friends anticipated that he might return to Germany. Adam von Trott – who, it seems, never learned of Wilfrid's death – had seen him as the man who would reintegrate the Jews into post-Nazi Germany.[85] But even before the deportations of German Jews began, Wilfrid had termed the return of Jews to Germany 'beyond reason'.

British friends in the Foreign Office and at Oxford thought he might become a permanent colleague, but Wilfrid already had his certificate for Palestine. His Zionist friends thought he might become an Israeli industrialist or a diplomat; but he had no such ambitions. His one explicit desire, to be a sculptor, he referred to ironically, as to all the things he most loved, as 'a hobby'.

After his death, Wilfrid's friends surmised how he would have reacted to later events: whether he would have been disillusioned and disappointed, or whether he would have rallied to the call for Jewish statehood and accepted the breach with England, as he had accepted the part destruction of his art collection, with 'a last reserve of grace and equanimity of mind'; or whether, in the end, the man who had found homes for so many fugitives might not himself have remained homeless at heart.

For the much-praised worldliness of Wilfrid Israel, his ability to cross cultural barriers, his skill as an interpreter, was deceptive. The man Beeley called 'an unaffectedly civilized European' remained, in the last analysis, a German Jew. Ironically enough, despite his early rebellion, the challenge of Nazism resolved much of his previous ambivalence towards his own community, and his fight within Germany was more effective than his efforts to mediate between German Jewry, or the anti-Nazis, and the outside world.

Wilfrid Israel never wholly freed himself of the attitudes of his class and demonstrated its chief virtue: the sense of the iron obligation of service. Privilege, too, was at least in part the source of his uncanny detachment, and helped him to function as an intermediary between the German Jews and their potential allies in the outside world; in this sense he appears today, perhaps, as an anachronistic figure. Yet the role of intermediary between the oppressed in authoritarian states, and the outside world, is anything but obsolete, nor is Wilfrid Israel's story irrelevant to the contemporary scene, in which persecuted minorities are still misunderstood, their appeals often disregarded, and demonstrations of support from liberal supporters outside often ill-conceived.

The romantic and contradictory portrait of Wilfrid which survived several decades was in many respects deceptive. The contradictions his friends and colleagues saw in his personality were not only explicable in terms of his heritage and experience; they were also, ultimately, less important than the great simplicity of the man's ideals. No one saw more clearly than Wilfrid himself that people considered his visionary side naïve, his ideas those of 'a blissful fool', his thought 'verging on mental crudeness'. But it was this singlemindedness which made him act. His apparent sophistication never obscured the clarity of his moral perception, nor did his sensitivity prevent him from accepting the reality of the horrors of Nazism. While many civilized men were unable to believe in the reality of the Holocaust, Wilfrid did so without hesitation.

Six years before his death, he wrote what must stand as a final comment on his life.

In the summer of 1937, after a journey abroad for the Hilfsverein, Wilfrid travelled to the Swiss mountains for a brief rest before returning to Nazi Germany. The village he chose, Soglio, was best known to lovers of German poetry. Rilke had spent several weeks there thirty years earlier, and, like Rilke, Wilfrid stayed in a seventeenth-century mansion from whose terrace he could look down over the chestnut woods, into Italy.[86]

Wilfrid wrote to Werner Behr on 19 June:

> In this little Eden, I am pervasively idle; I shall have to take myself in hand. The silence around me is astonishing; only the old mail coach lumbers up here from the valley twice a day, and even now there is not a single shop save for the grocery – no workshops, no barber – agriculture is the only profession considered dignified in this part of the world – take note of that!
>
> Yes, I am here alone. But I don't feel at all lonely, knowing that many people are close to me, and I to them, as so often has been confirmed in recent times.
>
> Should I shed tears of bitterness that 'great happiness' has not been granted me? All I know is that my life, for myself and others, has not remained empty. Is that of no account?[87]

Notes

Notes

The main sources are indicated in the acknowledgements. The following are the abbreviations used in the footnotes.

BOD	Board of Deputies Archives, London
CZA	The Central Zionist Archives, Jerusalem
DBFP	Documents of British Foreign Policy (printed volumes)
FLA	Friends Library Archives, London
FRUS	Foreign Relations of the United States (printed volumes)
ICJ	Institute of Contemporary Jewry, Hebrew University, Jerusalem
LBI	Leo Baeck Institute (New York, London or Jerusalem indicated)
JDC	Joint Distribution Committee Archives, New York
LBIY	*Leo Baeck Institute Yearbook*
PRO	Public Record Office, Kew, London: refers to all files beginning FO 371 (Foreign Office general correspondence), CAB (Cabinet Papers), PREM (Prime Minister's papers), CO (Colonial Office)
UNLA	UN Library Archives, Geneva
WA	Weizmann Archives, Rehovot, Israel
YIVO	YIVO Institute, New York
YVS	Yad Vashem, Jerusalem

Footnote references are not given for Israel's letters in private hands though the date and recipient are usually indicated. Letters in any of the above collections have detailed references.

1 Prologue: In Search of Wilfrid Israel

1 *The Times*, 8 June 1943.
2 John Beevor, *SOE: Recollections and Reflections* (London, 1981), p. 41.
3 For various theories, see Winston Churchill, *The Hinge of Fate* (London, 1951), closing paragraphs of volume; Ian Colvin, *Flight 777* (London, 1957); Ronald Howard, *In Search of My Father* (London, 1980).
4 The tribute was eventually published in *Wilfrid Israel 1899–1943* (London, 1944). A copy remains in the Wiener Library, Tel Aviv University.
5 Sir Michael Bruce, *Tramp Royal* (London, 1954), pp. 236–42.
6 Colvin, *Flight 777*.
7 *Wilfrid Israel 1899–1943*. The personal testimonies regarding his work in the

Hilfsverein are by Shlomo Adler Rudel, author of *Jüdisches Selbsthilfe* (Tubingen, 1974), and Werner Senator, a member of the Jewish Agency Executive who visited Berlin regularly throughout the 1930s and who died in 1958.

8 See *Manchester Guardian*, 28 May, 4 June and (weekly edition) 7 June 1956; *Encounter*, June 1969; Christopher Sykes's biography of Adam von Trott, *Troubled Loyalty* (London, 1968); and, for a partial account of Trott's life, H. Malone, *Adam von Trott zu Solz: the Road to Conspiracy against Hitler* (University of Texas at Austin, 1980).

9 Hans Reissner, 'The History of Kaufhaus N. Israel and Wilfrid Israel', LBIY, III (London, 1958), pp. 227–56.

10 Lionel Kochan, *Pogrom* (London, 1957); Joshua Sherman, *Island Refuge; Britain and the Refugees from the Third Reich* (London, 1973).

11 See, for instance, brief mentions in recent books such as M.R.D. Foot, *Resistance* (London, 1976); Martin Gilbert, *Auschwitz and the Allies* (London, 1981); Yehuda Bauer, *American Jewry and the Holocaust* (New York, 1981). The fullest (unpublished) account is in a Hebrew MA thesis by Chaim Avni, 'Hatsalat Hayehudim miSfarad ve Portugal', in the National Library, Jerusalem; Israel's mission is also briefly mentioned in Professor Avni's *Contemporary Spain and the Jewish People* (YVS, 1975), and Isaac Weissman's *Mul Eitanei HaResha* (Tel Aviv, 1968).

12 Peter Vansittart, *Living in London* (London, 1974); Stephen Spender, *World within World* (London, 1951); Christopher Isherwood, *Christopher and His Kind* (London, 1977).

13 See Herbert Strauss, 'Jewish Emigration from Germany', Part Two; LBIY, XXVI, p. 397 (London, 1982).

14 Ulrich Reusch, 'Die Londoner Institutionen der britischen Deutschlandpolitik 1943–48', *Historisches Jahrbuch* (Freiburg/Munchen), Vol. 100 (1980), pp. 318–443.

15 Werner Behr to Werner Senator, 18 March 1944, CZA, S7/950.

16 Wilfrid Israel's London papers are in the Wiener Library, Tel Aviv University.

2 The Last Heir

1 Author's conversation with Hilda Joachim, Richard Israel's daughter.

2 See *Herzl Diaries* (London, 1956), entry for 27 January 1896.

3 Hermann Adler, 'Judaism and War', *Anglo Jewish Memories and other Sermons* (London, 1909), p 111.

4 Separate volumes of the N. Israel albums survive in two collections: the Geheimes Staatsarchiv, Preussischer Kulturbesitz, Berlin, and the Wiener Library, Tel Aviv University.

5 Colin Holmes, *Anti Semitism in British Society, 1919–39* (London, 1979), pp. 12, 45.

6 Adler, 'Jew and Gentile', *Anglo Jewish Memories*, pp. 279–88.

7 For references to Conrad Alberti, see Gordon Craig, *Germany 1866–1945* (London, 1981), and Fritz Stern, *The Politics of Cultural Despair* (New York, 1965), p. 182n.

8 Steven Aschheim has pointed out to me that Walther Rathenau displayed similar contradictions. Rathenau, however, never played a role in the Jewish community.

9 Quoted in Lucy Davidowitz, *The War Against the Jews* (New York, 1975).

10 The account of the Israel firm until 1907 is based largely on Reissner, 'The History of Kaufhaus N. Isráel'.

11 The account of the Adler family is based on Marcus N. Adler, *The Adler Family*

(*Jewish Chronicle* publications, 1909); and H.D. Schmidt, 'Chief Rabbi N.M. Adler', LBIY, VII (London, 1962).

12 Weizmann to Perth, 12 December 1939, *The Letters and Papers of Chaim Weizmann*, Vol. XIX, p. 205.

13 Other contributors to the sketch of Wilfrid's youth are his nephew Vivian Prins, and Professor Siegfried Stein, whose father was an executive in the Israel firm.

14 Wilfrid's boyhood diary of the Italian journey is in Kibbutz Hazorea Archives.

15 Letter to Hans Reissner, 1941, LBI, New York, Israel Collection.

16 Letter to Maximilian Harden, 15 April 1918; I am grateful to the Bundesarchiv, Koblenz, for permission to reprint passages of this letter, which is in the Harden Nachlass. Other information on Harden is based on Eric Gottesgetreu, 'Maximilian Harden', LBIY, VII (London, 1962), and Helmut Rogge, 'Aus Maximilian Hardens publicistic 1912–22', *Publicistic*, No. 516, September–December 1961.

17 *Die Zukunft*, 2 December and 16 December 1905.

18 'Die Jüdischen Gefallenen des Deutschen Heeres, der Meutschen Marine und der Deutschen schutztrupper', *Philo-Lexicon* (Berlin, 1936).

19 Wilfrid Israel, 'Notes of Youth Aliya', January 1943, the Wiener Library, Israel Papers.

20 *Ibid.*

21 For an account of the Volksheim, see Eike Geisel, *Im Scheunenviertel* (Berlin, 1981), p. 19; see also Norman Bentwich, *Ben Shemen: a Children's Village*, UNESCO, no date given.

3 The Apprentice

1 Ruth Fry, *A Quaker Adventure* (London, 1926), Section VIII (Germany), Chapter LIV.

2 Marion Fox to Friends House, London, 20 July 1919, FLA, Germany Files 1919–23.

3 Ilse Scheffer to Fraulein Kolb, 1 February 1919, FLA, FWVR Files, Box 10, Parcel 2, Folder 3.

4 Harold Nicolson, *Peacemaking 1919* (London, 1937), Chapter III. Churchill was the exception, and urged lifting the boycott. See WSC to Sir Henry Wilson, 20 February 1919, in Martin Gilbert, *Winston Churchill* (London, 1977), Vol. IV, Companion Part I, documents January 1917–June 1919.

5 The German organization was the 'Hilfswerke für Deutsche in Ausland und Auslander in Deutschland'; see Fry, *A Quaker Adventure*.

6 The record of these negotiations is in FLA, FRWS Reports, 1919–23.

7 Elisabeth Rotten to Marion Fox, 18 June 1919, FLA, FWVR Files, Box 10, Folder 6 (correspondence with workers).

8 I am grateful to the late Professor T.H. Marshall for permission to quote from this document, Marshall Papers, 3/1, London School of Economics.

9 'Notes of conversation with Dr Rotten', The Hague, April, 1919, FLA, Germany Files 1919–23.

10 Details of Wilfrid Israel's meetings with the Quaker women are in Marion Fox's journal, FLA, Germany Files 1919–23.

11 Fry, *A Quaker Adventure*.

12 Letter from Dr Schlesinger (Nansen's representative in Berlin) to Lewis Strauss,

American-Jewish banker, 11 August 1923, UNLA, Nansen Office Papers, Divers 16, C 1120.

13 Wilfrid Israel's correspondence with Martin Buber is in Hebrew University Library, Jerusalem, Buber Archives, MS Varia 350/317. See Israel to Buber, 30 November 1932, and Buber to Israel, 5 December 1932. The drawings are not in the Buber Archives, but in LBI, New York, Israel Collection.

14 Israel to Buber, 27 February 1938, and Buber to Israel, 17 March 1938, Buber Archives, MS Varia 350/317. Buber had, however, supported the war.

15 Wilhelm Stahl, ed., *Schultheiss Europaeischer Geschichtes Kalendar* (Munich, 1922).

16 See Note 9.

17 Israel's friendship with these men is mentioned in Norman Bentwich's tribute to Israel, in *Wilfrid Israel 1899–1943*.

18 Open letter beginning 'Dear . . .', 15 November 1939. Wiener Library, Israel Papers. A copy is to be found in the George Bell German Church Papers in the Lambeth Palace Library, Vol. 24, 'Peace Aims Conference'.

19 Lenz und Fabian, eds, *Die Friedensbewegung* (*German Handbook of Peace Movements*) (Berlin, 1922), pp. 293–4.

20 Denkschrift der Deutsche Liga für Volkerbund, 26 April 1920, UNLA, Deutschefriedenscartelle (Fonds Quidde Papers) D. 113.

21 'The Coming Peace and the Jewish Question', Jewish Press Bureau, Stockholm, 31 November 1917, YIVO, D. Moshkowitz Collection, p. 8072.

22 See F.P. Walters, *History of the League of Nations* (London, 1965); for details of the Vilna crisis, pp. 107–8, 140–3.

23 These two documents were kindly lent to me by Mr T. Rechtmann.

24 Report of Dr Farrar, International Committee for Russian Relief, Geneva, 18 January 1922, UNLA, Registry Files 47/1752.

25 'Nansen's Place in History', Nansen memorial lecture given by Philip Noel Baker on 11 October 1961 and published by Oslo University Press.

26 These were reports from the Estonian Red Cross and Dr Schlesinger of the Berlin Central War Prisoners Bureau, UNLA, Registry Files, Classement 12, Dossiers 14182, 14309, 14502.

27 Nansen to J.H. Gorvin of the Supreme Allied Council in Paris, 27 July 1921, UNLA, Registry Files, Classement 12, Document 14407, Dossier 14182.

28 Israel to Philip Noel Baker (copied to Nansen and Massingham), 2 August 1921, UNLA, Registry Files, Classement 12, Document 14506, Dossier 14182.

29 Noel Baker to Israel, 8 August 1921, Churchill College, Cambridge, Noel Baker Papers, 4/610b.

30 Noel Baker's 'Nansen' papers used for writing his lecture (see note 25) have been placed in his Cambridge papers only recently, are still unsorted and thus not available to researchers.

31 The documents relating to this conference are in UNLA, Commission Files, Nansen Office Papers, Box 278. The conference was not reported in any of the major newspapers held in the Munich Institut für Zeitgeschichte.

32 *Krieg dem Kriege* (*War against War*) was first published in 1922. It was reprinted in Berlin in 1980; the Anti-War Museum was reopened by Tommy Spree, Friedrich's grandson, in 1982. For more details on Friedrich, see *Europaeischen Ideen* (Berlin, 1977), No. 29.

33 Oskar Kokoschka, *My Life* (London, 1974), p. 111.

34 The Indian (96-page) section of Israel's much longer diary of his travels, in typescript, is in the Kibbutz Hazorea Archives.

35 See Bernhard Kahn, 'My Trip to Russia', June–July 1925', YIVO, J.L. Rosen Files, (21). Israel probably accompanied either Kahn or David A. Brown, who toured the settlements a few weeks earlier. Letters Israel wrote to a Russian friend in 1941 indicate that they followed the same route. For another admiring report by Boris Bogen see same source in YIVO.
36 Israel, 'Youth Aliya', notes written in 1943, Wiener Library, Israel Papers.
37 Lehmann quote is from *Wilfrid Israel 1899–1943*.
38 Margot Klausner, 'Wilfrid Israel und seine Beziehung zur Habima', CZA, S7/1063.

4 Wilfrid in Weimar

1 *Deutsche Konfektion*, Heft 52, 28 December 1928. Copy in LBI, New York, Israel Collection.
2 Rilke, *Letters to a Young Poet*, translated by Reginald Snell (London, 1946).
3 R.W. (Robert Weltsch), 'Schawuoth und Delegiertentag', *Jüdische Rundschau*, 23 May 1928. Quoted in Donald L. Niewyk, *The Jews in Weimar Germany* (Manchester, 1980), p. 164.
4 Richard Lichtheim to Nahum Goldmann, 9 September 1942, CZA, L22/27. Lichtheim sent a copy of this letter to Wilfrid Israel in April 1943.
5 Walter Laqueur, *History of Zionism* (London, 1972).
6 *Wilfrid Israel 1899–1943*.
7 David Ben Gurion to Shalom Hektin, 16 September 1930, D. Ben Gurion, *Igarot* (in Hebrew, Tel Aviv, 1971).
8 See PRO, CO/733/175-67411 for details of Magnes's conversations with Chancellor. A copy of his cable to Felix Warburg is also in this file.
9 Weizmann to Isaac Naiditch, *The Letters and Papers of Chaim Weizmann*, Vol. XIV, p. 136; see also Weizmann to Felix Warburg, 22 November 1929, *ibid.*, p. 95.
10 Israel to Weizmann, 30 November 1929, WA.
11 Israel to Weizmann, 20 December 1929 and 5 January 1930, WA; see also Senator to Israel, 8 July 1930, CZA, 49/91.
12 Weizmann to Melchett, 21 November 1929, *The Letters and Papers of Chaim Weizmann*, Vol. XIV, p. 90.
13 Einstein to Weizmann (in German), 25 November 1929, WA.
14 Weizmann to Einstein, 30 November 1929, *The Letters and Papers of Chaim Weizmann*, Vol. XIV, p. 122.
15 Einstein to Weizmann, dated only 29 December, WA.
16 *Falastin*, 19 October 1929.
17 Israel to Einstein, 14 January 1930, Hebrew University, Jerusalem, Einstein Papers.
18 *Falastin*, 1 February 1930.
19 See, for instance, Israel to Weizmann, 6 June 1930, WA.
20 Cyrus Adler to Dr Bogen, 17 August 1923, YIVO, J.L. Rosen Files 1925.
21 The following account of Habima's adventures is based on Margot Klausner, *Yoman Habima* (in Hebrew; Tel Aviv, 1971), and on her unpublished diaries from the period. I am grateful to Mrs Miriam Spielmann for permission to use her mother's papers.
22 Laski's remark, based on visits to Blonie and Sochaszew, two villages near Warsaw, is from his account of a European journey in August 1934, YIVO, D. Moshkowitz Collection, File 76, p. 9921.
23 The account of the visit to Poland is based on Mordechai Shenhabi's recollections, as told to the author. The dates of Wilfrid Israel's Polish trip can be exactly

calculated from his letters to Weizmann dated 10 February and 22 August 1930, WA.

24 See Weizmann to Felix Warburg, 22 November 1929, *The Letters and Papers of Chaim Weizmann*, Vol. XIV, p. 99.

25 Said-Ruete to Weizmann, 24 November 1929, WA; Israel to Weizmann, 21 February, 5 May and 9 September 1930, WA.

26 Said-Ruete's reports are dated 20 December 1929, 11 January, 17 January and 7 February 1930, WA.

27 Said-Ruete to Israel, 1 September 1930, WA.

28 Israel to Weizmann, 9 September 1930, WA. His friends in Egypt were Charles de Menasce and Ralph Harari.

29 The correspondence between Senator and Israel is in Senator's private file, CZA, S49/91.

30 Shenhabi to Israel, 3 November 1932, Shenhabi Papers, Kibbutz Artzi Archives, Kibbutz Merhavia.

31 Isherwood, *Christopher and His Kind*, pp. 55–60.

32 Spender, *World within World*.

33 *Ibid.*, p. 131.

34 Israel to Senator, 25 April 1932, CZA, S49/91.

35 See Gustav Horn, ed., *Juedische Jugend im Uebergang – Ludwig Tietz (1897–1933) Sein Leben und Seine Zeit* (Tel Aviv, 1981).

36 Senator to Israel, 26 June 1932, CZA, S49/81.

37 Israel to Shenhabi, 30 January 1932, Shenhabi Papers, Kibbutz Artzi Archives, Kibbutz Merhavia.

38 Recha Freier, *Let the Children Come* (London, 1961), p. 16; and author's conversation with Mrs Freier.

5 The Visible Darkness

1 Israel, 'Youth Aliya'.

2 Unsigned testimony, FLA, Germany Files, 29 June–December 1933, GE 9. Wilfrid's arrest: testimony of Heidi Spree, Friedrich's daughter, who visited the Parochialstrasse on that day with her mother (author's conversation with Tommy Spree, Heidi's son – Berlin). Wilfrid's friends assert that he did not tell his family or friends of the incident.

3 Werner Behr tribute, from *Wilfrid Israel 1899–1943*.

4 Arnold Paucker, *Der Jüdische Abwehrkampf im der letzen Jahren der Weimarer Republik* (Hamburg, 1968), p. 88.

5 Reissner, 'The History of Kaufhaus N. Israel', p. 243.

6 A pamphlet on the Wecke group is to be found in the papers of Stafford Cripps at Nuffield College, Oxford. Cripps was in touch with the SPD Reichsbanner militia leader, Holtermann, and raised some money in an ineffectual effort to help socialist resistance in Nazi Germany.

7 Behr, released, told these details to his brother-in-law, Hans Feld. They are also confirmed in the testimony of Rosa Dukas, the sister of Einstein's secretary and an employee of the Israel firm (YVS, Bell Kadurie Papers, 01/299). Wilfrid Israel gave an identical account to Hans Neumann (George Newman).

8 Reissner, 'The History of Kaufhaus N. Israel', p. 243.

9 Accounts of several N. Israel employees.

10 Reissner, 'The History of Kaufhaus N. Israel'.

11 Isherwood, *Christopher and His Kind*, p. 97.
12 Dukas testimony, see Note 7.
13 Reissner, 'The History of Kaufhaus N. Israel'. Reissner does not make it clear whether or not Berthold acceded to the demand.
14 Author's conversation with Rafael Buber.
15 Author's conversation with Alfred Front.
16 Einstein to Paul Ehrenfest, 14 April 1933. Quoted in Otto Nathan and Heinz Norden, eds, *Einstein on Peace* (Schocken, 1968).
17 Author's conversation with Efrem Kurtz.
18 Letter to the author from Sir Con O'Neill, 31 August 1981. O'Neill was Third Secretary at the British Embassy in Berlin during the period. This is the general practice according to international law.
19 Kayser to Israel, 29 October 1932, Buber Archives, Ms Varia 350/317.
20 Author's conversation with M. Shenhabi.
21 Karl Schleunes, *The Twisted Road to Auschwitz* (Chicago, 1970), Chapter I, p. 93; see also Gustav Horn interview, ICJ, File 41.
22 Reissner, 'The History of Kaufhaus N. Israel'. Among the surviving papers of the Central Bureau where Wilfrid Israel's name is mentioned, see Zentralauschuss Report, April–December 1933, LBI, Jerusalem, Adler Rudel Files; and at an early meeting, CZA, A 142 (Blau Files) 86/3, dated May 1933.
23 Horn interview, see Note 21. Also author's conversations with Horn.
24 For a detailed study of the Werkleute, its philosophy and origins, see Eliahau Maoz, 'The Werkleute', LBY, IV, 1959, pp. 165–82.
25 Author's conversations with Gustav Horn and Wolf Mattesdorf, among those arrested with Wilfrid.
26 *The Times*, 26 June 1933.
27 Reissner, 'The History of Kaufhaus N. Israel'.
28 Leo Baeck to Sir Osmond D'Avigdor Goldsmith of the Central British Fund, 6 September 1933, LBI, Jerusalem, Adler Rudel Files, Correspondence, Zentralauschuss - CBF, (E 108).
29 Minutes of meeting at home of Paul Baerwald, 15 May 1933, Rabbi Jonah Wise, JDC, Germany General 1933 (14–47) January–July.
30 See, for example, correspondence between Neville Laski and Sidney Salomon, in BOD, C 11/12/14. Salomon was head of the Jewish Defence Committee. See also telegram to Laski from Berlin-Jewish community, dated 30 March 1933, in BOD, C 11/12/12 (1933–5), probably written under Nazi dictation. Menahem Kaufman interviews with Dolf Michaelis, Zionist banker, 10 June and 26 June 1981, in ICJ, Oral Evidence Department, 175/17.
31 See Senator plan, dated 24 July 1933, CZA, S7/216; Jonah Wise minutes in JDC (see Note 29); Laski interview with Karl Melchior and Ludwig Tietz, 11 June 1933, YIVO, D. Moshkowitz Collection, Folder 75, p. 9806.
32 'Conversation with Dr. Kahn', 31 March 1933, YIVO, D. Moshkowitz Collection, Folder 75, p. 9764.
33 This is mentioned, without details, in a conversation between Dr Preyse of the Reichsbank and James McDonald, as recorded by the latter, on 14 November 1934 (reference to a plan of Warburg's dated the previous year), CZA, Bentwich Papers, A255/539. The 'preliminary talks' are mentioned in Werner Senator's memo to JDC (see Note 31); this is also found in JDC, Germany General, July–December 1933.
34 Senator to JDC, 6 April 1933, in CZA, S25/9809.

35 Hyman to Baerwald, 20 April 1933 (Senator report attached), JDC, Germany General, January–July 1933.
36 See Note 31.
37 Weltsch's famous article, 'Wear the Yellow Star with Pride', appeared in the *Jüdische Rundschau*, 4 April. The exhortation was metaphorical: the Nazis did not force the Jews to wear yellow stars until the early war period. Weltsch's comment to Buber on Wilfrid is in a letter dated 22 April 1933, *Buber Letters* (Heidelberg, 1973), Vol. II, p. 478.
38 Report of meeting on 29 June 1933, by Israel Cohen, CZA, S25/9703.
39 Report of Laski visit to Vansittart, same date. YIVO, D. Moshkowitz Collection, Folder 75, pp. 9846–9.
40 See Note 29.
41 Yehuda Bauer, *My Brother's Keeper* (Philadelphia, 1974), pp. 108, 125–6.
42 Kahn to Joint, New York, 14 August 1933, JDC, Germany General, July–December 1933; see also Evelyn Morrissey (administrative secretary to JDC) letter in same file, dated 16 August 1933.
43 For close analysis of British policy in 1933, see John P. Fox, 'Great Britain and the German Jews 1933', *Wiener Library Bulletin*, Vol. XXVII, 1972. See also Sherman, *Island Refuge*, and Martin Gilbert, *Sir Horace Rumbold: Portrait of a Diplomat 1869–1941* (London, 1973), pp. 379–82.
44 'Proposals of the Jewish Community as Regards Jewish Refugees from Germany', Appendix I to memorandum by the Home Secretary, 7 April 1933, Cabinet paper 96/33. Quoted in Sherman, *Island Refuge*, p. 30n. By way of comparison, American Jewry set up a National Refugee Service in June 1939 for the support of refugees, see Lyman C. White, *300,000 New Americans* (New York, 1957), p. 151.
45 'Economic Position of the Jews in Germany' (interview with Wilfrid Israel and G. Lubinski, 13 December 1933), LBI, Jerusalem, Adler Rudel Files, E. 108.
46 Summary of Jewish Refugee Organization Conference, October 1933, BOD, C 11/12/14.
47 David Wyman, *Paper Walls* (Amherst, Mass., 1968), p. 6.
48 Report in *The Times*, 11 October 1933.
49 Catchpool report and correspondence, dated Whitsun 1933, FLA, Germany Files, GE9.
50 Bentwich account of visit to Berlin, 22–25 November 1933, CZA, L 13/171.
51 Foley's intelligence background in SIS was confirmed to me by Colonel J. Beevor, author of *SOE: Recollections and Reflections*. For Foley's early contacts with the Israels, author's conversation with Agnes Schneider, who lived with the family at that time.
52 Baeck to McDonald, 28 November and 2 December 1933, UNLA, High Commissioner for Refugees Files, C 1606.
53 Bentwich to Stephany of CBF, 16 January 1934, UNLA, *ibid*.
54 The journey is noted in a private letter dated 22 January 1934, in correspondence with the Central British Fund (CBF), from Brown's Hotel in London later that week, and evidence of Wilfrid's prolonged contact with the High Commission's office in London is contained in an exchange of letters between J. Cohen of the Jewish Refugees Committee and André Wurfbein, one of McDonald's colleagues, December 1934 and 6 January 1935, UNLA, High Commissioner for Refugees Files, C1606.
55 See Sherman, *Island Refuge*, pp. 45–6.

56 Israel to M. Stephany and others at CBF, 29 January 1934, LBI, Jerusalem, Adler Rudel Files, E 114.
57 Israel to Stephany, 17 February 1934, and Stephany to Israel, 20 February 1934, LBI, Jerusalem, Adler Rudel Files, E 115.
58 Kurt Battsek of Jewish Refugees Committee to Norman Bentwich, 16 June 1935, including copy of plan submitted, according to context, in June–July 1933, UNLA, High Commissioner for Refugees Files, C 1606. Battsek was also the representative of the Hilfsverein in London.
59 See 'Ten Years of Hazorea' (in Hebrew) in Hazorea Archives.
60 Israel to Shenhabi, 25 June 1934, Shenhabi Papers, Kibbutz Artzi Archives, Kibbutz Merhavia.
61 Israel to Stephany, 15 November 1934, LBI, Jerusalem, Adler Rudel Files, E 126.

6 Double Lives

1 See Leonard Baker, *Days of Sorrow and Pain* (New York, 1978).
2 Gustav Horn, ICJ, 41/11; see also Max Nussbaum testimony, YVS, 01/222.
3 'A Question to the Single One', written in 1931, published in 1936 (in German). In *Between Man and Man* (London, 1947).
4 Michaelis interview, see Chapter 5, Note 30; see also Benno Cohn's Eichmann trial testimony, *Mishpat Eichmann; Eduyot Alef* (Jerusalem, 1974).
5 Reissner, 'The History of Kaufhaus N. Israel'.
6 Author's conversation with Frieda Grimm, nurse with N. Israel firm.
7 Yosef Yishuvi (Hugo Rosenthal), *Hinuch VaMasoret* (in Hebrew; Jerusalem, 1960). See also Rosenthal to Otto Hirsch, 20 March 1934, Herrlingen to Reissner, 3 March 1936, and Israel to Rosenthal, 26 February 1935, YVS, 08/59.
8 William L. Shirer, *The Rise and Fall of the Third Reich* (London, 1960); Yishuvi, *Hinuch VaMasoret*.
9 Bell Kadurie, 'The Struggle of the Reichsvertretung against Excessive Taxation', YVS, II, 1958.
10 Author's conversation with Eva Michaelis; see also E. Michaelis, 'Saving Children 1933–39', ICJ, 16/27.
11 Author's conversation with Eliezer Be'eri (Ernst Bauer). The children are mentioned in Israel's letters to Shenhabi, Shenhabi Papers, Kibbutz Artzi Archives, Kibbutz Merhavia.
12 Israel to Youth Aliya, Jerusalem, 10 January 1935, CZA, S75/72.
13 Henrietta Szold to Edwin Samuel, 8 May 1935, CZA, S75/39. Judische Waisenhilfe, Berlin, to Hans Beyth, Jerusalem, 9 April 1935, CZA, S75/80.
14 Michaelis, *op. cit.*, Note 10.
15 Shenhabi to Israel, 3 January 1936, and Israel to Shenhabi, 20 January 1936, Shenhabi Papers, Kibbutz Artzi Archives, Kibbutz Merhavia.
16 Diana Hopkinson, *The Incense Tree* (London, 1968), pp. 34–7.
17 See Trott biographies mentioned in Chapter 1, Note 8.
18 Israel to Bentwich, 23 May 1935, UNLA, High Commissioner for Refugees Files, C 1606 (Germany Committee).
19 Bentwich to Sherman at Jewish Refugees Committee, 26 June 1935; Battsek to Bentwich, 16 July 1935; Bentwich to Kahn at Joint, Paris, 26 July 1935, UNLA, *ibid.* See also Battsek to Bentwich, 27 February 1936, CZA, A 255/404.
20 See Martin Gilbert, *Plough My Own Furrow: The Life of Lord Allen of Hurtwood* (London, 1965), pp. 356–62, 384–6.

21 Lothian to Weizmann, 18 June 1935, with Weizmann memo, 11 June 1935, CZA, L 13/165.
22 Max Warburg to Sir Osmond D'Avigdor Goldsmith, 18 May 1935, LBI, Jerusalem, Adler Rudel Papers, E 134.
23 Verbatim notes on meeting of Jewish organizations with German Deputies, Harmonie Club, New York, 14 June 1935, LBI, New York, ARC2 464/1989.
24 Stephany of CBF to Bentwich, 30 October 1935, UNLA, High Commissioner for Refugees Files C 1606 (Germany Committee).
25 Bentwich to Allen, 1 October and 14 October 1935, CZA A 255/325.
26 Reissner, 'The History of Kaufhaus N. Israel', p. 246.
27 Mills to FO, 6 October 1935, PRO, FO 371/18859 C 7555/111/18.
28 *Ibid.* Mills report, dated 27 January 1936, PRO, FO 371/19919 C 541.
29 Phipps report to FO, enclosing Foley memorandum, dated 23 January 1936, PRO, FO 371/19919 C 467. The 'enclosed correspondence' is not in the file.
30 For details on the Warburg-Wirtschaftsministerium talks, see the correspondence between Martin Rosenblueth, head of the German Department at the Zionist Federation's offices in London, and Georg Landauer, head of the German Department at the Jewish Agency in Jerusalem, CZA, S 25/9810 (deals with transfer of capital from Germany) and S 7/217. For brief summary, with references to several important letters, see Abraham Margalioth, 'The Reactions of the Jewish Public in Germany to the Nuremberg Laws', YVS, XII, 1977, pp. 81–3; Margalioth, however, makes no mention of Weizmann's and Ben Gurion's opposition to the plan.
31 Hubert Pollack, 'Captain Foley und andere Berichte', YVS, 01/17. Evidence of Pollack's personal work for Foley is in his private letters, for which I must thank the late Mrs Thea Pollack.
32 Record of talk with Samuel by Lord Cranborne at FO, dated 17 January 1936, PRO, FO 371/9919 C 301.
33 Marks to Weizmann, 31 December 1935, CZA, S 25/9810; J.L. Cohen to Weizmann, 16 December 1935, CZA, S 7/242.
34 Marks to Weizmann, *ibid.*
35 Herbert Samuel to Edwin Samuel, 17 December 1935, Israel State Archives, Jerusalem, Samuel Papers.
36 See, for instance, Elisabeth Wiskemann, *The Europe I Saw* (London, 1968), p. 37.
37 Weizmann to Marks, 15 December and 31 December 1935, CZA, S 25/9756.
38 Weizmann to Samuel, 31 December 1935, *The Letters and Papers of Chaim Weizmann* (1979), Vol. XVII.
39 'DBG' (Ben Gurion) to Marks, 31 December 1935, CZA, S 25/9756.
40 The Gentile bankers involved were: Constantine Benson; Sir Andrew McFadyean, a colleague of Siegmund Warburg in London; Sir William McLintock, and members of the Abel and Hamlin firms. See memo appended to Rosenblueth's letter to Landauer, 24 December 1935, CZA, S 7/242.
41 See Note 32.
42 Phipps to FO, 17 January 1936, PRO, FO 371/19919 C 455.
43 *Ibid.* FO minute by Orme Sargent.
44 *New York Times*, 6 January 1936. Otto Tolischus, the *Times* Berlin correspondent, confirmed the story, quoting unnamed government sources, on the following day, *New York Times*, 7 January 1936.
45 Samuel at Temple Emmanuel, 28 January 1936, House of Lords, Samuel Papers, B 15/17/19.

46 *Cincinatti American Hebrew*, cutting in House of Lords, Samuel Papers, B 15/17/19.
47 See Abraham Margalioth, 'The Rescue of German Jewry during the Years 1933–39: The reasons for the delay of their emigration from the Third Reich', *Rescue Efforts during the Holocaust*, YVS conference proceedings, 1977.
48 McDonald to Weizmann, 4 June 1935, UNLA, High Commissioner for Refugees, Files, C 1606.
49 For text of plan, see 'Tentative Four Year Plan', CZA, J.L. Cohen Files, A 173/464; see also CZA, S 7/516.
50 See CBF Annual Reports 1936–8, CZA, 51084. Also Council for German Jewry (CGJ) Report, signed J.L. Cohen 1937, CZA, S 7/516; CGJ meeting 28 October 1937, S 7/516, and CGJ protocols, S 7/740. For details of American failure to raise funds, see Namier to Samuel, resignation letter, 13 April 1937, CZA, S 7/387. For Joint response to Namier's criticisms, see Kahn to Hyman, 12 May 1937, and Hyman to Felix Warburg, 10 June 1937, JDC, General Files 1365/915.
51 Bentwich, *Wanderer Between Two Worlds* (London, 1941), p. 264.
52 See Pollack testimony, Note 31. For more details on Bartenstein, see Jewish Central Information Office, Amsterdam, Circular, 1935, warning refugees in Switzerland against him, YVS, P 13/74.
53 For Kareski's involvement (no mention of Israel), see H.S. Levine, 'A Jewish Collaborator in Nazi Germany: the Strange Career of Georg Kareski', *Central European History*, September 1975, pp. 251–81.
54 J.L. Cohen to Weizmann, 16 December 1935, CZA, S 7/242. For fuller first-hand account of incident, see Rosenblueth to Landauer, 16 December 1935, CZA, S 7/217.
55 Dr A.L. Lilienthal to Central British Fund, 13 March 1936, LBI, Jerusalem, Adler Rudel Files, Zentralauschuss correspondence,
56 Norman Rose, *Vansittart, Portrait of a Diplomat* (London, 1978), pp. 196–9. For other critical views of the Allen and Lothian visits, see Ralph Wigram's comments in PRO, FO 371/18832, C 2518/55/18, 9/3/35.
57 Rose, *Vansittart.*
58 Vansittart's account of the visit, 'A Busman's Holiday', September 1936, Churchill College, Cambridge, Vnst 1/17. I am grateful to Professor Norman Rose for drawing my attention to this memoir.
59 Baerwald to Kahn telegram, 1 May 1936, and Kahn to Baerwald telegram, 5 May 1936, JDC, Germany General, 1936/7 14–46.
60 The following account is taken from David Glick, 'Some were Rescued – Memoirs of a Private Mission', *Harvard Law School Bulletin*, December 1960, LBI, New York.
61 *Ibid.* See Israel to George Bell, 19 May 1937, Lambeth Palace Library, Bell German Church Papers, Vol. 28.
62 Rosenblueth to Landauer, *Streng Vertraulich* (Most Secret), 27 October 1937, CZA, S 7/558.
63 Bauer, *My Brother's Keeper*, p. 146.
64 Strauss, 'Jewish Emigration from Germany', Part Two.
65 Author's conversation with Arnold Horwell (Horwitz).
66 Author's conversation with Professor Yehuda Bauer. George Bell assessed the Christian 'non-Aryans' at 700,000.
67 See Guenter Lewy, *The Catholic Church and Nazi Germany* (London, 1964).
68 Corder Catchpool to Friends, London, 7 July 1936, FLA, Germany Files, GE 9.

69 Ronald Jasper, *George Bell, Bishop of Chichester* (London, 1967), p. 135.
70 Report on non-Aryan Christians, January 1937, Bell German Church Papers, Vol. 34.
71 Israel to Bell, see Note 61.
72 Jasper, *George Bell*, p. 141.
73 Details of Laura Livingstone's life from Address by Archdeacon of Chichester at a memorial service for Miss Livingstone, on 1 December 1969 at Christ Church, Chelsea. I am grateful to Mrs Eadle of the Wings of Friendship Association for this document.
74 Jasper, *George Bell*.
75 Cranborne to Bell, 27 July 1937, Bell German Church Papers, Vol. 28.
76 J. Roger Carter to Friends, 13 June 1939, FLA, Germany Files, GE.
77 Laura Livingstone Report, September 1937, Bell German Church Papers, Vol. 34.
78 For details of 'South American settlement for Refugees' see Bell German Church Papers, Vol. 33.
79 Bell German Church Papers, Vol. 28.
80 See, for instance, correspondence between N. Laski and Wickham Steed, etc., over the case of Fischer (Hecht), BOD, President's Papers. Oskar Wassermann had similar charges raised against him.
81 See Chapter 10.
82 Laura Livingstone to Arnold Horwell, 22 February 1945.
83 Philip Bernstein, 'The Fate of German Jews', *The Nation*, 23 October 1937.
84 Dr Hans Klutmann, *Jugendholungsheim Schwanenwerder, Ein Kleine Chronik* (Berlin, 1981), p. 9.
85 Lehmann in Ben Shemen cabled Wilfrid and Lola Hahn Warburg in Berlin, 12 June 1936; see also Lehmann to Landauer, 30 May 1936, CZA, S 75/193.
86 Israel to Robert Weltsch, 8 April 1937. Copy in Shenhabi Papers, Kibbutz Artzi Archives, Kibbutz Merhavia.

7 Flood Warnings

1 Buber to Israel, 17 March 1938, Buber Archives, Ms Varia, 350/317.
2 G.E.R. Gedye, *Fallen Bastions* (London, 1939), pp. 304–5.
3 *Ibid.* The last detail is taken from another eye-witness account.
4 Leni Yahil, 'Jews in German Concentration Camps before World War II'. I am grateful to Professor Yahil for having allowed me to examine her detailed paper in manuscript.
5 Report in *Correspondance Juive*, anthology of press cuttings, referring to dates 1–21 June 1938. Published 6 July 1938. Wiener Library, Tel Aviv University.
6 Extract from Berlin Consular Report (Foley), 16 July 1938, PRO, FO 371/21635 C 7092.
7 Background to Wilfrid Israel's letter to Samuel is taken from Yahil, 'Jews in German Concentration Camps'.
8 Israel to Lord Samuel, 28 June 1938, House of Lords, Samuel Papers. General Political Papers, A 155X.
9 R.T. Smallbones, British Consul General, Frankfurt, to Otto Schiff of Central British Fund, 30 November 1938; Smallbones urged Schiff to press USA and Home Office for visas, describing conditions of 8,000 men in Buchenwald, many of whom

had been waiting for release since June. BOD C11/12/25, JFC Papers filed by country (Germany).

10 Walter Poller, *Medical Block, Buchenwald* (London, 1961): describes identical conditions to those detailed in Israel's letter.

11 Yahil, 'Jews in German Concentration Camps'.

12 See Chapter 8.

13 Bentwich to Bell, 15 July 1938, CZA, A 255/401.

14 Harvey to Ogilvie Forbes, 15 October 1938, PRO, FO 371/22536 W 14375/104/98; Ogilvie Forbes to Harvey, 25 October 1938, *ibid.* Ogilvie Forbes mentions his frequent meetings with Israel in note to Randall, 31 October 1938, PRO, FO 371/22535.

15 'Papers concerning the Treatment of German Nationals in Germany 1938–9', Germany No. 2 (1939), HMSO CMD 6120. Statement by Herr X, member of 'charitable organization in Germany'.

16 Ogilvie Forbes, see Note 14.

17 M. J. Creswell minute, 8 November 1938, FO 371/22536/W 14375.

18 Walter Schwartz, *Späte Frucht* (Hamburg, 1981).

19 Foley to Werner Senator, 19 April 1945, CZA, S 7/915.

20 Benno Cohn's testimony in *Mishpat Eichmann, Eduyot Alef* (Jerusalem, 1974).

21 Pollack, 'Captain Foley und Andere Bericht'.

22 Pollack to Aluf Mishne Benjamin Givli, 2 August 1960. I am grateful to the late Mrs Thea Pollack for this letter.

23 Reissner, 'The History of Kaufhaus N. Israel'.

24 Author's conversation with Dolf Michaelis; see also Michaelis testimony in ICJ, Oral Evidence Department.

25 Pollack, 'Captain Foley und Andere Berichte'.

26 Author's conversations with Yosef Amir (Friedrich Altmann).

27 Max Warburg, *Aus Meinen Aufzeichnungen* (New York, 1952; privately printed), p. 154, LBI, New York.

28 Perowne to Foreign Office, 16 June 1938, PRO, FO 371/21686 C 5928.

29 Speaight at FO to Adler and Perowne, 27 June 1938, *ibid.*

30 Correspondence between FO, Adler and Perowne and British Embassy in Berlin, 13 October and 20 October 1938, PRO, FO 371/21688 C 12118 and C 12718.

31 Memo signed Bismarck, 21 June 1938, Auswartiges Amt Archives, Bonn, Aktenband Inland II A3B 83–20, Band 5.

32 According to the report to the German Restitutions Committee submitted on 20 June 1971, a contract was drawn up between Emil Koester AG and N. Israel on 7 July 1938. Herbert Israel reached England on the previous day, according to a refugee file which survives at Osmond House, an old age home for German-Jewish refugees in North London (File No. 12447). For the subsequent official obstruction, see memo attached to Wilfrid Israel's letter to Ogilvie Forbes, dated 4 November 1938, PRO, FO 371/21688 C 14154.

33 *Daily Telegraph* and *Morning Post*, 14 July 1938, London.

34 *Der Stürmer*, August 1938.

35 For a detailed account of the obstacles put in the way of prospective immigrants to the USA, see David Wyman's comprehensive *Paper Walls* (Amherst Mass., 1968).

36 Winterton to Halifax, 28 June 1938, PRO, FO 371/22528 W 8870.

37 DBFP, Series D: 1937–8, pp. 455–8. Ribbentrop's answer was transmitted to Halifax in rather garbled terms by Henderson. See Sherman, *Island Refuge*, pp. 112–13.

38 Makins's memo, 'Emigration from Germany and other Central European Countries, possible action by HMG', dated 18 November 1938, PRO, FO 371/22536 W 15905.
39 See Note 36.
40 Weizmann expressed his opposition to settlement elsewhere than Palestine, for fear of stimulating anti-semitism, in a conversation with Winterton on 24 June 1938, CZA, S 25/9778. Winterton also warned Weizmann off participating: Winterton to Weizmann, 29 June 1938, WA. For the failure to organize a united Jewish delegation, see Ruppin and Goldmann to Landauer, 12 July 1938, CZA, S 25/9778.
41 Record of inter-departmental meeting at Foreign Office, 30 June 1938, PRO, FO 371/22528 W 8713/104/98282.
42 Sherman, *Island Refuge*, p. 118.
43 *Manchester Guardian*, 9 July 1938.
44 Letter (marked only Berlin, 18 February 1938) to Council for German Jewry, signed Wilfrid Israel and Otto Hirsch, CZA, A 255/539.
45 Council for German Jewry, draft memorandum for Evian, CZA, S 7/518. Two-thirds of emigration at this period, the draft notes, was unassisted.
46 Reichsvertretung delegates' meeting with Lord Winterton and Sir Michael Palairet, 18 July 1938, PRO, FO 371/22531 W 9619.
47 Henceforth, for the sake of brevity, the 'Evian Committee'.
48 Corder Catchpool to Friends, London, enclosing Israel memorandum to Halifax, Samuel and Board of Deputies, 31 August 1938, FLA, Germany Files, June 1929–December 1939, GE 9. Halifax and Samuel had a meeting the following week, contents undisclosed; see Samuel to Edwin Samuel, 9 September 1938, Israel State Archives, Samuel Papers, Record Group 100.
49 Conversation between Lord Winterton and Max Warburg, 2 September 1938, PRO, FO 371/22533 W 11759. The meeting with German Foreign Ministry officials is untraceable.
50 Memo dated 24 November 1938, Leith Ross to FO, PRO, FO 371/22537.
51 The account of the Israel-Makins meeting is in Makins's memo dated 18 October 1938, PRO, FO 371/22535 W 13823.
52 Author's conversation with Lord Sherfield (Roger Makins), who had no recollection of Israel.
53 'Note on visit to Germany' 17–19 February 1939, CZA, A 255 (Bentwich papers)/394: interview with heads of Reichsvertretung who told visitor (unnamed) that 'the authorities require an emigration of 100,000 a year'. This took place after the setting up of the special office by Heydrich within the Ministry of the Interior.
54 Makins's note on Evian Committee, 28 October 1938, PRO, FO 371/25536 W 14168. Banker mentioned is Aufhauser (spelt Aufhausen).
55 See Chapter 8.
56 Description of Godman in Kirkpatrick to Makins, 7 November 1938, PRO, FO 371/22536 W 14808/104/98.
57 Rublee plan in FRUS 1938, Vol. I, p. 809. Letter dated 27 October 1938. See also note by Lee (Board of Trade), describing plan and his comments, dated 26 October 1938, PRO, FO 371/22536 W 14456.
58 *Ibid.*
59 Memo by Pinsent in Treasury, British Embassy, Berlin, 15 November 1938, PRO, FO 371/22536 W 14984.
60 FRUS, 1938, Vol. I, p. 817, dated 9 November 1938.
61 See Halifax to Stanley, 3 November 1938, and Stanley to Halifax, 22 November

1938, PRO, FO 371/22535 W 13673/104/98 and FO 371/22538 W 15482/104/98. The idea foundered because of the opposition of the Board of Trade, who thought it would militate against British exporters. This was apparently the end of Wilfrid's proposal to Halifax. Sherman, *Island Refuge*, p. 161, is incorrect in stating that this discussion preceded the Rublee proposal.

62 See memo by Fishboeck, Austrian Minister of Economics, Labour and Finance, dated 14 November 1938, Nuremberg Trial Documents, NG 1522, YVS, Jerusalem. Rublee did not visit Berlin until 1939.

8 Command Performance

1 Judge Berthold Loewenstein testimony, Wiener Library Collection, Oral Evidence, P IID 103. The informant was a Reichsbanoberinspektur Engelke in the Ministry of Economics, whose name was added in YVS, 01/1–9.

2 'Notes on Conditions of Jews in Germany and Austria Made by a Recent Visitor from Palestine' (probably Werner Senator or Georg Landauer, both of whom visited Berlin after the pogrom), CZA, S 7/902.

3 DBFP, 3rd Series, Vol. III, Cable No. 294, p. 262. Wilfrid is clearly the 'representative of principal Jewish organization, who is British born'. See Kochan, *Pogrom*.

4 Protocols of the Political Office of the Jewish Agency, London, 13 November 1938, CZA. This also reports that Wilfrid, Benno Cohen and one other Jewish leader (probably Julius Seligsohn) were free. Leo Baeck was also free at this time.

5 DBFP, 3rd Series, Vol. III, Cable Nos. 297 (p. 264) and 299 (p. 266); and Strang minute, 10 November 1938, for Kirkpatrick remark, PRO, PREM 1/326.

6 Ernst Kramer, 'Ein Amerikaner in Buchenwald', *Die Welt*, 9 November 1978. Herr Kramer's translation.

7 See Note 2.

8 Ogilvie Forbes to Halifax, 16 November 1938, DBFP, 3rd Series, Vol. III, Cable No. 313. The following description is reconstructed from the evidence of many eye-witnesses, some of whom are named in the text.

9 Reissner, 'The History of Kaufhaus N. Israel' (who does not name Baranowski, merely referring to the Commandant of Sachsenhausen); also author's conversation with Dr Eva Reichmann.

10 Nuremberg Trial Documents, PS 1816.

11 Author's correspondence with Ursula Borchard Sklan. For details on Richard Latham, see Peter and Leni Gillman, *Collar the Lot* (London, 1981).

12 See FO minute in reply to Commander Fletcher in Commons debate on 21 November 1938, PRO, FO 371/21637 C 14382, 23 November 1938. Ogilvie Forbes's report on the damage to Israels is in PRO, FO 371/21688 C 661, 10 November 1938.

13 PRO, FO 371/21637 C 14015, 17 November 1938.

14 Ogilvie Forbes to FO, 7 December 1938, PRO, FO 371/21638 C 15076.

15 Details are contained in the family's appeal to the German reparations authorities, kindly shown to me by Mrs Bertha Heilbut. No reparations were paid, as the firm stood in what is today East German territory. East Germany recognizes no debts of this kind.

16 Copy in possession of Mrs Salka Behr.

17 See Note 15.

18 Georg Landauer to Henry Montor, New York, 2 December 1938, marked 'Strictly Confidential', CZA, S 7/756.

19 Baker, *Days of Sorrow and Pain*; Foley's help is mentioned in Bell Kadurie,

'November Pogrom in Berlin', YVS, III, 1959; author's conversation with Arnold Horwell (Horwitz).

20 See Judith Tydor Baumel, 'Jewish Refugee Children in Great Britain 1938–45', unpublished MA thesis, University of Bar Ilan, 1981. I am grateful to Ms Baumel for this information.

21 The Samuel delegation is described in PRO, FO 371/22536/W 15037, 17 November 1938. The Cabinet meeting of 16 November 1938 is in Cabinet No. 55 of 1938, Conclusion 5, Cabinet papers 23/96.

22 'A ten-year survey, 1933–43; Friends Committee for Refugees and Aliens', FLA. Wilfrid is described anonymously in this account written by Bertha Bracey, head of the Friends Emergency Committee in 1938, and identified in letter to the author dated 12 November 1981. At the time of writing, it was dangerous to name Wilfrid.

23 Bracey letter, *ibid.*

24 House of Commons Debates, 21 November 1938, Hansard, Cols. 1429–39.

25 Report by W.R. Hughes of Quakers, 16 December 1938, PRO, FO 371/24074 XC/A1 8187.

26 *Ibid.* Report by Ben Greene on two trips to Germany. See also reports by Apollonia Rissek and Joan Clapham.

27 *Ibid.*

28 *The Times*, 3 December 1938.

29 Baumel, 'Jewish Refugee Children'.

30 PRO, Cabinet No. 59 of 1938, Conclusion 6, Cabinet papers 23/96.

31 Baumel, 'Jewish Refugee Children'.

32 See correspondence between Neville Laski and others in BOD, E3/532. Also *Jewish Chronicle*, 23 June 1939. Lack of finances is the usual explanation for delays. However, see Marks to Samuel, 9 December 1938, CZA, S 7/730: Marks believed that 70,000 children could be emigrated at a cost of £2 million. By the summer of 1939, the Baldwin fund had raised 40 per cent of that sum.

33 See Note 26.

34 Council for German Jewry, Report of Children's Movement, CZA, S 7/740, 1 January 1939.

35 *Ibid.* See also CZA, S 7/730 and PRO, FO 371/24085 W 6550/55/48.

36 Baumel, 'Jewish Refugee Children'; Sherman, *Island Refuge*, pp. 243–4.

37 Sherman, *ibid.*

38 ICJ, Oral Evidence Department, 17/27, Adler Rudel testimony.

39 For many moving case histories, see Karen Gershon, *They Came as Children* (London, 1966).

40 The figures are from Bentwich, *Jewish Youth Comes Home* (London, 1944).

41 Report from German office of Friends to Paul Sturge, London, 20 November 1938; notes on German Trip by Robert Yarnall, 7 December 1938, FLA, Germany Files, 1929–39, GE 9.

42 Bauer, *My Brother's Keeper*, p. 123; see also Wyman, *Paper Walls*, pp. 75–98.

43 Halifax memo, 15 November 1938, PRO, FO 371/21637 C 13900; FRUS 1938, Vol. 1, 840.48 Refugees, Welles Report, p. 289; Lindsay's own account of conversation, dated 18 November 1939, PRO, FO 371/21637 C 4092.

44 Henry Montor memorandum to Leo Herrmann, marked 'Very Confidential', undated, but clearly immediately pre-Evian, CZA, S 7/574. Montor explains that Hull did not intend German refugees to come to the United States, and that only half the refugee quota reached the USA in 1937, because they could not prove they

had sufficient funds. The raising of such funds, Montor (head of a Zionist news agency) explains, should be devoted to enabling Jews to go to Palestine.

45 Roosevelt to Taylor, 13 November 1938, quoted in Henry Feingold, *The Politics of Rescue*, p. 42, F.D. Roosevelt Library Papers/Official File 3186.

46 PRO, FO 371/21637 C 14083, 18/11/38. (Otto Schiff, of the Council of German Jewry, made enquiries at the Home Office in late October. CGJ Protocols, 24 October 1938, CZA, S 7/740. He appears to have been discouraged.)

47 *Ibid.*, Rowe minute.

48 Bruce's account in *Tramp Royal*, pp. 236–42. His report to Patrick Reilly of the Foreign Office is in Reilly memo, 2 December 1938, PRO, FO 371/22538, W 15893/104/98.

49 For example, Baker, *Days of Sorrow and Pain*, pp. 231–2. The description of bloodthirsty mobs suggests that the pogrom was spontaneous, rather than, as it was, highly organized and carried out by the SA and the SS. Bruce's accounts of meetings in the following week with Wilfrid and 'Beck' (*sic*) correspond to the known facts.

50 Foley to FO, 15 December 1938, PRO, FO 371/32540 W 16623.

51 PRO, FO 371/22539 W 16410/104/98, 7 December 1938.

52 CGJ Protocols, 3 January 1939, CZA, S 7/740. Hirsch subsequently accompanied the British Jews to the Home Office.

53 For detailed account of Richborough, see Judith Tydor Baumel, 'The Kitchener Transmigration Camp at Richborough', *YVS Studies*, XIV, Jerusalem, 1981. Foley detail from Pollack, 'Captain Foley und Andere Berichte'.

54 CGJ, 'Training Abroad', Adler Rudel Report, 8 December 1938, CZA, S 7/782.

55 'Plan for assisting emigration of Jews from Germany', PRO, FO 371/22539 W 16205, 8 December 1938.

56 *Ibid.*, minutes.

57 See Feingold, *The Politics of Rescue*, pp. 45–68.

58 Rolf Vogel, *Ein Stempel hat Gefehlt* (Munich, 1977), p. 210 (interview with Schacht, 16 January 1970).

59 Rublee-Wohlthat plan is contained in Gilbert to Hull, 5 February 1939, FRUS 1939, Vol. II, pp. 77–81, and in PRO, FO 371/24076/14920.

60 Senator to Friedrich Altmann, 12 March 1939, CZA, S 7/708.

61 Ogilvie Forbes to Halifax, 14 December 1938, PRO, FO 371/21639 C 15541.

62 Sherman, *Island Refuge*, p. 204. These figures are based on estimates to June 1939, drawn up in Sir John Hope Simpson's *Refugees: a Review of the Situation Since September 1938* (London, August 1939).

63 Pollack, 'Captain Foley und Andere Berichte'.

64 Benno Cohn testimony in *Mishpat Eichmann*.

65 See Chapter 7, Note 9.

66 Pollack, 'Captain Foley und Andere Bericht'.

67 'Note on Conditions of Jews in Germany and Austria Made by a Recent Visitor from Palestine' (undated, context indicates it was written end of 1938), CZA, S 7/902. See Note 2.

68 *Ibid.*

69 Benno Cohn testimony in *Mishpat Eichmann*.

70 Pollack, 'Captain Foley und Andere Bericht'; Arthur Prinz, 'The Role of the Gestapo in Obstructing and Promoting Jewish Emigration', YVS, II, 1958; according to research by Professor Konrad Kwiet, the Robert Bosch Werke in Stuttgart provided between 1–2 million reichsmarks between late 1938 and 1940 to

finance the escape of Jews in immediate danger (letter from Kwiet to the author, 3 October 1982).

71 This assessment is based on a number of recently collected documents analysed by an Israeli scholar, Dr A. Hildesheimer, in his 'The Central Organization of the German Jews in the Years 1933–1945: Its Legal and Political Status and Its Position in the Jewish Community' (in Hebrew), unpublished Ph.D. thesis, Hebrew University, Jerusalem, 1982. I am grateful to Dr Hildesheimer for permission to examine his manuscript. The relevant documentation is mentioned on pp. 132–5.

72 The Council of German Jewry applied to the Foreign Office at this time asking for an official ban on exporting funds to Germany, PRO, FO 371/21637 C 14087, 18 November 1938.

73 Prinz, 'The Role of the Gestapo in Obstructing and Promoting Jewish Emigration'.

74 Foley to Ogilvie Forbes, 17 January 1939, PRO, FO 371/24079 W 1017/519/48.

75 Prinz, 'The Role of the Gestapo in Obstructing and Promoting Jewish Emigration'.

76 High Commission for Refugees to Oungre of HIAS-ICA, 16 March 1939, ICA, London, HIAS-ICA Papers.

77 HIAS memorandum, 2 May 1939, 'Memorandum on Irregular Emigration from Germany', ICA, London, HIAS-ICA Papers.

78 Kirkpatrick minute, 13 February 1939, PRO, FO 371/24087 W 2600.

79 Lehmann in *Wilfrid Israel 1899–1943*.

80 The exact date can be ascertained from Israel's letter to Einstein, Note 89. Wilfrid, according to a letter sent from London to Ursula Borchard in Berlin on 8 May 1939, had made an unexplained flying visit to London ten days earlier.

81 HMSO, Cmd. 6019, 1939, paragraph 14.

82 Vogel, *Ein Stempel hat Gefehlt*, Document 85 (Report by Wohlthat to Central Emigration Office, dated 29 April 1939), p. 270. Warburg's role is confirmed in a letter from Georg Landauer to Ruppin in a report from Berlin dated 17 February 1939, CZA, L 13/152. See also Ralph Weingarten, *Die Hilfeleistung der Westliche Welt bei der Endlosung der deutschen Judenfrage. Das IGCR 1938–39* (Bern, Frankfurt, 1981).

83 Vogel, *ibid.*, Document 86 (Schumburg, Auswartiges Amt, to Ribbentrop, 16 May 1939), Auswartiges Amt Archives, 83-24B 16/5).

84 There are two records of the first meeting. The British record is in PRO, FO 371/24983 W 8144, 23 May 1939; and the American in FRUS, 1939, Vol. II, Refugees 1617, pp. 840–48 (Kennedy to Hull, Pell Report). The British record, which does *not* correspond to the catalogue listing in the PRO, indicates Israel's insistence. Feingold, *The Politics of Rescue*, who clearly used the Pell record, calls this a 'panic-stricken delegation'.

85 Sherman, *Island Refuge*, p. 254, quoting Kennedy to Hull, FRUS, 1939, Vol. II, 134.

86 The record of the second meeting is in FRUS, 1939, Vol. II, Refugees 1817, pp. 840–48 (Kennedy to Hull, 19 May 1939).

87 Hull to Rublee, 9 November 1938, FRUS, 1938, Vol. I, p. 817.

88 PRO, FO 371/24080 W 2146, 7 February 1939.

89 Israel to Einstein, 29 May 1939, Hebrew University, Jerusalem, Einstein Archives.

90 Hopkinson, *The Incense Tree*, p. 165.

91 Sherman, *Island Refuge*, p. 255.

92 Hirsch to Meyer, 6 July 1939, and Meyer to Wilfrid Israel, 18 July 1939, YVS, 08/11.

93 Hanna Karminski to Dora Segall, 20 August 1939. Courtesy of Mrs Segall.

94 Author's conversation with Agnes Schneider.
95 Bell in *Wilfrid Israel 1899–1943*.

9 'Merely Transitional'

1 Eva Michaelis, Youth Aliya, Report, 25 August–7 September 1939, CZA, S 75/746.
2 Adler Rudel to Youth Aliya Executive, 27 September 1939, CZA, S 75/909.
3 See Feingold, *The Politics of Rescue*, pp. 81–2, and Bauer, *American Jewry and the Holocaust*, pp. 61–2.
4 Moshe Sharett, *Yoman Medini* (in Hebrew; Jerusalem, 1974), p. 492.
5 Israel to Trott, 20 November 1939. Courtesy of Clarita von Trott.
6 Letter beginning 'Dear ...', unsigned, dated 15 November 1939, Bell German Church Papers, Vol. 28. The identical letter is in Wiener Library, Israel Papers; the style is recognizably Israel's.
7 For a detailed description, see *Britain's New Citizens*, Association of Jewish Refugees 1941–51 (London, 1951).
8 Leib Jaffe, *Katavim, Igarot, ve Yomanim* (in Hebrew), ed. Binyamin Jaffe (Jerusalem, 1964), entry for 16 April 1941.
9 Israel to Louis Oungre, 3 March 1940. This and other documents relating to Israel's visit to Palestine are in I C A Archives, Huleh Files.
10 Israel to Trott, 9 April 1940. Courtesy of Clarita von Trott.
11 Lehmann did not serve the full term: he was released by 1943.
12 Israel to Ruppin, 28 June 1938, Israel to Rosenblueth, 28 June 1938, and Israel to Werner Senator, CZA, S 7/537. The story of Hazorea's trials are in this file and in S 7/259.
13 Douglas Philips to Clive Burt at FO, 28 May 1940, and R.T. Latham to Jennifer Williams at HO, PRO, FO 371/25244 W 8040/7848/48.
14 'How British Policy Towards Refugees Helps Hitler', 6 July 1940, Liverpool University, Rathbone Papers, XIV.2.17 (1.65).
15 For two recent books on internment, see R. Stent, *A Bespattered Page* (London, 1980), and Gillman, *Collar the Lot*.
16 This is the assessment of Vera Craig (Schaerli), secretary of the Parliamentary Committee for Refugees, who worked closely with Wilfrid Israel, Eleanor Rathbone, and others. Author's conversation with Vera Craig.
17 Central Council for Jewish Refugees, Report for 1940, CZA, J.L. Cohen Papers, A 173/63. Minutes for the Sub-committee for Internment, dated 16 July 1940, in CZA, A 173/53, mention Israel's detailed account of conditions in the camps, although his report is missing. This paper also indicates that he had neither expenses nor auxiliary staff until mid-August.
18 House of Commons Debates, 10 July 1940, Hansard.
19 'Summary of impressions gained on second visit to the camps in the Isle of Man', 31 July 1940, signed Israel, Bell German Church Papers, Vol. 33.
20 Vera Craig, see Note 16.
21 See Eleanor Rathbone, Parliamentary Committee on Refugees (PCR) Report on activities up to March 1941 and Rathbone's Report on Parliamentary Committee for Refugees sent to Leicester conference, January 1941 (*ibid.*). See also Parliamentary Committee for Refugees, 'Treatment of Refugees', second and third memoranda, CZA, Adler Rudel Papers, A 140/250. Provenance not indicated, but identical with reports of the PCR held by Vera Craig.
22 Report by Wilfrid Israel on conditions in the men's internment camps, 18–29

December 1940, CZA, Adler Rudel Papers, A 140/249. The 13-page report covers conditions in six camps, a statistical survey, and general recommendations.

23 Letter from Louis Graham Harrison, secretary to Sir Osbert Peake, Home Office, to Reverend Henry Carter, chairman of Refugee Joint Consultative Committee, 18 August 1941, Osmond House Papers (CBF), London, General, 22 February 1945. Osmond House is an old age home for German-Jewish refugees.

24 Adler Rudel Papers. Hermann Berlak account of internment, CZA, A 140/250.

25 The paper in question appears to be Zander, 'The Power of the Spirit in Internment', FLA, IFOR 7, 1941.

26 Israel to Reissner, 22 January 1941, LBI, New York, Israel Collection.

27 Israel to Werner Senator, 8 March 1941, CZA, S 7/2014.

28 Author's conversation with Eva Michaelis.

29 Protocols of the London office of Youth Aliya, CZA, S 75/1718, 11 June 1940.

30 *Ibid.*, 4 March 1941.

31 Mrs D.B. Greenberg, head of American Youth Aliya, to London Office, 20 March 1941, CZA, S 75/1718.

32 Protocols of the London office of Youth Aliya, CZA, S 75/1718, 18 March 1941.

33 See entries in above Protocols between October 1941 and March 1942.

34 Israel to Reissner, 17 November 1940, LBI, New York, Israel Collection.

35 Israel to Ruppin, 12 July 1941, Klausner Papers, private collection of Mrs M. Spielmann.

36 Note on 'Contemporary English Art', Wiener Library, Israel Papers. He was clearly interrupted in the middle of writing.

37 Vansittart, *Living in London.*

38 Peter Vansittart, *Enemies* (London, 1947).

10 A German Patriot

1 Royal Institute of International Affairs, Reports, 1939–45, Chatham House, London. This is the source of the general description that follows.

2 Makins minute, 6 March 1941, PRO, FO 371/26419, C 2510.

3 Nicolson, *Peacemaking 1919.*

4 Quintin Hogg, 7 November 1940, Chatham House Reports.

5 Nigel Ronald of FO at 'meeting in Orme Sargent's room', PRO, FO 371/32481 W 1671, 3 February 1942 (see also FO 898/29, January 1941).

6 E.M. Forster, 'Tolerance' (1941), in *Two Cheers for Democracy* (London, 1951).

7 House of Commons Debates, 29 January 1941. Churchill was answering a question by Labour MP, Geoffrey Mander.

8 House of Commons Debates, 1 January 1941, Hansard.

9 Ministry of Economic Warfare, memo to FO, 8 January 1942, PRO, FO 371/32481.

10 For a detailed account, see Anthony Glees, *Exile Politics during the Second World War – the German Social Democrats in Britain* (Oxford, 1982), particularly Chapters 4 and 7.

11 House of Commons Debates, 29 May 1941, Hansard.

12 See Martin Gilbert, *Finest Hour: Winston Spencer Churchill 1939–41* (London, 1983), p. 944 and fn., 1070.

13 Harrison minute, 12 December 1941, PRO, FO 371/26585 C 13723.

14 Author's conversations with the late Professor Marshall. In the following account of Wilfrid's contribution to Marshall's papers, I have checked his testimony against

the notes and papers in Wiener Library, Israel Papers, and Marshall's papers in the PRO.

15 PRO, FO 371/32481 W 335, 8 January 1942.

16 Lord Gladwyn, *Memoirs* (London, 1972); post-war planning 1942–3 is discussed from page 109.

17 See Victor Rothwell, *Britain and the Cold War* (London, 1982), pp. 42, 87; and Glees, *Exile Politics*.

18 Orme Sargent minute, 15 October 1942, PRO, FO 371/31499 U 1019/26/72.

19 Richard Law, PRO, FO 371/31499 U 1019/26/72.

20 Eden to Viscount Astor, chairman of RIIA, 7 December 1942, Chatham House Reports.

21 Toynbee to Nigel Ronald, 9 March 1942, PRO, FO 371/32482 W 3614. Also author's conversations with Marshall.

22 PRO, FO 371/32482 W 3614. See also Toynbee to Ronald, 15 March 1943, PRO, FO 371/36633.

23 Author's conversations with Sir Frank Roberts and Dr Lothar Kettenacker.

24 Author's conversation with Marshall.

25 'Main Groups and Some Personalities Among Refugees from Germany and Austria', Wiener Library, Israel Papers.

26 Wickham Steed in *Die Zeitung*, 19 May 1941; note by Israel, Wiener Library, Israel Papers.

27 Strang memo, PRO, FO 371/26559 C 7108, quoted in Glees, *Exile Politics*, p. 148.

28 Correspondence between Israel, Ollenhauer and Vogel, Friedrich Ebert Stiftung, Bonn, SPD Archives. Israel letters dated 22 August, 5 September and 14 September 1941 and 2 January 1942. Israel to Ollenhauer, 27 September 1941, encloses a questionnaire on the German opposition.

29 'Material on Structure and Grouping of Oppositional Forces in Germany', Part II, 'Some Notes of Mine on Three Stages', 17 November 1942, Wiener Library, Israel Papers.

30 See Glees, *Exile Politics*; *Gollancz in German Wonderland* (London, 1942). *The German Workers Movement and German Nationalism*, Executive of the SPD in London, 1942. Institut für Zeitgeschichte, Munich. Hans Jaeger Papers, 1f2 ED 210/23. Israel to Hans Vogel, 4 October 1942, Friedrich Ebert Stiftung, Bonn.

31 See Note 29. Israel clearly thought little of the Reichsbanner Schwartz-Rot-Gold, the militant wing of the Liberals and Social Democrats.

32 Israel to Marshall, 17 November 1941; 'extract from a letter written in 1941'; notes to his paper, 'German Self Re-education' (PGP 44), 9 March 1942; Chatham House protocols from debates on reconstruction and re-education (PGP 55 and 61), August and September 1942; Israel memo to Zimmern; Zimmern to Israel, 22 July 1942, and Israel to Zimmern, 4 August 1942, Wiener Library, Israel Papers.

33 Report of conversation between FRPS German Section and Dr Ernst Wolff, 14 January 1942, Wiener Library, Israel Papers. For study of the contribution of German-Jewish refugees to FO policy, see Reusch, 'Die Londoner Institutionen', *Historisches Jahrbuch*. Reusch dates Wolff's contribution from a later period. Author's correspondence with Dr Dietrich Mende and also Marshall.

34 See various essays and Chatham House Political Group Papers Nos. 44, 55, 59 and 67, Wiener Library, Israel Papers.

35 Author's conversations with Marshall.

36 The paper, 'What to do with Germany', dated 28 May 1942, is now in Professor Marshall's papers at the London School of Economics.

37 For various accounts of these approaches, see Peter Hoffman, *The History of the German Resistance* (University of Massachusetts, 1977). Bell's own account of his Stockholm talks is in *Wiener Library Bulletin*, Vol. XI, 3–4, 1956, pp. 21–3.
38 Author's conversation with David Astor.
39 See Note 29.
40 For Visser 'T Hooft's own account, see 'The View from Geneva', *Encounter*, July 1969. The memorandum, which is unsigned, is in PRO, FO 371/30912 C 5428/48/18, headed 'Strictly Private and Confidential'; Marshall's comments are appended in a memorandum in the same file headed 'Note on the Memorandum attributed to Rauschning', but also refers to 'the document appended' (the Trott memorandum), obtained from Arnold Toynbee. The Rauschning memo, with comments dated 12 May 1942, is in PRO, FO 371/30931 C 4912/241/18.
41 See Lothar Kettenacker, 'Die Britische Haltung zum Deutschen Widerstand Wahrend des Zweiten Weltkriegs', in Kettenacker, ed., *Das Andere Deutschland* (Munich, 1977).
42 Cripps-Eden exchange of letters in PRO, FO 371/30912.
43 PRO, FO 371/26544 C 12966, 23 September 1941.
44 'EW' memorandum dated 25 June 1942, headed 'Most Secret', PRO, FO 371/30912 C 6464.
45 Confidential unsigned memo, 'Freiherr Adam von Trott', in PRO, FO 371/30912 C 5428/48/18.
46 *Ibid.*
47 Israel 'Notes on the Churches', 27 May 1942, Wiener Library, Israel Papers.
48 Marshall comments in PRO, FO 371/30912 C 5428/48/18. Israel's remarks in Chatham House PGP Paper 44, 'German Self Re-education', Wiener Library, Israel Papers.
49 Anthony Eden, *The Reckoning* (Cambridge, 1965), pp. 333–5.
50 Isobel Cripps to Wilfrid Israel, 24 July 1942, Wiener Library, Israel Papers.
51 See Chapter II.
52 See Note 31.
53 Author's conversation with Sir Frank Roberts.
54 FRPS Paper, 'Measures of Security against Germany – Dismemberment and Truncation', 12 January 1943, was submitted to Harrison on 15 January 1943; PRO, FO 371/34456 C 670. A copy of the original paper, with Israel's notes, is in the Wiener Library, Israel Papers. Harrison's version is the third part of the War Cabinet Paper, 'The Future of Germany', PRO, FO 371/34457 C 2864.
55 Chatham House PGP 59, Addendum. Wilfrid's own contribution is marked in the copy in the Wiener Library, Israel Papers.
56 Marshall to Roberts, Marshall memorandum attached, PRO, FO 371/34456 XC/A 18476.
57 The memorandum is the first part of 'The Future of Germany', see Note 54.
58 PRO, FO 371/34457 C 3667, 3 April 1943.
59 PRO, FO 371/34456 C 2233, 1 March 1943.
60 The paper's conclusions reproduce those of Israel's in his 'Notes on the Weimar Republic', dated 16 February 1943, Wiener Library, Israel Papers.
61 Bell to Israel, 19 December 1942, Bell German Church Papers, Vol. 28.
62 Israel to Bell, 10 October 1942, *ibid.*
63 Israel to Bell, 28 December 1942, *ibid.*
64 See Chapter 7, Note 61.
65 PRO, FO 371/34452 C 3150/279/18.

66 Jasper, *George Bell*, p. 275.
67 The full text of the debate is in House of Lords Debates, 10 March 1943, Hansard, Cols. 535–82. Israel's words quoted by Bell in Col. 538.

11 The Adviser

1 Briefing for visit by Colonel Beck, Polish Foreign Secretary, by Sir Howard Kennard, British Ambassador in Warsaw; also Makins's minute, PRO, FO 371/24084 W 5796, 11 April 1939.
2 Stein, Notes of Informal Conversation at Chatham House, 20 January 1940, BOD, E 30/40 (RIIA 1930–40).
3 Beeley to Brotman, 2 February 1940, BOD, E 30/40 (RIIA 1930–40). Also PRO, FO 371/27133 (Mr Beeley's situation) E 205/205/31, 18 January 1941.
4 See Elie Kadourie, *The Chatham House Version* (London, 1970).
5 Weizmann to Coupland, 16 November 1939, *The Letters and Papers of Chaim Weizmann*, Vol. XIX, p. 187.
6 Sharett, *Yoman Medini*, pp. 512–13; see also Harry Sacher to Weizmann, 21 November 1939, WA.
7 *Ibid.*
8 'Programme of the Jewish Section of the FRPS 9/9/41', signed H.B., Wiener Library, Israel Papers.
9 Conversation with Professor Zander. Zander, probably because of Wilfrid's behaviour at these meetings, was not favourably impressed by him.
10 Conversation with Professor Hourani. I am grateful to Professor Hourani for providing me with his 1946 pamphlet, written for the Arab League, 'Is Zionism the Solution of the Jewish Problem?', which reflects his thinking at that time.
11 Beeley to Bentwich, 22 June 1943, CZA, A 255 (Bentwich Papers) 630.
12 Author's conversation with Eric Lucas.
13 'Jewish Emancipation', Wiener Library, Israel Papers.
14 'Great Britain and Palestine', accompanying papers indicate written by Beeley. FRPS Paper, RR X-4-II FO 371/27133 E 7595, 18 November 1941.
15 The resemblance between the thinking of Ahad HaAm (Ginsberg) and Israel is striking; Wilfrid mentions his name only once – in the Indian diary of 1925. For a brief exposé of Ahad HaAm's thinking, see David Vital, *The Origins of Zionism* (Oxford, 1975).
16 'The Present Position of World Jewry with Particular Reference to Eastern Europe', PRO, FO 371/32680 W 5837, 18 April 1942.
17 Colonial Office minute to 'Great Britain and Palestine' (see Note 14), para. 26.
18 PRO, FO 371/29227 W 1341, 10 December 1941. For the fate of AgroJoint in the Soviet Union, see Bauer, *American Jewry and the Holocaust*, p. 127, and the same author's *My Brother's Keeper*, pp. 103–4.
19 YVS, Schwarzbart Papers, Schwarzbart Diary, entry for 31 August 1941.
20 *Ibid.*, entries for 2 September and 3 September 1941.
21 *Ibid.*, entry for 2 September 1941.
22 *Ibid.*, entry for 9 March 1942.
23 Notes on meeting with Dr Schwarzbart, Wiener Library, Israel Papers.
24 Author's conversation with Sir Harold Beeley.
25 'Movements of Jewish Population in Europe Since the Outbreak of Hostilities', March, May and July 1942, Wiener Library, Israel Papers.

26 Author's conversation with Arieh Handler, worker for Jewish youth groups and colleague of Wilfrid's in relief work.
27 Author's conversations with Beeley and Marshall.
28 PRO, CAB 72/19/14, February 1942.
29 69th meeting of FRPS research sub-committee on international organizations dated 30 May 1942. Beeley suggests consulting Mr Israel 'who had experience of food relief in practice'. Reference is also made to Chatham House work 'on immediate measures', a report on which had gone to the Leith-Ross Bureau (i.e. the APWRB). Sir Charles Webster Papers, London School of Economics, 8/6 (RIIA).
30 See PRO, FO 371/32659 W 2530, 20 February 1942.
31 PRO, FO 837/15.
32 PRO, FO 371/32660 W 15241.
33 See John P. Fox, 'The Jewish Factor in British War Crimes Policy in 1942', *English Historical Review*, Vol. XCII, CCCLXVII (London, January 1977), pp. 88–92.
34 Author's conversation with Linton.
35 Rathbone to Churchill, 29 March 1943, PREM 4 51/8.
36 Weizmann-Moyne conversation is in PRO, FO 371/27128 E 4474, 1 August 1941. Ben Gurion-Moyne conversation, 21 August 1941, is in PRO, CO 733/446/760333/41.
37 Boyd of the Colonial Office to Baxter of the FO, 24 December 1941, PRO, FO 371/27129 E 8556. I am grateful to Dr Ronald Zweig for pointing out this incident to me, and for access to his 1978 Cambridge Ph.D. thesis, 'British Policy to Palestine, May 1939 to 1943: the Fate of the White Paper'.
38 Weizmann to Churchill, 14 September 1941, PRO, PREM 4 52/5.
39 Gabriel Cohen, *Churchill and Palestine, 1939–42* (in Hebrew; with English abstract; Jerusalem, 1976).
40 'War Cabinet; Jewish Policy', 30 September 1941, signed M (Moyne), PRO, PREM 4 52/5.
41 Cherwell to Prime Minister, 25 June 1942, *ibid.*
42 The Colonial Office had circulated a Cabinet paper on this subject in September 1941, 'Jewish Policy', PRO, WP (G) (41) 104. The quotation is from Sir Maurice Peterson, Assistant Secretary of Eastern Department, 13 August 1942, PRO, FO 371/31379 E 4772. Zweig, 'British Policy to Palestine'.
43 'Some Controversial Points on Questions regarding Jewish Post-War Re-Construction', 15 January 1942, Wiener Library, Israel Papers.
44 PRO, FO 371/32659 W 1338, 27 January 1942.
45 PRO, FO 371/30885 C 9844, 14 September 1942.
46 Gorvin minute, 1 March 1943, PRO, FO 371/35298 U 933, and Walker minute, 2 January 1943, PRO, FO 371/36694 W 124.
47 Walker minute, 16 May 1942, PRO, FO 371/32680 W 7259.
48 Randall to Emerson, 9 January 1942, PRO, FO 371/32659 W 397.
49 Emerson memo, PRO, FO 371/32659 W 4740, 27 March 1942.
50 Ronald minute, *ibid.*
51 Record of Inter-departmental meeting on 9 December 1942, at Foreign Office, PRO, FO 371/32660 W 16802/397/48.
52 War Cabinet Files and PRO, CAB 65/33 6/43, 11/1/43, Cab. Concl. 4. and CAB 65/33 33/43, 22/2/43, Cab. Concl. 4. See Leonard Dinnerstein, *America and the Survivors of the Holocaust* (New York, 1982), p. 10, Chapters 4 and 8 for the inadequacy and callousness of the treatment provided.
53 Martin Gilbert, *Exile and Return* (London, 1978), pp. 275–8.

54 YVS, Schwarzbart Diary, entry for July 1943.
55 Lichtheim to Goldmann, 9 September 1942, CZA, L 22/27, enclosed in Lichtheim to Israel, 7 April 1943, CZA, L 22/152.

12 Last Call

1 Author's conversation with Joseph Linton.
2 Israel to Reissner, 16 April 1942, LBI, New York, Israel Collection.
3 *Ibid.*, 27 September 1942.
4 See CZA, S 75/1273/1, and 1361 for individual case histories.
5 CZA, Z4/15161, quoted in Martin Gilbert, *Auschwitz and the Allies*, p. 79.
6 Michaelis to Szold and Landauer, 11 December 1942, CZA, S 75/1642.
7 Israel to Reissner, 8 January 1943, LBI, New York, Israel Collection.
8 Israel to David Hopkinson, 10 November 1942.
9 Jewish Agency Political Office London, minutes, CZA, 1942/3 302/25 and 303/25, entries 28 December 1942 and 14 February 1943.
10 Toynbee to Ronald, 15 March 1943, PRO, FO 371/36633 15001.
11 Latham minute, 1 February 1941, PRO, FO 371/27132 E 204, quoted in Zweig, 'British Policy to Palestine'.
12 See PRO, CO 733/396/75 113/46 (39) quoted in Zweig, 'British Policy to Palestine'.
13 Israel to Georg Landauer, 26 January 1943, CZA, S 75/1642. Berthold Simonsohn, 'Gedenkblatt für Dr Paul Eppstein', YVS 08/88.
14 PRO, FO 371/32680 W 14410, 28 October 1942. See also PRO, FO 371/32681 W 14673, 2 November 1942.
15 Protocols of Youth Aliya, 25 January 1943, CZA, S 75/1718. Protocols of the Political Office of the Jewish Agency, London 1942/3. Minutes for meetings on 15 February 1943 (Wilfrid Israel present), CZA, Z 4 302/26. Minutes for 15 March, 19 March and 28 March 1943, CZA, Z4 302/27.
16 Law minute, 16 December 1942, PRO, FO 371/30925 C 12716.
17 Protocols of Jewish Agency Executive Jerusalem (in Hebrew), 13 December 1942, CZA.
18 Bernard Joseph notes on above meeting, CZA, S 25/1510.
19 Protocols of Jewish Agency Political Office London, 23 December 1942, CZA, Z4 302/25.
20 Randall minute, 12 December 1942, PRO, FO 371/36282 W 16732.
21 Wasserstein, *Britain and the Jews of Europe 1939–45* (Oxford, 1979), pp. 206–8. See also Hoare to FO, 6 January 1943, PRO, FO 371/34736 C 203G.
22 Wasserstein, *Britain and the Jews of Europe*, pp. 207–8.
23 PRO, FO 371/36699 W 2140/391/48, 6 February 1943.
24 Boyd minute, PRO, CO 733/444/75872 26C (1942–3), quoted in Zweig, 'Britain's Policy to Palestine'.
25 Telegram from Lord Halifax to the Ambassador in Washington, 3 April 1943, PRO, FO, 371/36677 W 4943/80/48.
26 Emerson to Randall, 18 December 1942, PRO, FO 371/32660 W 17084.
27 PRO, FO 371/36686 27814, 25 April 1943.
28 See PRO, FO 371/36661 W 7640 and FO 371/36662 W 7131, 11 May 1943. See also Shlomo Adler Rudel, 'A Chronicle of Rescue Efforts', LBIY XI (London, 1966), pp. 213–41.
29 Jewish Agency memorandum dated 15 March 1943 is in JDC, Lisbon General letter 84, Katski to Joint New York, 31 March 1943.

30 Katski to Joint New York, 30 April 1943, see JDC, Lisbon General letter 111, for evidence of Israel's meetings with representatives of all these countries. Israel to Kullman, 23 April 1943, PRO, FO 371/36686 W 6285.
31 Correspondence Spaak to Eden, 7 October 1942, and Randall to Oliphant at British Embassy to Belgium, 9 November 1943, PRO, FO 371/32680 W 13392.
32 JDC, Lisbon General letter 214, 26 June 1943. The letter was censored and also appears in the British Files, PRO, FO 371/36704 W 12115, 2 August 1943. See also Note 28.
33 CZA, Z4/2008, 13 March 1943.
34 Wilfrid Israel, note on conversation with Schwarzbart, 12 February 1943, Wiener Library, Israel Papers.
35 Israel to Max Warburg, 11 March 1943, JDC.
36 Israel to Reissner, 19 March 1943, LBI, New York, Israel Collection.
37 Israel to Lichtheim, 7 April 1943, CZA, L22/152.
38 Author's conversation with Lieutenant Colonel James Langley.
39 Yehuda Bauer, 'American Jewry and the Holocaust', p. 206.
40 See Bauer, *ibid.*, p. 213. For Weissmann's version, see *Mul Eitanei HaResha* (in Hebrew; Tel Aviv, 1968).
41 Weissmann to World Jewish Congress, London, 22 April and 9 May 1943, YVS, Weissmann Papers, P3/A.
42 Israel to Lichtheim, 7 April 1943, CZA, L22/152.
43 Israel cable to Dobkin, 24 April 1943, CZA, S 75/1665.
44 See Bauer, *American Jewry and the Holocaust*, p. 215.
45 Wisla testimony in *Wilfrid Israel 1899–1943*.
46 Israel to Lichtheim, 28 April 1943, CZA, L 22/152.
47 Author's conversation with Minna Koss.
48 Israel to Werner Fuchs, First Secretary of Swiss Legation, Lisbon, 17 April 1943. Swiss Federal Archives, Berne, E 2200 Lissabon 7/12.
49 Szold to Israel, 12 April 1943, CZA, S 75/1665.
50 Israel to Szold, 24 April 1943, *ibid.*
51 PRO, FO 371/32682 W 1703, 18 December 1942.
52 Henderson minute, 14 April 1943, PRO, FO 371/36700 W 5346. For deportation figures see Martin Gilbert, *Holocaust Atlas* (London, 1982), Map 202.
53 Justice and Police Department, Berne, to Lisbon Legation, 27 May 1943, Swiss Federal Archives, E 2200 Lissabon 7/12.
54 International Red Cross, Geneva, to author, 4 January 1982.
55 Lichtheim to Israel, 19 May 1943, CZA, L 22/152.
56 Israel to Lichtheim, 28 April 1943, CZA, L 22/152.
57 Wohlwill, 'Privater Bericht über Wilfrid Israel's Tatigheit in Portugal und Spanien' (unpublished), Kibbutz Hazorea Archives. See also Wohlwill in Hazorea Anniversary publication on Wilfrid Israel, Kibbutz Hazorea Archives.
58 From diary of Siegmund Dispeker, one of the inmates. I am grateful to his son, Yoel Durkan, for allowing me to use these documents.
59 Hoare to FO, 6 January 1943, PRO, FO 371/34736 C 203G.
60 Wasserstein, *Britain and the Jews of Europe*, pp. 206–7.
61 Author's conversation with Rudolf and Eva Jones (Jonas).
62 Author's conversation with Shlomo Steinhorn. See also Bauer, *American Jewry and the Holocaust*, pp. 255–6.
63 'Liquidation of Refugee Problem in Spain', dated 22 May 1943, Israel memorandum

to Hoare, is in PRO, FO, 371/36639 W 8901. See Avni MA ms, 'HaFsalat Hayehudim miSfarad ve Portugal'.

64 Israel to Szold, 10 May 1943, CZA, S 75/1665.

65 Israel to Linton, 13 May 1943, CZA, Z4 2008. See also Israel to Dobkin, 25 April 1943, S75/1665.

66 Sandford to Bernard Joseph, 2 April 1943, paragraph 4, CZA, S75/2033.

67 *Ibid.*, Joseph to Sandford, 6 April 1943.

68 Minutes of Jewish Agency Executive, 25 April 1943, CZA.

69 Wohlwill, 'Privater Berichte über Wilfrid Israel's Tatigheit in Portugal und Spanien'.

70 *Ibid.*

71 *Ibid.*

72 Israel to Linton, 29 May 1943, CZA, Z4 2008.

73 Author's conversation with Lieutenant Colonel James Langley.

74 Howard, *In Search of My Father*, Chapter 1.

75 Colvin, *Flight 777*.

76 Freiburg Military Archives, RM 7/298 folio 848.

77 Randall minute to Israel memorandum, see Note 63.

78 Bauer, *American Jewry and the Holocaust*, p. 258.

79 Lowrie, *The Hunted Children* (New York, 1961).

80 Letter from Jorge Haestrup to author.

81 Wohlwill, 'Privater Bericht über Wilfrid Israel's Tatigheit in Portugal und Spanien'.

82 Author's conversation with Langley.

83 Author's conversation with Irmgard Smurka.

84 See Chapter 6, Note 73.

85 Author's conversation with David Astor.

86 See Rilke, *Letters*, translated by R.F.C. Hull (London, 1946). Letter to Countess Aline Dietrichstein, 9 August 1919.

87 Israel's letter, courtesy of Mrs Salka Behr.

Select Bibliography

Ayçoberry, Pierre, *The Nazi Question* (Routledge & Kegan Paul, London, 1981; Pantheon Books, New York, 1981).

Brock, Peter, *Twentieth Century Pacifism* (Van Nostrand Reinhold, London and New York, 1970).

Carr, E.H., *The Twenty Years Crisis* (Macmillan, London, 1946).

Carsten, F.L., *War against War: British and German Radical Movements in the First World War* (Batsford, London, 1982; University of California Press, Berkeley, 1982).

Craig, G.A., *Germany 1866–1945* (Oxford University Press, Oxford, 1978).

Feingold, Henry, *The Politics of Rescue* (Rutgers State University Press, New Jersey, 1970).

Gilbert, Martin, *Auschwitz and the Allies* (Michael Joseph, London, 1981; Holt, Rinehart & Winston, New York, 1982).

Gilbert, Martin, *Atlas of the Holocaust* (Michael Joseph, London, 1982; Macmillan, New York, 1982).

Gillman, Peter and Leni, *Collar the Lot! How Britain Interned and Expelled its Wartime Refugees* (Quartet, London, 1980; Charles River Books, Boston, 1981).

Hoffman, Peter, *History of the German Resistance* (Macdonald, London, 1977; MIT Press, Boston, 1977).

Laqueur, Walter, *A History of Zionism* (Weidenfeld & Nicolson, London, 1972; Holt, New York, 1972).

Lowrie, Donald, *The Hunted Children* (W.W. Norton, New York, 1963).

Nicholls, A.J., *Weimar and the Rise of Hitler* (Macmillan, London, 1979; St Martins Press, New York, 1969).

Niewyk, Donald L., *The Jews in Weimar Germany* (Manchester University Press, Manchester, 1981; Louisiana State University Press, Louisiana, 1980).

Parkes, James, *The Jewish Problem in the Modern World* (Thornton Butterworth, London, 1939).

Rothwell, Victor, *Britain and the Cold War, 1941–47* (Cape, London, 1982).

Schleunes, Karl L., *The Twisted Road to Auschwitz* (Andre Deutsch, London, 1972; University of Illinois Press, Illinois, 1970).

Sherman, A.J., *Island Refuge: Britain and Refugees from the Third Reich, 1933–39* (Elek, London, 1973; University of California Press, Berkeley, 1973).

Stern, Fritz, *Gold and Iron: Bismarck, Bleichroder and the building of the German Empire* (Allen & Unwin, London, 1977; Knopf, New York, 1977).

Wasserstein, Bernard, *Britain and the Jews of Europe, 1939–45* (Institute of Jewish Affairs, London, 1979; Oxford University Press, New York, 1979).

Wiskemann, Elizabeth, *Europe of the Dictators, 1919–45* (Collins, London, 1966; Cornell University Press, 1980).

Wyman, David S., *Paper Walls: America and the Refugee Crisis 1938–41* (University of Massachusetts Press, Amherst, Massachusetts, 1968).

Index

About the Author

Naomi Shepherd has been a political correspondent for British and American newspapers and magazines, including *The New York Times, The International Herald Tribune,* and *The New Statesman,* and has written for *Commentary* and *Present Tense.* Born in Britain, she is a permanent resident of Israel. This is her first book.